# THANKING
# FATHER TED

# THANKING FATHER TED

Thirty-Five Years of Notre Dame Coeducation

## 1972-2007

Thanking Father Ted Foundation, Inc.

Edited by Ann Therese Darin Palmer '73, '75 MBA

**Andrews McMeel**
**Publishing, LLC**
Kansas City

07 08 09 10 11 RR4 10 9 8 7 6 5 4 3 2 1

ISBN-13: 978-0-7407-7030-2
ISBN-10: 0-7407-7030-6

Library of Congress Control Number: 2007928189

ATTENTION: SCHOOLS AND BUSINESSES
Andrews McMeel books are available at
quantity discounts with bulk purchase for
educational, business, or sales promotional use.
For information, please write to: Special Sales
Department, Andrews McMeel Publishing,
LLC, 4520 Main Street, Kansas City,
Missouri 64111.

On His 90th Birthday, University of Notre Dame
Undergraduate Alumnae and Campus Celebrities
Thank Father Theodore M. Hesburgh, CSC, for the
Gift of Coeducation and Discuss the Impact of
Notre Dame Coeducation on Their Lives

This banner was strung across the South Dining Hall entrance in August 1972 to welcome the first coeds.

# CONTENTS

Father Ted with his mother and two sisters.

# INTRODUCTION AND ACKNOWLEDGMENTS

In March 2006, the Notre Dame Alumni Association asked a group of Chicago area alumnae to help plan the first-ever program for alumnae only. When we considered keynote speakers for this historic gathering, there was only one name on our list—Father Hesburgh. If it wasn't for Father Ted's vision and determination in opening up Notre Dame to coeducation, we wouldn't have had our undergraduate degrees.

After Father agreed, we decided to do something that we didn't think had been done before. We asked alumnae undergraduate degree recipients worldwide to send us letters individually thanking Father Ted for the gift of coeducation and telling him the difference it made in their lives. We collected four three-ring binders of letters and presented them to him at the luncheon, held at the Chicago Club on Thursday, May 11.

Two weeks before the luncheon, we realized we had the makings of a story that had never been published before: the history of Notre Dame's transition to coeducation, from the women's perspective. Recent women graduates or women students on campus today have no idea what it was like to be a coed pioneer. One reason is because there hasn't been a readily accessible collection of eyewitness accounts.

In addition, there weren't readily accessible accounts of what it was like from the perspective of the administrators and trustees. These individuals had been charged with taking one of the foremost male universities in the United States, waving a wand over it, and instantaneously turning it into a viable coeducational campus. So, for this book, we asked almost every living decision maker who transitioned Notre Dame to coeducation to give us their recollections. Twenty-five of them responded.

Notre Dame alumnae interviewed those who didn't want to pen their own recollections. We're very grateful to these alumnae: Kelly Murphy Bellinger '01 JD; Janet Carney O'Brien '77; Kathryn Faccenda '85; Sarah Magill Hamilton '86, a former editor in chief of the *Observer,* the campus newspaper; Eileen O'Grady Daday '77; Catherine Pieronek '84, '95 JD; and Monica Yant Kinney '93, another former *Observer* editor in chief. Carol Jambor-Smith, Law School director of external relations, helped us by interviewing Jim Roemer, dean of students during the coed transition.

From the moment we decided to incorporate a private foundation to publish *Thanking Father Ted,* we've received support from many in the Notre Dame community, starting with Father Ted and his administrative assistant, Melanie Chapleau. Whether it was a name, a phone number, prayers, some hospitality, some bucking up, they were there with whatever we needed.

We were received with the same encouragement and support in the Administration Building. It was University General Counsel Carol Kaesebier's idea to include photographs. She envisioned the book as being a scrapbook of coeducation campus life over the thirty-five years. To make this possible, she allowed us to use anything from the University Archives—pictures from the *Dome* yearbooks, articles from the *Observer* and the *Scholastic.* As a result, we were able to produce a much more visually interesting book for which we thank her.

In the University Archives, Charles Lamb and Elizabeth Hogan invested considerable time helping us hunt down what we needed. We also received help from Father Tom Blantz, CSC, former university archivist, and Erin Thornton '07, who used *Dome* yearbooks to fact-check for us. Thanks to Marty Schalm, College of Engineering graphic designer, for a stellar job laying out all of the photos and letters. Father John Jenkins's Chief of Staff Frances Shavers '80 and Associate Vice President/Counselor to the President Father Jim McDonald, CSC; Vice President of University Relations Lou Nanni; Director of Special Events and Protocol Pam Spence; Ave Maria Press President and Publisher Tom Grady; and American Studies Department Chairman Bob Schmuhl helped us in innumerable ways. In tracking down athletes, we owe many thanks to Rev. James Riehle, CSC, honorary Monogram Club president, and John Heisler, senior associate athletics director—media relations.

We've asked some of Notre Dame's most prominent male graduates and celebrities, as well, for their reflections. Many of them are fathers of Notre Dame alumnae. They've been keen observers of how the campus has changed from the all-male university they attended. The response was amazing. For example, the morning after we contacted Digger Phelps, Notre Dame's retired basketball coach, his handwritten note was faxed to us. The busier the man, it seemed, the faster they responded. Speaking about men, we also want to thank our husbands (many of whom are Notre Dame graduates, whom we wouldn't have met if Notre Dame hadn't become coed) for the support and love they gave us during this yearlong project.

Here in Chicago, thank you to Trustee Emeritus Newton Minow, who sent our manuscript to Kathleen Andrews, chairman of Andrews McMeel Universal, with a strong recommendation that she consider publishing it. We're grateful to Mrs. Andrews '62 MA, vice chairman of Notre Dame's Board of Trustees, for concurring with him, as well as to the entire Andrews McMeel Publishing team, especially Hugh Andrews '89, president and CEO; Dorothy O'Brien, managing director; and Kathy Massman Hilliard '81, '84 MA, publicity director.

Last year when we called Paula Cozzi Goedert, a Chicago-based attorney, head of Barnes Thornburg's not-for-profit national practice and mother of Robert '04, and told her of our plans, she immediately offered to serve as the Foundation's general counsel without charging us—a substantial gift. To help her, she recruited Kelly Bellinger, one of her associates and a 2001 Notre Dame Law School graduate. Kelly's great-grandfather, Ernest Morris, for whom the Morris Inn is named, was a Notre Dame trustee, as were her grandparents, Oliver Carmichael and Ernestine Morris Carmichael Raclin. Melissa Vallone, a copyright attorney in Barnes Thornburg's Chicago office, counseled us without charge on copyright issues for which we're most appreciative.

*Deo Gratias* to Monsignor Ken Velo of the Archdiocese of Chicago, who tracked down the identity of the priest photographed with Father Ted and Martin Luther King. Also in Chicago, we're grateful to Carolyn Vance, Paulita Pike's assistant and a 1984 Saint Mary's College graduate, who graciously volunteered to transcribe Father Ted's and Mary Davey Bliley's remarks at the May 2006 luncheon. Many thanks to Donna Shear, Northwestern University press director, and Robert B. Barnett, partner at Williams & Connolly, the Washington, D.C., law firm and literary representative to the stars there, for their advice and counsel.

Two weeks after we decided to do this book, Ann Therese was diagnosed with stage-3 breast cancer. That necessitated an immediate mastectomy, six months of chemotherapy, and almost six weeks of radiation. This book couldn't have happened without the medical expertise, magic potions, and unstinting support of the staffs of Northwestern Memorial Hospital's Robert H. Lurie Comprehensive Cancer Center, especially Dr. Steve Rosen, A.T.'s oncologist; Dr. John Butter, A.T.'s internist; and Lake Forest (Illinois) Hospital's radiation oncology department, especially Dr. Joe Imperato.

Finally, profits from *Thanking Father Ted* are being donated to the University of Notre Dame to fund a scholarship in Father Ted's name, as a 90th birthday present.

Thanks to everyone who has donated to the Thanking Father Ted Scholarship Fund in the Development Office including

Kathleen Walsh Anthony '85, '96 MBA
Lisa Becker '77
Barbara Beré
Gayla Molinelli Bush '77
Mary Davey Bliley '72
Claire Bula '01
Margaret Ann Capo '78
Ellen Carnahan '77
Susan Anderson Casper '76
Jean Collier '83
Darlene M. Palma Connelly '77, '80 JD
Americo Darin
   *In honor of Ann Therese Darin Palmer '73, '75 MBA and Mary Ellen Darin Tarpley '75, '80 JD*
Silvio Darin
Joan Dautremont-Gluck '74
Patrice Purcell DeCorrevont, '84
Deborah A. Dell '76
The Honorable Mary Catherine Rochford Demetrio '76, '79 JD
Judith A. Temmerman Donovan '77
Jean and Anthony Earley '47
Dr. Phillip J. Faccenda '51
The family of Dr. Phillip J. Faccenda '51
   *Maribeth Faccenda-Hough '82, Susan Faccenda Walsh '84, '88 JD, Kathryn Faccenda '85, Phillip John Faccenda '89, '92 JD, and Michael Anthony Faccenda '93, '96 JD*
The Honorable Carol A. Falvey '82
Mary Hesburgh Flaherty '79
Margaret M. Foran '76, '79 JD
Celeste Volz Ford '78
Anne Giffels '81
Marianne Morgan Harris '77
Elizabeth Keegan Hrycko '91
Amy Treder Kelliher '88
Tara C. Kenney '82
Donald P. Keough '85 Honorary
Sally M. Fischer LaPlante '73
The Honorable Diana Lewis '74, '82 JD
Roxanne O'Brien Martino '77
Patrick F. McCartan '56, '59 JD, '99 Honorary

Michael and Therese Koch McGraw '87
Andrew J. McKenna '51, '89 Honorary
Joan P. Mielski '79
Rosemary Mills-Russell '80
Josephine and Newton ('96 Honorary) N. Minow
John P. Mullen '57
 *In honor of Patricia Mullen '80, Mary Killeen Mullen '82, Neilli Mullen Walsh '84*
Mary Killeen Mullen '90
Dr. Mary Kay and John ('72) Mulvaney
 *In honor of Dr. Kerry Mulvaney Sheehan '98, Erin Mulvaney Callahan '04, and*
 *Katelyn Mary Mulvaney '08*
Dr. Elizabeth Neary '77
Notre Dame Club of Detroit
Janet Carney O'Brien '77
The Honorable Sheila O'Brien '77, '80 JD
Mr. and Mrs. Francis J. ('82) Oelerich III
 *In honor of Molly Oelerich '11*
Maureen O'Neill '77
Ann Therese Darin Palmer '73, '75 MBA
Laura Flaherty Palmer '80
Cindy Buescher Parseghian '77
Susan Oglesbee Payne '73
Jane Pfeiffer '91 Honorary
Ernestine M. Raclin '78 Honorary
Lee Ann Russo '77
Lee Ann '77 and Philip L. Russo Jr. '80
 *In honor of the late Philip L. Russo Sr. '44, '49 JD*
Johanna Ryan '73
Sharon Ryan '74
Dr. Carol Lally Shields '79, '05 Honorary
Sharon M. Sullivan '77
Elizabeth A. Toomey '81
Sherri Tubinis
Clare J. Twist, MD '82
Susan M. Valdisseri '84
Dick Vitale
 *In honor of Terri Vitale '94, '95 MBA and Sherri Vitale-Krug '96, '98 MBA*
Frank Wallmeyer '63
Julie Webb '73
The Women of the Notre Dame Class of 1977
Mary Ellen Woods '80

# 1

# Administrator, Trustee, and Women's Residence Hall Staff Reminiscences

# Thanking Father Ted Administrator, Trustee, and Women's Residence Hall Staff Reminiscences

Rev. Theodore M. Hesburgh, CSC '39
University of Notre Dame President 1952–1987

Rev. Ernest Bartell, CSC '53
University of Notre Dame Trustee 1973–present
Founding Executive Director, Helen Kellogg Institute
    for International Studies 1981–1997
Trustee 1973–2002
Emeritus Trustee since 2002

Susan Bennett '71 MA, '75 PhD
First Woman Assistant Rector, Badin Hall 1972–1973

Rev. Thomas E. Blantz, CSC '57, '63 MA
University Archivist 1969–1978
Vice President, Student Affairs 1970–1972
Department of History Chair 1980–1987
Trustee, Student Affairs Committee Member
    1970–1992
Trustee Emeritus since 1992

Thomas Carney '37, '69 Honorary
President, Alumni Association 1966
Trustee 1967–1986
Chairman Board of Trustees 1982–1986
Chairman, Student Affairs Committee 1967–1972
Trustee Emeritus since 1986

Kathleen Cekanski '75 JD
First Woman's Dorm Rector, Badin Hall 1972–1973
Rector, Breen-Phillips Hall 1973–1975

Richard W. Conklin '59 MA
Retired Associate Vice President for University
    Relations 1967–2001

Sister Barbara Couts, SC
Rector, Lyons Hall 1975–1978

Anthony F. Earley '47
National Alumni Board President 1966
Member, Advisory Council Admissions Office
    1970–1980
Trustee 1980–1993
Trustee Emeritus since 1993

Philip J. Faccenda '51
Special Assistant to the President 1967–1970
General Counsel 1970–1995
Vice President, Student Affairs 1973–1974
University Trustee 1972–1995
Trustee Emeritus since 1992

Elizabeth Fallon '76
Resident Assistant, Lyons Hall 1975–1976

John Goldrick '62, '70 MA, '84
Director of Admissions 1971–1984
Associate Vice President, Residence Life 1984–1991

Sister John Miriam Jones, SC '61 MS, '70
Assistant to the Provost 1972–1976
Assistant Provost 1976–1987
Associate Provost 1987–1989

Sister Jean Lenz, OFM '67 MA
Rector, Farley Hall 1973–1982
Rector, London Program 1982–1983
Assistant Vice President, Student
    Affairs 1983–2005

Carmen Leon '73 JD
First Woman's Resident Assistant,
    Badin Hall 1972–1973

John Macheca '62
Midwest Regional Development and Public Relations
    Director 1969–1973
Dean of Students 1973–1975

Mary Martha McNamara '73 JD
Resident Assistant, Walsh Hall 1972–1973

Newton N. Minow '96 Honorary
Trustee 1965–1977, 1983–1996
Trustee Emeritus since 1996

Jane Pfeiffer '91 Honorary
Trustee 1974–2003
Trustee Emeritus since 2003

Jane Pitz '72 MA
First Woman's Assistant Rector, Walsh Hall 1972–1982
Rector, London Program 1982,
    1984–1987, 1992–1995
Rector 1983–1984
O'Gara-Grace Graduate Women's Dormitory

Ernestine Morris Carmichael Raclin '78 Honorary
First Woman Chairman
1976 Notre Dame Capital Campaign
Trustee 1976–1998
Trustee Emeritus since 1998

Rev. James Riehle, CSC '49
Dean of Students 1967–1972
Chaplain, Notre Dame Varsity Sports Teams
    1975–present
Executive Director/Honorary
    President, Notre Dame Monogram Club
    1980–present

James A. Roemer '51, '55 JD
General Counsel 1972–1976
Dean of Students 1976–1985

Joanne Szafran '73 MA
Second Women's Dorm Rector (Walsh) 1972–1973

The Honorable Ann C. Williams '75 JD
First Woman's Assistant Rector, Farley Hall 1973
Trustee
Circuit Judge, U.S. Court of Appeals (7th Circuit),
    Chicago

*Father Theodore M. Hesburgh, CSC, retired University of Notre Dame president, was interviewed by Ann Therese Darin Palmer on February 5, 2007.*

*Years before you and the trustees decided to open up Notre Dame to women undergraduates, you'd already identified Catholic women as an area for serious academic research. What prompted you to do that?*

When I went to the Faculty Committee at Catholic University and they said, "What are you going to do your doctoral thesis on?" I responded, "I'm going to do it on the place of the laity in the Church." And they said, "That's not a serious theological subject."

I replied, "If people who represent better than 50 percent of the whole Church, if they're not a serious subject, then we better go back and find out what the word 'serious' means." I'm delighted to have done my thesis on the place of the laity in the church.

*Why was it important for Notre Dame to admit women undergraduates?*

Notre Dame was a great place, there was no question. But, there were times when it was a pretty raunchy place. There was something of the locker-room attitude about the residence halls. The language was pretty awful. The whole level of civility needed improvement, to put it mildly.

I grew up with three sisters. So, I was used to living with them, as well as my mother and my dad. We had a fine life. I did not have anything to complain about. They were wonderful ladies. My life is a lot richer because I was not just formed by my mother and father but by them. You can't live with three people like that and not be somewhat formed by them.

Anyway, I didn't have to have a picture drawn for me to know that if Notre Dame had one big failing, it was the fact that it was only addressing half of the Catholic Church. There are, in fact, more women Catholics than men if you add them all up. Some of the really great things that happened in the Church happened because of the imagination, the dedication, the zeal and generosity of women. Some were women religious, but other women, as well.

*So, what did you do?*

It struck me that if we are in the education business for higher education in the Catholic Church in America, we can't say we are doing this and ignore half of the American Catholic population. So, I began to make a few noises. It was obvious this was not going to be an easy thing to do.

I thought I'd finesse it by getting Saint Mary's into it. We were practically begun at the same time in the same decade back in the 1840s. If we did it by merging with them, it would automatically be a lot easier to sell than just our going coeducational out of the blue.

The sisters said right off, "Yes, we would like to join with Notre Dame." And I thought this was going to be easy. But I forgot my life with those three sisters.

And we met and we met and we met. Every time we came this close to an agreement, good Sister Gerald, who was the treasurer of their group, said, "Oh, I just remembered we have this item here, you will have to give us $1 million a year more." We could take that once or twice, but after the fifth time we were running out of even visions of money and resources.

And finally, one day after three solid months of discussions of how we were going to do it, after we agreed that we would do it, how we would join, I said one morning after we had our opening prayer, "Ladies, I think I can describe your point of view." And they said, "You can? Go ahead." So I said, "You have been saying for months now that you wanted to join with Notre Dame and it was often referred to as a kind of marriage of the two schools, which is typical, one school male and one school female." But then I said, "Having discussed the marriage now these last three months, I have come up with one impression. You say that you want to marry us." They all said, "Yes." "But you don't want to take our name and you don't want to live with us." And they said, "That's right."

And I said, "Well, that may be right, but that's not a marriage," and at that moment the merger was off, and we decided to go it alone, which was, you know, pioneering because we had never had women lay students there before, but now looking back that was a long time ago.

*What was the impact of that decision?*

It does my heart good because the experiment was right. Many other universities and colleges followed as they had on going under lay control. I think we are a much healthier place today. We are certainly a more intellectual place today. We are certainly a more cultural place today. And I have to say we are a better place today because about 50 percent of our students today are women. It may be 49 percent, but let's not quibble over 1 percent. But, the place is quite totally different. It is something you have to work at all the time. It is not automatic.

I just assumed having grown up with three sisters, the way they changed my life, the women coming to Notre Dame would change the lives of many of the men. And I also saw coming out of this, as you illustrate, some wonderful marriages and some wonderful friends and associates. But, nothing ever happens just automatically in this world. You have to work at it.

*What were some of your concerns during those first years of coeducation?*

I wanted women to have some downtime of their own. So you can have open halls all day long, but come midnight until after breakfast a women's hall is a women's hall, and men aren't welcome. Of course, the men have been screaming for years about this. They are not screaming quite so much today. But they say "This is terrible. Every school in the country has men and women in the same dorms."

They may be right. I may be wrong, but as I see it, there are times when women want to get in their pj's, sit on the bed, and talk women talk. It's important that women have women friends. The place to make women friends, best of all, I think, is in college when everyone is mature and your lives are beginning to take some definite shape. It's not conducive to women having women friends if they never have any time when they can just be women like we are today in this meeting. And coeducation is great, but not twenty-four hours a day. Some days, sometimes, you must be by yourselves.

I think that is true. For some reason, that rule has survived all these years. It certainly had a lot of critics. I have been called every name under the sun. But, I have a feeling that in the long run, it's the best thing for both sides because it preserves the privacy of women, but also to some extent the mystery of women, which is also important.

*Thirty-five years after the fact, has Notre Dame coeducation turned out as you anticipated?*

Notre Dame is a much better place than it once was. It was always a great place. I think it was a great place because it was under the name and patronage of a woman. We couldn't have a better patroness or be named after a better person.

We are named after the greatest human being who ever lived. People say, "You're crazy, Christ was the greatest human being." And I say, "Christ was human by nature, but as a person He was divine, the second person of the Blessed Trinity. So you can't compare a human being to the second person of the Blessed Trinity. Mary was the only person, as far as we know theologically, who ever conceived without original sin. Mary happens to be the holiest woman who ever lived because she was picked by God himself, not by me or somebody else, to be the mother of His divine son, and she was His prototype.

He grew up with her. She bathed Him. She diapered Him. She walked Him. She taught Him. She spanked Him, I'm sure once or twice. She was not above scolding Him, when He was lost in the temple, when He wanted to get away from the hum-drum life and have a little life of His own. Precocious, surely, but after all He was a son of God, as well as a son of Mary. But it's nice to think our school is named after the greatest person who ever lived or ever will live, that her name is Mary. And, we are lucky because it has a little pizzazz that we can say it in French—Notre Dame.

So, to all of the daughters of Notre Dame, I would like to say I can't tell you how proud I am of the fact that you all bear Notre Dame degrees. By your lives and your goodness, you have changed the world in many ways. There is no telling how much more you can change the world. But, I can tell you how much the world needs changing. It is getting to be a pretty coarse, ugly kind of place. It needs the kind of refinement that only women can bring to human life. I have to thank you for the enormous loyalty you've shown to Notre Dame. It was no mistake to bring you into the family and to make you full-fledged members, half the population. You've given Notre Dame a whole new mean-ing in the life of women and marriage and family and education, business, and law.

You continue to make this old guy very proud of all of you and where you are going and what you have done. As someone once said, "You ain't seen nothin' yet." It's gonna be even better.

ᶜᎦᶳ

*Rev. Ernest Bartell, CSC, '53 was a professor of economics from 1981 to 2003, as well as the founding executive director of the Helen Kellogg Institute for International Studies from 1981 to 1997.*

*An Economics Department professor emeritus since 2003, currently he is a faculty fellow of the Kellogg Institute for International Studies and of the Institute for Educational Initiatives.*

*Father Bartell was a member of the board of trustees from 1973 until 2002, when he was elected trustee emeritus.*

Although coeducation as an institutional policy at Notre Dame didn't arrive until midway through Father Hesburgh's term as president in the early '70s, the coeducational experience on campus didn't just suddenly pop up then.

In fact, the institutionalization of coeducation was preceded by a number of gender-related initiatives much earlier in his presidency, including some with which I was associated. As an example from the early '60s, Father Hesburgh was a strong supporter of a program of summer school work projects in the United States and Latin America for students, the Council for the International Lay Apostolate (CILA), which became an antecedent to the current Center for Social Concerns.

Although CILA's first service projects in 1962 grew out of campus conversation involving only male Notre Dame students about implementing Catholic social teaching, the organization uniquely and quickly grew to include Saint Mary's students, who participated in all CILA activities. In addition to the summer service projects, these activities included preparatory lectures, discussion and classes, Masses and retreats.

Not everyone was thrilled with the CILA initiatives. In a somewhat disapproving interrogation, the university officer for Student Affairs at Notre Dame once likened the coed CILA in its early days to "another bird-watchers' association," and I was reprimanded for encroaching on the turf of the university's Development Office when the Notre Dame Alumni Club of New York surprised us with an unsolicited financial contribution to CILA. At the same time, authorities at Saint Mary's were uneasy about the circumstances of fraternization between Saint Mary's and Notre Dame CILA members, e.g., during the three-day drives to project sites in Mexico. Once, when an overnight retreat to the shore of Lake Michigan had been planned under my direction, there was administrative resistance at Saint Mary's to granting permission for participation by Saint Mary's CILA members. Even when assured that a Holy Cross priest, yours truly, would be with the students at all times, the literal response was "You know you can't trust young priests these days."

So, the strong support for CILA from Father Hesburgh provided invaluable cover. Father Ted surprised us in the second year of CILA projects by arriving unannounced by car with Father Howard Kenna, then our Holy Cross provincial, in Tacámbaro, Michoacán, at the far end of an unpaved road in rural central Mexico. Despite the somewhat crude accommodations they had to endure, they spent several days with the student volunteers and were consistently supportive of CILA and its successor programs thereafter. Even in the relative rigid climate of seminary programs in those days, Holy Cross seminarians were subsequently allowed to participate fully in all coed CILA activities.

Of course, the opportunities for coeducational experiences on campus expanded greatly through the '60s with the growth of the "co-exchange" programs between Notre Dame and Saint Mary's. On one hand, the co-ex programs could be seen as a defensive reaction to growing sentiments in favor of coeducation emerging among the more selective single-sex private colleges and universities, both Catholic and secular. On the other hand, the success of the co-ex experience, despite its logistical limits, could and did also raise the level of interest in more expansive coeducational opportunities at Notre Dame. It was during this period that Suzanne Kelly led an initiative that included Frs. Dave Burrell, John Gerber, and myself to design and propose a coeducational "experimental" college within Notre Dame that would provide opportunities for more creative educational programming than could typically be generated within the traditional, somewhat hierarchical, university structure.

During these years of educational ferment, Father Hesburgh's own public stance toward coeducation can perhaps be described as one of letting "a thousand flowers bloom," neither passive nor directive. Then, in what appeared to be an unexpected lurch forward, in the dead of one winter the boards of trustees of Notre Dame and Saint Mary's met in the exhilarating warmth of Florida sunshine and abruptly declared a merger of the two institutions. The exhilaration soon dissipated in the cold light of subsequent negotiations when it became clear that the assumptions and expectations of officers of the two institutions were widely divergent.

The collapse of those negotiations almost inevitably set the stage for Notre Dame's independent decision to go coed. Nevertheless, the decision was not uniformly welcomed by all segments of the university community, especially among alumni and even among some long-serving faculty and staff. I recall speaking on the subject to several alumni clubs in the months before the final decision, when it seemed there was more vocal opposition than support. Almost invariably, when asked why they opposed coeducation, one or more alumni would respond with statements to the effect: "If you admit women, my son won't be able to get into Notre Dame." That reaction was so common that I learned to respond with a question: "May I ask how many of you have daughters?" These mild attempts at humor were not universally appreciated.

The fact that Father Hesburgh was not as publicly vocal on the subject during the long run-up to formal coeducation at Notre Dame as he was on other subjects, e.g., civil and human rights issues, may appear to some observers as ambivalence and doubt about coeducation. However, the fact is that it was only after the baby steps and missteps toward coeducation in the first half of the Hesburgh era that a necessary and sufficient consensus in favor of independently "going coed" within the Notre Dame community began to emerge. So, I prefer to conclude that Father Ted, always an astute judge of the feasible, simply and accurately gauged the timing to insure the success of so important a decision. The subsequent record of coeducation at Notre Dame today and his own demonstrated commitment to it should be sufficient and enduring evidence of his wise judgment.

*Susan Bennett '71 MA, '75 PhD was Badin Hall's first woman assistant rector from 1972 to 1973. During this period, she also served as representative to the board of trustees' Student Affairs Committee, representing women's dormitories.*

*A retired associate partner at Accenture, today she is a real estate associate in Palm Beach Gardens, Florida.*

Dear Father Ted,

Last fall I made a return trip to the campus, after having been away for several years. It was a moving and memorable time for me. I have returned for the occasional football weekend but this past year I took my eighty-three-year-old aunt with me, as visiting Notre Dame had been one of those "life objectives" she had for many years. It made the trip a bit different because it allowed me to reminisce about my graduate days there, as we toured the grounds and visited the buildings. Through all of this however, I realized that Notre Dame is much more than beautiful grounds and majestic architecture—it is an incommunicable spirit that has to be experienced. Even a day on campus can let one feel it. The leisurely weekend, ostensibly to allow her to experience the campus and fulfill a long-held wish, was equally important to me.

The boundaries have expanded well beyond the days of the early '70s, the grounds have been enhanced with phenomenal landscaping, the new buildings are marvelous.... The renovation of Sacred Heart is beautiful. The overwhelming and lasting impression, however, was the comfort of the "feel" of the place remaining intact. The dignity was there ... but so was the warmth. Passing the students on the quad made one feel the energy of youth ... wondering what great contribution would this one or that one be possibly destined to do ... whether in science, math, government, business, or social service either domestic or foreign. It was a feeling of going "home" for a visit.

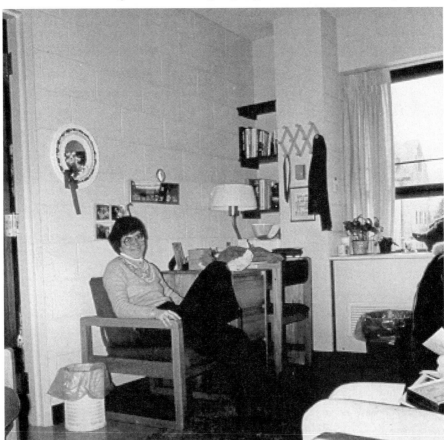

Susan Bennett, Badin Hall's first woman assistant rector.

It was great, on this tour, to see that Badin Hall had survived. The old bookstore across from it was long gone but Badin was still intact. Midway in my graduate studies, the decision was made to introduce coeducation to the campus. Badin Hall was identified as one of the first women's residence halls. I sought and accepted the position of assistant rector thinking I had a good background for the position while getting my PhD from the Department of Education and Psychology.

The campus was a virtual laboratory for "organizational change" and the residence hall a microcosm of adaptation to an evolving cultural environment. The selection process culled the best and brightest of the women applicants ... so many applications, so few spaces (in the 350 range the first year) that the cream really did rise. In an already strong academic environment, you had the exceptional women academic leaders entering the campus—well equipped to hold their own.

As assistant rector of Badin Hall in the first year of coeducation, I was given the opportunity to participate in university administration well beyond my "pay grade." There just were not that many women in any administrative capacity at that time so those of us that were there were asked to participate in multiple activities. I was elected to sit on the Student Affairs Committee of the board of trustees to represent the rectors of residence halls. This was an honor and a responsibility, since there were many issues those first years as the campus met the challenge of coeducation.

It was interesting to listen to discussions of the potential "cost" of coeducation ... not in building adaptation (though that was part of it) but in potential lost revenue. Would there be alumni who disagreed and would not donate? Would there now be intermarriage among grads and reduce the donating funds? Would there be women marrying non-ND students and having the male alma mater receive the larger or only donation? In the end, the decision had been made that the greater cost would be to bypass the coed decision and the board took the risk.

Having the best and brightest of the women applicants posed many challenges socially and academically to them in their new community. They were strong women; but, it was a battleground for acceptance not only with male peer students but also with some of the faculty in the early days. Today's students would not know what I am talking about because it is so commonplace. But, in those first years it was a major challenge for the early entrants. There were actually fewer women on campus the first year of coeducation than in prior years because the exchange program with Saint Mary's was cut back. Somehow many of the male students in those days preferred to socially relate to the "visiting women" than to those who had "moved in." It was difficult.

This also created a reaction from the women of ND as to the maturity of the ND men. It was truly a cultural clash in the beginning and not easy for the pioneers. The university was taking a giant leap from tradition. The reality of women on campus did not come easy to those who did not sign up for a coeducational

Badin Hall residents, September 1972.

experience, but nevertheless, they found themselves in the crosswinds of change.

The women received lots of attention. This was the good news and the bad news. It was difficult for many of them to handle the complexity of the environment they found themselves in. They not only had traditional adaptation to college and living away from home, but were now caught up in an historic event that was much more difficult than many of them anticipated.

Faculty members were not all on board in support of the move to coeducation either. In many classes, the faculty would talk about the women in the third person as if they were not there. Or, they would openly discuss the pitfalls to this change at the university. There was early discrimination, not necessarily in a legal sense, but certainly in a cultural sense. The administration did their best to address this but the attitude took time to change.

The media made a circus out of the first days of classes. All major networks were present looking for "the story." It was an open forum for the disgruntled and dismayed, but also for the committed! One can only imagine what it would have been like had the cable networks been up and running with the myriad of talk shows lining up at the gates.

This seems unreal today when we look at department chairs, heads of colleges like the business college, and other significant administrative positions being held by women. It seems impossible that back in the inaugural days, the administration had to go to residence hall rectors or assistant rectors to get a woman administrative representative for major trustee committees. In one sense, I was clearly the beneficiary of those times. It enabled me to have experience and exposure that I would not have had otherwise.

Father Ted never wavered in his commitment to that coeducation decision. He kept a watchful eye on the integration process of the new women of ND. He seized every opportunity to reinforce the positive aspects of this culture change without patronizing the women or placating the men. He was truly a role model for his faculty and staff. He was a source of strength for those of us fighting the daily wars and/or supporting the young women students.

Like the flag flying over the palace of London when the queen is in residence, the light in the upper corner of the Golden Domed–Administration Building was the beacon that told us Father Ted was "home." That corner light, which burned bright long into the night, gave us all a bit more comfort. It never went unnoticed. Somehow you knew all was well . . . or could be made well if necessary.

Sincerely,

Susan Bennett
Class of '71 MA, '75 PhD
Palm Beach Gardens, Florida

*Rev. Thomas E. Blantz, CSC, '57 served as university archivist from 1969 to 1978. During part of this period, Father Blantz, who also has a master of arts in history from Notre Dame (1963), served as vice president for Student Affairs from 1970 to 1972. He chaired the Department of History from 1980 to 1987.*

*Father Blantz was elected a trustee in 1970. He served on the board from 1970 to 1992, when he was elected a trustee emeritus. During his tenure as a trustee, he was a member of its Student Affairs Committee.*

The decision to admit undergraduate women into Notre Dame in the fall of 1972 was an excellent decision on the part of Father Hesburgh. During this time, I was both a trustee and vice president of Student Affairs.

There were probably several reasons for the decision to admit undergraduate women that fall. First, in the past many students had come to Notre Dame from single-sex high schools, but such schools were declining in number and students were now more comfortable and at home in coeducational classrooms. Second, many smaller Catholic women's colleges were being forced to close, chiefly for financial reasons. If sufficient opportunities were to exist for Catholic education for women, schools like Notre Dame needed to open their doors to them. Third, women were more and more taking their rightful places in the worlds of business, education, politics. If men and women were to work together successfully after graduation, they should begin preparing for it in college. Finally, Notre Dame was continuing its efforts to admit the most qualified student body possible. Opening admission to women would greatly increase that applicant pool.

There was a background of several years leading up to this decision. For most of the above reasons, and to reduce duplication of costs and efforts between the two institutions, Notre Dame and Saint Mary's College began a "co-exchange" program I believe in the fall of 1965, permitting a limited number of students from each school to enroll in classes on the opposite campus. The program expanded over the next few years. In the spring of 1971, the two schools announced their intention to unify by the close of the 1974–1975 academic year. As those so-called "merger talks" continued during the summer and fall of 1971, serious differences between the two schools emerged, I believe chiefly in the business and academic areas. The discussions were ter-

Father Tom Blantz (far left, facing the camera) at a 1970 board of trustees meeting. To his left are Trustees Dr. O. Meredith Wilson and Notre Dame Treasurer Father Jerry Wilson. To Father Blantz's right are (nearest camera) Trustee Chairman Edmund A. Stephan, Holy Cross Provincial Howard Kenna, and Executive Vice President Edmund P. Joyce. Standing is Trustee Jerome W. Van Gorkum.

minated that November. Notre Dame officials were still convinced of the benefits of educating men and women together, and thus made the decision to admit undergraduate women to Notre Dame beginning in the fall of 1972.

There were clearly challenges in preparing Notre Dame for undergraduate women that fall. In the area of Student Affairs, for example, there were questions of integrating residence hall life, student health services, athletic facilities, and so on. Anticipating a unification with Saint Mary's, we had hoped to rely primarily on the experience and proven expertise of Saint Mary's administrators. When the unification talks ended, we did ask a few of the Saint Mary's student leaders to continue to advise us in these areas. They were most helpful. Of course, some decisions we made were better than others—that is probably normal—and the women themselves can best evaluate where we succeeded and where we did not. But the basic decision of Father Hesburgh, to admit undergraduate women in Notre Dame itself once the unification talks with Saint Mary's College proved unsuccessful, was clearly the correct one. Notre Dame is a better place now for educating men and women together, and Notre Dame men and women are both making significant contributions today to the nation, to the Church, and to the world.

Sincerely,

(Rev.) Thomas E. Blantz, CSC

*Thomas P. Carney '37 was elected to the Notre Dame Board of Trustees in 1967 and was chairman of its Student Affairs Committee from 1968 to 1973, during the university's transition to coeducation.*

*Carney, president of the Alumni Association in 1966, was chairman of the board of trustees from 1982 to 1986.*

*He is the father of four Notre Dame graduates: Thomas P. Jr. '67, Sheila Carney Hopkins '74, James '75, and Janet Carney O'Brien '77, as well as grandfather to five additional graduates. Janet, a freelance writer, interviewed her father on November 7, 2006.*

*What was it like to be a trustee during the transition to coeducation?*

Probably the most stimulating experience as a member of the Notre Dame Board of Trustees was my tenure as chairman of the Student Affairs Committee during the late

'60s and early '70s. That was the time of the great student revolts and demonstrations across the country. It was during that time also that there was a great demand from the students for coeducation. I was in total sympathy with them. People have accused me of wanting coeducation because I had two daughters. An equally important reason was because I had two sons.

*How would you describe the coeducation process?*

I have to say that coeducation at Notre Dame was an evolutionary, rather than revolutionary, process. Shortly after I joined the board in 1967, coeducation discussions began. As women from Saint Mary's were integrated into classrooms at Notre Dame, the prospect of becoming a fully coeducational institution emerged as a reasonable next step. At the time, the focus was on merging Saint Mary's and Notre Dame into a single university.

*What was the reaction of alumni to the idea of coeducation? Did the university consult with anyone, while it was conducting talks with Saint Mary's about merging?*

There was some opposition from a small number of alumni but less than you might think. At the time, we had Rosemary Park, vice chancellor of UCLA and president emeritus of Connecticut College, on the board. She was the first woman to serve on the Notre Dame board and a proponent of coeducation. She, along with Lewis Mayhew, a Stanford educator and nationally renowned authority on higher education and change, coauthored a study in 1970 on the efficacy and logistics of forming a coeducational unit between Saint Mary's and Notre Dame.

The Park-Mayhew report was widely circulated through the Notre Dame community in the early months of 1971. By that time, the discussions were no longer about "why" Notre Dame needed coeducation, but rather "how"—how to blend faculty and administration, coed dorms vs. single-sex dorms, merging academic departments and so on.

*What was your role in the negotiation process? How would you characterize the negotiation process?*

I was a member of a small committee assigned to carry out the negotiations. It seemed to make a great deal of sense. Notre Dame favored the concept of a coeducational campus and Saint Mary's could benefit from what a University like Notre Dame had to offer.

In order to isolate ourselves from campus activities, several meetings of the committee were held at my home in Lake Forest, Illinois. The negotiations went smoothly for a time, but began to stall due in large part to concerns on the part of Saint Mary's administrators, who saw the value but also the loss in the prospect of absorption by the much larger Notre Dame institution. The negotiations fell through by the summer of 1971 and each school decided to go its own way.

That following Thanksgiving weekend the Notre Dame board officially voted to approve coeducation. In hindsight, it was probably the best decision either institution could have made. Notre Dame went coed in 1972. Saint Mary's has become a very successful all-female institution with a strong, nationwide reputation.

*When the first undergraduate women arrived on campus, were there any problems?*

As for the climate, once women began living on campus, I truly don't recall problems of any significance being brought to the attention of the board. It was a very smooth transition from a logistics point, mostly because so much groundwork had already been laid in anticipation of merging with Saint Mary's.

Janet Carney O'Brien '77, Dr. Thomas Carney '37, Sheila Carney Hopkins '74, and Mary Liz Carney at Sheila's graduation.

From what I could see, maintaining an all-male campus was far more fraught with problems that seemed to dissipate once a more normalized coeducational environment was created. The caliber of young women who came and continue to come to Notre Dame is second to none. Their arrival opened the door for every top student in the country seeking the kind of education Notre Dame has to offer. In the end, it's the education that brings students to Notre Dame. The fact that young men and women can share that education and campus living is just one more welcome element in their preparation for life outside of college.

*In 1972, Kathleen Cekanski was appointed the first woman rector of a residence hall at the University of Notre Dame. She was rector of Badin Hall from 1972 to 1973 and of Breen-Phillips Hall from 1973 to 1975. Today, Cekanski is city council attorney for the City of South Bend, Indiana. She was interviewed on November 16, 2006, by Ann Therese Darin Palmer.*

*You were appointed Notre Dame's first woman dormitory rector in spring 1972, when Badin was named the first women's dorm. Joann Szafran was the second women's rector, appointed to Walsh. What was your first year as Badin rector like?*

In spring 1973, the university flew both of us, Father Jerry Wilson, the university's treasurer, and Sister John Miriam Jones, the assistant provost, to Florida to update the board on how the transition to coeducation was going from our perspectives.

From my perspective, the biggest thing we had to do, as women rectors, was make each woman feel welcomed in her hall, the classroom, and the campus at-large. I also highlighted the areas that needed improving. We needed role models—more women on the faculty.

When I would attend gabfests, pizzafests, or popcornfests in Badin at night, the most common complaint I'd hear was women students weren't being called upon in classes. So, I decided to sit in on some of their classes to assess what was going on. One class I visited was Father Jim Shilts's physics class. He was also the assistant vice president of student affairs. When he saw me, he pointed out who I was and did something more people should have done. He talked about how great it was to have women on this campus and in his class. That helped a lot.

# A first look at the new rectors

by Anthony Abowd

The dawn of coeducation brings new faces to the rector and assistant rector scene at Notre Dame. The new dormitory staffs of Badin and Walsh are young, excited, very optimistic and totally female.

"It is not that women need Notre Dame, but that ND needs women," says Sr. Jane Pitz, assitant rector in Walsh, echoing the views of many ND administrators.

"This is a challenge," says Joanne Szafran, rector in Walsh.

"I'm very optimistic," says Kathy Cekanski, Badin's new rector.

Both Ms. Szafran and Ms. Cekanski are, naturally, the first female rectors in ND history. They are also the only rectors that are not members of any religious order. From this unique position they explain their qualifications and what the future has in store for their halls.

Szafran is presently a grad student in History at ND. Her undergraduate degree is from Merrimak College in Massachusetts. Last year she was the director of Holy Cross Hall at St. Mary's. This, she believes, is her greatest asset in her new position.

"From last year's experience IU can say that I am familiar with the environment. I know what is is like living with girls who go to school at ND," Szafran says.

In the months ahead, the new staff in Badin and Walsh will play a key role in establishing hall character. The new staffs inherited halls that had no hall government, no home rule and a set of entirely new residents.

"What's really a challenge," says Szafran, "is establishing a tradition and setting our own precedents. We have no example to follow. We are the first in line."

## 'What's really a challenge is establishing a tradition and setting our own precedents.'

Joanne Szafran is a ND grad student in History and the rector of Walsh Hall.

## 'I know what it is like living with girls who go to school at ND.'

Cekanski, an Ohio State graduate, is one of the "pioneers" females in the ND Law School. She is presently in her third year of law studies. Her law training and her status as a female member of ND for the past two years, she believes are her greatest assets.

"Throughout my law school experience I have been trying to break down barriers. This year should be similar. Also, as a lawyer, I am being trained to counsel and listen to people's problems. This should be very helpful," Cekanski says.

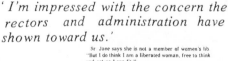

## 'I'm impressed with the concern the rectors and administration have shown toward us.'

Kathy Cekanski, a third year law student, is the new rector of Badin Hall.

Still the rectors are wary about problems. Probably the most formidable possibility is a panty raid on the new female halls. The staff expects some type of mass invasion because the dorms are much closer than St. Mary's dorms. They hope to adequately prepare the halls

The rectors are happy with the preparations made for coeducation. The halls are newly remodeled, and the Rockne Memorial and the ACC have female facilities. Even the bookstore has stocked ladies gym suits.

Sr. Jane says she is not a member of women's lib "But I do think I am a liberated woman, free to think and act as I see fit."

"I dislike the label 'women's lib,' but I do think women should be allowed to pursue a career the same as men," says Cekanski

"I believe in the equality of women," says Szafran. "Women should be recognized as real women and treated as such."

The new staff feels that the new coeds will be subject to close scrutiny in the months ahead. Sue Roberts, a new assistant in the Provost office, tells of her college experience which parallels the current ND situation

"I was one of twenty in a class of 1,000 men. You feel so visible as a woman that you are afraid to make mistakes," says Ms. Roberts.

ND women will probably be very visible for some time. As Notre Dame approaches this new era of coeducation, Szafran expressed one caution.

"I just hope that people don't judge too quickly. Remember, we have to establish whole new traditions here."

## 'The halls are just the right size.'

"The halls are just the right size. They are not too big. With the small female residences, we have twice the staff we would have if we had one big dormitory. I'm impressed with the concern the rectors and administration has shown toward us," say Cekanski.

"I really like the willingness of those people to try different things," says Szafran.

In such a prominent position for ND's coeducation program, the rectors and assitants face constant connection with women's liberation movement." Still the new residence hall staff members do not consider themselves hard-core women's libbers.

Sr. Jane Pitz is with Campus Ministry in addition to being the rector assistant in Walsh.

## 'I just hope people don't judge too quickly.'

From the *Observer*, August 1972 freshman orientation edition.

I also talked a lot to Professor Emil T. Hofman, the dean of freshman year. He was universally respected. He had a unique way of making a phone call here and there so that the animosity lessened.

Another area that needed attention was the ACC. Joann and I were both fencers and wanted to fence. We weren't allowed in either the ACC or Rockne Building. There were limited or nonexistent activities for women. Finally, we decided to go into the ACC to play handball. Whomever was on duty that night let us know that he didn't like us being there. We never played again. But, we needed to make a point.

That's also how we opened up skating for women at the ACC. Once a week, I'd take some girls skating. It started with a small group but grew in number every week. Activities like that were critical for meshing the men and women on campus.

The bookstore was another area. There wasn't much in the bookstore for women. There weren't any leisure magazines, books, or other casual reading. Back then, almost no one had a car. They needed to learn in the bookstore that girls didn't study all of the time. They needed leisure reading and other women's products.

Dr. Emil T. Hofman '53 MS, '63 PhD, '90 Honorary was dean of freshman year of studies from 1971 to 1990.

*How did the women deal with any verbal harassment or other gestures that might not have been the most welcoming?*

When I first started at Badin, I was also a third-year law student. I didn't expect the amount of contact that the girls would want to have with me both day and night. I don't know how I did both jobs.

One issue that we had to address was the amount of animosity that was verbally foisted upon them. They had to put up with some pretty cutting remarks, when they walked into class at first. Several of them were told that they were taking up the spot that would have gone to someone's brother. We dealt with that by being as positive as we could be until the boys got to know them. The girls couldn't retreat.

*What did you do to make sure that the girls felt welcome?*

It was imperative to get Father Ted involved at Badin as much as possible. He was at our welcome program. It was important for each of the women to hear from him why undergraduate women were needed at Notre Dame. They needed to hear him tell them that the university couldn't achieve academic excellence without them. That's the same argument he'd given to the trustees.

Many of the women had been questioning whether they'd made the right choice to come to Notre Dame and be part of the first group of women. They were questioning why put up with the innuendos, the pressure, the nastiness. He told us that night and reiterated it throughout the year that walking down this new path was worth the fight. If we were going to make a positive impact on the university, we had to make a stand. We deserved to be here. Father's eloquence and presence meant a lot to each of the women that night.

When he spoke to us that year, Father Ted would always, by analogy, compare what we were going through with what was happening worldwide. By then, he was a respected national and international leader who was on a lot of boards and commissions. He was able to tell us about the struggles happening in other countries where women didn't even have the opportunity to pursue higher education.

Why should we be complaining, when not only was the door open, but the sky was the limit? He said it would be tough, but we wouldn't have been selected if the university hadn't felt that we were ready to accept that call. Both what he said and the way that he said it made all of us at Badin feel good.

In his homilies and confabs with the Badin women that year, Father Ted would also talk about, "ever old, ever new." When you're making a significant change, trying to address how Notre Dame becomes a world leader academically and doesn't stagnate, you look at "ever old"—appreciate the past. But, you also have to be aware of what's the cutting of the new, "ever new." It's almost like the meshing of history—appreciate the past, as you're looking into the future.

*Was there anything that you experienced that year you hadn't expected?*

I wasn't expecting the utter depression that some girls experienced who felt that they couldn't cope. Through all kinds of hall events and just being there to talk, we made them feel that they weren't alone. Sometimes we'd pull in their roommates and ask them to help us. For the most part, we were able to address these issues. The other thing that I couldn't solve were the girls who were absolutely beautiful and never had a date.

*At the end of the first year, did you feel as if the year had been a success?*

There were more role models on campus, more women's activities. The golf course that had been restricted to only men under the terms it had been given to the university, was finally opened to women. There was a good spirit.

We were able to invite and attract quality speakers, such as Margaret Chase Smith, the only woman U.S. senator. It was critical for all of us to hear her stories. The girls could reflect on some of the heartaches they'd experienced and realize that it was worth it. She talked about how as a woman pioneer, you always have to be a lady and you have to be kind and considerate to each other.

At the end of that year, the majority of Badin women felt that we were one big family. When the decision was made that Breen-Phillips and Farley would be the next women's dorms on the north campus, very few women in Walsh or Badin were willing to leave. We had struggled and we grew stronger. Nobody wanted to give that up. We had pulled together to succeed.

I said that I'd throw my hat in the ring to be considered as one of the rectors of BP or Farley. When I was appointed rector of BP, I said that I wanted as many Badin women as could to follow me. About forty did.

*How critical was Father Ted to the success of Notre Dame coeducation?*

Father Ted's doctoral dissertation was on mediation. He was able to mediate among the board of trustees, convincing them coeducation would be not only a good thing for Notre Dame, it would be a great thing academically and socially. Donors wouldn't cut and run. He was able to open up Notre Dame's doors wider than they'd ever been opened before.

Without Father Ted's leadership and mentoring abilities, the university would not be what it is today. His door was always open to us—students and staff—until the wee hours of the morning. He truly has been a "Father" figure to us all. When I'd see his shining light on the third floor of the Administration Building late at night, I always felt more confident that he was doing everything humanly possible to make this the best place ever demographically and socially.

*Richard W. Conklin '59 MA joined Notre Dame's public information staff in 1967.*

*He spent thirty-four years at the university, often serving as its principal spokesperson.*

*Conklin's oral history with Father Hesburgh provided the basis for* God, Country, Notre Dame, *Father Hesburgh's best-selling autobiography. He also edited* Monk's Notre Dame *for retired University President Father Edward A. Malloy.*

*In 2001, Conklin retired as associate vice president of university relations. He received three presidential awards during his service, as well as the Alumni Association's James E. Armstrong Award in 1993.*

*His family was among the very first in which each member has a Notre Dame degree. His wife, Annette, received an MA in music in 1981. Their three children are Richard '86, Christina '88, and Marc '91.*

As I reached retirement at Notre Dame in 2001 as associate vice president for university relations, people would ask me if I were going to write a book. I would reply, "Faculty members are expected to write books; public relations people are expected not to write books." One area in which I wish I had kept notes, however, was the lead up to the university's decision to go coeducational at the undergraduate level in 1972. It was a fascinating time that unfortunately lingers in memory as fragments, some of which I share now.

I recall a Notre Dame trustees meeting at the Breakers in Florida that capped negotiations with Saint Mary's on a merger. I was present as amanuensis, on hand to prepare a joint statement at the conclusion of the meeting. The meeting was very tense. It was evident that the Saint Mary's representatives were reluctant participants. The atmosphere was not helped by the attitude of a few Notre Dame officials who did not hide the fact that they held the leverage in dictating merger terms. If Saint Mary's did not agree to merger, Notre Dame could always go coeducational on its own. The same option was not realistically open to Saint Mary's. The common wisdom at the time was that the Catholic women's college could not survive a neighboring coeducational Notre Dame. The end result was more like a tortured diplomatic communiqué than a joint statement. It went through several drafts. I eventually sent my much-marked-up final copy, a palimpsest of the day's ultrasensitive discussions, to the Notre Dame archives where it presumably rests today.

The staged photograph of Notre Dame and Saint Mary's representatives signing a merger agreement had no sooner appeared in newspapers than I sensed the whole thing was unraveling. One reason was evident from the start and famously summed up in Father Hesburgh's phrase, "They wanted to get married but did not want to take our name." The Holy Cross Sisters had recently given up or were in the process of closing educational apostolates in Saint Mary's-of-the-Wasatch in Salt Lake City, Cardinal Cushing College in Brookline, Massachusetts, and Dunbarton College of the Holy Cross in Washington, D.C. Saint Mary's, Notre Dame, was their last redoubt. They were not reassured by Notre Dame's promise to keep the name "Saint Mary's College" alive as part of the merged entity, knowing in their hearts that the larger and more prestigious Notre Dame would eventually swallow the identity of Saint Mary's. They came out of the Breakers meeting not with hope but with misgivings. A second reason received virtually no publicity. It was financial. Father Joyce, the steward of Notre Dame's fiduciary situation, reportedly had balked at the price tag the sisters subsequently had put on the physical property of Saint Mary's. He did not think Notre Dame could absorb the cost. The Holy Cross Sisters, with an eye toward subsidizing future retirements, did not think they could lower it. At the height of the back-and-forth between the two parties, I can recall a home Notre Dame football game where I carried sealed notes between Father Hesburgh, Edmund Stephan, trustee chair, and Father Joyce, seated in the old administrative box above the stadium press box, and Saint Mary's officials in their fifty-yard-line seats on the east side of the field.

For a brief time before the merger was called off, I was titularly responsible for news bureau operations at both Notre Dame and Saint Mary's. I learned two quick lessons. While it was the Congregation of Holy Cross for men, it was the Sisters of THE Holy Cross for women. Also, it was Saint Mary's College, never St. Mary's College. Sister Alma Peter, CSC, president of Saint Mary's, was made a vice president of Notre Dame. The breakup of the merger and the subsequent media frenzy was very difficult for her. She performed admirably during a painful time. It was also schizophrenic for me to be advising her on how to handle a situation created by my employer, Notre Dame.

The decision for Notre Dame to go coeducational on its own at the undergraduate level was surprising only in its quickness. Apart from the Clark-Mayhew report, there were virtually no formal studies on whether Notre Dame ought to go coeducational. But, it was a given that a coeducational Notre Dame was favored by Father Hesburgh, as well as key trustees. It was his unchallenged leadership and credibility that enabled the change to occur without deep and lasting divisions among the institution's trustees, alumni, and friends. It was a reminder of the influence he successfully brought to bear on an even more important decision five years earlier—the changeover to lay governance.

1971-1972 *Observer* Notre Dame Campus News Staff (left to right): Jerry Lutkus, Ann Therese Darin, George Lund, Anthony Abowd, Tom Bornholdt, Bill Sohn.

I can recall getting phone calls from my counterparts at universities such as Princeton and Dartmouth, where there was fierce opposition to coeducation, looking for the committee reports, studies, white papers, and so on leading to Notre Dame's decision to go coeducational. They were incredulous when told virtually none existed. Universities were divided then as now into president's universities, deans' universities, and faculty universities; clearly, Notre Dame was in the first group. Sure, some alumni were upset, but overall Notre Dame accomplished the transition to undergraduate coeducation with less friction than any of the Ivy League schools. There were some humorous moments, such as when male graduates returned to campus to find their former residence hall digs were now women's bathrooms.

I am often asked what it was like to be "the PR person for Father Hesburgh." My standard reply compares it to being the make-up person for Catherine Deneuve. There was not a lot to improve. However, I did make a contribution to framing the rationale for undergraduate coeducation. While his heart was always in the right place, Father Hesburgh's rhetoric too often emphasized the refining influence coeducation brought to a formerly all-male campus, as though the principle purpose of women was to civilize men. I do not think he realized how objectionable this was to many women, especially those with feminist sensitivities. Slowly but surely, I implanted a one-sentence rationale: "If Notre Dame was serious about educating for leadership in society, it realized it had to educate the other half of the human race."

The early days of coeducation brought forth the media era of "the firsts." This ranged from the first woman to become editor in chief of the *Observer* to the first woman to join the Irish Guard. We tried to be careful to avoid condescension while trying to chronicle these benchmarks to gender equality on campus. The media era of "the firsts" ended when a woman became student body president.

Early on in coeducation, Notre Dame was criticized for having quotas for female undergraduates. This restriction was actually dictated by the university's single-sex residence hall policy, but it also served to phase in coeducation, which helped the transition. The major aid in bringing around alumni was the realization that their daughters could now experience what they had experienced. I gave more than two hundred talks to graduates in my thirty-four years at Notre Dame. I met almost no one who thought the coeducation decision anything but positive.

The changeover to undergraduate coeducation also allowed Notre Dame to replace the bottom tier of male admissions candidates with a top tier of female matriculation. This was important in a time when the lure of all-male universities was waning, with fewer and fewer males opting for single-sex higher education. Some feared that Notre Dame would "tip" in favor of female enrollment when admissions became sexblind, i.e., when men and women were admitted in the same percentage as they were present in the applicant pool. That happened several years ago. Interestingly, Notre Dame, in contrast to virtually every other Catholic university, remains slightly male.

*Barbara Counts, SC, a member of the same religious order, the Sisters of Charity of Cincinnati, as Sister John Miriam Jones, SC, former assistant provost, came to Notre Dame to be the first woman rector of Lyons Hall in 1975.*

*While there, she taught math at Holy Cross Junior College and took graduate classes in pastoral theology. After three years, her congregation asked her to serve as provincial. She left Notre Dame and has been in Colorado ever since.*

*Today she is vice president of the Penrose–St. Francis Health Foundation in Colorado Springs.*

As Notre Dame went coed I was invited to be rector of Lyon's Hall by Sister John Miriam, SC. Being an avid football fan all my life I thought I knew Notre Dame intimately. That was my first mistake but not my last as I entered this male domain. My assignment was rector of Lyons Hall, known as the arch's dorm by the former male students because most of the architecture students lived there.

So Notre Dame was going coed and I was to be this thing called a rector, a term from some ancient monastic system. As I arrived Lyons Hall was being renovated for the women. The men were not happy that this old historic place was no longer to be a male domain with all the male mythology, so they left their markings of displeasure on the walls.

The atmosphere of the campus was predominantly male both in numbers and in attitude for both the women students and the women rectors. The Holy Cross presence dominated student life and was not inclusive of the women in the department, most of whom were religious who had just gone through Vatican II renewal.

Because the first women students were so few and academically from the top of their high school class, the men saw them as competition. Needless to say this atmosphere produced many a tear as the women established themselves as the "first." The pain gradually gave way to integration, inclusiveness happened, Notre Dame was coed.

One story about my meeting THE Father Ted. Most of the life of a rector happens between 10 p.m. and 4 a.m., so when break time comes one has the pleasure of "playing normal" by bathing and washing one's hair early in the evening. This is what I was doing during break when the students were gone. One more thing I need to mention is that I had made myself a bright red towel robe that covered all of me. So, here I am, red robe covering me totally, hair dripping, no shoes, music loud when a knock happens at my door. At first I was frightened because there was no one on campus, I asked who it was and to my surprise the answer was, " Father Ted and Mr. Stephan." Mr. Stephan was chairman of the board of trustees. He and Father Ted wanted a tour of a women's dorm.

I opened the door, as I was, and Father Ted, with eyes cast down, we in religious life call it "custody of the eyes," was obviously out of his comfort zone. Mr. Stephan, a married man with daughters, saved Father by being very much at home with me and my attire. Finally, Father Ted was able to say, "I like that robe, sorry I did not call first."

Barbara Counts, SC

*Head cheerleader from 1941 to 1943, Anthony F. Earley '47 is a former president of the Notre Dame Club of New York City (1956) and president of the National Alumni Board (1979).*

*A member of the National Alumni Schools' Advisory Board (to the Undergraduate Admissions Office) from 1970 to 1980, during Notre Dame's transition to coeducation, he was elected a trustee in 1980. He served until 1993, when he was elected a trustee emeritus.*

*Mr. Earley is the father of four Notre Dame graduates: Anthony '71, who has three additional Notre Dame degrees, including an honorary degree in 2006; Jeanne Earley Appelt '76 MBA, William '80 MBA, and James '90 PhD.*

*He is also grandfather to three Notre dame graduates: Michael Earley '04 JD, Daniel Earley '04, and James Patrick Earley '07.*

Members of the groups that made up the university family did not greet the decision for coeducation with enthusiasm. Dissident voices were heard from members of the CSC community, from the faculty, from the alumni, and from the student body. All kinds of dire predictions were made concerning the future of the university. What sur-prised me the most was the resistance to coeducation by the students then enrolled at the university. They were people in relatively the same age group as the female students who would enter the university. I remember walking across the campus one afternoon in the fall of 1973 or 1974 and hearing some of the most derogatory comments being made from one of the male halls about some female students who happened to be pass-ing by at the time.

One humorous incident in which I was directly involved concerned women's ath-letics. My daughter Jeanne Earley Appelt enrolled in the MBA program in the fall of 1974. As part of tuition help she was assigned to Farley Hall where Sister Jean Lenz, in addition to other jobs, put her in charge of the Farley Motel. A group of the Farley residents heard that Jeanne had been a physical education major at Indiana University and that she had taught phys ed at the high school level before coming to Notre Dame. Quite a few of the new undergraduate women had been athletes in high school. They asked Jeanne if she would help them start and also coach a women's basketball team. Jeanne agreed to take on the job, although basketball was not one of the sports she played at IU. After getting permission from the university administration to organize a team, she was told that she would have to get the approval for any funds that might be needed to support such an activity. The athletic director at the time was Moose Krause, a basketball and football legend at Notre Dame strongly anchored in the all-male tra-dition of the university. Moose explained that the athletic department had not set aside much of the department's budget for women's athletics and hadn't considered basket-ball at all. But he could probably dig up some funds for uniforms and local travel. I think they played Saint Mary's three or four times. He would also find them some time to use the athletic facilities for their practices and games. The team could only have club status. Jeanne was able to arrange some games with local schools not too distant from the Notre Dame campus. I don't know how successful the team was that first year. But I do remember Jeanne telling me that she was surprised at the number of girls who tried out for the team, their enthusiasm and particularly the amount of real basketball talent among them. They now had a jump start on the next season.

Plans for the 1975–1976 season started early. They were able to schedule games with a number of local colleges throughout Indiana including, I believe, Valparaiso. I'm not sure just how far afield from the campus they were allowed to go. Early in the sea-son, I had a call from Jeanne expressing great disappointment in the university. The pre-vious year, the girls noticed that, during the warm-up time before games, players on the other teams wore very attractive warm-up suits in their school's color with the school name. Notre Dame girls wore either old high school sweatshirts, sweatpants of various styles, or clothes purchased individually at the bookstore. She approached the athletic director asking if the university could furnish pregame warm-up suits for the team. Moose told them such expenditure was not in the athletic budget and besides girls' basketball would probably not go very far at Notre Dame. Dad ended up buying the warm-ups. Coeducation didn't come easy to Notre Dame.

One other amusing incident happened in the late '70s: discrimination complaints from the male halls. How come they didn't have a laundry room like the women's halls? This in spite of the fact that men had laundry service.

The trustees monitored the transition in several ways. There were reports from individual trustees about conversations they had with female students or with parents of female students. There were reports from the Student Affairs Committee of the board following their meetings with members of student government and representatives of other groups on the campus.

Some of the transition went quite smoothly and was accomplished much quicker than expected. Other things took much longer. As a former chairman of the Student Affairs Committee, I was appalled at how long it took the students to elect a woman president of student government. We had a number of women elected vice president, but to get to the next step seemed to take forever. It was one of the benchmarks I used to monitor our progress toward fully integrated coeducation. Have we arrived fully at that level? I would have to say almost. Sometimes I get the feeling that we are not fully there yet. It's nothing overt, nothing consciously done but an attitude or a thought process particularly among some of the male students, or certain members of the alumni, or even a few members of the faculty. I emphasize: This is a feeling I sometimes get, nothing I can point to specifically.

Tony Early, head Notre Dame cheerleader, 1941–1943.

As a university we have become more civilized, but I think the best example of the benefits of having become a coeducational university is just what the Notre Dame alumnae are doing here—thanking Father Ted.

Tony Earley '47

*Philip J. Faccenda '51 joined Notre Dame as special assistant to the president in 1967. Three years later, he was named vice president and general counsel. He also served as vice president of Student Affairs from 1973 to 1974.*

*Faccenda was elected a trustee in 1972. When he retired in 1995, he was elected a trustee emeritus.*

*He is the father of six Notre Dame alumni: Maribeth '82, Susan '84, Kathy '85, Peggy '86, Philip '89, and Michael '93. Susan, Philip, and Michael are also graduates of the Law School.*

*Kathy interviewed her father on December 16, 2006.*

It had been clear that Father Hesburgh was interested in educating women as well as men at the university because his thought was "Why should Notre Dame only educate half of the bright young Catholic community?" Notre Dame had been allowing Saint Mary's women to attend classes for five years (and vice versa with Notre Dame men attending classes at Saint Mary's) on an experimental basis. Father Ted's original thought had been to use the Loyola University model which was to have women's college affiliates—professional classes would be taken at Notre Dame, but female student residence and other classes traditionally associated with women would remain with the women's college. In addition to Saint Mary's, Father Ted had also had conversations with Barat College in Lake Forest, Illinois, proposing that Barat would have an opportunity to open a satellite campus in South Bend. At the time, a report was commissioned by Park-Mayhew to determine whether Notre Dame should be coeducational and, if so, in what time frame. The report that was presented to Notre Dame suggested an immediate merger in a time frame that was much shorter than had been anticipated.

The discussion with Saint Mary's broke down primarily because, as became evident at a joint meeting of the executive committees of trustees of both schools that was held in February of 1971 in Florida, the Saint Mary's and Notre Dame trustees had different impressions of what the merger would entail. Neither side truly understood what they were getting into. Notre Dame trustees, most of whom were familiar with for-profit corporate consolidations, mistakenly assumed a merger would take place in the same way and with the same result. The Saint Mary's trustees had a different impression of what would happen. Within a matter of months, the merger planning broke down.

With regard to whose decision it was to admit women to Notre Dame, after the negotiations with Saint Mary's broke down in the summer of 1971, Father Ted and then Provost Father Jim Burtchaell made the suggestion that women be allowed to attend Notre Dame. There was no vote among the trustees, as it was considered Father Ted's decision to make. The president of the board of trustees at the time, Ed Stephan, made the announcement at the next trustees' meeting and women were admitted the following fall.

Philip Faccenda with Father Ted in 1967.

The trustees had almost no apprehension to opening the university to women. Some rumbling was heard from alumni, but, truthfully, very little. Most of the complaints came from the student body. One of the primary complaints was in regard to the residence situation. Notre Dame has just recently gone to a "stay hall" policy where students stayed in the same hall every year. Previously, student loyalty was to their class, not their hall. With the "stay hall" policy, loyalty became more closely affiliated with the hall. With the announcement of the decision to admit women, it was also announced that no new halls would be built and there would be no coeducational halls, so some men would be displaced from their halls to accommodate women.

The biggest concern the trustees had with admitting women to the university was that Notre Dame was an all-male institution with all-male rules and expectations and had no infrastructure to accommodate women. The provost had a hands-on management style and coeducation became his top priority. He invited Sister Jean Lenz and Sister John Miriam Jones to help lead the effort. Frankly, without Sister John's and Sister Jean's help, it would not have been possible to accomplish what was done.

When Father Hesburgh asked me to add to my responsibilities the vice president of Student Affairs position in 1972, I recognized that the most important task was to create an infrastructure acceptable to women. We had many challenges, such as creating women's dorm life, taking all-male references out of materials, and being careful to be inclusive of women on various committees without overemphasizing gender. We wanted there to be an all-inclusive policy rather than a quota system. We had a major learning curve to deal with because, with the exception of Sister John and Sister Jean, no one else had any experience with the types of questions that needed to be answered for women students. We had no contact with other universities that had experienced a similar transition. We felt we were different enough that we needed to create our own answers.

As far as the benefits to coeducation at Notre Dame, you need only look around at collegiate life today. There are almost no single-sex universities in existence. Clearly this was the correct decision for Notre Dame.

On a personal note, I want to express to Father Ted how much his continuing friendship has meant to me and my family over the last forty years. Kathy and I thank him for the gift of his presence in our lives and in the lives of our four daughters and two sons, Notre Dame graduates all.

Phillip Faccenda

# GETTING STARTED

*Betsy Fallon leads the drive
to start women's athletics at Notre Dame.*

**September 15, 2006**

By: Ken Kleppel

Sit back, close your eyes, relax your head, take a deep breath, and dream.

Imagine you are an eighteen-year-old woman, entering Notre Dame as part of the first coeducational class in the university's one-hundred-thirty-year history. You are one of only 350 women on campus, and the opposite gender outnumbers you by a ratio of seventeen to one. Although you are welcomed, you still detect an undeniable tension between the sexes.

Imagine the year is 1972, and there is a social tsunami occurring around you with women's liberation, sexual revolution, and displays of feminism—but you are more concerned with rallies, net play, and perfecting your backhand.

Imagine in the same year the federal government passes Title IX of the Educational Amendments to the Civil Rights Act of 1964. The relevant language reads: "No person shall, on the basis of sex, be excluded from participation in, be denied the benefits of, or be subjected to discrimination under any educational programs or activity receiving federal assistance." Those thirty-two words will one day provide the margin of victory for your dream.

Imagine you play the sport you love and play it well enough to win—and you win often. Opportunities to compete at a higher level, however, are limited. At the end of the day, wins and losses on the court will not mean as much as wins and losses away from it.

Imagine you decide to form your own team, but you have no uniforms, issued equipment, transportation, or any funding whatsoever. You and your teammates sleep in vans or wake up at three o'clock in the morning to reduce the expenses incurred in traveling to away matches. While the interlocking "ND" cannot appear on the green warm-up jerseys with a white shamrock that your volunteer coach designed for you, the ideals of the university motivate your drive to succeed.

Imagine you petition the university to recognize this team with varsity status, so that it can achieve the support necessary for it to thrive, but you fail with each attempt.

Imagine that when the goal is finally attained, you have already graduated and never receive the accolades that accompany the success.

For Betsy Fallon, this was her dream and also her reality.

And accompanying Fallon in her pursuit of achieving varsity status for the women's tennis team on campus were teammate Jane Lammers; athletic directors in charge of club sports Rich O'Leary and Tom Kelley; professor, coach, and most vocal advocate, Dr. Carole Moore; volunteer coaches and classmates John Donahue, Tom Haywood,

Dave Wheaton, and Joel Goebel; student manager Andrea Moore; and the program's first head coach at the varsity level, Cathy Cordes.

Collectively, the heroic efforts of these students, faculty, coaches, and administrators enabled women's tennis to become Notre Dame's first varsity women's sport in 1976.

"We were able to make the sport what it really is—about individuals learning together and maximizing their potential and not strictly about winning and losing," says Fallon. "It was truly a group of us that made this possible. Together, we were committed to our goal and we were happier and healthier as a result of our efforts."

But while many indeed contributed, it is through the eyes of Fallon that the story is best told.

"Betsy is absolutely hands down the driving force behind women's tennis at Notre Dame," says Dr. Moore. "To recognize anybody else first is extremely shortsighted."

And for the first time in these three sets, her match will finally be won.

For a young woman growing up in Grand Rapids, Michigan, playing tennis was more than just recreation but rather a pastime for Fallon. After all, she had been playing since primary school, and traveled with the Junior Wightman Cup teams and competed in many district and state tournaments as a teenager.

The opportunity to compete on the advanced level, however, abruptly ended once she enrolled as a freshman in 1972.

"I did not think about the fact that I would not play sports," says Fallon. "To me, I chose Notre Dame because I received an academic scholarship and wanted to go to the best school possible. When I arrived, though, I was surprised that there was no structure to the sports women were playing on campus."

When her bid to qualify for the men's team failed, although she and eventual teammate Carol Simmons did win several matches in the tryout tournament, Fallon took the initiative to make a change.

Gathering interest from her classmates at meetings she conducted at Badin and Walsh halls, Fallon created the Notre Dame Women's Tennis Club. Although she did not receive sanctioned support from the university, Fallon scheduled her squad to compete against well-developed programs at nearby colleges and universities.

While many opponents were the beneficiaries of paid coaching, access to facilities, equipment, and uniforms, Fallon's team enjoyed none of these advantages. But as the Notre Dame women learned to compete as a team, help was on the way as others shared Fallon's dream.

That spring, Fallon sought the assistance of Dr. Carole Moore, an assistant history professor at the university and one of Notre Dame's first full-time female faculty members. Moore volunteered to handle scheduling, financing, and paperwork on behalf of the team, and served in this post for three years on a volunteer basis.

"I was taken back that there was no support for the women who played tennis," says Dr. Moore, who today serves as a professor of history, technology, and society, and a special assistant to the vice provost at the Georgia Institute of Technology. "I was anxious to take this on."

Using her sway as faculty, Moore aggressively advocated the position of women on campus and in athletics. While her initial hurdle was to reserve court time for practice and play, her eventual challenge was to provide the necessary support to help the women overcome both logistical and social obstacles that prevented their growth as a team.

"From 1972 through 1976, it was incredibly difficult," says Moore. "But the obstacles created camaraderie. A sense of leadership was forged in pursuit of their goal. If these women had not been as passionate and as proud of what they were accomplishing, nothing would have happened."

In the fall of 1973, Jane Lammers, a freshman, joined the squad and competed with Fallon as No. 1 and No. 2 singles. The pair would cocaptain the team for the next three years.

But they also thrived as a tandem away from the court. Together, they organized petition drives and fund-raisers to increase awareness and develop funding. Lammers also founded the Women's Athletics Association (WAA), a group comprised of the captains of the women's club sport teams, to serve as a collective voice for the advancement of women's athletics.

"We had to prove that we would be strong enough as a team to make it through competition," says Lammers. "Then we would receive support."

That support finally came, as the team's request to receive club status from the university was granted in the spring of 1974. Although the $700.00 provided to the team marked the first instance of university support, the sum was grossly inadequate to meet the expenses the team would incur.

Fallon, and the others, fought onward.

In the fall of 1975, Astrid Hotvedt, Notre Dame's first women physical education instructor, helped arrange a meeting between the WAA and Dominic Napolitano, director of non-varsity sports, along with Athletic Director Moose Krause, Assistant Athletic Director Colonel John Stephens, and Executive Vice President Father Edmund Joyce. At that conference the WAA petitioned that women's tennis, fencing, golf, and basketball receive varsity status. Attempts for all four sports failed.

Closely watching this historic encounter was Tom Fallon, men's tennis head coach and chairman of the Physical Education Department.

"On the part of the administration, there was ignorance as to how far the women's movement had come," says Coach Fallon, who bears no relation to Betsy. "On the other side, you had several vigilant women who wanted immediate recognition."

With each letter from Moore petitioning for recognition and as a growing number of institutions began to comply with the requirements that Title IX imposed, the university was now aware just how far the movement had progressed in three years.

The momentum continued on the court, as well. In Fallon's senior year, the club added eighteen members, including six freshmen, who defeated rival Saint Mary's College, and finished second at the Ball State Invitational, by virtue of wins over DePauw, Ball State, and Indiana State.

Fallon graduated in May 1976. For her efforts, she received a plaque of appreciation at the WAA Honors Banquet in what would be her farewell celebration.

The tennis team would play its first match as a varsity unit four months later.

That fall, Cathy Cordes, from an applicant pool of two hundred, was appointed the varsity team's first head coach. Cordes led the Irish to a 7–3–1 record in its maiden season, in which she hosted the Notre Dame Tennis Tournament and the Irish Invitational to showcase her program. Lammers, appropriately enough, served as the team's first captain, and along with Mary (Shukis) Behler would win the program's first monograms.

"Everything that we did as a team was important to establish credibility," says Cordes, who became athletic director at Saint Mary's College after her first season at Notre Dame. "Everybody was very welcoming and we had a lot of support from the Athletic Department."

After one year of service in the Jesuit Volunteer Corps, Fallon moved to Chicago and earned a masters degree in business administration from Northwestern University. For the past thirty years, she has worked in hospital administration and health care. Today, she is the vice president of marketing and planning for Brooks Rehabilitation in Jacksonville, Florida, is married to former professional player Cecil Mella, and is a proud mother.

As Fallon prospered, so too did the program she fought so valiantly to create.

Today, women's tennis is fully funded and receives the maximum number of scholarships allowed by the NCAA. Over the course of the past thirty years, a total of eight Division I and two Division II All-Americans have competed in pacing the squad to eighteen conference championships and appearances in eleven straight NCAA tournaments.

"What women learn through athletics helps them be successful throughout life," says Fallon. "You will always face challenges. Athletics teaches you how to react to these, and how to deal with success when you achieve it. Women's sports keep that balance and Notre Dame still graduates kids that exemplify it."

While the record books may begin in 1976, Fallon's efforts—and those of each individual referenced above, among others—will not be forgotten.

There is no more need to imagine. The match is over, and it belongs to Betsy.

Reprinted from the Notre Dame–University of Michigan 2006 Football Program with the permission of the University of Notre Dame Sports Information Department.

*Elizabeth Fallon '76 was one of the first woman resident assistants in Lyons Hall where she served from 1975 to 1976.*

*She also organized the first women's tennis teams, was the captain and number-one player in 1973–1974, 1974–1975, and 1975–1976.*

Dear Father Ted,

Our connections go way back. My uncle had predicted that ND would admit women when I was a young girl. He was a friend of Ara Parsegian's, had played tennis for ND, and was Father Joyce's roommate in the '40s. So, when I enrolled at ND in the fall of 1972, I was making him and my deceased father very proud.

Thinking I was applying to a merged Saint Mary's/Notre Dame, I learned that you had other things in mind. I was accepted and given a scholarship. As a legacy daughter, I made the choice and didn't think about the disadvantages of being a pioneer.

It's been thirty-five years, and many friends, teachers, and memories remain dear and fresh in my mind. I loved Badin Hall freshman year. We were a small, close dorm. We went everywhere in small groups, feeling conspicuous all the time. We made lots of friends on the South Quad, but most of us had very few dates. Unfortunately, it is true that some upper classmen told us that "we were ruining the tradition" and held up cards to rate our looks in the dining hall. We retreated to the safety and closeness of Badin Hall, feeling confident in our abilities most of the time.

As much as we wanted to stay in Badin, many of us were asked to move to North Quad sophomore year. As the first women on that quad, we once again felt out of place. We hoped that better manners would arrive in the North Dining Hall, too.

As a junior, given the chance, my group of friends returned to South Quad in Lyons Hall. Then, the men complained that the women always got the best dorms. You continued to support us, and we knew it. I was a resident assistant senior year. I counseled younger classwomen whose social life was much better than mine. Even with those ratios, I never had many dates. I suspected that the Saint Mary's students had better social lives because they were not as threatening a presence. It didn't help much that I was a "jock" and also a bit outspoken. I made the best friends with men who tested me and listened to my beliefs; some are still dear friends at ND.

Like many women at ND who were athletes, we were ready to compete but ND wasn't ready for us. I had played competitive tennis all my life. Other than good grades and a loving family, tennis was my life. I was allowed to play on the boys' team in high school because we had no girls' sports and someone took the high schools to court. At ND, the awkwardness began in gym classes—imagine being outnumbered seventy to three in a swimsuit!

My freshman year, I organized some matches against friends at Saint Mary's and held meetings to jump-start a tennis team. Sophomore year, I tried out for the men's team (hoping I could get some support if I made that team). Not making it, I went back to organizing a women's team. I was the captain and number-one player for most of the next three years. We were fortunate that Professor Carole Moore, an articulate and smart feminist, and one of the few women professors on campus, agreed to help and coach us for free. Many of the men helped us, too.

One of the ugliest moments was having to wait for tennis courts, while negotiations occurred between administrators. We had to "borrow" tennis balls from the men's team because we didn't have enough. We sold baked goods, movie tickets, and pizza muffins to pay for our travel expenses. We paid for indoor court time because the ACC was too crowded. We bought our own uniforms, but we weren't allowed to put an "ND" on them since we weren't a recognized team.

In 1975, we gained club status with a $700 budget. We competed in full schedules and tournaments, often against varsity teams with scholarship players, all over the Midwest. We had more and more success (and fun) as more and more women joined us. Our friends in basketball, fencing, and flag football were building programs, too, led by the efforts of determined women.

However, our requests for recognition as varsity teams were denied. We felt, and I still do, that the Athletic Department was afraid that we would take away from their programs. They forgot, I think, that the women would add richness and diversity to the sports program at ND, providing a balance and perspective needed during those early years.

The balance and environment improved in many ways during my years at ND. We became more comfortable and welcomed. The animosity with SMC decreased. We made friends and learned lessons about values, compassion, and community, among many. You were an amazing symbol of those values and gave us the gift of our education there.

When I graduated, I cried in gratitude for the friends I had made through the tennis team, classes, and many activities. I was recognized by my teammates and have been very grateful for all that I learned. My best teachers and friends at Notre Dame made indelible marks on my character. Some like you and Fathers John Dunne, Tim Scully, and John Jenkins are still changing lives.

Thank God you let women into ND. Asked once "what do women think?" in class, I realized that many of the students and profs hadn't had women in class since grade school. We had wonderful women leaders who trailblazed with us—women like Kathy Cekanski, Sister Barb Counts, Sister Jane Pitz, and Sister Jean Lenz. They taught me to be myself and not to be afraid.

I've had six nieces and nephews at ND, and none of them experienced less than a 50/50 ratio. They don't even know what we accomplished, starting with your enlightened vision. I hear the stories of those years are in the "archives" of the library! Just ask any of us—we loved each other and the school passionately. The women were ambitious, had high expectations, and were often frustrated by the hierarchy. But, coeducation has been a success. I celebrated more for the women's basketball team's national championship than for any football game. It felt like the biggest victory to me.

I hope the women's teams continue to hold the highest standards for which ND is known. Father Ted, you started all of this. I don't know if you realized how uncomfortable you would make people. In the years since I've graduated, it seems to me that some at ND don't realize or forget that it struggled to embrace women fully on campus. It would make me feel better if we could get the story across. We were there, we loved it, and we remember!

I hope that ND grads, and especially women, don't forget what it was like before there were equal opportunities at ND. Those times provide a reminder that we must always support fairness and equality, even when it is inconvenient. You have done that throughout your life, for which you are to be congratulated.

Sincerely yours and God bless,

Betsy Fallon
Class of '76

*John T. Goldrick, a triple Domer, served as director of undergraduate admissions from 1971 to 1984. Goldrick '62 has a masters in counseling '70 and law degree '84, and also has served as associate vice president for residential life from 1984 to 1991.*

*Currently he is vice president for enrollment management and student life at the University of Portland, and is also affiliated with the Congregation of Holy Cross.*

*Goldrick is the father of two Notre Dame graduates: Sean '93 and Shaheen Goldrick Hemsey '94.*

"Thanking Father Ted"
John T. Goldrick, '62, '70, '84
Director of Admissions 1971–1984
Associate Vice President for Residence Life 1984–1991

Imagine . . . I'm sitting in Beirut, Lebanon, at the American Community School where I had only a few months before begun a new job as counselor to seventh and eleventh grade students, and I am opening my mail. To my surprise, I find a letter from Notre Dame's provost, Father Jim Burtchaell, inviting me to return to Notre Dame to run the Admissions Office. Needless to say, I was surprised and honored. But it was only after accepting the job that I was sent a subsequent letter informing me that Notre Dame and Saint Mary's College would be unifying, that the first two offices to be unified were the two admissions offices, and that I was to be the director of both operations. It was only after this letter that I wondered, "What have I gotten myself into?"

The Saint Mary's Admissions Office had been directed for quite a few years by Sister Raphaelita, who reminded me countless numbers of times that she served as Saint Mary's director through numerous admissions directors at Notre Dame. Nor did she recognize that I was in any way running her Admissions Office, even though she sent one of her counselors to work in the Notre Dame office. So, from August to November 1971, we collaborated as best we could to look toward what unification would mean. Then one morning in November, the provost asked me to drive with him to Saint Mary's campus. We went directly to Sister Raphaelita's office in LeMans Hall where Father Burtchaell proceeded to inform the two of us that we needed to work out a solution to notify applicants for admission that the ND/SMC unification process was being dissolved, and that Notre Dame would be admitting its first female freshmen as part of its new decision to become a coeducational institution in its own right.

To that end, we contacted all female applicants allowing them the option to choose to apply for admission to Notre Dame, to Saint Mary's College, or to both institutions with the same application. As it turned out, 1,174 women chose (one way or the other) to apply to Notre Dame; I was informed that we would have only 125 places for women in the freshman class. We also were permitted to grant Notre Dame degrees to women who (while previously enrolled at Saint Mary's) had pursued majors offered only at Notre Dame, as well as to admit women as upper-class transfer students to fill whatever spots might be available to transfer students. In order to fill the available freshman places, we offered admission to 175 applicants, and by the grace of God, we enrolled exactly 125 freshman women in the class entering in 1972.

But wait, nothing was to go that well, at least not without a serious glitch. It seems that we in the Notre Dame administration somehow forgot about the fact, that when we enrolled 125 freshmen plus additional transfer women, then the residence halls where they would be residing need to be vacated by the men who had previously lived in those halls. And so, only a short time before "coeducation" became a reality, male students were informed that they were being moved out of their "homes" to other residence halls. As you might expect, the uproar was loud, and the stage was set for making the transition to coeducation a little less smooth than it otherwise might have been.

Fast-forward to commencement four years later when the first females who had been admitted as freshmen were graduating. I was invited to be the speaker at a special

# *THE OBSERVER*

Less sun and more cold. Temp: 15 degrees wind: 15 mph. You figure out the wind chill factor.

Volume VI, No. 64

serving the notre dame- saint mary's community

Wednesday, January 26, 1972

## Admissions Office: 1100 coed applications

by Jack Kelly

The ND Admissions Office is presently processing all female applications to both ND and SMC, according to Admission Counselor Anne Hollander.

Miss Hollander, an employee of St. Mary's, is responsible for all applications from females. Under the present applications system, females petitioning for entrance into either ND or SMC receive the same application form. When applying the women may choose to apply for admission only to SMC under St. Mary's rules and standards, to Notre Dame under ND's stan-

dards, or to both schools.

Miss Hollander siad "The office has received over 1100 female applications, of which Notre Dame has accepted 29." ND has not finalized any further acceptances.

Miss Hollander siad that she did not have "any particular bias" towards St. Mary's. "I try to be unbiased, and to refer the girls to the school which would fit the girls the school which would fit the girls desired curriculum," she said "I am employed by St. Mary's but as my title says I'm an admissions counselor."

Notre Dame Admissions Director John Goldrick, said "the admissions guidelines, which are setup in the Notre Dame Report number six, are such that we can

accept 200 girls for transfer and 125 girls as freshmen." SMC is yet to establish their quota for acceptance.

"Their is no special consideration for females. They receive the same consideration as males-that is according to quota only the most qualified are accepted." Goldrick continued.

To date 25 per cent of applicants have applied only to SMC, 25 per cent to ND only and 50 per cent to both, ND and SMC, Goldrick said.

Both Miss Hollander and Goldrick said that applications for females had increased and that the ND admissions race had become, in Goldrick's term "exceptionally tough."

John Goldrick, ND admissions director, is accepting applications to ND from both men and women.

dinner referred to as the "senior women's dinner" that was held shortly before commencement weekend. We were actually graduating 123 of the 125 women who had entered four years earlier, plus other women who had entered as transfer students during that four-year period. So, there were approximately 400 women at the event, and I was there (the single male present) to speak to those assembled. I have to admit I ate little, primarily because my stomach and I were fighting fright and nervousness. So when I stood up to speak, I mentioned that I was very nervous, primarily because I had never before found myself to be the only male in a room filled with four hundred women. As soon as I had made that remark, a voice from the back of the room shouted, "Now you know how it feels!" Fortunately, the laughter in the room relaxed me so that I gave my remarks easily, and I think we all had a good time.

That Father Hesburgh and the board of trustees decided to admit women to Notre Dame, in spite of the "de-unification" with Saint Mary's College is, I believe, one of the finest and most courageous decisions (considering its all-male history and traditions), which brought Notre Dame into a period of academic excellence and growth that has helped it become the great and renowned university it is today. Indubitably, becoming fully "coed" was a slow and sometimes painful process, for both men and women students. But being a part of those initial coeducational years, and watching that growth (slowly but surely) happen for the institution as well as the students, are integral facets of my fond and enjoyable memories from my many years at "du Lac." Thank you, Father Ted!

᪥

*Sister John Miriam Jones, SC, '61 MS, '70 PhD was Notre Dame's first high-level woman administrator. She was appointed assistant to the provost (1972–1976), assistant provost (1976–1987), and associate provost (1987–1989).*

*Her chief responsibility was the integration of women undergraduates into the university. In addition, she dealt with faculty affairs, coordinated foreign study programs (1980–1982), was director of military affairs (1982–1984, 1987–1989), and coordinated services for disabled students.*

*During her time at Notre Dame she also served as assistant professor of microbiology.*

In the fall of 1972 I gathered all 365 women students in the Badin Hall Chapel and tried to convey to them my own enthusiasm about this pioneering effort. A place I had come to love while in graduate studies was opening its doors to undergraduate women for the first time. One of the campus quips at that time was that after 130 years with a woman atop the Golden Dome, women were finally beneath it. We were making history! The reaction to my excitement was muted. The women's stance was something like, "We didn't come to be pioneers making history. We're here to be Notre Dame students." This is exactly what they also told the national TV crews who were covering the event on campus that first weekend. It turned out that just being a student was hard to do.

Those three hundred-plus women were on campus with about 6,200 men undergraduates, many of whom seemed to view them more as a curiosity than as fellow students. A few years before, during my own graduate studies, the men undergraduates had demonstrated to have women admitted, but somehow, once it happened, many found it hard to be welcoming. There was a nightly rating system in the dining hall; catcalls from the windows of the men's halls; run-throughs in women's halls; something akin to noninclusion in the classrooms; leaving our women in the dorms over the weekend while dating those from Saint Mary's. And in the classroom where "being a student" was designed to happen, it was not unusual for one woman to be the only woman present and, as a consequence, uncomfortable. In an effort to be accepted the women began to mimic their male counterparts—dress, language, parties, playing touch football.

Even on a restless campus there was never a doubt among Notre Dame decision makers that the move to coeducation was a correct one. On many occasions Father Ted spoke of it as one of the two most important decisions of his presidency, the other being the establishment of a lay-led board of trustees. I witnessed tremendous goodwill among administrators responsible for making the necessary changes. And yet some of what was done led the women to feel too special and a bit overprotected. In that first year no halls other than Badin and Walsh had hall security monitors, outdoor spotlights, locks on the outside doors, curtains, or even laundries.

My own sensitivity was heightened as I witnessed the struggle the women were having. I came to realize that much of what was happening was a localized reflection of what was happening in American society in the '70s as women fought for equality in the workplace and in the political realm. My own awareness didn't help our women

Legendary actress Helen Hayes and Sister John Miriam Jones, SC, at the dedication of the Pasquerilla West in 1981. It was the first dormitory specifically built for women.

feel any better, but I think it allowed me to help prepare them for what awaited them beyond the campus. Shortly after their graduations I began to hear how, once again, they were a minority among the men around them in graduate school or in the workplace, but this time they felt uninhibited and confident of themselves and their abilities. The Notre Dame experience had given them a strong dose of self-confidence.

In those first years we established a Women's Council and discussed freely what their discomforts were. Together we looked for solutions. With their input, and often in their company, I sought out those who could help to make necessary changes. We began to move in the right direction, but changing attitudes is a slow business. Thus, it took some time for the women to feel that they were a valued part of the place. In 1982 we made a campus-wide effort to celebrate "ten years of men and women learning together." We put up posters, held discussions, and scheduled a speakers' series of Distinguished American Women. Father Ted was the celebrant and homilist for a well-attended Mass of celebration in Sacred Heart. At the end of that year I finally heard the words I had been waiting for—"I really feel that I belong here."

Indeed, women do belong. They have made an unequaled contribution to Notre Dame. Today the university is a truly human place largely because of its women students. They have enabled deep and lasting male/female friendships; they have brought a balance to every classroom and to the campus itself; they have translated being a Notre Dame student into a unique feminine form; they have led the way in self-giving and service.

In May of 2006, I was delighted to read a remark made by that year's valedictorian, Catherine Distler. She recalled that in her freshman year a Notre Dame friend had explained to her that every person is responsible for caring for everyone else. It changed her life and brought her to believe that "people are reason enough to want to change the world for the better." I haven't met Catherine but I am proud of her as I am proud of those women who began it all and of all those who followed and who bring this dimension of caring to a place that so values it.

This book is about gratitude to the place, and especially to Father Ted. Those early women of Notre Dame have every reason to be grateful. In 1997 they placed a rock at the Grotto to attest to their gratitude. Many friendships they made there are sterling and solid. They received a quality education in a formal sense and also an education for life—lessons that enabled them to be their own women. They didn't give up when things were difficult. Rather they grew in self-discovery, personal assurance, and leadership.

I, too, want to thank Father Ted. As president he presided over all my Notre Dame years that were richly graced in a thousand ways. Among the graces was the privilege of working with this man of such firm faith. He is a man with passion for the place and its people. That attitude is easily contagious. I learned from his leadership to take the broad view, to let the big vision govern the details. He taught me the importance of a reverence for the history that grounds us and needs to guide us. I admire his amazing loyalty to people, and pray that lesson rubbed off on me. For all of this I thank you, Father Ted, but especially for your unyielding belief in the presence and goodness of women, and your vigorous determination to see it through.

John Miriam Jones, SC

*A 1967 theology masters of arts graduate, Sister Jean Lenz, OFM, was rector of Farley Hall from 1973 to 1982, when she left campus to be rector in the London Program. During this period, she also served as an adjunct instructor in the Theology Department.*

*Upon her return from London, she was appointed and continues to serve as assistant vice president for Student Affairs.*

Dear Father Ted,

What an honor to join this grand chorus of gratitude for you, your vision, and your strong conviction that led to coeducation at Notre Dame.

As I began to search for words to thank you, I was drawn more and more to preserving the memory of a special day in your life. It was the first meeting of the Leadership Initiative for Alumnae in the Chicago region held last May 11, 2006. It made sense that you were slated to be the main speaker, but as you know, that was just the beginning of a delightful occasion that turned into one grand historic thank-you party.

From the moment you stepped in the Chicago Club off Michigan Avenue, I watched you meet and greet and call by name so many of the women who came to share your company and to thank you personally for their Notre Dame heritage. Although it was an historic moment when undergraduate women arrived on campus in the fall of 1972, this spring luncheon in the Windy City was another whole layer of history. There you were, decades later, welcoming some of the same women you first met more than thirty years ago. You had always hoped your decision would all work out for the best, and on this day over two hundred of the first generation of Notre Dame women proved you right.

As you approached each one, it was quite obvious that you cherish them and are so proud of them. It showed in all your conversations. They represent so well the major professions in society, and so many other fields of interest, many of them combining marriage and family obligations. You see them as strong laity in the Church. And lest we forget, the women have earned four national sports championships. I can never forget the time you said to me so wholeheartedly, "Jean, the women have done it all. I knew they would!"

Sister Jean Lenz, rector of Farley Hall 1973–1982.

When you stepped up to the podium to speak that day, the women were all eyes and ears, some sitting with former roommates and others with best friends from Notre Dame. You had all kinds of information to share with them, but you especially delighted them when you mentioned meeting some of their sons and daughters now at Notre Dame. Imagine, a second generation of women on campus, with one of them student body president for the 2006–2007 academic year.

A bit more history was made as you were leaving the podium in the midst of audience applause. You stopped in your tracks. You suddenly remembered that you had something else you wanted to say. The room settled into a surprised silence as you stood tall and said with such thoughtfulness, conviction, and clarity, "There is one other thing that I want you to know. The Church doesn't teach this, but I want you to know that I would have no problem with women priests." When I think back, I wonder if your first public announcement that Notre Dame was going to admit undergraduate women didn't have a tinge of that same shock value. One thing I have learned over my years at Notre Dame is that you always stay close to the future, Father Ted.

While there were endless words of thanksgiving expressed in that Chicago dining room, you were also presented with four leather notebooks filled with still more messages, more notes, and letters filled with thanks from Notre Dame women across the country.

Finally, how fitting that this thanksgiving festival turned into your 90th birthday celebration and this book.

Thank you Father Ted for oh, so much!

With much love and gratitude,

Jean

Jean Lenz, OSF
Assistant Vice President for Student Affairs

*Carmen León '73 JD was a resident assistant in Badin Hall from 1972 to 1973, its first year as a women's dorm. She is a Miami attorney.*

Dear Father Hesburgh,

In 1960, I arrived in Miami, Florida, from Cuba as a political refugee without any money or any English. Who could have predicted that within ten years, I would be one of the first women on campus with a full tuition academic scholarship to the University of Notre Dame Law School!

My "Notre Dame experience" started at the Law School where I was warmly welcomed by the faculty, staff, and most of my classmates; although, some were initially shocked to have females in their classes. The week of my first Thanksgiving at Notre Dame was very memorable and a true example of the "Notre Dame family." While I was at the Law Library, I saw a member of the faculty talking quietly to the law students. They wanted to know if any students were staying in town for the holiday and inviting them to their homes for Thanksgiving. I was one of the lucky ones!

In 1972 the announcement came that undergraduate women students were to be admitted to Notre Dame. I then became a resident assistant at Badin Hall, one of the first dormitories converted to a women's dorm. The students at Badin were a combination of Saint Mary's transfers entering their sophomore and junior years and true freshman. They were eager to study at Notre Dame and break apart the sex barrier. These students received a lot of support from the faculty, administrators, and Badin Hall staff, where we had an open door policy.

Among the reasons that I attended Notre Dame was because of its national reputation and your work, Father Hesburgh—in civil rights and social justice. While at Notre Dame, I had the unique experience of meeting people from across the United States and several countries who truly became one community. I made enduring friendships. The ethics and social justice taught to me by my parents were broadened by Notre Dame and made a part of my professional life. After law school, I worked several years in the area of poverty law. Today, I only do legal work part-time and dedicate most of my working hours coordinating a program for adult refugees/asylees in the local public school system.

On several occasions I have returned to Notre Dame and each one has been memorable. My last visit was for 2001 graduation when my niece, Rebecca Trujillo, received her BA. Her two-year-old already shouts, "Go Irish!"

In conclusion, my years at Notre Dame changed my life, broadened my perspectives, and provided a professional formation ruled by ethics, moral law, and social justice. None of these would have happened without your guidance at Notre Dame. Thank you for all you have done for me and the other female students at Notre Dame.

Happy Birthday!

Carmen L. León
Class of '73 JD

Father Ned Joyce, President John F. Kennedy, and Father Ted.

*John Macheca '62 was head of Notre Dame's Midwest Regional Development Office and head of its Midwest regional public relations from 1969 to 1973, when he was appointed dean of students. He served as dean of students from 1973 to 1975, during Notre Dame's transition to coeducation.*

*Two of his four children are Notre Dame graduates: Margot '88 and Mark '91.*

Dear Father Ted,

"Thank you" . . . reputedly the two most powerful words in the English language, somehow
don't seem forceful enough to express my feelings for all you have done for Our Lady's University during your ninety years!

However, it is a privilege to be given
this special opportunity to participate in our
collective expressions of appreciation for all
your contributions to the quality of the Notre
Dame life experience.

Undoubtedly, of the things we are aware
of (You've done so much that we'll never know
about!), your role as an agent for change was
most important; in particular, the university's

John A. Macheca.

transitions to both lay governance and coeducation, in my mind, have been the most
significant. But it's the latter that impacted my life the most. For instance, the opportunity to work for you as the first lay dean of students probably wouldn't have happened
without coeducation. Also, my daughter, Margot '88, would not have been able to become the proud and loyal Notre Dame alumna that she is today.

Much more importantly, Notre Dame would have been deprived of its greatest
potential; namely, to recruit, admit, and educate the best possible applicants. That realization started on the first day of the first semester of the 1973–1974 academic year,
when I became dean of students. I met students who thought Notre Dame would
never be an option for them. Those women were part of a tradition of "university en-
hancement" that even Father Cavanaugh, Jim Frick, Bill Sexton, and Lou Nanni, as a
group, would envy. The women of Notre Dame had an appreciation for the opportunity
they had earned that was unprecedented and it evidently endures to this day.

From the dean's perspective, it was a privilege and a joy to work with them. They
were all "student leaders." They were instrumental in replacing the *Student Rule Book*
with *Du Lac, A Guide to Student Life* that, for the first time, provided Notre Dame students with a truly positive perspective on their lives on campus. More importantly, as
people would say these days, "The women not only talked-the-talk, they also walked-
the-walk!" They brought out the best in Notre Dame. They challenged us to think and

do things in different, better ways. They always wanted to take things to a new, enhanced level of quality for student life.

Father Ted, you have been an inspiration to all of us and have endowed us with an immeasurable legacy of love and respect for our fellow man . . . and woman! Thank you again!

Devotedly yours in Notre Dame,

John A. Macheca
Class of '62

*Mary Martha McNamara '73 JD was a resident assistant in Walsh Hall during the first year it was a woman's dormitory. Today she is an attorney in Alexandria, Virginia.*

In my third year of law school, I was selected to be a resident assistant in Walsh Hall after the university designated it as one of the women's dorms. The integration of women into the Law School had been accomplished a few years prior but, when I arrived in 1970, the number of females on the campus was hardly noteworthy. Although our numbers were few, the talent of my female colleagues was abundant.

Nothing compared, however, to the undergraduate women who came to Walsh Hall in the fall of 1972. I was awed by the sheer brilliance of my group of student residents on first-floor Walsh. And, despite their genius, they were the most delightful group of women you would ever want to call friends. They hardly considered themselves to be the pioneers that they were. Rather, they simply embraced the university as all Notre Dame students have throughout its history.

These women had such positive attitudes that they made my job easy. I cannot recall any particular problems we experienced. It seemed like what issues we had were typical of what any college freshman might have, i.e., homesickness, breakups with high school beaux, discipline to study when no written homework was due, etc. When I remember back, I think of the many nights, particularly the first semester, when we had our own floor parties and made our own fun as friendships flourished among the women in our hall. Although there were not many boys hanging around Walsh that first year, it is my understanding that things warmed up thereafter and several of "my girls" ended up marrying their Notre Dame sweethearts.

If Father Ted is responsible for bringing these outstanding women to Notre Dame, then I must say thank you—and bless you—for the vision you showed! My son is currently an undergraduate at Notre Dame. As I watch him progress through the school, I can appreciate more than ever the contribution that the female undergraduates have made to make the university the strongest it has ever been.

Mary Martha McNamara
Class of '73 JD

*Newton N. Minow, former chairman of the Federal Communications Commission, was a University of Notre Dame Trustee from 1965 to 1977 and from 1983 to 1996, when he became a trustee emeritus. He is a senior partner at Sidley Austin Brown Wood in Chicago.*

*He was interviewed by phone on November 8, 2006, by Ann Therese Darin Palmer.*

*Did the trustees have any apprehensions about opening up the undergraduate enrollment to women? If so, what were they?*

Some trustees were apprehensive. Tradition was a factor. Concern about safety for women was a factor. But, these concerns were outweighed by the promise of an enriched environment on campus for both men and women.

And, these concerns proved unfounded. The benefits of coeducation made Notre Dame a better place in every way.

*How did the trustees monitor the transition to make sure that the incoming women undergraduate students were satisfied with what they were experiencing?*

I was chairman of the Student Affairs Committee. At the end of the first year of coeducation, we invited some of the undergraduate women to talk to us. There were four of them.

When we asked them how everything was and whether there were any problems, they replied that there weren't. When we asked them if they had any complaints or suggestions, one woman asked to speak about the food. She asked if there could be more cottage cheese and Tab in the dining halls.

I couldn't believe that after the first year of coeducation, this was the only complaint.

*How long did it take for undergraduate women to be considered a normal situation, not something unusual?*

By the end of the first year, there had been a remarkably fast adjustment.

I attribute much of this phenomenon to Father Hesburgh. He has a sensi-

Father Ted and Newton N. Minow at the 1996 spring commencement, where Minow was awarded an honorary Notre Dame degree.

tivity, an ability to put himself in another person's shoes that's remarkable. He's got empathy and understanding. I think he transmitted that to his staff and they transmitted that to the women. They also told the boys they'd better behave.

*Looking back on the university's transition to coeducation from a thirty-five-year vantage, would you do anything differently today than you did then?*

"I would have done it fifty years earlier. Having both genders together enriches their education, as well as enriching the growth to maturity of young men and young women because they're going to be living in the same world.

We should all be very proud of the fact that Notre Dame is coeducational. When coeducation was originally considered by the trustees, the intention was that women undergraduates would comprise 40 percent of the student enrollment.

Today that number is up to about 50 percent.

The women are doing as well or better than the men academically. It's made Notre Dame a better place.

༻

*Jane Pfeiffer, the retired chairman of NBC (National Broadcasting Company), was the second woman to join the Notre Dame Board of Trustees.*

*(The first was Dr. Rosemary Park, a renowned educator, specializing in women's higher education issues, who was elected in 1971. She coauthored with Dr. Louis Mayhew a comprehensive report advising Notre Dame on how to incorporate women undergraduates into its enrollment.)*

*Pfeiffer served from 1974 to 2003, when she became a trustee emeritus. She was interviewed by phone on November 30, 2006, by Eileen O'Grady Daday '77, a columnist for the* Daily Herald, *a metropolitan Chicago daily newspaper.*

Like the young coeds newly attending the university, Pfeiffer was a high-achieving woman, a pioneer in some of the country's largest corporations. Prior to joining the NBC television network, she was vice president of communications at IBM. While she worked her way up through the management ranks there, among her assignments was serving as Bermuda site manager for NASA's computer complex.

However, it wasn't as much her business credentials that drew her invitation to join the board, as it was her close working relationship with the Reverend Theodore Hesburgh.

"He is the dearest and finest person I know," says Pfeiffer. "We have been friends for a long, long time."

She joined the board of trustees, after having served with Hesburgh on the Rockefeller Foundation, during the '60s at the height of the civil rights era. Hesburgh later served as the foundation's chairman from 1977 to 1982. The foundation expands opportunities for the poor and disenfranchised, and helps ensure that the benefits of globalization are shared more equitably.

Hesburgh's decision to admit undergraduate women to Notre Dame is directly related to his work as a charter member and subsequent chairman of the U.S. Civil Rights Commission (1969–1972) and his work as chairman of the International Federation of Catholic Universities (1963–1970).

As Civil Rights Commission chairman, Father Ted was driven to lobby for equal rights for all citizens, she says. That extended to a full participation in the Catholic Church and its institutions of higher learning. At the International Federation of Catholic Universities, Father Ted led a movement to redefine the nature and mission of the contemporary Catholic university.

Pfeiffer also cites Father Ted's family life, "a family of strong women," as another reason he favored coeducation. "Father Ted was very close to his mother and sisters, and they all were well-educated women," says Pfeiffer.

While Pfeiffer was not involved in the decision to admit women, she was there during the first years of coeducation.

"One of the biggest things I remember trustees wrestling with were the percentages," she says. "As the number of female applicants increased, I was astounded that we were turning away women who were eminently qualified. It appeared to me that it was harder to get into Notre Dame as a woman, than as a man."

Pfeiffer, a graduate of Holy Cross Academy in Washington, D.C., and the University of Maryland's Speech and Drama Department, credits her liberal arts education with giving her "self-confidence and ability to think on my feet, while honing my stage presence," all important factors in success in the business world, she says.

When Pfeiffer joined IBM in 1955, she trained in systems engineering. In 1966, she was the first woman selected to become a White House Fellow, one of the most prestigious national fellowships. When she returned, Pfeiffer achieved a national

Father Ted, Martin Luther King Jr., and Monsignor Robert J. Hagarty of the Archdiocese of Chicago at a Prayer Service at Soldier Field in Chicago, 1964.

reputation as a highly successful business executive, who brought IBM into television as a major sponsor of public affairs programming.

Pfeiffer left IBM in 1976 to become an independent consultant to such major companies as RCA (which owned NBC at the time) and educational institutions. When NBC picked her as chairman of the board in 1978, The *Los Angeles Times* called her "perhaps the most powerful woman in America."

*Jane Pitz '71 MFA served as the first assistant rector of Walsh Hall in 1972, while being part of the first Campus Ministry Team. She lived in Walsh until the summer of 1982, when she went to London where she also lived with students.*

*Since that first Notre Dame assignment in London, she has worked both in London and at Notre Dame as a rector in the London Program, rector of O'Hara-Grace, the women's graduate student dorm on campus, and director of the Holy Cross Associates Program for the Holy Cross priests.*

*She left the university in 1995 and resides in South Bend, where she is an artist.*

Dear Father Hesburgh,

Life at Notre Dame began for me as a graduate student in the summer of 1964. The university was an exciting place for religious women and men during those summers. The Church was coming alive with the documents of the Second Vatican Council. There were folks on campus who were sharing their theology and pastoral insights with students in impromptu nightly gatherings. We were alive with a spirit, the Spirit, and saw opportunities for the future of the Church and religious life and for each of us personally. At that time, Notre Dame summer experiences were the center of my year. I looked forward, after the year's teaching, to gather with the men and women who dreamed and envisioned. Never in those summers did I envision that I would be working at the university in pastoral care with undergraduate students. But it happened!

During my last semester as a graduate student, you came to the decision to create the opportunity for women undergraduates to be educated in academics and life at Notre Dame. And that has made all the difference in my own life. Fathers Bill Toohey and Jim Flanigan approached me to join them in creating residence halls (Walsh and Badin) for women and to work in campus ministry. Suddenly my life was changed.

The summer prior to opening the halls we, the future staff, went through the buildings with Father Jerry Wilson. He was very solicitous for those women to come and wanted to have things in place that would make life easier for them. Mirrors in the corridors seemed a minor element but he saw their importance! And so we had mirrors. The Mor-

ris Inn was procuring new furniture and a new look so we inherited the chairs and tables and lamps that had been there. The urinals were removed. We had thought we might use them as planters! But gone they were. He saw to that.

The physical surroundings were being prepared but the real moment came when we received the list of women who would be living in our halls. Roommates and rooms would have to be assigned. Who were these women? What would life be like with them? What were they anticipating? We had overwhelming questions but the male rectors helped us sort them out and some of the men who had lived in Walsh prior to being "moved out to make room for women" came early that autumn and helped us. In fact, they were on hand to actually move women into the hall—bag and baggage! With help from them, we found out about hall meetings and life on the campus in the residence halls and what was expected of us.

Those women, those first women (and many after them) have become part of my life's journey. When we initially met and began the first semester, we together figured out what we were about in that venture. The questions were many. The answers came gradually. From "what to do when the fire alarm goes off" to more serious questions regarding life and future and to their present struggles with being such a small band of women among so many men. Just recalling these images brings a sense of pride and warmth. To have been there at the beginning was an honor. At the time, it seemed just to be happening day-to-day. Some of these women have become lifelong friends. I am welcomed into their homes, spend vacations with them and their families, celebrate life events with them.

I remember meeting with Emil Hoffman over a problem a freshman woman was having. Sometime during the meeting, in frustration, he pointed to a structure of a chemical molecule atop his shelving and said, "That is easier to figure out than the women I'm teaching!" In the beginning, this frustration was felt from both sides in the classroom. "Why am I being singled out, as the spokesperson for all women?" was a common lament, when a Walsh resident returned from a class. Being the only woman in a physical education class was difficult at best. But gradually, over the years, all this ceased. And, in its place, gratitude for being at the university, for having a place there among its students and alums, replaced any of the early feelings.

On a personal note, Father Hesburgh, the experience of being at Notre Dame in the beginnings of coeducation, growing up in that environment of a place that oozed tradition and was filled with deeply held values and spiritual life, brought me to a sense of who I am today. The coworkers with whom as a team I got to chart pastoral care on the campus, the marvelous and dedicated faculty who named me as friend, the religious of Holy Cross who became my brothers—all these persons, in addition to the students, have accompanied me (and I, them) on a journey that has been blessed and has borne much fruit. You have been an essential part of that over these many years. I'm deeply grateful.

Fondly,

Jane Pitz
Class of '71 MFA

*Ernestine Morris Carmichael Raclin is chairman emeritus of the board of directors of 1st Source Corporation and 1st Source Bank in South Bend. In addition, she was the first woman director of First Chicago Corp. (First National Bank of Chicago), as well as the first woman director of NIPSCO Industries Inc. (Northern Indiana Public Service Co.), People's Energy Corp. in Chicago and Midcon Corp.*

*She was elected a trustee in 1976 and served until 1998, when she became a trustee emeritus. She received an honorary Doctor of Laws from the university in 1978.*

*Mrs. Raclin is the first woman chairman of Notre Dame Capital Campaign, having headed the 1976 campaign, which raised $150 million. Her granddaughter, Kelly Murphy Bellinger, a 2001 Law School graduate, interviewed her by telephone on December 18, 2006.*

*Do you recall when the first time was that you met Father Ted?*

I feel as if I've known Father Ted my whole life, but I think I first met him in the '40s, when he was counseling World War II veterans, studying, and living at Notre Dame.

My initial impression was that he was doing an outstanding job in a difficult assignment.

*Your husband, Oliver Carmichael, was a trustee, when the university went coed in 1972. After his death, you were elected a trustee in 1976. What do you remember were the trustees' concerns, during this period?*

My husband would talk to me about the trustees meetings, when he'd come home. He was a former women's college president, Converse College in Spartanburg, South Carolina, Father Joyce's hometown. In fact, we lived about three blocks away from Father Joyce's parents, when we lived there.

My husband was concerned about how the first women would feel in what was obviously a very male environment, a male-dominated university. I remember him saying that there was some feeling of intimidation at first.

When I became a board member, one of the things that I noticed was that the undergraduate women didn't reach out to us women trustees. None of them ever called me. So, we, women trustees, made it a point to visit the women's dormitories to speak with the women. During these meetings, their main concerns were the living conditions, particularly the lack of closet space.

*You were the first woman to chair a Notre Dame Capital Campaign in 1976. Why were you selected?*

Father Ted asked me if I'd be the chairman. I'd been chairman of the Notre Dame Women's Advisory Council. Before women were members of the different college advisory councils, when the men, who were members came to campus for meetings, the women would meet separately.

Because I have had significant experience in fund-raising and have a love affair with Notre Dame, I agreed immediately to be the capital campaign chairman. In fact, that's how I'd start my talks—talking about how much Notre Dame means to me, its specialness and uniqueness.

*Was this Notre Dame's first capital campaign or did others precede the one you chaired?*

There had been one before that my husband had chaired. Being chairman involved making fifty to sixty appearances at fly-ins. These were on-campus visits by about forty potential donors. John Ryan, a Notre Dame Trustee from Pittsburgh, helped me. Because I lived in South Bend, it was easy for me to do this.

We would talk to the potential donors during meetings, have slide shows, walk them around campus showing them different things like LOBUND.

*Do you think that the university had become coed had much of an impact on the success of the capital campaign?*

I can't say, for sure, that it helped us to get the money any faster, but from the questions I got during these fly-ins, it was clear that people were delighted that Notre Dame had gone coed. As to how that translated into what they gave I don't know.

*You grew up in South Bend and have been visiting Notre Dame almost your whole life. When you visit the campus, what do you see as being the impact of undergraduate women? How is the campus today different than the campus of 1971?*

It's the best of both worlds. It's much more normal to have men and women on the same campus.

At one time, Notre Dame and Saint Mary's had considered merging. What eventually happened was a better result. It preserved the best of all worlds. It preserved Saint Mary's, which is unique and wonderful. And, you also have coeds at Notre Dame. For women, this is the best of all worlds.

*How would you describe Father Ted's presidency?*

I think the university has been very fortunate to have leaders at different points of time who have been so perfect for the university.

Father Ted was a visionary at a time when it needed that vision of expanding. Part of that vision was opening up the university to undergrad coeducation. He would tell me that it was going to change Notre Dame, but change it for the better.

He opened the gates to Notre Dame and brought the country in. It became nationally and internationally known because Father Ted was on so many different boards and represented the university in such a fine way. He brought people, who'd never been to Notre Dame, who would never have come to Notre Dame except for him, there.

*Rev. James Riehle '49 CSC, was dean of students (1967–1973), when Notre Dame went coed. He was also a rector of Sorin Hall (1965–1965), and Pangborn Hall (1971–1985).*

*As the longtime chaplain of Notre Dame's sports teams, Father Riehle has celebrated the football team's Saturday pregame Mass, since 1967. Executive director of the Monogram Club for seventeen years, Father Riehle is now honorary president.*

*A keen athlete in his own right, reportedly in an early '70s faculty hockey game, Father Riehle body-checked football coach Ara Parseghian and survived to tell about it.*

*Father Riehle was interviewed in his office on September 15, 2006, by Ann Therese Darin Palmer.*

*Did you hire any women staff or make any modifications at all in student policies or the dean of students' office, in anticipation of women living on campus as undergrads in 1972?*

I didn't see the need to do anything. At the time, I had one male assistant dean of students.

What happened, when women arrived, bore me out. I was expecting nothing was going to happen. And, that's exactly what happened. I never had a disciplinary case involving a woman.

*When were the first Notre Dame alumnae elected Monogram Club members?*

As soon as women, who'd earned athletic letters, started graduating, they were eligible to join the Monogram Club. The first women joined in 1976 for athletics in the 1975–1976 season.

They included Mary Behler, Catherine Buzard Sazdanoff, Jane Lammers, Christina Marciniak, and Kathy Valdiserri. Their monograms were in tennis and fencing.

Prior to this group, there were some Saint Mary's College graduates who earned a monogram in cheerleading. The Monogram Office does not have those names.

*How did the male Monogram Club members react?*

It didn't bother them at all. In fact, shortly afterward, women started serving on the Monogram Club Board. The first woman director of the Monogram Club was Anne Cisle Murray '74, who was a cheerleader from 1972 to 1974.

*How many Monogram Club members are there today? How many are women?*

There are 6,776 current living monogram winners. Of those, 1,390 are women.

This year for the first time, we have a woman Monogram Club president, Julie Pierson Doyle '85, a varsity volleyball team player. She played on the team during its second and third years in existence.

*How has Notre Dame women's athletics changed in the last thirty-five years?*

We've won national championships in basketball, fencing, and soccer. ND women athletes have gotten a lot of positive recognition.

These women have also become great role models. I'm talking about Jackie Batteast '05 and Ruth Riley '01, former captain of the Detroit Shock, which won the Women's National Basketball Championship in 2006. She was captain of the women's basketball team here when we won the national championship in 2001. She won a gold medal in the Olympics.

She's a great ambassador for Notre Dame—a good student, an excellent athlete. She represents everything that a Notre Dame student athlete should be. She came from a small farm town to Notre Dame on a scholarship. She's shown that if you work hard, the sky's the limit.

Another role model is Dr. Carol Lally Shields '79. She's a distinguished eye oncologist in Philadelphia. She played basketball and was captain of the first varsity women's basketball team. She was the first woman to win the Byron Kanely Award for excellence in academics and leadership, the highest honor given to ND student athletes. She was given an ND honorary degree in 2005.

*James A. Roemer '51,'55 JD actually may be considered a triple Domer. As a high school student at Holy Cross Seminary, Roemer drove Father Ted to the "county poorhouse" weekly where Father Ted said Mass for its residents.*

*He'd known Father Ted before this assignment. Roemer's dad was a Notre Dame philosophy professor. Father Ted visited the Roemer household occasionally, when Roemer was growing up.*

*The South Bend attorney was appointed university general counsel in 1972 and dean of students from 1976 to 1985. He served as the director of community relations for fifteen years afterward. For seventeen years, concurrently he was adjunct associate professor in the Law School, teaching street law and municipal law.*

*His son, former Congressman Timothy Roemer, has a master's degree (1981) and PhD in government and international studies (1985).*

*He was interviewed on December 16, 2006 by Carol Jambor-Smith, Notre Dame Law School director of external relations.*

1972 was a momentous year in the history of Notre Dame because you and the trustees made the decisions that were necessary to allow women to enter this university. At the time, you asked Phil Faccenda to serve as the vice president of Student Affairs; you and Phil then asked me to serve as the general counsel of the university. My office was across the hall from you in the Main Building.

Before this time, I hadn't had the privilege of knowing you except during the times when I, then a teenage seminarian, would pick you up to drive you to the "county poorhouse," now known as Portage Manor, to celebrate Mass. At that time, you were the chaplain for Vetville and a theology professor at Notre Dame. I will always fondly remember our drives, conversation, and breakfasts afterward.

Then about 1976, you and Father Jim Burtchaell, CSC, the provost, asked that I become the dean of students. For the next nine years, I had the privilege of being in your office maybe once a week since you were always vitally interested in any important issues that involved your students.

Father Joyce, a wonderful priest and maybe your dearest friend, was always interested in student behavior too, especially if it involved the Athletic Department, which he followed very closely.

I remember the conversations we would have about matters that involved my office; I always wanted to have you know what the issues were and what my thoughts were about the issues. There was only one occasion when you courteously asked me to reverse a position I had taken on a particular case, and you had solid personal reasons that I respected.

I was constantly amazed at the common sense you consistently applied to all the issues that we discussed.

I remember one occasion late at night when I knocked on your Corby Hall room to discuss a problem involving prominent athletes. You heard me out and then said, "Jim, you treat them the same way that you would treat any other student here at Notre Dame." That's all I needed to know.

In my nine years as dean of students, I saw maybe thousands of male students and only hundreds of women students. There was no question in my mind that we males got into more difficulty, especially drinking, than the females!

In more recent years, during dinners which Mary Ann and I have had with you at Ann and Bill Sexton's, we've talked about the ordination of women. I was pleased to see you argue for that change in the Church, even though it will not happen in our lifetimes. Women have an innate sense of caring and compassion for other people that we men do not so easily practice. I have observed you in your relationships with women and you have always been comfortable treating them as equally important in every respect.

Father Ted, I remember knocking on your door late at night one time up at Land of Lakes, Wisconsin. In the course of a long conversation, I asked you what would happen to you upon your death. Where were you going? You responded that a person grows in length by the love he's given and enjoyed in a lifetime. You added that he then grows in breadth by the service that he has rendered to others in that person's lifetime. In that measure of depth and breadth, he enters forever into life hereafter. I really appreciated that graphic vision, which condensed in so many short words volumes of theological reflection and vision.

Last night, as I was thinking about what I would write in this letter, I rewatched the television tribute to you. I was not at all surprised by the many tributes that were offered by women graduates and women students. You have touched many, many lives, mine included.

I have never known a priest who has lived out his life so consistently and beautifully as a priest and as a human being. It has been my privilege to have had a relationship with you for these past sixty years.

There was so much talk about women at Notre Dame this year that often the real gift of co-education was lost. For the first time in Notre Dame's history, men and women could have an outlet outside of a dating relationship. Hopefully, now that the first year is over, the excitement of co-education can end, and the education of men and women can begin in earnest.

Father Ted, Joanne Szafran, and Sister John Miriam Jones in Walsh Hall, 1973.

*Joanne Szafran '73 MA was the second woman appointed to be a rector of a woman's dorm. She served as rector of Walsh Hall from 1972 to 1975. Walsh Hall was one of the first two women's dorms on campus. The other was Badin.*

*Joanne also earned a master of arts in teaching from the George Washington University in 1976. She's spent thirty years with the federal government in Washington D.C. She has worked at the National Archives, as well as the Departments of Treasury and Agriculture. Since 1990, she has worked in the Office of Inspector General for the General Services Administration.*

*She was interviewed by Monica Yant Kinney '93 a former editor in chief of the* Observer *and a reporter for the* Philadelphia Daily News, *by phone on January 15, 2007.*

*How were you selected to become a women's dorm rector?*

I was older. I had been in Thailand with the Peace Corps before I came to Notre Dame. I was thirty-two, in graduate school majoring in history, in charge of Holy Cross dorm at Saint Mary's.

A lot of my students from Holy Cross transferred and moved with me to Walsh Hall. A lot of the women were very loyal to Saint Mary's. It was very hard for them to come over, to leave their old social friends behind.

*What did you have to do to convert Walsh to a woman's dorm?*

There was a lot to do to get the dorm ready for the women and the projects were behind schedule. The big thing the workers had to do was install washers and dryers in the basement.

A security system had to be put on the doors—we were very, very conscious of security, with a few hundred women and thousands of guys. Walls had to be painted. The bathrooms had urinals that had to be removed. What I remember most is how behind schedule all the projects were. Were we every going to get this done on time?

Notre Dame had such a strong dorm tradition. If you were from Walsh, you lived there for four years. You're a Walsh guy. Well, it was different for the woman. We had to build a community, build our own identity. The first year, we had 173 women in Walsh, 116 in Badin.

*What were those first days like, when the women arrived?*

Moving in that first year, the chaos didn't seem as bad as move-in day at Saint Mary's because there were fewer residents at Walsh Hall. The dads who'd graduated from Notre Dame were familiar with the dorm. Many of the mothers had graduated from Saint Mary's. I know those Dads were proud, some of them saying, "My daughter's going to Notre Dame and I lived in this dorm."

Most of the students would go to RAs first with their problems—they'd come to me only when it was pretty serious. I insisted on being called Miss Szafran. I wanted them to know I was in charge of the dorm. I could be very isolated, so I would walk the halls, to visit.

*What were some of the biggest issues you faced?*

Security was just such a big issue. Keys—who should get one, who is coming in and out. Don't let somebody in just because they're knocking on the door. My fear was, we had 173 women in this dorm and 6,000 guys on campus. Will we have panty raids? Would someone wander in off campus?

We had the Detex system to unlock doors. The first year, it was on all the time. By the third year, we took it off from noon to 6:00 p.m.

In the beginning, there was some tension because the former residents of Walsh Hall resented that women were living in their dorm. They were set to settle into Walsh for four years and had to move. There were some unhappy campers.

So, we invited the previous residents to a Halloween costume party with the women in Walsh. That way, they could get to know each other. It was still by and large, a little sticky that first year. They didn't like it. I could see why.

That first year, we lived in a fishbowl. There were TV cameras interviewing as students moved in. I was surprised by this, and it was very overwhelming for the students. The students had to play a social role. On football weekends, we invited alumni back to visit the hall. They wanted to see what the women looked like living in Walsh Hall. It was exhilarating, but most of the students were very stressed.

Before coeducation, there were actually MORE women on campus, because of Saint Mary's students. So the pressures mounted for the new ND enrollees because they were so exposed.

*What was it like academically?*

The women were very competitive in the classroom. They worked—you didn't slough off. They were overwhelmed, and many of them would get many requests for dates with guys. They had dilemmas—do I say yes or no? How do I handle this? Some of them would laugh it off. They didn't want to settle down with just one person.

They wanted lots of friends, but were worried, "How will this look if I say no?" Thankfully, that settled down by the second year. They weren't such a novelty.

I never heard about classroom troubles. There was no doubt there were some chauvinist teachers. The absence of female faculty and administrators made it harder. Where were the role models for these students? They weren't there. I'm sure some students were unhappy that first year, but I don't remember anybody leaving for that reason.

*What was one of the high points of the year?*

I remember Father Ted coming to visit us at Walsh Hall that first year. It was a very, very special visit, for him to come to the dorm. He was nationally known, traveled all over the world. We always knew when he was in his office, because we could see the light on. If the light was off, he was traveling. When the light was on in his office in the Administration Building, students would go there, in the middle of the night, and ask the security guard if they could see him. He always said yes.

Father Ted and Coretta Scott King at "Toasting Father Ted," benefiting the South Bend Life Treatment Center, 1999.

*Seventh Circuit U.S. Appellate Court Judge Ann Claire Williams, '75 Law, was the first assistant rector of Farley Hall, when it became the third women's residence hall in September 1973. She is the first African-American to serve on the Seventh Circuit Appellate Court.*

*In 1985, Judge Williams became the first African-American appointed to U.S. District Court for the Northern District of Illinois, which sits in Chicago. She became the first African-American president of the Federal Judges Association in 1999.*

*Judge Williams is a Notre Dame trustee.*

Dear Father Ted,

I first heard about you when I was a little girl in Detroit and was watching television with my family. My mom pointed you out, marching, hand and hand, with Dr. Martin Luther King Jr. and other leaders of the civil rights movement. She told me that you were the president of the University of Notre Dame, and I was very impressed. Little did I know that many years later, I would be a direct beneficiary of your commitment to civil rights, justice, and coeducation at Notre Dame.

You were responsible for opening the doors of the Law School to women in the late '60s and to undergraduates in 1972. There were nineteen women in my law school class and one woman faculty member. And although I had some appreciation for the visionary and bold steps that you had taken, it wasn't until the next year when I became the first assistant rector at Farley, the third women's residence hall, that I really felt the sweeping impact of your momentous decisions.

My dear friend, Sister Jean Lenz, Farley's first rector, who still lives in my old room, and I braced ourselves when the doors opened and students moved in. I remember so clearly all the dads, brothers, alumni, and other young men—some in tears, gnashing their teeth—reminiscing and commenting that it would never, ever be the same. And others who shared your dream, joyful, proud, and beaming because their daughters would breathe, live, learn, pray, and become women at Notre Dame.

But it was a tough time. There were only about eight hundred women on campus compared to roughly eight thousand men. Every weekend we were astounded that so many girls were sitting in their rooms or just hanging out together. That was because the boys assumed that the girls had so many invitations that they would not be able to get a date. When we first began giving hall parties, it was just like high school—the boys leaning on one wall, and the girls on the other.

Because the boy-girl ratio was so bad and we wanted to accommodate girls who were visiting from other schools or girlfriends of ND students, we opened the Farley Motel—a large open space in the basement of Farley, with lots of bunk beds. Jean Early was the resident assistant and host to hundreds of young women who paid a dollar a night to experience some of the magic of the Notre Dame family. I even remember arranging weekend visits where we bussed in young women from historically black colleges for dances and other activities because there were only a handful of black women on campus.

Also, that was the year that male streakers, baring all, started flashing and running around campus late at night. When Sister Jean and I heard the girls squealing, we raced to make sure doors were locked and windows were shut tight. The last thing we needed was streakers in the dorm.

Going to Mass and hearing your homilies or seeing you speak around campus was also an amazing and inspiring experience that raised the message of being our brother's and sister's keeper to the highest level. Your guiding light blazed so brightly here at Notre Dame and on the national and international stage. You were a charter member and former chair of the United States Civil Rights Commission. And because of your leadership, the Law School opened the Center for Civil Rights School, where I worked as a research assistant. It was and continues to be a beacon of hope for all who seek justice.

So, as we celebrate your 90th birthday and the thirty-fifth anniversary of coeducation at Notre Dame, I, a fortunate beneficiary of your great legacy, will continue to dedicate my life to working toward the example you set of striving for justice, equality, and community. Thank you, Father Ted, for reaching out your hand to the millions of people you've touched at Notre Dame and across the world, and thank you from a little girl who had big dreams that you helped make come true.

With love and best wishes,

The Honorable Ann Claire Williams
Class of '75 JD
U.S. Circuit Court Judge, 1999–present
U.S. District Court Judge, 1985–1999

# 2

# NOTRE DAME CELEBRITY REMINISCENCES

# Celebrity Letters

Lydia Antonini '97
Director, Digital Entertainment, Warner Bros.-Warner
  Premiere, California

Patricia Ann Romano Barry '84
First Notre Dame Woman Class President

George Blaha '66
Play-by-Play Broadcaster, Detroit Pistons, Michigan
  State University Football

Kathleen A. Blatz '76
Former Chief Justice, Minnesota Supreme Court

Mary Davey Bliley '72
First Woman Undergraduate Degree Recipient

Elizabeth C. Brown '08
Student Body President 2007–2008

Shannon Boland Burkhart '98
Former Communications Manager, White House
  Press Office

Ellen Carnahan '77
Managing Director, William Blair
  Capital Partners LLC and Seyen Capital LLC,
  Chicago, Illinois

Susan Andersen Casper '74
First Woman President, Walsh Hall 1972–1973

The Honorable Tracy Kee Christopher '78
District Court Judge, Houston, Texas

Tom Clements '75
Quarterback, Football Team 1972–1974
National Champions: 1973

Jean Collier '83
President, Notre Dame Alumni Association 2003

The Honorable Kathleen Gallogly Cox '76, '79 JD
Judge, Baltimore (Maryland) County Circuit Court

Patrice P. DeCorrevont '84
Managing Director, JP Morgan Chase & Co., Chicago,
  Illinois

Joya De Foor '77
Treasurer, City of Los Angeles, California

The Honorable Mary Katherine
  Rochford Demetrio '76, '79 JD
Associate Circuit Court Judge, Cook County, Illinois

L. Franklin Devine '75
Producer, *60 Minutes,* CBS News

Reverend Anne M. Dilenschneider '77
Pastor, United Methodist and United Church of Christ,
  Montara, California

Julie Pierson Doyle '85
First Woman President, Notre Dame Monogram Club
  2006–2007

The Honorable Carol A. Falvey '82
Circuit Court Judge, Citrus County, Florida

Peggy Foran '76, '79 JD
Senior Vice President, Associate General Counsel,
    and Corporate Secretary, Pfizer Inc., New York,
    New York

Celeste Volz Ford '78
CEO/Chairperson, Stellar Solutions Inc., California
Chairman, Fitzpatrick College of Engineering
    Advisory Council

The Honorable Carol Hackett Garagiola '77
Chief Judge, Livingston County (Michigan)
    Probate Court

Steve Garagiola '77
Anchor/Reporter, WDIV-TV, Detroit, Michigan

The Honorable Piper D. Griffin '84
Judge, Civil District Court, New Orleans, Louisiana

Susan Darin Hagan '76
First Woman Editor in Chief, *Dome* Yearbook, 1975
    Edition

Madeleine Hanna '08
Editor in Chief, *Observer* Newspaper 2007–2008

Melinda Henneberger '80
Author, *If They Only Listened to Us: What Women
    Voters Want Politicians to Hear* (2007)
Former Rome Bureau Chief, the *New York Times*

Lou Holtz
Head Football Coach 1986–1996
National Champions: 1988

Reverend John I. Jenkins, CSC, '76, '78 MA
President, University of Notre Dame 2005–

Tara Crane Kenney '82
First Woman Student Body Vice
    President 1981–1982
Managing Director, Deutshce Bank Asset
    Management, Boston, Massachusetts

Donald R. Keough '85 Honorary
Chairman, Notre Dame Board of Trustees 1986–1992

Monica Yant Kinney '93
Editor in Chief, *Observer* Newspaper 1992–1993

Brooke Norton Lais '02
First Woman Student Body President
    2001–2002

Kathleen C. Laurini '82
Deputy Director, Space Life Sciences Directorate,
    NASA Johnson Space Center

The Honorable Diana Lewis '74, '82 JD
Trustee, Circuit Court Judge, Palm Beach County,
    Florida

James R. Lynch '67
Captain, Notre Dame Football Team, 1966
National Champions: 1966

Sally Stanton MacKenzie '76
First Woman Editor in Chief, *Scholastic* Magazine
    1975–1976
Romance Novelist, Maryland

Sarah Hamilton Magill '86
Editor in Chief, *Observer* Newspaper 1985–1986

Rev. Edward M. Malloy, CSC '63, '67 MA, '69 MA
President, University of Notre Dame, 1987–2005

Kathryn Sobrero Markgraf '98
Captain, ND Women's Soccer Team 1997–1998
2000 Silver Olympic Medalist, Women's Soccer
2004 Gold Olympic Medalist, Women's Soccer

Roxanne M. O'Brien Martino '77
President and CEO, Harris Alternatives LLC, Chicago,
    Illinois
Chairman, Mendoza College of Business Advisory
    Council

Patrick F. McCartan '56, '59 JD, '99 Honorary
Chairman, Notre Dame Board of Trustees
2000–2007

Mary Margaret McCarthy '80
Director, National Immigrant Justice Center,
    Heartland Alliance, Chicago, Illinois

Andrew J. McKenna Sr. '51, '89 Honorary
Chairman, Notre Dame Board of Trustees 1992–2000

Rosemary Mills-Russell '80
First Notre Dame Undergraduate Woman Editor
    in Chief *Observer* Newspaper 1979–1980

Joe Montana '79
Quarterback, Football Team 1975–1979
National Champions: 1977
Quarterback, San Francisco 49ers
Four-Time Super Bowl Champions

Mary Killeen Mullen '90
Manager, Special Events, Tampa Bay Buccaneers

Kristy Zloch Murphy '96
Television Actress, *The West Wing*

Anne Cisle Murray '74
First Woman Director, Notre Dame Monogram Club
    1978–1984

Coley O'Brien '66, '69 JD
Quarterback, Football Team 1964–1966
National Champions: 1966

The Honorable Sheila M. O'Brien '77, '80 JD
Justice, Illinois Appellate Court

Joseph I. O'Neill III '67
Trustee, Managing Partner, O'Neill Properties
    Limited, Midland, Texas

Maureen O'Neill '77
Director of Development, School of Law, University
    of Oxford, Oxford, England

Kerri Ochs Oxley '04
Trustee, Medical Student, Yale University

Ara Parseghian
Head Football Coach 1964–1974
National Champions: 1966, 1973

Cindy Buescher Parseghian '77
President, Ara Parseghian Medical Foundation,
    Arizona

John Paxson '83
General Manager, Chicago Bulls
NBA Championship Teammate 1991–1993

Richard (Digger) Phelps
Head Basketball Coach 1971–1991

Regis Philbin '53
Emmy Award–Winning Host, *Live with Regis and Kelly*

Cecilia Prinster '76
President-Elect, Notre Dame Alumni Association
   2007–2008

Heather Rakoczy '93
Director, Notre Dame Gender Relations Center

Ruth Riley '01
Member, San Antonio Silver Stars, WNBA
Olympic Gold Medal Winner
NCAA Irish Women's Basketball Championship Team
Member, Detroit Shock, 2006, WNBA Champions
   2006

Shayla Keough Rumley '76
Trustee, Attorney, Atlanta, Georgia

Laura Jonaus Schumacher '85
General Counsel, Abbott Laboratories, North Chicago,
   Ilinois

Elizabeth Shappell '07
Student Body President 2006–2007

Frances L. Shavers '90
Chief of Staff, Special Assistant to the President,
   University of Notre Dame

Dr. Carol Lally Shields '79 '05 Honorary
Captain, Women's Basketball Team 1978–1979
First Woman Varsity Athlete Recipient
Byron Kaneley Award for Excellence in Academics
Ocular Oncologist, Philadelphia, Pennsylvania

Elizabeth Bishop Shields '03
Student Body President 2002–2003, London,
   England

Carolyn P. Short '77
Former General Counsel, U.S. Senate Judiciary
   Committee
Partner, Reed, Smith, Shaw & McClay, Philadelphia,
   Pennsylvania

Hannah Storm '83
Cohost, *The Early Show,* CBS News

Joe Theismann '70
Quarterback, Football Team 1968–1970
Super Bowl XVII Champion
1983 NFL Most Valuable Player

Anne Thompson '79
Chief Environmental Correspondent, NBC News
New York, New York

Elizabeth Anne Toomey '81
First Woman President, Notre Dame Alumni
   Association
Residential Realtor, Seattle, Washington

Kelley Tuthill '92
Anchor/Reporter, WCVB-TV, Boston, Massachusetts

Dr. Claire J. Twist '82
Pediatric Hematologist Oncologist, Lucile Packard
   Children's Hospital at Stanford University,
   Palo Alto, California

Susan Valdiserri '84
Professional and Executive Coach, IBM Corporation,
   Chicago, Illinois

The Honorable Martha Vazquez '75, '79 JD
U.S. District Court, New Mexico

Dick Vitale
ESPN Sportscaster/Father of Two Notre Dame
   Alumnae

Dr. Eleanor M. Walker '84
Radiation Oncologist, Henry Ford Hospital, Detroit,
    Michigan

Charlie Weis '78
Head Football Coach 2005–
Assistant Coach, New York Giants and New England
    Patriots
Four Super Bowl Championships

Kenneth L. Woodward '57
Retired Religion Editor, *Newsweek* Magazine

The Honorable Susan Zwick '77, '80 JD
Circuit Court Judge, Cook County, Illinois

ear Father Hesburgh,

Often the bravest decisions in life are the ones that go unnoticed and uncelebrated by the masses. I consider your decision to make the University of Notre Dame into a co-educational university to be one of those unnoticed and uncelebrated decisions. Hopefully, all of these thank-you notes from the women of Notre Dame can help to correct that oversight.

The decision to make Notre Dame coed not only created great opportunities for women throughout the world, but it also gave the men of Notre Dame the opportunity to work with women and to recognize their ability to contribute on equal footing to the progress of our university, our nation, our world, and the Catholic religion.

Your decision to always look forward toward change and to bring the university along in that journey has made Notre Dame a place where great men and women learn, discern, and wrestle with what it means to always be moving toward a deeper peace and joy in communion with the world.

I am proud to be a part of your legacy and I thank you for laying the foundation that has made my journey possible.

Sincerely,

Lydia Antonini
Class of '97
Director, Digital Entertainment, Warner Bros.-Warner Premiere, California

☙

Dear Father Hesburgh,

Please allow me to join the thousands of women who genuinely thank you for all you have done for Our Lady's university. I will always remember your encouragement as I was running for the office of president of the Class of 1984. Although Notre Dame had not had a female president up until that time, I felt we were ready for a change. There were many who tried to discourage me but little did they know that an encouraging word from you was all I needed to stay the course.

I will always remember the night of March 3, 1983, first because I had found out our ticket had won, but most importantly because of the congratulatory call I received from you.

You have always been an ardent advocate for all human rights so it is only appropriate that you championed the cause for women at the university dedicated to the greatest woman of all.

**The Observer**

VOL. XVII, NO. 110          the independent student newspaper serving notre dame and saint mary's          FRIDAY, MARCH 4, 1983

Class officer elections

# Romano, Hockett, Broussard win

BY KEVIN BINGER
*Campus Campaign Reporter*

Tricia Romano became the first female senior class president in yesterday's runoff balloting for class officers.

Vince Hockett won the job of junior class president, and Lee Broussard will be the next sophomore class president.

Romano's ticket won with 631, or 54.2 percent of the ballots cast. The opposing ticket, led by Bill Dawahare, garnered 534 votes.

Hockett, who finished second by nine votes to Mike Schmitt in the first election Tuesday, made up ground in Wednesday's campaigning, earning 559 votes, 51.8 percent of the number cast. Schmitt's ticket finished with 521 votes.

Runners-up in the first election rarely win in the runoff, according to Pat Borchers, Ombudsman spokesman.

Broussard's margin of victory over his oppponent, Vito Gagliardi, was approximately 200 votes.

"It feels great, I'm excited," said Romano about her election as the first female class president. "But that's not our full purpose."

Romano learned the news at about 9 p.m. last night as she walked into the second floor Ombudsman office in LaFortune. Her first reaction was to call home. "I've got to call my dad. He said I'd never make it, not a girl."

"We, want to get started right away," Romano said. "Disorientation week is going to be our first event, right away at the beginning of the year."

Romano stressed the experience of her ticket, which includes Eric Wiechart, vice president; Pat Berry, secretary; and Bill Kirk, treasurer.

"We know what's going to happen," she said. "We're going to have a good year."

According to Kevin Stierer, Judicial Coordinator and part of Lloyd Burke's team investigating junior class balloting, Vince Hockett's victory will probably stand despite some ballot shortages. John Decker, presidential candidate of the *Mob* ticket claimed that there were sophomores in several dorms who who

See RESULTS, page 3

# House passes package of recession relief

WASHINGTON (AP) — The House passed $24.95 yesterday a $4.9 billion package of recession relief designed to provide temporary employment for nearly one million people as well as food and shelter for the neediest.

The plan was attached to $5 billion in funds needed to assure continued payment of unemployment benefits. Together, these provisions constitute the first major anti-recession initiative of the 98th Congress that took office two

measure yesterday, the bill drew sharp criticism from Republicans who complained about "pork barrel" provisions that funneled funds to the districts of influential House members, as well as from Democratic liberals who complained what the bill did not do enough to deal with the long recession.

"If you want to vote for pork, this is it," said Rep. Delbert Latta, R-Ohio.

"This bill is a frenzied feeding at the public trough," agreed Rep. Judd

*A high flying Dave Rectenwald shows his dynamic style of one-step defense techniques on his way to achieving his 1st degree black-belt at the ACC. Rectenwald is a four year member of the Notre Dame Tae Kwon Do Club (Photo by Larry Petras)*

Thank you for all you have done for me personally and for all women of Notre Dame.

You will always be in my heart and prayers.

Yours in Notre Dame,

Tricia Romano Barry
Class of '84
First Notre Dame Woman Class President

Dear Father Hesburgh,

What you have done for ND over the years is nothing short of sensational. Your timing was always perfect and your decision making superb.

While I was in school, you continued to build Notre Dame's academic reputation, while actually upgrading our football team in the process by bringing the brilliant Ara Parseghian to campus.

You seem to know, with God's help for sure, when the timing was right to make a move. A few years after my graduation, you did the right thing again for our school, when you brought young women to the campus.

It's hard to imagine Notre Dame without coeds these days. They helped us raise the bar once again—helping to make Our Lady's university truly one of the finest in the world. I don't see any loss of that awesome Notre Dame spirit. On the contrary, what I have noticed is that the Notre Dame campus has become so much more refined with the addition of women to our student body.

Thank you for another courageous and correct decision.

Happy 90th Birthday, Father Ted.

Sincerely,

George Blaha
Class of '66
Play-by-Play Announcer, Detroit Pistons and Michigan State University Football

Dear Father Ted,

It is wonderful to have this opportunity to tell you that you and your vision for Notre Dame, some thirty-plus years ago, have profoundly affected my life. I am very grateful to you and will always count you as a person who made a difference to me and countless other women.

One of my earliest memories growing up was my father's undying loyalty—and enthusiasm—for his alma mater, the University of Notre Dame. Little did I know that I, too, would graduate from this remarkable university in 1976. How lucky I was to have the doors of Notre Dame opened to women!

While I have many memories to choose from, one of the most meaningful experiences I had at Notre Dame was being chosen to be a part of your "experimental values/ethics class" to see if a requirement for a values seminar should be integrated into the curriculum for every Notre Dame student. You visited the class on its opening night as a testament to your personal commitment to the goal that every student grappled with and appreciated the ethical challenges presented by daily living. To this day I can remember your recounting the true story of a former student—then CEO of a large international company. The CEO had sought your advice on how to handle a business transaction in a foreign country, a transaction that involved many ethical issues. You carefully laid out the competing interests and left the discussion regarding the resolution to us. How wise you were in choosing this approach to emphasize the personal examination necessary to solve complex issues in a thoughtful and integrated way. I was enormously pleased when the value/ethics class became a requirement in later years . . . just one more remarkable piece of your legacy.

Twenty-two years after graduating from Notre Dame, I became chief justice of the Minnesota Supreme Court. I was the first woman to have held this position in Minnesota. I know that my education at Notre Dame and the institution's deep commitment to justice and scholarship not only prepared me for this position but also guided me as I strove to meet the demands of daily life. Your challenge to us that what we believe and value must be reflected in how we act has been both an inspiration to me as well as a guiding light.

Thank you for your excellent leadership. Thank you for the difference you and Notre Dame made in my life. Every time I am asked where I went to college, I am proud to answer the "University of Notre Dame."

With deep respect,

Kathleen Blatz
Class of '76
Former Chief Justice, Minnesota Supreme Court

Dear Father Ted,

All female undergraduates owe the success of coeducation to your foresight and determination, but none more than me. Due to your vision and the guidance of Dean Vincent Raymond, head of the Business College, I was permitted to be the first and only female undergraduate to receive a Notre Dame degree in the Class of 1972.

In 1968, when I took the train from my home in Columbus, Montana, to Chicago, en route to starting college as a freshman at Saint Mary's, little did I dream what was ahead of me. I arrived in Chicago during the horrific riots at the Democratic Presidential Convention. We were in the throngs of the Vietnam War protests, and there were so many angry people confronting the young freshman from a town of 1,000 people.

I was happy to be attending Saint Mary's. As a Catholic growing up in Montana, I'd been a minority my whole life. I was a math major my freshman year. Solving math problems did not quite fit me. Sophomore year, I was a history major. Neither, I learned, did writing term papers fit me. That's when I decided to major in business.

At the beginning of my junior year the merger was full speed ahead between Notre Dame and Saint Mary's. I went into Dean Raymond's office and said, "Dean Raymond, I want to graduate from the University of Notre Dame." He replied, "Red, sit with me and we're going to plan your curriculum and you're going to graduate as a marketing major in business from Notre Dame." That was the beginning of my junior year, and I began working toward my Notre Dame degree.

The fall of my senior year I was nostalgic but moving forward. Then, after Thanksgiving vacation, I received a huge shock. The merger wasn't going to happen. Notre Dame would admit women the following fall. In the *Observer,* Father said, "You (Saint Mary's) want to marry us, but you don't want to take our name or live with us. The sisters agreed and we decided to make Notre Dame coeducational some other way." I did what I had done when I wanted to become a business major. I went into Dean Raymond's office and said, "Dean Raymond, what am I going to do? I am a senior, all my credits are at Notre Dame." Dean Raymond said what he always said, "Stick with me, Red, we are going to get you out of here."

I went home that Christmas to the family ranch. I was the oldest of seven and at that time my father had three kids in private schools. I went home to tell him the merger was off. He looked at me and said, "And where are you going to graduate?" And I said, "Don't worry, Dad, they are going to take care of me."

Early in 1972, I received a letter from Sister Alma, president of the Saint Mary's College. In that letter she wrote that I would not receive a degree from Saint Mary's, and I was not to attend any graduation ceremonies at Saint Mary's. These were the ceremonies of my friends with whom I had just spent the last four years of my life.

That spring was extremely tedious. Other deserving women were protesting their inability to receive Notre Dame degrees. I went to Dean Raymond. "Dean, should I be protesting?" He would reply as he always had, "Mary, we are going to take care of you." In April, Dean Raymond called me into his office. He said, "Red, you're going to graduate—not only are you going to graduate but you will be the first female undergraduate from the University of Notre Dame and the only female in your class."

Because I had fulfilled all of the university's requirements for a degree in business

# THE OBSERVER

only one word for it: wel

Vol. VI, No. 53

serving the notre dame - st. mary's community

Tuesday, November 30, 1971

# Merger hopes killed; speculation rampant

by Ann Therese Darin
Observer Associate Editor

Informed sources revealed over the long weekend that plans for a Notre Dame-St. Mary's merger, in the offing for almost a year, have been scrapped by Trustees of the two schools.

Edmund A. Stephan, chairman of Notre Dame's Board of Trustees, and Mother Olivette Whelan, chairman of St. Mary's Board, are scheduled to issue "an important announcemnt" through the university office of public information this afternoon.

Notre Dame President Theodore Hesburgh said that two seperate statements are being prepared. One was released to the ND faculty this morning. The other statement will be released at 2 o'clock this afternoon.

Hesburgh declined to comment on the contents of the two statements. He said that they were prepared by representatives of both schools.

Reportedly the statement will indefinitely suspend unification. In the same release, sources revealed that the University will announce its intent to accept women students for the 1972-73 academic year.

Although the statement allegedly will not stipulate the number of women to be admitted, some university administrators approximated the number at 400.

The statement supposedly says that the University will not terminate coeducational programs with St. Mary's College SMC, however, may have to start paying for present coexchange services which include cafeteria exchange, shuttle bus transportation between the two campuses, tuition per credit hour for coexchange classes, and fees for the use of university computers to program students schedules, payrolls, and report cards.

While the two schools still desire unifications, the statement allegedly contends, the Trustees are still far apart on terms.

Stephan could not be reached for comment. In Chicago, his secretary revealed he will be in Russia until Dec. 7. Likewise Mother Olivette Whelan was unavailable for comment.

ND Trustee's secratary, Paul F. Hellmuth, claimed he had not yet received notification of the plans yesterday afternoon in Boston.

William Cahill, a 10-year member of the St. Mary's Board, however, denied that the two boards had terminated unification plans. Cahill attended the Ad-Hoc meeting on unification Nov. 20-21, with St. Mary's representatives P. Jordan Hamel and Srs. Olivette, Alma, and Gerald. Notre Dame's representatives to the meeting included Rev. Theodore M. Hesburgh, president; executive vice-president Rev. Edmund Joyce, Provost Rev. James T. Burtchaell, Trustees Student Affairs Committee Chairman Thomas Carney, and Stephan.

In Chicago, Cahill said that, "I felt the meeting was very satisfactory. In fact, there is another meeting planned before Christmas."

"I can't speak for Notre Dame," he

continued. "We certainly haven't withdrawn at St. Mary's though."

He felt, however, students are "overemphasizing" the finances of the merger. He indicated faculty contracts and merger of administrations are critical points.

"The joint budget alone is a tough problem," he related. "as for SMC faculty contracts for next year, Notre Dame originally agrees to issue them. They didn't realize at the time, the depth of the problem. There are personnel problems to be resolved – and you can't put a general solution to specific problems."

P. Jordan Hamel the other lay SMC member of the Ad-Hoc Committee, will be out of town (Chicago) until Dec. 2. It could not be ascertained whether he attended the meeting. Some SMC faculty have indicated that all of the listed representatives did not attend the meeting which may have thrown its results into jeopardy.

While Cahill felt the merger would be continued, apparently other SMC representatives to the Ad-Hoc Committee believed differently.

In Boston, the consulting board of the college region for the Sisters of the Holy Cross, owners of the college property, sent a telegram last weekend to the Ad-Hoc Committee meeting.

According to one sister present at the meeting, the wire said the board, "deplored the breaking off of the merger." SMC representatives present at the assembly included Srs. Alma, acting president, Elena, theology instructor; and Franzita, English instructor.

Late last week Sr. Alma sent letters to all SMC professors describing the tensions. In the letter, she indicated she would meet today at 1:00 pm with SMLC department chairman to discuss the situation.

She also scheduled meetings with the rank and tenure committee (2:00 p.m.) and with the faculty (4:30 pm). At the faculty meeting, Mother Olivette Whelan will speak.

Notre Dame officials, however, denied they had planned any meetings to inform their faculty of the changes.

Notre Dame students may receive letters from Fr. Burtchaell in their mailboxes confirming the actions of the administration today or tomorrow.

**Edmund Stephan**  Chairman of the Notre Dame Board of Trustees, scheduled to issue "an important announcement."

**Fr. Hesburgh**  President of the University, "two statements being prepared," for release this afternoon.

**Sister Alma**  Acting President of St. Mary's, informed faculty of tensions, will meet with SMC faculty this afternoon.

## Transfering?

Although university admissions officials admitted they were as unclear an anyone on campus about the coeducation announcement, they clarified admissions procedure for upper class transfer students.

John Goldrick, an admissions officer, indicated an applicant must have 30 hours of credit from an accredited college or university.

Students wishing to transfer or even thinking about a move should contact the admissions office to arrange an appointment with a counselor.

administration and Saint Mary's didn't offer a similar degree, I was able to graduate from Notre Dame.

My parents came out to graduation from Montana. My dad asked me "How are we going to know which one you are? Are you going to be the one with the long hair?" In 1972, that didn't distinguish me from my other long-haired classmates! But, they did find me—when I was called up on stage to receive my diploma from Father Hesburgh. Father, I still remember being up there and getting kissed by you. Thank you for one of the proudest moments of my life.

Since 1972, my Notre Dame degree and fellow alumni have transported me throughout the United States and Europe. The Notre Dame degree is a passport creating opportunities throughout the financial world. Whether in New York City negotiating eastern European financing or working in Vienna, I was mindful I was the person from a town that still doesn't have a stoplight to this day.

Father, I can only begin to repay you and the university by giving back to the community. This spring I used the marketing savvy I got at Notre Dame to do just that. I chaired Virginia Commonwealth University's Massey Cancer Center Benefit for Breast Cancer Research here in Richmond. (The president is Eugene Trani, a fellow Domer.) It was the first time a non-Catholic had chaired the event. And, it raised the most money the event has ever made!

Thank you, Father, for the honor and privilege of being the first female undergraduate from the University of Notre Dame.

Yours in Notre Dame,

Mary Davey Bliley
Class of '72
First Woman Undergraduate Degree Recipient

Dear Father Hesburgh,

As a future graduate for the Class of 2008, I am honored to be among the select and privileged individuals to have attended the University of Notre Dame. While I am looking forward to being a Notre Dame alumna, I am most proud to be a woman attending one of the finest universities in the nation.

# THE OBSERVER

*The Independent Newspaper Serving Notre Dame and Saint Mary's*

VOLUME 41 : ISSUE 93     WEDNESDAY, FEBRUARY 28, 2007     NDSMCOBSERVER.COM

## Brown chooses new chief executive

*Sheena Plamoottil's selection solidifies all-female team in student government's top three*

**By KAITLYNN RIELY**
Associate News Editor

JESSICA LEE/The Observer
Junior Sheena Plamoottil was selected by student body president-elect Liz Brown to serve as chief executive assistant.

Student body president-elect Liz Brown and vice president-elect Maris Braun took one of their first steps as student government leaders Tuesday when they announced Pangborn senator and Senate Social Concerns chair Sheena Plamoottil as their Chief Executive Assistant (CEA).

Plamoottil will fill the position Brown currently holds under the Lizzi Shappell-Bill Andrichik administration.

Brown called Plamoottil the "best person for the job" and said she has followed her progress closely in the Senate.

Plamoottil redefined the Social Concerns committee at the beginning of the year, Brown said, and "she really took the committee and ran with it and has gotten some good things accomplished."

The selection of Plamoottil fills the top three positions in the student government with women, something that has never before happened at Notre Dame.

Brown said she is happy to be part of history, but said the choice of Plamoottil was

*see CEA/page 6*

## Students give thanks to donors

*Letters to be written to benefactors*

**By STEVE KERINS**
News Writer

Students are giving thanks today for the nearly $68 million received by the University for scholarships this year by partaking in "Thanksgiving in February," an event organized by the Development Office allowing students to personally thank individual donors.

"'Thanksgiving in February'

---

For as long as I can remember, I dreamed of going to Notre Dame. My siblings and I had enough Notre Dame apparel to last a lifetime and were fortunate enough to attend home football games on a regular basis. However, my biggest inspiration for attending Notre Dame is rooted in my parents' experience as graduates of the Class of 1980. My parents were close friends throughout their time at Notre Dame and were married a few years after graduation. Their experience under your leadership is truly a highlight of their lives, and my father still talks about the handwritten note he received from you during his time as an undergraduate.

But what stuck out most about my parents' time at Notre Dame is my mother's experience as a member of one of the first class of varsity athletes. I remember my mother bringing her fencing gear to show-and-tell when I was younger, and I was always struck by her strength and confidence as she spoke of her college years. It was certainly not easy to be among the few female varsity athletes, but because of this experience my mother has grown into a remarkable and truly amazing role model.

As the fourth female student body president and the first to serve with a female vice president, I am proud to follow in my mother's footsteps. While my mother exemplifies the spirit and challenges of the first female students, my recent election reflects a shift in the standing of women at the University of Notre Dame. My running mate and I were able to run a successful campaign without answering a single question regarding our gender, largely because of the impressive legacies of so many other successful female undergraduates. I am extremely honored to hold this position at Notre Dame, and truly believe that it is a direct result of your insightful leadership during your tenure as president.

Words cannot express how grateful my mother, father, and my entire extended family are of your work at the University of Notre Dame. I thank you from the bottom of my heart for your tireless efforts to make Notre Dame what it is today.

Sincerely,

Elizabeth C. Brown
Class of '08
Student Body President 2007–2008

Dear Father Hesburgh,

It is hard for me to believe that it will be eight years ago this month that I graduated from Notre Dame. Not a day goes by that I don't draw upon the education I received there, talk to a friend from Farley Hall, and look back on my time spent in South Bend with wonder and awe.

While women were admitted to the university four years before I was born, stories of Notre Dame as an all-male institution have been passed on to me through my dad ('71 BA, '74 JD). As his oldest child, it was always my dream to follow in his footsteps—and I am eternally grateful to have had that chance. I want to express my deepest gratitude to you for your role in making the admission of women to the undergraduate program a reality. In my life alone, the Notre Dame experience has made all the difference in the world, and I can't imagine the cumulative positive effects of thirty-four years of women under the Golden Dome!

Not only has my academic instruction allowed me to excel, but the deepened sense of faith and the personal connections that I developed at Notre Dame have shaped my life in profound ways. I have enjoyed a rewarding career in political communications and worked at the White House for five years. I even had the chance to experience the thrill of a presidential campaign. I have friends from Notre Dame

spread across the country that I connect with on a daily basis, and others that I am constantly meeting anew through the ND connection. I met my husband Joe Burkhart ('98 BA) our senior year, and our first child, Will, was born last September. Life has been wonderful and I know that I am truly, truly blessed.

I firmly believe that I am the strong, Catholic woman I am today because of the University of Notre Dame. The university itself and the phenomenon of its extended community are unlike anything I have ever known. I will tell anyone who wants to listen about my time there, and I am already bombarding a cousin who will start in the fall with pointers and advice.

Father Hesburgh, thank you again for opening its classrooms and dormitories to women. Through our own unique Notre Dame experiences, generations of female Domers have benefited from all that the university has to offer and are seeking to give back in a similar way.

Sincerely,

Shannon Boland Burkhart
Class of '98
Former Communications Manager, White House Press Office

Dear Father Hesburgh,

I am a 1977 graduate, an accounting major in the College of Business. Most importantly, I write to thank you so much for pushing to have women admitted to Notre Dame. I am fortunate to have enjoyed—and continue to enjoy—much success in the business world. I am coleader and a managing director at William Blair Capital Partners in Chicago. We are a successful private equity fund. There are still very few women, especially of my tenure, in this industry. It wasn't until years after I graduated from Notre Dame that I realized that Notre Dame has been a very big part of my success.

Being in that class of about three hundred women entering the school in 1973, I will never forget what it felt like to be a minority! It was a great experience and I learned so many tips and tricks that have all served me well. I don't think I could have been successful in this business if I had not learned at an early age how to get along, focus, and succeed as the only woman in the room. Back in 1973, my dorm, Breen Phillips, still had urinals in the bathrooms!

Not only did I learn to fit in and excel in an unusual situation, I learned how to enjoy it. I met terrific friends—both men and women—who I still value today. And, the solid culture and overriding sense of integrity that Notre Dame represents serves me every day. It was and still is an environment that values these principles and represents them in the finest sense. All businesspeople should be so fortunate.

So, in closing, I thank you sincerely for your trailblazing position and enabling the many women graduates like me to benefit for life. It has been a wonderful gift!

Sincerely,

Ellen Carnahan
Class of '77
Managing Director, William Blair Capital Partners LLC and Seyen Capital LLC, Chicago, Illinois

Dear Father Ted,

It is with the "fondest of memories" that I think back to fall of 1971 when you made that visionary decision that the University of Notre Dame would go forward with co-education on their own and accept the first three hundred women to make up their freshman, sophomore, and junior classes in the fall of 1972.

I remember that you did not hesitate one minute in this decision even in the midst of opposition from various university groups. In fact, I remember many a football weekend speaking with disgruntled alumni and trying to convince them that coeducation was indeed the progressive path for the university. I don't know if I had an impact or not, but being one of the fortunate women who was accepted as a junior to be a part of coeducation the first year, to live on campus in Walsh Hall, and to watch history in the making, now that was exciting! So, I decided to get connected in the Notre Dame community and take in as much as I could during those formative years.

I was very involved in all facets of "coeducation" through advisory councils, public relations, dormitory president, and resident assistant, which had a huge impact on my personal confidence, social skills, lifelong relationships, and really my entire life. Of course, at this time we had our challenges as well, since this was "new" to all of us, but with your administration's unending support we plowed through the daily experiences together and paved our own way.

Your administration was so approachable, partnering with us to make this as smooth a transition as possible. In retrospect, for the first few years I don't think outsiders could see noticeable differences with the acceptance of women, except our mere visibility, but internally so many things were happening to solidify our presence on campus. Thanks to you, all Notre Dame students since that time have reaped the benefits from your inspirational decision and Notre Dame is a better place.

It still amazes me that after thirty-five years of coeducation, people still ask me what it was like and are interested in my experiences being part of such a unique group of women. Of course, I usually ask them how much time they have, as I could go on and on.

It was really about the total experience—being the only woman in a class, dorm life, the excitement of football weekends, relationships with fellow students, ratio of seventeen men to one woman, talking to Father Riehle about life in general, going to the Rock to play racquetball with Father Toohey, Mass in the dormitory, meetings with Sister John Miriam, getting advice from Jane Pitz, meeting my husband in Coach Leahy's Economics class and getting married at Sacred Heart and much more. It was such a close community and we all participated in it. It's the blending of all of these ingredients that made it such a wonderful and special place to me! I was definitely in the right place at the right time. I took advantage of what was given and at the same time I felt as though I gave back to the extent I could.

On a personal note, I still remember all the wonderful talks we shared, you telling David and I about Bear Bryant's comments after the 1973 Sugar Bowl in New Orleans.

Again, I thank you for sharing your Notre Dame with me and it continues to be

Susan Andersen Casper '74 with Father Ted, Twenty-Fifth ND Women's Reunion, 1997.

a lifelong experience. It was an honor to be a "pioneer" under your leadership and your vision proved to undoubtedly be the right one. God bless you, Father Ted, and Happy 90th Birthday!

Warmest regards,

Susan Andersen Casper
Class of '74
First Woman President, Walsh Hall 1972–1973

Dear Father Hesburgh,

My brother graduated from ND in 1966 and I was ten years old when I went to his graduation. I fell in love with the school and knew that by the time I was ready for college that ND would be coed. I followed the plans for ND and Saint Mary's to merge and was disappointed when that didn't happen but then ND decided to accept women and once again my plan was on track. I am a member of the Class of 1978, and was in the second class of freshman women accepted.

I loved ND and made so many wonderful friends that I still keep in touch with today. I enjoyed being a pioneer in the coeducation process and thank you for putting that process in place.

The Honorable Tracy Lee Christopher
Class of '78
District Court Judge, Houston, Texas

Dear Father Ted,

It would be easy to drift into sentimentality about the days of old when Notre Dame was only men and camaraderie defined life on campus. But looking back also reminds me that your leadership was always about change and how that change could transform our lives into something new and glorious.

My success story as a man was written largely during my years at Notre Dame, so I will be forever grateful to you for the culture of change your nourished during your tenure.

Have a blessed and wonderful 90th birthday.

Sincerely,

Tom Clements
Class of '75
Quarterback, Football Team 1972–1974
National Champions: 1973

Dear Father Hesburgh,

Thank you does not seem to be enough to tell you how much my four years as an undergraduate at Notre Dame started me on a path to transform my life. My introduction to Notre Dame was listening to football games on the radio in the '60s with my dad and my older brothers. My dad's dream was to have one of his ten children attend Notre Dame. I was the first one who had the opportunity to apply, and being the ninth of the kids, we had more resources to help me make the dream a reality. When I received my acceptance letter in March of 1979, it was a cause for celebration not just in my family and hometown, but for all of my relatives back in Scranton, Pennsylvania. My parents grew up in Scranton, met in high school, and married after my Dad returned from World War II. Moving their growing family to Connecticut in 1952 for employment opportunities was difficult for my dad as he was seventh of eight kids in his close family and my mom was the oldest of five. The calls to Scranton to tell all of the extended family of my acceptance were special. My Uncle Bobby asked to speak to the "one who is going straight to Heaven." That's when it hit me that attending Notre Dame was so much bigger than getting an education. And it never occurred to anyone to question why a "girl" was the first to go in our family.

Looking back on my years on campus from 1979 to 1983, I don't think I took complete advantage of all that Notre Dame had to offer. I studied hard, played intramural sports, and I loved being a part of the fraternity that was Lewis Hall (Go Chicks!), playing flag football all four years and serving as president my junior year. But what I found through my involvement in the local alumni clubs is that Notre Dame never stops giving. I feel like I never left. I've been involved with the Fairfield County Connecticut Club since 1983 and helped convince my younger sister to attend and she received an MBA in 1987. I joined the Alumni Association Board in 2000 and was fortunate enough to serve as the president from 2002 to 2003, which also allowed me to serve on the board of trustees for two years.

We have the next generation attending Notre Dame right now. My oldest nephew is on campus and finding his way through all that Notre Dame has to offer. He'll have his lifetime, like I do and the other 120,000-plus alumni, to learn from and serve Our Lady's university. What a wonderful journey ahead of him! He would not be at Notre Dame if I had not gone and been able to benefit from the Notre Dame experience and then include my family in it.

When I served on the board of trustees, I brought along my mom to the meeting in Naples, Florida, a few years ago. Although my dad never saw his daughters graduate from Notre Dame (he died my senior year), my mom has been able to continue to live their dreams and lead a life full of service and faith and provide her family with a wonderful role model. She met you at the trustee meeting and then commented that now she could die and go to Heaven. She passed away recently and she reminded me before she died of the wonderful impact that Notre Dame has made on my life. Although I'm the "one who is going straight to Heaven," I still have a long way to go to earn my way in. Thank you for opening up Notre Dame for women like me and the generations of men and women we are influencing because of our relationship to Notre Dame.

God bless you, Father Hesburgh.

Jean Collier
Class of '83
President, ND Alumni Association 2003

Dear Father Hesburgh,

I am writing to join my many alumnae friends to express my gratitude to you for the changes you brought to the University of Notre Dame in your time there as president.

I was fortunate to be admitted in 1972 in the first class of freshmen women at

Notre Dame. While I knew that was a privilege, I had no perspective at the time how important that unique opportunity would be in my life. I've reflected on that more recently. In part, that introspection was triggered by my thirtieth reunion weekend on campus last year. It was reinforced by several visits to the campus to visit my daughter, who is now a sophomore at Notre Dame.

I recall clearly the fall of 1972 when I arrived as a freshman on campus. Women were a distinct minority. I was the only woman in many of my classes. Although I worked out with the men's diving team, there was no available women's team. In fact the only varsity team available for women that year was fencing. Although the university celebrated the arrival of women, there was a strong undercurrent of resentment among many of the alumni. One of the things I love about Notre Dame is its strong traditions, and the sense of history you feel on the campus. The trade-off for that is the resistance that exists when you try to implement change.

Without your commitment, leadership, and vision, coeducation would not have occurred at Notre Dame in my era. Without the benefit of a Notre Dame education, I am convinced my personal and professional lives would have been vastly different.

I spent seven years on campus, completing both my undergraduate and law school education. I lived on campus for five of those years, and worked in a legal aid clinic in southern Michigan during my last two years in law school. In addition to the excellent educational opportunity, Notre Dame built in me a commitment to public service and to excellence that has served me well in my adult life. I am convinced that Notre Dame's reputation for excellence is a big part of what opened doors of professional opportunity for me, which ultimately led to my appointment to the bench in Maryland.

I truly loved my time at Notre Dame. I absolutely benefited from the fact that I was there in an era of transition, at a time when women were not fully integrated into campus life. Those experiences taught me how to compete and to excel in atmospheres that were not always familiar or comfortable. They also taught me how to persevere while in an atmosphere that was in transition. And those lessons were invaluable in my early professional roles.

I marvel at how different the Notre Dame campus is today. My daughter's experience mirrors mine in so many ways, and yet the social atmosphere is now so much more "normal." Women bring so much to the campus environment. They round out the educational and social milieu when they are in significant numbers. Obviously that was part of your vision in the early '70s, and you must be gratified to see it come to fruition.

When I was on the campus last year, I had the pleasure of attending the Mass that you celebrated at the end of the reunion weekend for the Class of 1976. You spoke of coeducation as one of your proudest accomplishments. You have lived a life that is filled with accomplishments, but for those of us who were the beneficiaries of your vision, we would agree.

I have been blessed in many ways in my life. My time at Notre Dame was an important one of those blessings. Thank you for your vision, and the opportunities it provided to me.

Very truly yours,

The Honorable Kathleen Gallogly Cox
Class of '76
Judge, Baltimore (Maryland) County Circuit Court

Dear Father Ted,

I wanted to take a few minutes to thank you for all that you have done for those of us who were lucky enough to have attended and graduated from the University of Notre Dame. I was lucky enough to have been accepted into the Class of 1984 where I met some of my lifelong friends, including my roommate Susan Faccenda Walsh.

I knew of you long before I arrived at ND, as my father Phil Purcell '35 knew you and Father Ned very well. I also had two uncles and my two brothers, Philip and Paul, pave the way before I arrived in South Bend. Having so many connections to ND before I even started classes made it feel like my home away from home.

I laugh when I remember my parents telling the story of you and Ned traveling cross-country in your RV and stopping in Salt Lake. My mom and dad loaded you two up with frozen dinners (with very specific instructions taped to the top) to put into your freezer for the next leg of your journey.

You have given so many of us the gifts of your leadership, vision, and friendship. Notre Dame would not be the world-class institution it is today without your hard work and amazing ability to tackle difficult and sometimes unpopular issues.

Thank you for your persistence and your compassion.

You are truly a man of God. YOU ARE ND!!

With much love,

Patrice Purcell DeCorrevont
Class of '84
Managing Director, JP Morgan Chase & Co., Chicago, Illinois

Dear Father Ted,

I wanted to take this opportunity to thank you for your vision, leadership, encouragement, and kindness. I would not be where I am today without my experiences at Notre Dame. When asked about factors leading to my success, Notre Dame is number three after my family and being an army brat. Thank you, Father Ted, for your vision to bring women to Notre Dame enabling us to have the ability to enter the workplace.

I came to campus alone. My parents would have come with me, but I asked to go alone, appreciating the expense, but more importantly I remember feeling that if they came, I didn't know if I could say good-bye. But I was not afraid! I was proud, filled with hope and excited about the future. When I arrived at Breen-Phillips, I saw a man with his daughter. When he saw me, he asked if I could take his daughter's suitcases to her room. I learned that before coeducation came to Notre Dame, a number of African-American women worked in the dorms, at the laundry, or in the dining halls. This alumnus had made just that assumption. As a young, African-American woman, my parents had shielded me from much of the biases of the time. In our home, people were to be judged by their character. Now some thirty years later, because of you Father Ted, at Notre Dame events and activities, it is assumed that I am a Notre Dame alumna. Thank you for your vision.

In my sophomore year, one finance professor shared that he had never had any girlies or colored in his class. Another proclaimed that if he had any blacks who were articulate (in his chemistry class), he would encourage "them" to go to law school. Thank you, Father Ted, for your leadership. Because you led the charge for coeducation, I chose to go to Notre Dame and had to leave my sheltered and protective upbringing. The thick skin and a passion to succeed that came as a result, is why, despite all the challenges, I have been successful as the first woman city treasurer of the City of Los Angeles.

But nothing had the profound impact on my life as the late night meeting with you. I had learned that a friend was to be dismissed from the university. I was sad and depressed. I somehow found myself at the Administration Building, and then at your office door. It was very late, but you were there. I don't remember the exact conversation, but I do remember that you took the time to reassure a lonely young woman. I felt that my words mattered and that you had listened. Although I don't remember the details of that night, I do remember that you bolstered my resolve to help others.

You made me feel special, determined, brave, and strong. As I write this, my heart is still filled with appreciation. Thank you, Father Ted, for your encouragement and kindness. It is a privilege to have been a beneficiary of your vision for coeducation. Because of that vision, I have survived and succeeded as a person and a professional and look back at my years at Notre Dame with appreciation. I realize as I look back, that I now understand the meaning of "in place of parents." For me, the phrase is a definition for you. Thank you for guiding me by direct and indirect example. I still consider you my mentor and my priest. Thank you, Father Ted, and may God continue to bless you.

Joya ("JJ") De Foor
Class of '77
Treasurer, City of Los Angeles, California

Father Ted receives the Congressional Gold Medal of Freedom in 1999. With him are (left to right) President Bill Clinton, Senator Strom Thurmond, and Speaker of the House of Representatives Dennis Hastert. From 1789, when George Washington became its first recipient, until today, only 165 people have received this honor.

Dear Father Hesburgh,

I want to thank you for opening the doors of Notre Dame to women and allowing me to be a part of something special, the Notre Dame family. My education was superior. I made lifetime friends that are very dear to me. Most importantly, I met my husband Mike Demetrio and became a part of the Demetrio family with their strong ties to Notre Dame through three generations. Your caring ways sustained my mother-in-law Madeleine Demetrio throughout her life. For that, I will be eternally grateful.

When I return to campus now, I feel the power of the place. It is one of spirit, peace, and belonging. Your decision to allow women as students has impact way beyond the four years I spent as an undergraduate.

I thank you for showing us how to lead our lives. As students, we learned the power of prayer through your sermons and celebrations of the Eucharist. You and Father Joyce taught us the importance of loyalty and friendship. You inspired us to correct social injustices and to fight for equality.

Happy Birthday.

With deep appreciation,

The Honorable Mary Katherine Rochford Demetrio
Class of '76, '79 JD
Associate Circuit Court Judge, Cook County, Illinois

The most remarkable thing about Notre Dame's transition from an all-male institution into a coeducational university is how unremarkable the whole thing seemed, both then and now.

There was nothing traumatic about the change, at least for us men living on the South Quad. It all seemed natural, normal, and familiar.

For those of us who had summer jobs on campus, cutting grass and keeping WSND FM on the air, there were some new and odd sights during those humid months. We saw a coin laundry added to the lower level of Badin. Who ever thought of having a self-service laundry when you could send everything over to the hot water ministrations of St. Michael's?

The bizarrely huge Walsh Hall urinals appeared one day, discarded near the

bookstore basketball court. They appeared more porcelain sarcophagi than plumbing fixtures.

But, there seemed nothing odd about the sight of the Notre Dame women when they arrived at all. After all, many of the new students in our midst were not strangers. They were our friends from co-exchange classes with Saint Mary's. They were our colleagues at WSND, or the *Observer*, or campus theater productions, or any of the dozens of other activities and groups on campus. We knew them from the library, or the Huddle, or the lurching bus rides past the Holy Cross Fathers' cemetery through the chained gate and across then U.S. 31 to the other campus.

Years earlier, we had shared notes with many of our now fellow Domers for Jonathan Ziskind's world history lectures on our campus, or explored poetry with them in Miss (not, Ms. or Dr.) Noel's classes at Saint Mary's.

The welcome barbeque outside the South Dining Hall that fall of 1972 had more the feeling of a family reunion than a social revolution. There were new women students, along with familiar faces, but somehow, it felt they belonged.

Of course, coeducation was a revolution. In the end, this was to be no quiet merger with Saint Mary's, but a new coeducational Notre Dame. Both campus and classroom changed fundamentally for the better with coeducation. Our Lady's school is a better place with our ladies' presence.

That untraumatic transition is a tribute to the Hesburgh way. In coeducation, as in so many other areas during the Hesburgh years, progress was a steady, logical, and inevitable road. Thanks, Father Ted, I am grateful you took all of us along on the trip.

L. Franklin Devine
Class of '75
Producer, *60 Minutes,* CBS News

Dear Father Ted,

As an alumna who entered Notre Dame as a freshman in 1973 I want to wish you Happy Birthday and thank you for your efforts in support of coeducation at Notre Dame.

I wanted to go to Notre Dame as long as I can remember. As I entered high school, my parish priest, Msgr. Paul O'Dea, told me that he believed it just might be possible. I was so excited to be able to apply early decision in my senior year—and to be accepted right before my December 8 birthday.

I have so many memories: good friends, challenging professors, top-level general program and premed classes, study marathons at the library, late nights at the Grotto, playing on Notre Dame's first field hockey team, being one of three women in my PE class, teaching swimming for PE and being one of the first women lifeguards at the Rock, playing guitar at the Breen-Phillips Masses, my roommates, campus ministry, the beauty of the campus. . . .

But two memories stand out.

One was a visit three of us made to you late one night with ice cream cones—including one for you—from the Huddle. Your light was on, so we had decided to stop. And you took the time from what you were doing to talk with three women students. I had the sense that there was nothing more important to you in that moment than the three of us. Thanks you for valuing us.

The second memory is from the year of our twenty-fifth reunion (2002). A group of eight women (1977 grads) from Breen-Phillips came to visit you after the reunion dinner. At that time, you shared with us your three reasons for hoping that the dorms at ND would continue to be women-only and men-only. The reason that touched me the most was your understanding that women make friendships differently than men do. You spoke about women's need for time and protected space to build relationships. All of us there, who have maintained our friendships over the years and distance, had experienced that gift of time and space while you were president of Notre Dame. And, as you probably know, most of the women of our class are in touch by e-mail on a regular basis. In 2005—when we all turned 50—we kept a weekly e-mail list going so we could congratulate each other on that milestone. Thank you for giving us a gift that will continue for our entire lives.

You gave us the gift of being valued, first as students and then as alumnae of Notre Dame. For me, that gift has translated into the valuing of others. First, in my role as a pastor and spiritual director for both United Methodist and United Church of Christ congregants, I help people find themselves and others as valued persons in God's greater story. Second, in my role as a clinical psychology PhD intern, I work with adolescent girls in our county's juvenile justice system. The program is the first of its kind in the country; it is based on principles of restorative justice and gender-specific approaches to recovery and trauma. Most of these girls are at-risk, and have been repeatedly traumatized. Part of my work with them is hearing their stories and letting them know they are valued. Finally, in my full-time work as the assistant director of a psychosocial residential program, I work with those who are "least," persons who are working through acute psychiatric crises, and who usually have extremely limited resources. Again, this work is about valuing individual persons, seeing them as worthy of care and attention just as they are. I help create supportive relationships for these persons so they are able to return to independent living and meaningful roles in the wider community.

I bring the spirit of Notre Dame—a bold spirituality that is linked to justice through relationships that value each person as a unique child of God—to my daily work and prayer. Thank you so much for making it possible for me to be a Notre Dame alumna!

Happy 90th Birthday!

Fondly,

Reverend Dr. Anne M. Dilenschneider
Class of '77
Pastor, United Methodist and United Church of Christ, Montara, California

## Notre Dame Alumnae Prayer

Gracious and loving God,
we thank you
for the blessings of Your creation
and Your presence among us
morning, noon, and night.

We thank You, too,
for the blessings of our families
through whose love we have known
Your abiding support.

Today, we thank You
for Notre Dame, our mother,
who nurtures us in love
and sustains us as her daughters.
She has enriched us with the gift of sisters
who accompany us as we grow in love—
in heart and mind, in soul and strength.

In this hour,
we especially remember
our faithful sisters,
whom You have received into Your arms.
We thank You
for the gift of their lives
and the joy of their presence among us.
We now trust them to Your eternal care.

We also trust our lives, like theirs, into Your hands,
and our souls into Your keeping.
We pray that we, too,
may live lives of courage and love
until that glorious day
when we meet again as sisters,
face to face, in our eternal home.
Amen.

—Reverend Dr. Anne Dilenschneider '77

*Reverend Dilenschneider wrote this prayer for a Mass in celebration of the Class of '77 women's fiftieth birthdays at Notre Dame on May 22, 2005. Since then, the Class of '77 women pray this prayer together when they gather and use it in other communications to honor their milestone events.*

✑

Dear Father Hesburgh,

For a long time, growing up in a "Notre Dame" family meant spending New Year's Day dressed in blue and gold cheering for the Irish along with my four sisters. Even though we were living in Portland, Oregon, there was an understanding that we had a strong connection to this place in Indiana. However, until I was twelve, my knowledge of Notre Dame did not extend much beyond football and the fact that my dad had graduated from there in 1950.

It was probably not coincidental that my father, a devoted Domer, chose to have all five of his daughters visit campus during his twenty-fifth reunion, just a few years after Notre Dame went coed. It was on that visit, at the impressionable age of twelve, that I first fell in love with the beautiful campus and first felt the pull of the Dome. That pull would eventually lead me to follow my oldest sister, Ann Marie, to Notre Dame where I would spend four years of my life, and build a lifetime of commitment to a place that stills feels like a second home.

My desire to stay connected to the university after graduation led me to get involved in the Monogram Club board, where eventually I had the honor of being nominated to serve as the first female president of the club. The fact that there is now a female president of the Monogram Club says very little about me, but says volumes about the role of women at Notre Dame in general, and the strength of women's athletics in particular.

Julie Pierson Doyle '85 is inaugurated first woman president of the ND Monogram Club in 2005. Reprinted with the permission of the Notre Dame Sports Information Department.

Things have changed a lot since the days when I played volleyball for the Irish. The days of players driving the vans to away games and PE teachers moonlighting as Division I coaches are long gone. Since the time when, under your watch, women were first admitted to Notre Dame, women's varsity programs have grown to thirteen teams, with seven national championships—two in soccer, four in fencing, and one in basketball. None of this could have been possible without your vision and courage.

Thank you, Father Ted, for your belief that Notre Dame would be a better place as a coed institution and thank you for the conviction to stand by that decision every step of the way. My father thanks you, my sisters and I thank you, and someday my own daughters may thank you as well.

Yours in Notre Dame,

Julie Pierson Doyle
Class of '85
President, Notre Dame Monogram Club 2006–2007

Dear Father Hesburgh,

I am writing to thank you for your efforts in making Notre Dame coeducational so many years ago. I can honestly say your work changed my life in very dramatic ways. I graduated from Notre Dame with a bachelor of business administration degree in accounting in 1982, the tenth class of women at Notre Dame.

After graduating from Notre Dame, I attended the University of Florida Law School where I received my JD in 1986. Following law school graduation, I began practicing law in Ocala, Florida. I became a partner in a litigation firm in 1988 and practiced for nearly twenty years before being appointed to the circuit court bench by Florida Governor Jeb Bush in November of 2005. I truly believe that having a degree from Notre Dame helped with my professional advancement.

As I look back upon my education and career in the practice of law, I can say without hesitation that the four years I spent at Notre Dame were the most significant, formative years. Not only did I receive an outstanding education but Notre Dame instilled in me the values and beliefs that have been my guiding influences, both professionally and personally. I still keep in touch with many of my former classmates. My twenty-fifth reunion was this year. Once again, a most heartfelt "thank you" for being instrumental in allowing women to attend the world's finest Catholic university.

Very truly yours,

The Honorable Carol A. Falvey
Class of '82
Circuit Court Judge, Citrus County, Florida

Dear Father Ted,

I really cannot begin to tell you how grateful I am for your efforts to make Notre Dame coed. I know, in so many ways, that my education at Notre Dame shaped my outlook and supported me as I strive to be a competent, thoughtful, ethical, and compassionate business leader.

I learned so many things at Notre Dame but the most important influences were the things that were constantly reinforced: giving back to our community and our world, integrity, honesty, a life of meaning, and the importance of treating everyone with respect.

Because of this foundation, I never have to think twice about telling those at my company to "do the right thing" and to go beyond the legal requirements. Nor do I have to remind people how important it is to give back to the community: They see it as part of me, and my family's life. As importantly, that foundation has given me the courage to only select or remain at an organization that has the same values.

Lastly, as a woman in business and law, I cannot think of any place that could have given me a better education or a preparation to deal with all that comes your way.

Thank you from the bottom of my heart.

Love,

Peggy Foran
Class of '76, '79 JD
Senior Vice President, Associate General Counsel, and Corporate Secretary,
    Pfizer Inc., New York, New York

ᥫᮗ

Dear Father Ted,

I don't remember thinking at the time that it was a big deal to be a woman at Notre Dame. However, looking back and comparing it to today's Notre Dame certainly does make me feel like I was more of a pioneer than I thought. My daughter graduated from Notre Dame last year, so I guess that makes me less of a "recent grad" than my mind chooses to acknowledge (I have been "frozen in time" with the memories of my Notre Dame experience seeming like just yesterday). It was fun and unsettling at the same time to realize that some of my classmates, and my husband's classmates also had children attending Notre Dame with our daughter. The university gave us all opportunities to live vicariously through our children and relive our Notre Dame experiences together during the four years that our children studied at Notre Dame.

I studied aerospace engineering at Notre Dame from 1974 to 1978. There were no other women in my aerospace major. In fact, there weren't many women in the other engineering majors either. We got to know each other well as we were easy to spot, but it was awkward for us because people learned our names more quickly than we could remember their names, since we stood out in the mostly male crowd. This was either an advantage or disadvantage with our professors and fellow engineers, depending upon if we were prepared for our professors to call on us in class or if we were being approached socially by a male fellow engineer. I have great memories of fun projects, like the engineering team that designed an airplane, as well as the many wonderful people that I met in my other activities (theater, community service, interhall activities, etc.).

I am now the CEO of Stellar Solutions, Inc., an aerospace engineering business I founded in 1995. I feel the technical training I received at Notre Dame prepared me well for the jobs I held prior to starting my own business. I also think Notre Dame instilled in me a strong sense of ethics and integrity that are of equal importance to me. Notre Dame gave me the added advantage of being trained for the "real world" of engineering (i.e., lots of men and very few women). There weren't many women in engineering in any of the jobs early in my career, so the predominately male environment at Notre Dame truly prepared me for my experiences in the real world. My engineering career seemed just like my experience at Notre Dame (i.e., being the only woman was no big deal).

I'd like to thank you, Father Ted, for making Notre Dame what it is today, and for the opportunities and recognition I have been given by the university. I also want to express my appreciation for the opportunities afforded my daughter at Notre Dame, as well as the many women of Notre Dame who will come after us.

Celeste Volz Ford
Class of '78
CEO/Chairperson, Stellar Solutions Inc., California
Chairman, Fitzpatrick College of Engineering Advisory Council

Dear Father Ted,

Through your vision and gift of coeducation at Notre Dame, you recognized and promoted the dignity and role of women as scholars and leaders. You challenged a venerable status quo that limited opportunities for women. You understood the value of making available to women the unique and extraordinary opportunities for personal growth and meaningful contributions to society that a Notre Dame education provides.

Father Ted runs with the 2002 Winter Olympic torch outside the Joyce Athletic and Convocation Center.

My Notre Dame education nurtured critical thinking and commitment to justice and service. It opened the doors to postgraduate educational and professional experiences that position one to "make a difference." I am mindful of that privilege and draw upon the gifts of my ND education to try to honor that obligation.

Through my ND experience I have received the gift of friendships with dear, fun, funny classmates who still make me laugh as hard as when we sat on the floors of Breen-Phillips, talking throughout the night until we were surprised to hear the birds chirping at sunrise. And, ND introduced me to my best buddy, my husband of thirty years, Steve. I believe that the environment of the ND community, and the nature of our relationship at ND, laid a foundation of respect, kindness, humor, and love that has helped us embrace the joys and weather the not-so-joyful aspects of marriage and parenthood.

So, Father Ted, on your 90th birthday, I wish you a wonderful and Happy Birthday. I send a deep and heartfelt THANK YOU for your gift of coeducation at Notre Dame, a gift that has enriched my life beyond measure.

Sincerely,

The Honorable Carol Hackett Garagiola
Class of '77
Chief Judge, Livingston County (Michigan) Probate Court

Dear Father Hesburgh,

In 1973, my freshman year, coeducation was a relatively new phenomenon for Notre Dame, and completely new for me. Upon receiving my letter of acceptance, as a senior at an all-boys Catholic high school, I recall thinking three things:

1. A coeducational environment would provide a rich depth and variety of perspective as I sorted through issues like gender equity and social justice.

2. How to better explore and understand the complex dynamics of relationship than through open and frank dialogue with young women seeking similar insights.

3. Girls *and* Notre Dame football? This is going to be great!

After thirty years of marriage to one of my freshman year classmates, it remains clear that I was right on all counts. Thanks, Father Ted.

Steve Garagiola
Class of '77
Anchor/Reporter, WDIV-TV, Detroit, Michigan

Dear Father Ted,

As an African-American female, my experience at Notre Dame was probably a little different from my non-African-American counterparts. For me, Notre Dame was vastly different from the life I had lived in New Orleans. I grew up in a predominately African-American community and had attended African-American institutions my entire life. Coming to Notre Dame where less than 10 percent of the student body was African-American was a little bit of a shocking experience. As the eldest child, I understood that failure was not an option, but that realization did not make things any easier. My college experience would have been much more difficult if the university had not respected my different heritage.

Throughout my four years at Notre Dame I was active with student government activities and was most active with the Black Cultural Arts Council (BCAC). Thus, I had an opportunity to meet with you fairly early during my academic career. I do not know if you remember those meetings, but I do. During that first meeting, I was pleasantly surprised that you not only knew who I was, but actually knew of my background and my campus activities. This made me feel special.

What I learned during that first meeting was that you had a commitment to helping the Black Cultural Arts Council achieve its goals and it was clear that during your reign, the university would always be mindful of the special needs and concerns of African-Americans. In short, Father Ted, you not only talked a talk of inclusion of minorities and women, but I believe that this inclusion was necessary for the university to be a success. I thank you for that commitment.

While I was a senior I came to realize that you made everyone you met feel special. You were always willing to listen to our needs, to respect our differences, and to try to respond to those needs. There was no them and us. Having now graduated and gone on to a life that includes service to my community, I thank you, Father Ted and the university for helping me to realize that I did not have to ignore my heritage or my gender, but that I could be proud of who I am and allow my differences to compliment my personal and intellectual growth.

Thank you, Father Ted, your life continues to be an inspiration to me and to many others.

Sincerely,

The Honorable Piper D. Griffin
Class of '84
Judge, Civil District Court, New Orleans, Louisiana

Dear Father Hesburgh,

It's been thirty-five years since I decided where I most wanted to go to college, and it's hard to imagine what my life would be like if Notre Dame had not been that choice— had not even been an option for me.

Choosing to go to Notre Dame was consciously accepting a challenge. I think we all knew that first year was going to be different. I don't think we understood how much we, and everyone else on campus would have to learn to "roll with the punches." Enduring football Saturdays when alums returned to see their room that had "gone to the girls," wasn't that bad, but being the target of sophomoric beauty ratings in the dining hall was belittling. Being one of two women in a class and having to provide the "female perspective" when asked, was tiring. Alumni, faculty, male students, and the "new" female students all had to make the adjustments asked of them those first years.

After twelve years in an all-girl elementary/high school, I needed to experience life in the real world, and I believe that Notre Dame also was moving into the real world with your decision to admit women. There was much to be learned, and we did it together.

I look back on my four years and can see how far I came because of that challenge, how much my sense of humor developed (it had to!). And now, I truly realize how blessed I have been because of my time at Notre Dame. My husband of twenty-seven years is a Double Domer, four of our five children hold or will hold undergraduate degrees from Our Lady's university, and most of our good friends we have met through the Alumni Association.

But it's the values Notre Dame promotes that reinforced what my parents and the nuns taught me, that bring me to where I am in my life. I'm happy to be a woman who chose to stay home, raise a family, volunteer for church, schools and community organizations, and accept foster infants into our home. Through work in marriage preparation and foster care, I have met so many wonderful people that I might never have encountered in our community—expanding our real world. And I have a good marriage and five delightful young adults who are good human beings.

There are still times when I am reminded of how lucky I

Susan Darin Hagan '76, First Woman *Dome* Editor.

was to be in that first class of entering freshmen women and of being the first female *Dome* editor, but they don't compare to the times when I realize how fortunate I was to be applying to college when you were deciding that Notre Dame needed to enlarge its "real world."

Thank you, Father Ted, for allowing Marty and I to meet, and for our sons and daughters to attend Notre Dame. Without you, this would not have been possible!

Sincerely,

Susan Darin Hagan
Class of '76
First Woman Editor in Chief, *Dome* Yearbook, 1975 Edition

⚡

Dear Father Ted,

I said yes to Notre Dame after realizing it had the happiest students I'd seen. It wasn't a labored decision—although the search certainly was—and I dropped my acceptance into the mail with a relatively clear head, grateful to reach some resolution on how I was going to spend the next four years of my life.

But that doesn't mean I've never considered the "what ifs" and "where elses." Where else could I be? What if I hadn't picked Notre Dame? What if I never even had the option? Because this second home wouldn't have been here for me, or for us—for thousands of us—were it not for Father Hesburgh. For current students, it doesn't seem like a big deal that Notre Dame has both men and women. That's standard. Coeducation is something that happened forever ago, and after all, our school isn't ex-actly considered normal. (Parietals.) So was adding a gender even that earth shattering of a development?

Except for Notre Dame, it was. On a football Friday sometime last fall, I was walking across God Quad on my way back to Lewis Hall. An older man, probably in his seventies, was coming from the other direction. As we approached each other, he stopped in front of me. "I'm sorry to stare," he said, smiling, "but I'm still not used to seeing women around here!"

Today, we talk about what direction Notre Dame will take in the future. How should the campus develop between new dorms, renovated and expanded academic buildings, and even a planned "college town" district lining Eddy Street? How much emphasis should the university place on research, compared to its traditional focus on undergraduate education? And how do we preserve Notre Dame's Catholic character while striving to be unique in so many ways?

These are debates I've watched surface over a handful of semesters. Father Hes-burgh, you led this university for thirty-five years. How you dealt with thirty-five years of questions—questions of weight, with answers that determined the future and suc-cess of the university—is beyond my comprehension.

But you've made it all sound natural. You've played off the tough calls as simply what's right and you've done it so good-naturedly.

"I had started to notice that the longer I was at Notre Dame, the more brutish the men were becoming," you told students at a panel discussion in the spring of 2005.

"Without women, men degenerate into something less than human. That's why God put women here, because he didn't want the world to be a zoo."

Maybe that's the case. Maybe Notre Dame was on a fast downward spiral into the basest behavioral depths of the animal kingdom. But I'm sure there were plenty of people who disagreed with coeducation—there always are.

There are innumerably more, however, who were thrilled. Three years after committing to this school, it's hard to pick my where else. Probably Georgetown. I'm sure I'd still be enjoying myself.

But what I'd be missing!

Thank you, Father Hesburgh.

Maddie Hanna
Editor in Chief, *Observer* Newspaper, 2007–2008

Dear Father Ted,

In a lifetime known as the '70s, I fancied myself quite the feminist—even if I did wear kneesocks and love the Virgin Mary. And at the time, I would not have sworn that you were such a true friend to the movement.

On one occasion in my junior year, a friend invited me to have dinner with his fellow seminarians, and the guest of honor that evening was you. After the meal, there was time set aside for questions and answers. I did not raise my hand, being there by invitation after all. But you asked me if, as the only woman present, there wasn't anything I wanted to know.

OK, then: Why *weren't* there more of us in the university as a whole, and when *would* Notre Dame have sex-blind admissions? To your credit, you did not placate me, or pretend you were working on it. You said, "Women at Notre Dame are like flowers in the springtime." But welcome as we were, women did not tend to fund their alma maters, so the ratio of men to women was a business decision.

I was not wild about this answer, I have to tell you. Yet I see things differently now, appreciate candor over blah-blah, and results so much more than rhetoric. What matters, of course, is that you opened the door to us, even under pressure to keep it barred and that is more than I could possibly have appreciated at the time.

As for all that followed, I'm not sure when you changed your mind—or when I did, either. But first impressions are overrated, don't you think?

With thanks and admiration,

Melinda Henneberger
Class of '80
Author, *If They Only Listened to Us: What Women Voters Want Politicians to Hear* (2007)
Former Rome Bureau Chief, the *New York Times*

Dear Father Ted,

Many years ago *Reader's Digest* had a monthly feature titled "most unforgettable person I ever met." I often thought "Who would I write about if they ever approached me?" After meeting you, Father Hesburgh, and spending time with you, there is no doubt you are the most unforgettable person I ever met.

My reasons for choosing you Father Ted are numerous and varied. Let's start with your intelligence and memory. You led Notre Dame for thirty-five glorious years and your decision to make Notre Dame coeducational is just one example of your vision. You felt Notre Dame could not become a great educational institution if Our

Lou Holtz and Father Ted at "Toasting Father Ted," 1999.

Lady's school eliminated one half of the most talented people in the world. You made a difficult, but proper, decision. Thanks to you, today Notre Dame is one of the fifteen best academic institutions in the country.

It was fascinating to listen to you talk about your relationship with popes, presidents, Mother Teresa, entertainers, politicians, foreign dignitaries, etc., and it was not only educational, but entertaining as well.

Your love of people and Notre Dame is unsurpassed. You told all Notre Dame students that if the light in your room was on, your door was open to them. Not only was your door always open to visitors, but your heart was open as well. Your relationship with Father Ned was the most remarkable one I have ever witnessed. As the last football coach you and Father Ned hired, I can assure you that you never did anything but encourage me and make me feel like I was part of the Notre Dame family. This ability to make me feel welcome is not shared by a large number of people.

Without a doubt, Father Hesburgh, I feel your greatest quality is your love of God. You may be the most religious person I have ever met. To be in your presence meant I was in the presence of someone special. If you were to be canonized for sainthood I would not object.

I now realize I could write a book about the great things I know and admire about you, Father Ted, but time and space do not allow me to do this. I will simply say I am a better person because of my relationship with you. A big question I ask about a person is, "If you hadn't showed up who would miss you and why?" I think we all agree, if you hadn't showed up, I would miss you, Notre Dame would miss you, this country would miss you, and the world would miss you. Thank you, Father Ted, I have been blessed to know you.

Sincerely,

Lou Holtz
Head Football Coach 1986–1996
National Chapions: 1988

Dear Father Ted,

It is with gratitude and admiration that I congratulate you, on the occasion of your 90th birthday, for the many gifts you bestowed upon the university as its president, especially your bold decision to open Our Lady's university to undergraduate women thirty-five years ago.

As a Notre Dame undergraduate in the early '70s, I can speak from experience when saying this radical transformation significantly enriched the educational experience here, made life better and fuller for its students' personal lives, and has ultimately benefited the university and the world. Having women in our classrooms, laboratories, and dining halls, engaging them as peers and as friends, and witnessing the development and maturity of the students and the institution because of their presence only confirmed for me the wisdom of your decision.

Now that I sit in the president's chair I appreciate the decision all the more. I understand better the vision and courage it took to break with 130 years of tradition, the firm decisiveness for Notre Dame to go forward on its own terms when negotiations with Saint Mary's College had broken off, and the steady will, judgment, and faith needed to guide the institution through a difficult transition.

The university and the entire Notre Dame family are indebted to you for elevating so significantly and so gracefully the life of this institution through the inclusion of so many talented and dedicated women. And I feel deep appreciation personally. I

Father Ted, Father Malloy, and Father Jenkins.

have inherited a student body in which the ratio between men and women is divided evenly; a campus with twenty-seven residence halls, thirteen of which are female; and a robust athletic program bolstered by strength and excellence in women's sports, including three national championships. For more than three decades Notre Dame's women have excelled impressively in academics, service, and in extracurricular and leadership activities on campus. Notre Dame's women alumni have succeeded in public service, in medical centers, courtrooms, boardrooms, the media, and other professional spheres as well as contributing to family, community, the Church, and society.

As a student, faculty member, and now president, I have been a direct beneficiary of your move to include women in the Notre Dame undergraduate experience and I'm grateful to you for that. And I can attest that what once may have seemed to many like a break from tradition to the other half of the population, and they have, in turn, carried these traditions, values, and principles to all corners of the globe. Through you, what was once prophetic and a struggle has become right and natural.

May God continue to bless you and Our Lady, Notre Dame, protect and keep you.

Fraternally yours,

Reverend John I. Jenkins, CSC, '76, '78 MA
President, University of Notre Dame 2005

Dear Father Ted,

*Feliz Cumpleaños!* I feel so blessed to be writing to you on this occasion, as your birthday is the perfect time to celebrate your life, and to remind us of all that you have accomplished throughout the years. Thirty-plus years later, we ND women are the proud legacy of your having had the vision and the courage so many years ago to break the mold and allow us to attend Notre Dame. The Notre Dame community fostered and grew under your good guidance, and the men and women that now serve as Our Lady's emissaries are proof positive that coeducation is the best environment for both men and women to learn how to live and work together. We women of Notre Dame are indeed blessed and thankful for having been given this opportunity to grow and serve in the spirit of Our Lady.

You have set an example for all of us, the men and women of Notre Dame, of the importance of service to God and others above self. I trust you are aware of how you have inspired me to pursue the path I have chosen, of developing a love for Latin America as you have, and of serving others through my various nonprofit pursuits. I consider myself blessed to have had you as a mentor and guide, and the year I served as the first woman student body vice president was one of my most rewarding. I am thankful for your support at that time, and for encouraging me to represent the women student body as their spokesperson for the Tenth Anniversary of Coeducation. The many women who have followed me in helping lead our great university are proof of how far we have come.

Your legacy will live on in all of the women of ND who were made to feel equals on campus—whether in the classroom or the athletic arena. It was your continued support that inspired a group of women swimmers to fight for our own team soon after I began my freshman year. I vividly recall being in your office with Moose Krause, the university's athletic director, advocating for pool time and for a club team. You were supportive then, and four years later we "graduated" to a varsity status. Today the seeds of our effort have grown into a Division I program and much acclaim.

Father Ted with Tara Crane Kenney '82.

# The Observer

VOL. XV, NO. 104          an independent student newspaper serving notre dame and saint mary's          WEDNESDAY, MARCH 4, 1981

### Garner 63.6 percent

# Murday, Kenney triumph

**By MIKE O'BRIEN**
*Staff Reporter*

Notre Dame students yesterday elected Don Murday and his running-mate Tara Kenney to the offices of student body president and vice-president.

Also elected were four new representatives to the student senate, Clare Padgett in District 1, Brian Callaghan in District 2, Tom Weithman in District 4, and Matt Huffman from off-campus.

District 3 saw the only really close race of the day as Carl Carney and Patricia Hiler survived the challenge of three other candidates to advance to a runoff election tomorrow.

Murday and Kenney polled 63.3 percent of the SBP vote to overwhelm the opposition ticket of Pat Borchers and Rosemary Canino, which garnered 19.2 percent of the ballots. Write-in candidates pulled 17.4 percent of the total vote.

The victorious ticket carried all but one of the residence halls as well as winning a large majority of the off-campus vote.

A quiet Murday attributed his victory to his "door-to-door" campaign and said he planned on a good deal of administrative work before taking office on April 1. He added that his immediate priorities were, however, "sleep and school."

The new SBP, who calls Avon, New Jersey his home, is a junior business major currently serving as president of Carroll Hall. Kenney, who is the president of Lyons Hall, is a junior from Adrian, Michigan.

Padgett, the new senator from District 1 (St. Ed's, Lewis, Holy Cross, Carroll, Sorin, Walsh, and Alumni) is a sophomore from Lewis. She received 61.4 percent of the vote to defeat St. Ed's junior Richard Navarro, who had 38.6 percent.

In District 2 (Stanford, Keenan, Zahm, Cavanaugh, BP, and Farley), Keenan freshman Brian Callaghan beat Zahm junior Edward Bylina 62.8 percent to 37.2 percent.

The vote total in District 3 (Dillon, Badin, Howard, Morrissey, Lyons, Pangborn, Fisher) was Carl Carney 26.7 percent, Patrica Hiler 23.2 percent, Tom Cushing 21.8 percent, Bob Zimmerman 17.4 percent, and David DeJute 10.9 percent. Carney is a Fisher sophomore and Hiler is a sophomore from Lyons.

Tom Weithman, a junior from Grace, gained 57.9 percent of the District 4 (Flanner, Grace, Pasquerilla East and West) vote to defeat sophomore Karen Corbett, who lives in Pasquerilla West.

Junior Matt Huffman ran unopposed in the off-campus Senate race.

Total voter turnout for the election was over half of the student body as 3,656 people cast ballots.

---

Thank you, also, Father, for continuing to impress on us the importance of fostering peace, democracy, and economic development in our world. I am proud to serve as a director of the Kellogg Institute for International Studies, and am constantly reminded of your mission to create a lasting institute to bring about necessary change. The Kellogg and Kroc Institutes are the hallmarks of your, Father Ned, and Father Bartell's remarkable vision for our world. Our work is far from done, but will continue to be inspired by your example.

Your dedication to God, to Country, and to Notre Dame (to paraphrase a well-known book) has given us all a moral compass to live by. Whether in our professional lives, or more importantly in raising our families and within our communities, the lessons you helped impart while we were at Notre Dame have shaped who we are. We are the women of Notre Dame, and we are a powerful, spiritual, and responsible group who cherish life and seek justice and truth.

Finally, I am reminded that first and foremost you have always been a priest, and for that the Notre Dame family is eternally grateful. My husband Gary and my three boys also thank you for continuing to pray for us; we are blessed.

May you enjoy this day, and all of the days ahead knowing that you are loved by us all.

Happy 90th Birthday and may God bless you always,

Yours truly,

Tara Crane Kenney
Class of '82
First Woman Student Body Vice President 1981–1982
Managing Director, Deutsche Bank Asset Management, Boston, Massachusets

Dear Father Ted,

Writing to you about your decision to open the doors of Notre Dame to women deserves a library, more than a book or letter. But, Father Ted, you already have the library.

As a proud father of Mary Shayla, one of the 125 women who arrived at Notre Dame in 1972, I have a special reason to be writing to you.

In addition, my son Michael found the woman of his life, Jinny, at Notre Dame and married her in the Basilica.

My daughter, Eileen, a few years later, arrived on campus and a couple of decades after that, two granddaughters, Betsy and Katie, are now enjoying life at Our Lady's university.

Scatter Michael, Patrick, and Clarke in the mix and we're a coed family in the greatest coed university in the world. Shayla is now a trustee of the university, and Eileen is a member of the Snite Museum Council.

I remember a sunlit morning at the Grotto in late August of 1972. You were celebrating Mass on a temporary altar with Father Ned at your side, and the 125 incoming freshman girls and their families, including Mickie and me, standing with them.

As you began the Offertory, you lifted your head and turned to Our Lady on the Dome. You said, "Mary, I want to apologize for waiting 140 years to bring your daughters to your university." Our Lady knew . . . you knew . . . we all knew . . . that Notre Dame would never be the same. It would forever be a better Notre Dame.

Father Ted, you have received more honors and awards than any other single human being, but you will never get enough thanks for that momentous decision.

Mickie and the entire Keough family joins me in thanking you.

With respect, admiration and affection.

Sincerely,

Donald R. Keough
Class of '85 Honorary
Chairman, Notre Dame Board of Trustees 1986–1992

Dear Father Ted,

I was the first woman in my family to go to college. What a gift that I got to do it at Notre Dame, a place that teaches men AND women to think with their heads and their hearts.

I'm now a mother and a journalist. My husband—a fellow Domer, '94—chose to stay home with our toddler daughter. Our twist on the traditional family was born at ND. And all three of us are better for it.

Monica Yant Kinney
Class of '93
Editor in Chief, *Observer* Newspaper, 1992–1993

Dear Father Hesburgh,

When I think of you, I am filled with admiration and hope. Admiration for all that you are and have been to so many—a mentor, a visionary, a friend and priest. And hope, that one day I can be as convicted, spiritual, and wise as you.

Thank you for your mentorship and guidance during my undergraduate years at Notre Dame. You continually challenged me to grow as a leader and as a human being. Whether it was over lunch at the Morris Inn, in a meeting about student life, or during Mass with my friends and family in the library chapel, you always sent me off with much to think about—a personal challenge.

In particular, I remember our first meeting. It was 2000 and I had just been elected student body vice president. Brian O'Donoghue (the student body president) and I met you for lunch at the Morris Inn. There had never been a female student body president in the nearly thirty years since you admitted undergraduate women to Notre Dame, and you were keenly aware of this.

I remember you describing with pride your decision to bring coeducation to Notre Dame. You told us that it had always seemed a bit of a contradiction that a university named after Our Lady didn't have any women students. And that after being close to us and helping us all these years, she was probably asking, "Where are all the ladies?" Then you told us that you felt the mission of coeducation would be complete

# THE OBSERVER

*The Independent Newspaper Serving Notre Dame and Saint Mary's*

VOL XXXIV NO. 89           HTTP://OBSERVER.ND.EDU

## ND elects Norton first female student body president

### ◆ Student voter rates lower than primary election

**By LAURA ROMPF**
Assistant News Editor

Brooke Norton did what Al Gore couldn't. By capturing 56 percent of the vote in Thursday's run-off, the current vice president became the first female student body president at Notre Dame.

"I am excited for this opportunity," Norton said. "This year is the 30th anniversary of women being admitted into Notre Dame, and we will have our first female student body president. I am very honored to have that privilege."

Norton is the first vice president to win the University's student body elections since incumbent Dennis Etienne won the presidency in 1973. Ryan Becker, along with running mate Nikki McCord, captured 42 percent of the vote in Thursday's run-off. Becker said he was proud of his campaign staff and thanked his supporters.

"I'm really proud of the race we ran," Becker said. "We picked up 500 votes today. It shows how hard we worked in the past week. I'm very

proud."

Becker gave special thanks to Zahm Hall which had the highest voter turn-out on campus and awarded Becker 154 votes compared to Norton's 18.

"We have nothing to be ashamed of," Becker said. "Obviously, we wish we could've won, but we can walk out of here and hold our heads high."

Brian Moscona, the vice president-elect, said he is excited for the opportunity to serve the student body.

"We're going to work our butts off to make this a better campus and a better place for the student body," said Moscona. "I think there's a lot of good we can do."

The run-off election had a lower voter turnout than previous student body elections. While 3,801 students voted in Monday's primary, only 3,249 voted Thursday, amounting to a little more than 40 percent of the student body.

Norton, whose parents were on hand for the announcement Thursday night, thanked all her supporters and said she looks forward to accomplishing all the Norton/Moscona platform goals.

"It was all the little things that made this happen," Norton said. "I want to thank all of those who did the work."

SARAH FUCHS/The Observer
**Brian Moscona and Brooke Norton (l to r) are congratulated by Son Nguyen at the McKenna Center for Continuing Education following the announcement of their victory in the student body presidential/vice presidential race Thursday night.**

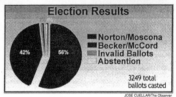

### Election Results

- Norton/Moscona
- Becker/McCord
- Invalid Ballots
- Abstention

42%   56%

3249 total ballots casted

JOSE CUELLAR/The Observer

---

when a woman led the students of Notre Dame as student body president. And you thought I should consider it.

Your encouragement that day and in the year following helped give me the confidence to run for student body president. It also instilled in me that in serving the students of Notre Dame, I was carrying the torch of the first class of 365 undergraduate women, who paved the way for me.

Thank you for bringing coeducation to Notre Dame. We ARE forever grateful.

And thank you for continuing to inspire the sons and daughters of Notre Dame du Lac. You gave me the following advice, and it still adorns the student body president's office today:

"Don't make decisions because they are easy or cheap or because they are popular—
make them because they are the right thing to do."
— Father Theodore Hesburgh, CSC

With heartfelt thanks,

Brooke Norton Lais
Class of '02
First Woman Student Body President 2001–2002

Dear Father Ted,

Fifteen years ago today, my daughter was born. She came into the world reluctantly, having to be induced two weeks past her due date. The night I was scheduled to report to the hospital for the inducement, my husband and I had a nice dinner at a restaurant in Washington, D.C., near the White House. After dinner, as we prepared to leave the

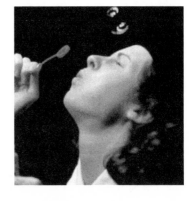

restaurant, we saw you as you were leaving at the same time. I introduced myself as a Domer, and the daughter of a Domer. My dad, Peter J. Cannon (Class of 1956), knew Father Ted through Notre Dame activities. When I told you that we were leaving the restaurant to go to the hospital, you blessed my unborn daughter. Your blessing gave me the comfort and strength to face the uncertainties in my immediate future. Looking back now, I see that your actions on that night, and while president of Notre Dame, have had an impact on my daughter's life.

At fifteen, my daughter is developing into a wonderful young woman. She is starting to think about college and is very interested in Notre Dame. She is interested in the world around her and finding her place in it. I know that she would thrive in the environment created by you at Notre Dame and I am thankful that as a woman, she will have the opportunity to apply.

With this in mind and with heartfelt thanks to you, I wish the following for my daughter on her fifteenth birthday:

-  a rich life with true friendships, a fulfilling career, and a loving family
- a worldview that allows her to understand and be compassionate
- the strength to deal with the inevitable bumps in the road
- the faith in herself that allows her to keep the smile on her face and continue to make those around her happy

My dad and I can each describe what Notre Dame contributed to making us the people we are today. I wish the same for my daughter someday.

Kathleen C. Laurini
Class of '82
Deputy Director, Space Life Sciences Directorate, NASA Johnson Space Center

U.S. Air Force Brigadier General James R. Beale with Father Ted, who'd just flown in an SR-71 near Sacramento, California.

Dear Father Ted,

The best advice you gave me and I would want to share with my colleagues in the Notre Dame female family:

When you have problems, troubles, or are not sure of your decisions:

Say: COME HOLY SPIRIT!!

It is the best advice you ever gave to me. I obtained a new job. And otherwise felt that my life journey was because of the Holy Spirit's intervention and your advice.

Thank you.

Fondly,

The Honorable Diana Lewis
Class of '74, '82 JD
Circuit Court Judge, Palm Beach County, Florida


P.S. Your Mass in a very small room in London for a trustee meeting is also memorable; my family's first connection with you for the Lewis Bus Stop is now history but great folklore; and your great stories and adventures as president are my greatest memories . . . which I hope you will share.

Coretta Scott King, Joan Kroc, Father Ted, Ann Landers (Eppie Lederer), and Father Joyce at "Toasting Father Ted," 1999

Dear Father,

"Bless me, Father, for I have sinned."

Thank goodness I was never asked to pay for one particular sin in my youth. In fact, the opposite occurred. The 1967 transgression I'm referring to was my boneheaded, wrong-thinking opposition to the decision to make Notre Dame coeducational.

Not content to merely agree to disagree on the issue, I encouraged organized resistance. "Better dead than coed" was our rallying cry. I thought it just perfect for soon-to-be-graduated seniors with time on their hands! In the end, our righteous indignation was given the at-

LB  CAPT. JIM LYNCH      NOTRE DAME

Reprinted with the permission of the Notre Dame Sports Information Department.

tention it deserved. We were treated as the noisy gang that couldn't shoot straight; and the well-thought-out move to women on campus became a reality.

My "better dead than coed" gang and I got on with our lives and soon became much more productive members of society. In my case, two of three children were female and all bright enough to matriculate at our university. The obvious end to the story and this letter is that Megan Lynch graduated Notre Dame in 1990 and Kara Lynch graduated in 1993. Not only was I not punished for my transgression, I was rewarded with more Notre Dame tradition and love than I deserve.

So—thank you Father Ted—for all you have done and continue to do for our university. It's a privilege to know you.

Sincerely,

James R. Lynch
Class of '67
Captain, Notre Dame Football Team 1966
National Champions: 1966

# BETTER DEAD
# THAN COED

**EMOTIONAL MISOGYNY**
An inalienable student right?

### THE SACRED GRIDIRON

"The ridiculousness of 2,000 signing a petition against cheerleaders! Where were those 2,000 when academic freedom and the speakers policy were being discussed!" This bitter statement came from a high Administration official last weekend. Similar frustrated comments were echoed by student leaders and Administration officials (one being no less than Fr. Hesburgh in remarks at a recent discussion with the newly elected class presidents).

The Senate motion provoking the various emotional outbursts around campus was moved by Larry Broderick, senator from Howard. Broderick, a cheerleader, explained that under his plan the girl cheerleaders would not receive Notre Dame monograms, would appear only in home games, would be carefully selected for appearance and agility by the ND cheerleaders themselves. His motion was passed in the Senate 17-14 on this basis. That did not prevent the Senate's constituency from reacting, however.

By the following evening, a petition for reconsideration of the motion was circulated in the dining halls. The petition, initiated by off-campus senator Rick Hunt, was signed by 2,000 students. The petition itself particularly assailed the principles of representation which had been violated by some of the senators.

One of the most violent reactions was in Cavanaugh Hall where outrage was aimed at senators Chuck Goria and Bill Meyer. Both had taken polls of their sections before the Senate considered the measure. Their limited polls showed that the majority did not favor the proposal. Nevertheless, Goria and Meyer backed the motion, and for one night anger reigned in Cavanaugh with posters all over the hall favoring impeachment of the two senators. By the next morning, impeachment efforts had fizzled.

Protest flourished elsewhere, though; by the end of the week, a bulletin was distributed in the halls. Headlined — "Who's Number One? Do you want

girl cheerleaders? Has anyone ever asked you?"—the bulletin charged the Senate with disregarding "over 75 years of tradition, while justifying their action with dubious political procedure." The sheet further expressed a concern for preserving this "cherished" autonomy and further noted that a referendum would be held on Monday, May 1. It was signed by Mike Bradley (former SCHOLASTIC Sports Editor), Jim Purcell (VP, Class of '67), and Jim Lynch.

Before the referendum returns were in that night though, the Senate reconsidered the "cheerleader" proposal. The original motion was passed again by a vote of 18-16.

But behind the facade, consternation still lingers in the Senate. A number of solons who switched to opposing the proposal felt that the real issue was representing their halls. Others felt that the students' failure to react on the more mature and academic issues while reacting to such a minor concern in the athletic spectrum was discouraging. Many felt that maybe the students were more concerned with athletics than academics. "Maybe students rights are defined as defending minor traditions . . . they seem to have missed the real issues in students rights . . . ," said a senator.

—*T. D.*

⚬

Dear Father Hesburgh,

When I was asked, as the first female *Scholastic* editor, to write this letter, I did what any good former journalist would do—I pulled out my old yearbooks and bound copies of the magazine. I came to two immediate conclusions—you and I looked a lot younger back then and plaid pants—not to say plaid jackets!—should be outlawed.

I've always felt a little awkward writing paeans to Notre Dame, because I've always felt a little bit of the odd woman out. I did not grow up wanting to go to Notre Dame. My parents were rather skeptical when I applied—Chicagoans, they considered Notre Dame a football school (and that was not a compliment). But I wanted to go to a coed Catholic college that wasn't urban, and, at least in 1971, there were not many schools that met those criteria. Neither did Notre Dame when I applied, but in December I got the letter announcing that the Saint Mary's/Notre Dame merger had been called off. Notre Dame moved up on my list.

I came to campus in the fall of 1972, a dreamy writer-wannabe from an all-girls' Catholic high school in Washington, D.C. Notre Dame was a culture shock. It was midwestern and it was very male. Only 125 of the 1,600 freshman were female; if I remember correctly, the total undergraduate female population was about 350, smaller than the previous year when Saint Mary's students could take classes without paying a separate fee.

As I've told my friends, one girl does not make a gym class coed—at least from the girl's perspective.

Many of the professors and administrators viewed us as pioneers, but I thought of myself as simply a college freshman. I learned the fight song. I went to a few football games, though the rah-rah football mania of the place never really appealed to me. I ate lots of popcorn first in Walsh and then in Farley, had deep discussions about the meaning of life, worked on the magazine, got very interested in literary theory, and worried about what I was going to do when I graduated and entered the real world.

Watching my sons go through college—and no, none of them went to Notre Dame, but then, none of the six of us (me, my husband, and our four sons) has the same alma mater—I sometimes marvel at how different things are today. When I graduated from Notre Dame in 1976, there were still no varsity women sports on campus. There was no viable student center—LaFortune then was a dingy, unwelcoming place—where men and women could socialize. And of course there was no Starbucks, no Internet, no personal computers. (I'm certain I would have pulled fewer all-nighters if I hadn't had to write all those English papers with a typewriter and correction paper.)

Did I love every minute of my four years at Notre Dame? No, but I doubt I would have loved every minute of any college experience. My fondest memories are of my friends, of talking late into the night, of walking the lakes (often alone during a football game!), and of going to Mass in Farley and the other residence halls.

What I value most about my time at Notre Dame, I found articulated by you in the 1973 *Dome*. You wrote in part:

"Lastly, a liberal education should enable a person to humanize everything that he or she touches in life, which is to say that one is enabled not only to evaluate what one is or does, but that in addition, one adds value consciously to relationships that might otherwise be banal or superficial or meaningless; relations to God, to one's fellow men, to one's wife or husband or children, to one's associates, one's country and world."

Sally Stanton MacKenzie '76, first woman *Scholastic* editor.

Notre Dame gave me the gift of four years to believe that things mattered, that there was significance beyond the obvious.

Where have I gone since I graduated? To law school, briefly, where I met my husband. (I, tongue in cheek, say I didn't get my JD, but my MRS.) To the federal government where I wrote regulations for the School Nutrition programs. (Remember ketchup as a vegetable?) And then out of the paid work force, staying home to raise my sons; writing school newspapers and class plays; managing the community swim team; leading the Cub Scout pack; doing a variety of other volunteer duties where I tried to add value to the banal, the mundane. Now as my nest empties, I've finally turned to the dream I had even before I arrived at Notre Dame—I'm writing novels. (Not that I ever thought I'd be writing romance novels, but the spirit moves in mysterious ways.)

So thank you for having the vision to open the university to women and to allow me to spend four years at that special place.

Sincerely,

Sally Stanton MacKenzie
Class of '76
First Woman Editor in Chief, *Scholastic* magazine, 1975–1976
Romance Novelist, Maryland

Dear Father Ted,

One Sunday afternoon in October 1985 you presented a lecture in the Center for Social Concerns, and afterward, I ambushed you. As only a college student can be, I was incensed about the injustice of a disciplinary action the university had taken against two of my friends. Your response to being accosted was to invite me for a walk.

We ambled around St. Joseph's Lake for the next hour and a half. To this day, I remember that you were calm yet resolute, always the teacher, the strolling embodiment of grace. The respect you showed me that day is a lesson I try never to forget, one of dignity.

Of course, human dignity as an unconditional gift from God was a lesson to which you dedicated your life. For numerous decades, through numerous organizations, and on numerous continents, you worked to lift people up, to show them that they are, by their being, worthy of honor and respect.

Back at home, at Notre Dame, you did the same thing. By opening Notre Dame's doors to women in 1972, you raised the dignity of women and men. You insisted women would make Notre Dame a better university. Thank you for that humbling respect and incredible opportunity.

At the end of that Sunday walk in 1985 you offered to buy me a soda. I think I was too overwhelmed at the time to accept. If I could have that moment back now, I would raise my glass to toast you and the dignity you encourage in all of us.

As ever,

Sarah Hamilton Magill
Class of '86
Editor in Chief, *Observer* Newspaper 1985–1986

# Hamilton named as editor

Sarah Hamilton, a junior from Scotch Plains, N.J., has been elected editor-in-chief of The Observer for 1985-86.

She will assume her duties March 25.

Hamilton, who served as a news editor this year, said she is excited about the The Observer's potential.

"This year we have worked on developing wide coverage of both campuses, always keeping in mind objectivity and fairness," Hamilton said. "Next year this philosophy will become routine."

The editor-in-chief, Hamilton said, must understand all facets of the newspaper - its responsibilities as a business, its duties as a newspaper, and its role as a service to Notre Dame and Saint Mary's.

*Sarah Hamilton*

Joining the University's budget system last year was a necessary evil, Hamilton said. "From a financial standpoint, budget unit control encourages professional and consistent business policies and practices," she said. "But we are always concerned with our editorial independence because the people we are reporting on should not be holding our money."

Father Ted and Pope Pius XII.

Pope John Paul II and Father Ted.

Pope Pius VI and Father Ted.

*Rev. Edward A. ("Monk") Malloy was president of the University of Notre Dame from 1987 to 2005.*

*On February 7, 2007, Catherine Pieronek '84, '95 JD, director of academic affairs and director of the women's engineering program in the College of Engineering, asked him about his experiences with Notre Dame coeducation.*

When I became president, in my inaugural address, I included among my priorities that Notre Dame become effectively coeducational in its common life. In order to achieve this goal, we worked hard on a number of fronts: (1) we celebrated a "Year of Women" with multiple activities; (2) we gave increased attention to hiring women faculty; (3) we significantly added to the number of women in the central administration (at the officer level) and in major academic leadership roles; (4) we targeted an increase in the number of women on the board of trustees and advisory councils; (5) we put in place a wider range of programming in student affairs (including areas related to women's health and safety); (6) we expanded significantly the number of female intercollegiate athletic options and upgraded the support structure; (7) we had a number of women commencement speakers and honorary degree recipients; and (8) most of all we kept it as a high priority for eighteen years.

While there was initial opposition to becoming coeducational, I think that it has become such a characteristic of the university that most people just take it for granted. It has increased the academic quality of the school, diversified its social life, improved its commitment to service learning, and otherwise made Notre Dame a better institution.

Like all transitions in higher education, I am sure that things could have been done better and our goals achieved more rapidly. But I am thankful that we have seen the improvements that have taken place. As an institution, we are named after a woman and it seems fitting that women now play such an essential role in our common life.

Dear Father Hesburgh,

Without you, my life would have been different. My athletic dreams may have never been realized. My happiness would have been unknowingly lacking without the richness of my college relationships. My faith would never have been challenged and ultimately enhanced had I not been exposed to the rigor of a Catholic education. Without your decision to allow women into Notre Dame, my life would have been less fulfilled.

I have traveled the world, competed in front of thousands of spectators, represented and made my country proud by being an Olympic gold medalist, and have lived experiences beyond my wildest dreams. Yet the experience I hold closest to my heart is my time at Notre Dame.

Thank you for giving me the opportunity to attend such a wonderful institution—a nurturing home which drives students to be their best. The faculty and administration are equally concerned with the intelligence and moral fiber of the student body. Thank you for giving me the chance to see, live, and be a part of the culture you created.

Sincerely,

Kathryn Sobrero Markgraf
Class of '98
Captain, ND Women's Soccer Team 1997–1998
2000 Silver Olympic Medalist, Women's Soccer
2004 Gold Olympic Medalist, Women's Soccer

Kathryn Sobrero Markgraf '98.
Reprinted with the permission of the Notre Dame Sports Information Department.

Dear Father Hesburgh,

Your courageous decision to transform the University of Notre Dame into a coeducational institution changed it and all those who came in contact with it from that point on. You were and are a visionary.

My life has been full of blessings. While some of them would have occurred whether I went to Notre Dame or not, I suspect most of them would not have happened. Your decision put in motion life-altering events for many, including me.

The news of your decision to make Notre Dame coeducational reached my small Catholic girls' high school like wildfire. I was determined to apply for admission.

I entered the university as an energetic sixteen-year-old, having already met my husband-to-be the weekend that I interviewed on campus (Rocco was then a freshman). Our twenty-seven-year marriage is still going strong. Our oldest, Dan, is now a sophomore at Notre Dame and living in Stanford Hall. Tommy, our youngest, is making his First Holy Communion this year and is already a huge Irish fan.

I support the university in as many ways as possible—feeding students during breaks, cheering its teams on, and currently serving as the chairperson of the Mendoza College of Business Council.

My years at Notre Dame were magical in so many ways. I found an area of study that I enjoyed and excelled in—accounting. I made friends that remain an integral part of my life—from vacations together, becoming godparents to each others' children, to social events shared. Many of us live in the same parish and our children have become close friends.

After beginning my career in public accounting, I completed my MBA at the University of Chicago and transitioned into the investment field. Today I am the president and CEO of an $8 billion investment firm.

Thank you for making this all possible.

Sincerely,

Roxanne M. O'Brien Martino
Class of '77
President and CEO, Harris Alternatives LLC
Chairman, Mendoza College of Business Advisory Council

Dear Father Ted,

Thank you for recognizing that Notre Dame would never be a great university if we excluded half the talent in the world from the university.

Your decision to admit young women to Notre Dame, which I know you consider to be one of your most significant accomplishments as president of Notre Dame, has served to enrich the Notre Dame experience for all of our students. You must also be very proud of the Notre Dame women who have gone on to distinguish themselves in so many ways.

As chairman of the board of trustees I am pleased to participate in this tribute to you and to the women of Notre Dame.

Sincerely,

Patrick F. McCartan
Class of '56, '59 JD, '99 Honorary
Chairman, Notre Dame Board of Trustees 2000–2007

Lois McCartan, Father Ted, and Patrick F. McCartan, Notre Dame Board of Trustees Chairman, at the U.S. Capitol in 1999, when Father Ted received the Congressional Gold Medal of Freedom.

Dear Father Hesburgh,

"Competent, Compassionate, and Committed: the three Cs." These were your parting words to me and the Class of 1980, twenty-seven years ago at our graduation. Those words have remained with me and serve as my road map. It is an honor to write this letter to you as I often think of you and your leadership in protecting human and civil rights.

For nearly nine years, I have served as director of the National Immigrant Justice Center, a not-for-profit organization based in Chicago, which provides direct legal services to and advocates for immigrants, refugees, and asylum-seekers through policy reform, impact litigation, and public education. My position allows me to use my legal skills to ensure due process protections for the most vulnerable in our community and to work with men, women, and children who have amazing faith and courage. Prior to becoming the director of the National Immigrant Justice Center, I served as a pro bono attorney for the center while practicing law.

Today, as our country attempts to respond to immigrant rights crisis, I am reminded of your leadership in immigration and refugee reform, dating back to 1979. Since September 11, 2001, the basic civil and human rights of immigrants and refugees are under attack. A two-tiered system of justice has evolved: one for citizens and another for noncitizens. Immigrants face exploitation, arbitrary detention, deportation without due process, and separation from families. In the name of national security, we have dehumanized members of our family, denying them their human rights due to their legal status.

I came to this job with a vision. . . . a vision that began many years ago while a student at Notre Dame under the influence of your Catholic social justice teachings. You inspired me then and continue to inspire me today! Your leadership and your commitment to build a more just world and to ensure the dignity of each human being serve as a guiding force. I am proud to be a member of a dedicated group of men and women who litigate, educate, and advocate on behalf of those whose rights are being violated. The National Immigrant Justice Center has nearly seven hundred pro bono attorneys and a significant number are Notre Dame graduates. These attorneys provide legal representation to detained asylum-seekers, advocate with members of Congress, and educate their community on the need to protect and promote the human rights of the most vulnerable in our community. The National Immigrant Justice Center has a team of dedicated staff members, and many of them are also Notre Dame graduates.

Another virtue that you taught me was the importance of good people. Msgr. Jack Egan and Peggy Roach were two such people. They inspired and motivated me and many others to live out the Gospel. I felt blessed to have spent time with them in Chicago. Father Hesburgh, you have a true gift in bringing good people together to forge a more just society. That gift has had a profound and positive impact on so many lives.

Finally, I will never forget the spring day in 1980 when a group of students, led by Don McNeill, CSC, met with you and the board of trustees to present our proposal for the Center for Social Concerns (CSC) to open its first permanent home—the recently vacated WNDU building. Prepared with an architectural model and talking points, we enthusiastically presented the proposal to you and the board. You understood the need for the University to have a visible, accessible, and dynamic center to engage students in local, national, and international social justice issues. Today, the Center for Social Concerns is a vibrant campus space linking students and faculty in critical interdisciplinary analysis and active service learning. This is yet another component in your legacy of justice.

I truly believe that my position as director of the National Immigrant Justice Center gives me the best opportunity to seek justice for all. I am able to combine my commitment to serve compassionately with the competency achieved in my professional skills. Few people have such a privilege. With that privilege comes responsibility. I thank you for providing me with a strong foundation and the desire to fulfill that responsibility.

With gratitude and blessings,

Mary Meg McCarthy
Class of '80
Director, National Immigrant Justice Center, Heartland Alliance, Chicago, Illinois

Dear Father Ted,

I am one of those who join many others in thinking of you as the greatest living American. Newt Minow and I had that very conversation this week, and he is only one of many with whom I have had that conversation.

There are so many notable things that happened to the university during your thirty-five wonderful years of leadership and your continued presence.

You guided the university through both charted and uncharted waters. You had the courage to turn the leadership over to a predominantly lay board of trustees. Clearly you observed that to be the future governance of Our Lady's university. Only five years after you provided lay governance, you gave us powerful leadership in opening Notre Dame to women. Coeducation at Notre Dame is the best of all academic opportunities.

It is a different campus today then that of many years ago. Your leadership has helped to provide so much for us to be thankful for. Just think, in your thirty-five years as Notre Dame's president, the United States of America has had eight presidents. You had a role in each of those administrations.

Speaking on a personal note, I am gratified not only by my education at the University of Notre Dame, but also honored that I have two daughters and two sons with Notre Dame degrees and now working on the next generation with one granddaughter a graduate, one grandson a student, and many more anxious to come.

Thanks, Father Ted, for all that you have done for all of us. For the university helping elevate it to its prime standing among academic institutions and for attracting such an impressive faculty and for creating an atmosphere that students worldwide are attracted to.

It has been ninety great years, Father Ted, and many more important ones to come. Congratulations!

Kind regards,

Andrew J. McKenna Sr.
Class of '51, '89 Honorary
Chairman, Notre Dame Board of Trutees, 1992–2000

Dear Father Hesburgh,

Thank you for having the wisdom, courage, and perseverance to bring coeducation to Notre Dame. Of all of your numerous achievements, this is the one for which thousands of women thank you. As the force behind the change, you touched all of our lives and raised the university to a higher level.

In the fall of 1976, when I arrived at Notre Dame as a freshman, coeducation was still in its infancy.

Rosemary Mills-Russell '80, first ND undergraduate woman *Observer* editor in chief.

During my four years at the *Observer*, I watched, participated in, and sometimes criticized, its evolution. It did evolve, and succeed, through discussion and debate and developing sensitivity to those around us. These are some of the skills that the women of Notre Dame then carried into the rest of our lives and used in our personal and professional lives. Not having come from an ND family, I was unaware what being an ND grad would mean. In the intervening years, I have learned that there is a special bond among all of us, especially the women. It comes from cheering for the same sports teams and against certain others. It comes from being part of a group that worked hard to be accepted. It comes from shared memories of a very special place, even if they occurred at different times. Most importantly, it comes from sharing a silent but obvious recognition of the importance of our faith in our lives. There are many fine universities in this country, but I am convinced that only Notre Dame, in her challenging education of the mind and spirit, has such a deep, lifelong impact on each student. Thank you for giving women the opportunity to be part of the Notre Dame community.

Sincerely,

Rosemary Mills-Russell
Class of '80
First Notre Dame Undergraduate Woman Editor in Chief, *Observer* Newspaper
    1979–1980

Dear Father Hesburgh,

Many years ago as a child, I had a dream of attending the University of Notre Dame. I truly had no understanding of what Notre Dame was all about, but I did know it was something special even though I had never stepped foot on campus. I knew certain things and people were symbols of the university and they were as follows: the Leprechaun, the Golden Dome, Touchdown Jesus, Ara Parseghian, and you. At a young age, these symbols were very important and I rarely thought of one without the others, but their importance also varied as the years passed.

Football was a large part of my life and having the opportunity to play for Notre Dame was a dream come true. I realized I was fortunate to be at Notre Dame and playing football for Ara, but there was more to Notre Dame than football. Being at

ND under your tutelage was an honor. Your vision not only for ND, but for the world, was far more important than any football game ever played. Notre Dame is a very special place and a winner. As they say "winning begins at the top." The sports programs flourished under you, as did the students and the university. Never has Notre Dame been as visible and dominant as your years at the helm.

Thank you for all that you have done for the university, the students (oh yes, let's not forget your opening of the doors to women students), our faith, and me.

Joe Montana '79, ND football team quarterback 1975–1979.
Reprinted with the permission of the Notre Dame Sports Information Department.

Happy Birthday, Father Hesburgh!

Joe Montana
Class of '79
Quarterback, Football Team 1975–1979
National Champions: 1977
Quarterback, San Francisco 49ers
Four-Time Super Bowl Champions

Dear Father Ted,

Growing up the youngest child of Diane and Jack Mullen (Class of '53, business council, chairman/Kroc Institute) who have had the blessing of knowing you for years, you can well imagine that some of my most vivid memories from when I was very little center around Notre Dame. Scenes play out in my mind of closing up our summer home to the sounds of ND football on the portable radio and my dad shouting "Oh, geesh" every time a play did not go the way of the Irish; watching cars get packed in the late summers as big brother and sisters headed from New Jersey to dorm rooms in Alumni and Walsh; staying at the Morris Inn for game weekends and getting big Go Irish buttons from their lobby gift shop. . . . As I grew older, memories included Masses at Sacred Heart; meeting both you and Father Joyce at pregame receptions; Alumni Association events and certainly, dreams of one day walking the campus as a student.

Fortunately, dreams came true and unbelievingly, I came to the campus with my parents in August of 1986. I still have a letter one of my brothers wrote to me just before I left. In it, he called Notre Dame "one of the truly great places in the whole world." He could not have been more accurate and I could not have been more blessed. I am humbled with recollections of midnight trips to the Grotto; quiet 11:30 p.m. Sorin Masses on weeknights, sessions on the second floor of the library; room picks and road trips with roommates and so much more.

Notre Dame was never just a college to go to or a place at which to get an education. It was, and continues to be, a lifelong experience. I am grateful every day for my Notre Dame education and for the family I am a part of as an ND graduate. I could not be more thankful for having grown up amongst that family, sharing such a passion for the school, the campus, the beliefs, and the education that is Notre Dame. I know that I am a better person for having Notre Dame to call my own and I am hopeful that as one of her ambassadors, I am able to make some small contributions to our world in honor of Notre Dame, my parents, and in honor of you.

Thank you for everything you have done so tirelessly to make Notre Dame this place, this home, this life for so many young men and women. If we shine, it is because of your tremendous example. You are loved and respected.

Very fondly,

Mary Killeen Mullen
Class of '90
Manager, Special Events, Tampa Bay Buccaneers

Dear Father Ted,

My father and mother moved to South Bend, Indiana, when I was five weeks old so that my father, William Zloch, could attend law school at Notre Dame. My parents were very close with you and wanted my brother and I to somehow be a part of your life. My mother came up with the idea of sending you a Valentine card each year from me. Of course, at five weeks old, I had no idea what was going on, but when I became older and had met you a number of times, I grew a great fondness toward you.

You were truly my Valentine. Every year I looked forward to picking just the right card to send to you. The best part to me was I would always get a Valentine (letter) back from you. I felt so loved, so special.

During my attendance at the University of Notre Dame, you and I would see each other every so often. I once ran into you outside of the library with my golden retriever Jacob. I remember you looking at me like I was crazy to have a dog in the library, but you put your hand on Jake's head and gave him a blessing per my request anyway!

After graduation, my road was very rocky. I was living in New York City pursuing an acting career. I guess I should say I was pursuing a waitressing career. I called you, who always, I mean always, had time to speak with me. I'll never forget what you said. "Kristy, you need the hide of a mule to pursue acting, but you can do it through Christ." After that conversation I moved to Los Angeles, worked hard, prayed daily, and landed an acting job on *The West Wing* for six years. I met my husband and have recently given birth to a beautiful miracle named Maddin Sullivan Murphy.

You have been one of the strongest forces in my life since childhood . . . five weeks

1965–1966 football team quarterback and now U.S. District Court Judge Bill Zloch '66 '74 JD, William Thomas Zloch '96 JD, Nancy Fitzhugh Zloch (Saint Mary's College '67), and Kristy Zloch Murphy '96.

to be exact. I love and respect you. I feel so very blessed that God gave the University of Notre Dame a man like you. I feel that you represent the best of Notre Dame.

Father Ted, you have and will always be my Valentine.

I love you,

Kristy Zloch Murphy
Class of '96
Television Actress, *The West Wing*

Dear Father Ted,

In the fall of 1972, I was one of your first 365 women to be enrolled at the University of Notre Dame. Thinking of that exciting time brings back many fond memories. May I take a walk with you down memory lane?

As a child growing up in the Notre Dame tradition (Don Cisle '45), I was proud to be among the first class of women. I was honored just to be there and to be making history. I loved the "pioneer" role. From the beginning I was involved in the transition work with the administration and Sister John Miriam Jones and her new staff of women. Walsh Hall was not exactly "five star" but living in the legendary residence hall was special to me because it was where my dad lived a generation ago. Joanne Szafran and Jane Pitz provided us with all we needed, including a lot of love and encouragement.

At this point I should thank you and perhaps Dean Raymond for accepting the largest number of transfers from Saint Mary's in the College of Business. In my opinion, our professors and "fellow" classmates accepted us rather easily. I felt the transition in the academic arena was seamless. I love the story of Dr. Cho (Stats) calling all of us coeds "Mister____," followed by his engaging smile.

Another thrill and little bit of luck was that I was a cheerleader for the Fighting Irish for three years. As a cheerleader, I had the good fortune to travel the country to attend away games and to participate in many alumni-sponsored functions and pep rallies. When alumni learned that I was one of the new "coeds," I was usually besieged with questions because everyone was curious about the transition. This "unofficial" role suited me just fine and I was delighted to answer their questions and to spread

the good news. Notre Dame people love Notre Dame people, and
I witnessed that from one coast to
the other.

As for our coaches in those
days, you sure picked some real
winners. Coach Parseghian and
Coach Phelps were not only great
at their jobs, but they were amazing personalities, with wonderful
families. My senior year they provided Irish fans with a National
Championship and an awesome
upset against UCLA. I remember going to Father Joyce's office
to "insist" that the university pay
for the cheerleaders to attend the
Sugar Bowl. As I entered his office,
he sensed my anxiety. Before I sat
down, he congratulated me on the
great news that the cheerleaders
were to be part of the official party

Anne Cisle Murray '74. Reprinted with the permission of the Notre Dame Sports
Information Department.

representing the University of Notre Dame. The rest is history and created a lifetime
memory. Your good friend was a wonderful man.

Throughout the excitement of coeducation and cheerleading, the greatest
joy I experienced was the opportunity to meet and get to know so many wonderful people—fellow students who remain my dearest friends today, as well as those
who worked for the university. My friendships encompassed the entire campus, from
the administration to the Athletic Department. I worked for Fr. Jim Riehle in the
housing office. He remains my dear friend to this day. Father Riehle officiated at
my wedding and baptized two of our children. I was blessed to know John Goldrick
in Admissions, Dr. Jim Frick in Development, Father Tom Blantz in Student Affairs, Bob Ackerman in Student Activities, Jim Gibbons in Special Events, Brother
Conan in the bookstore, Roger Valdiserri in Sports Information, Father Toohey
in Campus Ministry, Dean Broderick in the Law School (great pep rallies!!) . . .

and too many more to mention. It was truly a wonderful place, brimming with incredible people who embraced coeducation and loved Notre Dame. This is the secret—we all love Notre Dame!

In the spring of 1974, as graduation approached, I attended my final cheerleader banquet. Father Tom Blantz, who was our moderator, presented me with an official "Monogram" as I had completed the requirements and I was to soon graduate from the University of Notre Dame. I was technically the first woman to receive a Monogram and my name appears on the wall in the JACC Monogram Hall of Fame. It was a few years later that another wonderful man, "Moose" Krause called and invited me to be the first woman to serve on the Monogram Board of Directors. Moose said that he, Father Riehle, and Harvey Foster all agreed that it was time and that they would be honored to have me as the first woman board member. It was a humbling but proud experience, and one I will remember always.

As you recall, in 1997 the university honored the first group of women to arrive on campus in the fall of 1972. On a glorious afternoon, we presented you with an inscribed rock at the Grotto. It stated: "In thanksgiving to the Blessed Virgin Mary, we are and forever will be grateful daughters of Notre Dame du Lac." That statement remains as true today as it was when we first arrived on campus in 1972. We then attended a memorable Mass in the Basilica of the Sacred Heart. I remember thinking at the time, how wonderful it was that as a Catholic university we can celebrate and thank God for all His blessings upon us. We are ND.

It's now 2007 and I have a son who graduated with the Class of 2007. I also have a daughter (Class of 2003) who recently married a wonderful young man from the Class of 2002!! We played "Notre Dame, Our Mother" at the recessional and all these memories will fill my heart. . . . How does one ever explain it?? It really is true that one does not go to Notre Dame for four short years—you become part of Notre Dame for a lifetime.

Father Ted, I thank you for the profound impact you and Notre Dame have had on my life, and the lives of so many others. I thank you for always making yourself available and for teaching us to show sincere interest in others and to care for them. You are ND.

Anne Cisle Murray
Class of '74
First Woman Director, Notre Dame Monogram Club 1978–1984

Dear Father Ted,

I arrived at Notre Dame in the fall of 1965. The first time I saw you was at Washington Hall when you welcomed our freshman class. It was a cold fall night and as we left the Hall I remember hearing someone ask his friend, "What is the difference between God and Father Hesburgh? God is everywhere, Father Hesburgh is everywhere but Notre Dame." Years later I came to appreciate why this humorous characterization was so misdirected and wrong. As the president of the University of Notre Dame, you had established yourself as an intellectual and moral leader whose ideas and guidance were sought by not only corporate America but our governmental leaders, as well. Your excellent work and visibility with the U.S. Civil Rights Commission through the '60s was instrumental in facilitating passage and then acceptance by the public of the historic civil rights legislation of that era. Your contributions on the national issues of the day have been well recognized and applauded and helped establish Notre Dame as a national university.

I want to thank you for your leadership in another area. You and Father Joyce always believed that the University of Notre Dame could be first in academics as well as first in athletics. These are not mutually exclusive goals. You succeeded in making Notre Dame a center of academic excellence while also encouraging athletic excellence under Father Joyce's leadership. Since I had the distinct privilege of playing football for Ara and the university, I saw this first hand and was a strong proponent of this view. As you know, there is nothing inconsistent with outstanding academic institutions pursuing and fostering great athletic tradition. Notre Dame has a distinguished history of athletic and academic excellence and you added immeasurably to that tradition in your tenure as president.

Thank you, Father Ted, for your support, friendship, and lifetime of service to the university.

Sincerely,

Coley O'Brien
Class of '66, '69 JD
Quarterback, Football Team 1964–1966
National Champions: 1966

Back Row: The Honorable Wayne Andersen; Father Ted; The Honorable Sheila O'Brien '77, 2007 Rev. Charles F. Sorin Alumni Award Winner for Distinguished Service to the University. Front Row: Thomas O'Brien; Maureen Andersen; Noreen Andersen; Mary Andersen. Alumni Weekend 2007.

Dear Father Ted,

Our grandparents left Mayo and Kerry with faith.
Our parents worked a lifetime with hope.
You helped make their dreams, and ours, come true.
And, we love you for it!
We are grateful beyond words.
Thank you, thank you.

Fondly,

The Honorable Sheila O'Brien
Class of '77, '80 JD
Justice, Illinois Appellate Court

Patti O'Brien Reising
Class of '82

Ellen O'Brien, MD
Class of '82

⚬ᘒᕽ

Dear Father Ted,

It is my pleasure to write to you about the decision you made thirty-five years ago to include women in the undergraduate study program of our university. My only regret is that I graduated five years before your momentous decision. Nevertheless, I have seen Notre Dame change since the election to go coed and it has been nothing but for the good. I remember my father was on the board of trustees at the time when you and the board made the decision. While the overwhelming majority of people that contacted my father about the decision were for coed education, there were of course a few against, some of them rather vocal. They said "Notre Dame would never be the same" and that "you have ruined one hundred-plus years of male tradition." Of course, they were right. In one sense Notre Dame will never be the same. No place should stay the same and should all adjust to the times within the confines of their goals. Notre Dame has been so positively changed by the presence of women. I will be the first to admit that my years at Notre Dame were wonderful but in a sense not as good as they could have been. We have come to a much better place since Notre Dame became coed.

My firstborn is a girl, Catherine. We call her Casey. She was also able to attend

President George W. Bush and Father Ted at Commencement 2001.

the university. Hers was a wonderful experience. While not intending to, she met her husband there and both of them are devoted followers of the university. I do recall my father and I talking about the fact that they had decided to make Walsh Hall a female dorm. Both of us had lived in Walsh and had a very strong love for the hall. I will admit though that when Casey was born I saw the wisdom of the decision although she spent her four years in Farley Hall.

Father Ted, I honestly think that, throughout the history of Notre Dame, students there have received a first-class college education. However, the perception in other people's minds was, before your arrival, that Notre Dame was a good regional Catholic university with a national reputation in sports. You, of course, have changed that and we can now be proud of the fact that Notre Dame is one of the top schools in the world. You and the people you surround yourself with changed all that and we will be forever grateful, and I do think history will record that one of your great decisions was making Notre Dame coed.

Sincerely,

Joseph I. O'Neill, III
Class of '67
Trustee, Managing Partner, O'Neill Properties Limited, Midland, Texas

My Dear Uncle Ted,

Here I am joining my sisters from Notre Dame in thanking you for bringing women into the ND community. For this and so many other decisions you have proven an insightful leader of our university. Your leadership extends far beyond ND which resulted in bringing the world back to campus. Obviously, I know you as an uncle as well as a priest and a president emeritus. You sent me a telegram from one of your far-reaching travels on my First Communion day and you celebrated my marriage some thirty years later. You have ever been an example of living one's faith, even down to the photographs of you and three popes that hung in our home throughout our youth. Your midnight calls to Mom updating her on your life while catching up with hers were exciting touchstones of a life in full throttle. (Riding with you in that Mustang of yours should never be repeated but illustrated that I had learned to resort to prayer in times of trial.)

Molly Kinder '01, first woman Irish Guard.
Reprinted with the permission of the Notre Dame Sports Information Department.

Families are funny, though. Your visits to upstate New York would always mean excitement. Our visits to ND would give us access to you and your office, which always felt like a gift. I was the first female member of our family admitted to Notre Dame. When I arrived at ND, I felt awkward about visiting you as I learned that you were more than an uncle. You were a very important man! I assumed you were too busy with the running of our major university. I didn't tell a soul that I was your niece (although it was known she was among us and so I had fun joining in the speculation as to who that niece was). One Friday night in early November, you called my dorm room. I was out but my roommate, Marilyn Tomasko, answered the phone and took the message "Have Maureen call her Uncle Ted." You left a campus number. I went to your office that night and you asked all about life on campus. What was it like to be one of the first women? How were the boys treating me? You laughed to learn that the Sorin men would hold up cards one to ten when women passed rating their looks and chalked it up as growing pains (theirs as well as ours!). You were impressed to learn how many women were participating in sports and extracurricular activities. You were so eager to learn how it was working from one who would speak to you as a member of the family. I came more regularly after that and with some of my dorm mates.

There was a day in my freshman year when I was accepted into the Innsbruck program against all odds. The thirty-six students were gathered as a collective and told the plan that would consume their life for the next year. I was surrounded at that point by people, many of whom remain my finest friends and who have seen me through many a memorable and defining day. On that memorable day, I came to your office to let you in on my joy. I brought with me a small handful of friends all destined for Europe and you spoke of your time in Rome as a student and what that meant to you. You told of what you missed at Notre Dame but carried all that our alma mater offered with you, like a warm cloak in winter. We were heady with anticipation. I felt so blessed to be part of the ND community. Although I couldn't know it then, it was Notre Dame and all that followed that led me on happily throughout what has been my life.

Some twenty-seven years later many of us gathered to have Mass in your office on our reunion weekend. You were keen to hear our stories, interested to learn what had become of us since living at Notre Dame. I remarked at that point that I had never really left ND. I have worn the ring on my finger since graduation as a daily reminder of my belonging to a community so unique, supportive, spiritual, giving, and thoughtful. I have simply brought ND with me to share with those less fortunate.

A few months ago, one of my English friends asked me what it was like attending a Catholic university. I am surrounded by those who would argue that there was no finer experience than Oxford University. I explained that being educated in an

Standing: Janet Noble, Stephanie Urillo, Anne Dilenschneider, Mary Moira, Maureen O'Neill, and Marilyn Sammarco. Below are Terry Malony, Father Ted Hesburgh, and Linda Curgian. This was taken in his office at their twenty-fifth college reunion on June 8, 2002.

environment filled with the passion of one's faith and the rigor of intellectual challenge was a privilege beyond any I have known since.

We have you to thank for your wisdom and good common sense in admitting women. As I am sure you know, last year we all electronically "feted" one another on the celebration of turning fifty. The ND women's community was never more united. We are a modern-age family and we have you to thank for your leadership, your convictions, and for your willingness to convert Walsh Hall (and others) to women! God bless.

Much love and many thanks,

Maureen O'Neill
Class of '77
Director of Development, School of Law, University of Oxford, Oxford, England

Father Ted,

As I sit at the Grotto amidst the delicate snow of this winter night, I'm compelled to reflect on a few transforming elements of Notre Dame life: the unspoken secrets and subtleties of our campus that serve as the lifeblood of the university. The scene of the Grotto evokes memories of the life-altering moments that regularly occur in this sacred space.

I recall one reflective evening at the Grotto with my college roommate. She began sharing accounts of her grandfather, who had the pleasure of working with you at a threshold moment in the living history of Notre Dame. Father Ted, it was your virtues and strength that paved the way for women's admission. At the time, many were resistant to opening the classroom doors to women. However, you remained unceasingly resilient. Powerful figures were adverse to the progressive and universal ideals you willingly embraced. My roommate's grandfather personalized these stories of your immense courage, perseverance, prudence, and will.

This coeducational landmark, in Notre Dame's narrative, transformed the lives and opportunities for generations to come. As I sit here, watching the snow softly cover Our Lady's mantle, I can't help but think of her warm joy as she saw you so courageously responding to such a call. This educational reform allowed her to look down on the everyday scenes of the Grotto and view women gradually lighting their own votives, dedicated as students to the vision and mission you so boldly forged.

Father Ted, Mother Teresa, and Tim O'Meara, Notre Dame Provost.

Marriage proposals between Domers are commonly shared amongst the candles of the Grotto. Oftentimes, such engagements are the culmination of countless evenings couples share in prayer and reflection before the Grotto scene. Marital unions within the Notre Dame family are the genesis of holy families that serve as testaments of selfless love to our society. Beyond the classroom dynamics, women's presence at this university marked a cultural transformation that facilitated these profound lay vocations to serve our Church and society at large. Father Ted, these beautiful unions and their powerful witness to our world are a result of your passion and vision for Our Lady's university.

Father Ted, as an undergraduate I seized your ever-present "open door policy," which invites all members of the Notre Dame family to visit your office at will. It was weeks prior to my embarking on my first excursion to Mother Teresa's Home for the Dying in Kolkata, India. After reaching your office and being graciously welcomed, you took precious time to share your reflections on Mother Teresa's words and inspirations. Your words cultivated a unique lens for viewing my time of service and prayer with her beloved Missionaries of Charity. Those moments in the presence of the poorest of the poor deepened my perspective on interpersonal relationships and prompted my personal calling to medicine and public service. Your wisdom and reflections catalyzed this powerful experience. I continue to be grateful that Our Lady nudged me from the Grotto bench to your doorstep.

Now, five years later, serving as the youngest university trustee, your open door policy remains. I am regularly blessed with your insights and guidance on my evolving vocation. I also have the honor of viewing other trustees gain similar fulfillment and direction from your counsel. Their profuse gratitude is an expression of your compelling presence in their family lives and professional paths. This beyond-warranted respect manifests most strikingly in trustee meetings; where the vacillation on a particular topic is immediately extinguished with your recommendations and reflections.

Beyond these Notre Dame encounters, I've had the privilege of beholding the global impact of your life of service. My Notre Dame experiences served as a springboard for further educational and public service pursuits. Regardless of country, creed, or academic circle, people across the globe invariably inquire on your happenings. I have witnessed this immense respect from Vatican officials, to Maryknoll missionaries in Thailand, to government officials in India, to Harvard Fellowships committees, to Yale medical professionals.

The shining presence of the statue of Our Lady serves as the epicenter of the Grotto scene. She lovingly gazes on all who seek her intercession. Our Lady also stands as a vivid witness to the feminism the women of Notre Dame strive to embody; one of the loving presence, strength, selflessness, and generosity. She has interceded for me, through your guidance, to travel the world serving in her name. From the desolate remote areas of Thailand and Honduras, to the streets of Kolkata, to the boardroom of Notre Dame, to the hospital medical wards of Yale, and now to the forums at the Kennedy School of Government, she has called for service. Your vision and courage incited these transformational opportunities.

Tonight, I light another votive, to share my deepest gratitude for your influence. The Grotto's reflection, I am confident, will continue to illuminate this university in your name and Our Lady's.

Yours in Notre Dame,

Keri Ochs Oxley
Class of '04
Trustee, Medical Student, Yale University

Dear Father Ted,

You have made many important decisions during your lengthy and remarkable tenure as president of Notre Dame. My family and I were the beneficiaries of one and the women of America another; the latter with huge impact.

Your willingness to take a chance on me as your football coach and include us as members of the Notre Dame family has had a profound effect on all of our lives. For that, we are eternally grateful.

From my vantage point, I have been able to evaluate firsthand the positive effects that have resulted from your decision to make Notre Dame coeducational. My daughter and daughter-in-law became graduates and like other Notre Dame women, have benefited enormously from your decision. This book celebrating your 90th birthday is filled with accolades from women graduates and speaks volumes about their appreciation for

Father Ted, Ara Parseghian, Father Ned Joyce hear that the 1969 Cotton Bowl Committee has chosen Notre Dame.

allowing them the Notre Dame experience. Women have made remarkable progress in all fields and you played a significant part in that movement.

Happy 90th Birthday.

Your old football coach,

Ara Parseghian
Head Football Coach 1964–1974
National Champions: 1966, 1973

Dear Father Ted,

Thank you for sharing with our family the Notre Dame community: the community that has showered our family with prayers, the community that has cried tears of sorrow while our hearts have broken, the community that has held us up while we have staggered in our pain.

My husband and I, both graduates of 1977, never expected that the Notre Dame community would play such a strong and significant role in our family when we first married. We started our married life with the expectations of raising a large family with children we hoped would be caring and loving individuals. Little did we expect that one day three of our four children would be diagnosed with a rare disease that would eventually claim their lives.

You have always led by example. Throughout your tenure at ND, you have always put the needs of others above your own and emphasized the necessity of helping those in stress. My family can attest that you were very successful in teaching the Notre Dame students to lend a helping hand. We have been blessed by the Notre Dame family time and time again.

Notre Dame graduates have helped to sponsor research into the disease that claimed our children. They have donated millions of dollars and contributed many hours into organizing fund-raisers. They are responsible for the advances in understanding the disorder and moving the research toward a treatment and a cure.

You also gave us a special moment that I am forever grateful. My family including my husband, Mike, our children, Ara, Marcia, and Christa had come to celebrate Mass with you in your office. We were still feeling the jagged, searing pain of the recent death of our second son, Michael. You embraced us in our sorrow with your gentle words. After Mass you paused and looked at Mike and I and asked if we would like our two daughters to be anointed. You quietly blessed and anointed them without frightening these young children who were just slowly coming to the realization that they were also dying.

That anointing also helped me in my spiritual anxiety. It helped to ease some of the confusion that comes with the many "whys" surrounding the illness and death of a child. The anointing helped me to understand how important it would be to celebrate each precious moment with my children.

Thank you for these gifts,

Cindy (Buescher) Parseghian
Class of '77
President, Ara Parseghian Medical Foundation, Arizona

Dear Father Ted,

Let me be one of the many in the Notre Dame community to congratulate you on the momentous occasion of your 90th birthday and the thirty-fifth anniversary of coeducation at Our Lady's university.

When I reminisce about my career at Notre Dame, I think fondly of many aspects of my four years on campus. Obtaining my bachelor's degree in business marketing stands out as my greatest accomplishment. In my twenty-plus years since graduation, I have applied many of the concepts acquired in the classroom in professional life.

While at Notre Dame and since then, I was able to enjoy a measure of success on the basketball court. During each season, Coach Phelps asked you to say Mass and sit on our bench during a home game. This to me was one of the highlights of each year.

In your homily, you always made the analogy that illustrated how the lessons from the readings for that day directly related to athletics but, more importantly, to our lives after Notre Dame. For this, I thank you.

When I enrolled at Notre Dame in the fall of 1979, women had already emerged as a very important segment of our student population. Whether it was in the classroom, in the dining halls, or at social/cultural events, women brought a unique dimension to the student body. As a student and athlete myself, it has been especially gratifying in recent years to see the success of so many of our women's teams, most notably basketball, fencing, and soccer.

To me, one of the greatest accomplishments during your tenure as president was the inclusion of women in the university's student body. With your foresight and leadership, in one simple word, they "completed" Notre Dame.

I echo the sentiments of so many others in the Notre Dame family. You are truly the essence and embodiment of what this university means to me and to all alumni— women and men alike.

John Paxson and ND Basketball Coach Digger Phelps

Sincerely,

John Paxson
Class of '83
General Manager, Chicago Bulls
NBA Championship Teammate 1991–1993

Father Theodore Hesburgh was named president of Notre Dame in 1952. Two decades later he made the decision to go coeducational. After all, Notre Dame means Our Lady. Why not women at her school? Today nearly half the university student body is coed.

Knowing that varsity athletics was important, Father Ted made me chairman of the Basketball Department to build a Division I women's basketball team. Mary DiStanislao was hired as the first coach. Muffet McGraw replaced her to bring our first National Champions in 2001. In the last two decades we have become very competitive at the national level in women's sports at Notre Dame.

To me, Father Hesburgh is a living saint. What Mother Teresa was as a nun, Father Hesburgh is as a priest. He has a power of inspiration that he is able to convey to people. He can inspire people to dream and go beyond their own perceived limits. He has done this to many women and to me who have known him on and off campus.

Sincerely,

Richard "Digger" Phelps
Head Basketball Coach 1971–1991

Basketball Coach Digger Phelps.

Dear Father Ted,

You are one of the giants of our lifetimes. I remember, like it was yesterday, working in the Huddle, the campus milkshake/ice cream place (no longer there), and I looked out the side window and saw you, the new president of Notre Dame with a shovel in your hand turning the ground over for the first new building of your reign. What a great-looking man, a dead ringer for Tyrone Power. To me that was the beginning of your story at Notre Dame—the story continues to this day.

Years later I went back to Notre Dame to cover President Ronald Reagan's speech on campus. It was his first after the assassination attempt that almost killed him. How

Larry King, Father Ted, and Regis Philbin in the football stadium press box.

gracious you were in your introduction. How proud I was of Notre Dame that day. And on my way to the Convocation Center to see his speech, I saw for the first time, the young ladies of our school. For someone who came out of the dark era of all boys, it was quite a shock. But how great these girls looked and what a terrific addition they were. And it was the first time I thought of the possibility that my two daughters, Joanna and Jennifer, might one day be a part of Notre Dame as well. Of course you made that happen. You paved the way for coeducation. You paved the way for so much of today's Notre Dame. We can never thank you enough. Happy Birthday, Father Ted. We all love you.

My best,

Regis Philbin
Class of '53
Emmy Award–Winning Host,
*Live with Regis and Kelly*

Father Ted, Regis Philbin, and retired football coach Frank Leahy.

Dear Father Ted,

When I arrived at Notre Dame in August of 1972, it was a dreary rainy day, but I was struck with how green and lush the campus was, especially in contrast to the desert climate of my small rural hometown of Grand Junction, Colorado. I wasn't coming there to be a pioneer or to prove anything about women. I came because I wanted a college that challenged me academically and offered me the opportunity to explore and express my Catholic faith. Your gift of coeducation at Notre Dame opened up not only the doors of the Golden Dome, but of the world both inside myself and beyond the horizon of the time and place in which I lived.

My most treasured memory of you is from the summer of 1974, when I was going into my junior year at Notre Dame. I was working at a small grocery store in Aspen and I read in the local newspaper that you were attending the Aspen Institute as a featured speaker. As a gesture of hospitality, I left a note at your hotel welcoming you to my beautiful home state, and I offered to take you to dinner if your schedule would permit. I was totally shocked when you called and accepted my invitation. I (boldly) asked if you would like to join me and some family members at our nearby cabin on the river, thinking you might like that instead of going to a restaurant. We had a delightful family evening enjoying the crisp mountain air, exchanging stories (including a few fishing tales), and hearing about your many involvements and adventures. Your warmth and wisdom engaged us all, and I marveled at how your world spanned the distance of being with me and my family on our cabin deck to dining with presidents and popes. It was a special experience of belonging to the Notre Dame family.

The following day was your departure from Aspen, and you asked if I could give you a ride to the airport. When I picked you up, you brought along a friend of yours, Lester Brown, who was also at the conference. As we were standing near the landing strip waiting for the small planes to board, you told me about Mr. Brown's work addressing the devastating world food crisis. I recall how he noticed a small injured bird on the ground and picked it up, cradling it gently in his hands. As the three of us looked at the little bird in poignant silence for a moment thinking about its fate, I thought of the fate of the millions of people around the world who would suffer that day. It was time for boarding, so we said our good-byes and I watched the two of you walk toward the planes. Then I got in my car and went to work.

There was something about that brief introduction to Lester Brown, whom I had never heard of before, and briefly hearing about his work from you that inspired me to learn more about hunger issues. When I got back to campus in the fall of 1974, I connected with some other students who were also interested in the world food crisis, and what

Ceyl Prinster '76, president-elect, Notre Dame Alumni Association, 2007–2008, Father Ted, and Ceyl's daughter, Megan Sheehan '06.

evolved was the World Hunger Coalition, an organization that is still active on campus today. Little did I know at the time that at the Aspen Institute that summer, Lester Brown was working with you and other influential people in attendance to found the Worldwatch Institute, which has had a profound influence in the fields of food security and sustainable development. For you to "bring me along" like a member of the family is a tribute to your fatherly and priestly mindset that is inclusive and affirming, and which sows seeds of connectedness and inspiration wherever you go.

I am grateful to you, Father Ted, for what you did to make Notre Dame a possibility for me, and now also for my daughter, Megan Sheehan '06, who is a second-generation Notre Dame woman. We know that the best way to thank you is to do what we learned so well at Notre Dame—to seek God, study the world, and serve humanity.

God bless you, Father Ted, on your 90th birthday. All of us in the Notre Dame family will love you forever.

Ceyl Prinster
Class of '76
President-Elect, Notre Dame Alumni Association 2007–2008

Dear Father Hesburgh,

I once read an anonymous quote, "The purpose in life is finding out who you are, and the meaning of life is giving it away." Truly, words seem completely inadequate to thank you for the gift of coeducation at Notre Dame. Being part of the Notre Dame family has been my vehicle for discovering the purpose and meaning for my life.

Although I grew up just over an hour away from campus in Schererville, Indiana, I never imagined that I would attend the university. Yet, during the late '80s and early '90s, I found myself welcomed into the Notre Dame family. During my time as an undergraduate, the ratio of men to women was four to one, so most of my friends were men with whom I shared mutual academic and service interests. However, I also became close to several extraordinary women in my own dorm, Lyons Hall.

Following graduation, I moved to Nashville, Tennessee, to get a master's of divinity at Vanderbilt University and worked for five years in the domestic violence movement with both victims and perpetrators. As part of my field education, I served as lay pastor of an inner-city church and as a hospital chaplain, both of which helped me to discern my vocation. Also, I volunteered as community service coordinator on the board of directors in the Alumni Club of Nashville.

In 1998, I returned to Notre Dame to work in Student Affairs and as rector of Pangborn Hall until 2005. It was truly a privilege to share so intimately in the lives of nearly 1,000 women over those seven years. While working for Student Affairs, I became immersed in the larger campus culture in ways that did not exist when I was an undergraduate—most importantly through the Gender Relations Center (GRC). That's the newest department in Student Affairs, the only such center in the nation's top twenty universities, and the first and only one of its kind within collegiate student affairs offices nationwide. I am the founding director.

The GRC was the outgrowth of proposals written by Brooke Norton, first female student body president (2001–2002), and Kaitlyn Redfield, Pangborn Hall senator (2003–2004). They realized that the creation of a department exclusively aimed at women's issues might be passé in 2004, since the student population was nearly half women and half men at that time. They felt the needs of women matriculating into a formerly male institution had changed after thirty years of coeducation. In an effort to design a cutting-edge initiative, Kaitlyn recommended the university create a "Gender Relations Center" to put women and men in dialogue with each other, thereby ideally encouraging collaboration between the sexes on issues of gender and sexuality as they relate to the Catholic tradition. In September 2004, at the charge of Father Mark Poorman, vice president for Student Affairs, and under the direct supervision of associate vice president for Student Affairs, Ann Stockmann Firth ('81, '84 JD), the GRC opened its doors in LaFortune.

In three years, the GRC has addressed a variety of issues affecting our university women and men. This includes: dating and relating, competition and perfectionism, hook-up culture, femininity and masculinity, sexuality and sexual health, body image and eating disorders, homosexuality and homophobia, sexism and stereotyping gender roles, domestic violence and abuse, violent and controlling behaviors, marriage and divorce, and sexual harassment and sexual assault. It's become a place where women and men can engage in respectful dialogue and explore issues of identity, relationships, and equality. Ultimately, the GRC hopes to follow in your footsteps, as we seek to create a healthier climate for women and men at the University of Notre Dame in the new millennium.

Because of you, I was afforded the ability to be an undergraduate student at the University of Notre Dame, and I was also presented the opportunity to become connected to extraordinary life experiences, mentors, and role models. They have moved me to become better than I thought I could be. Because of you, I was given the most precious gift—a Notre Dame education that challenged me to become an integrated human being with a sense of purpose and meaning in the world. The moment of grace in this particular story is that my vocation has led me back home to Notre Dame. I am most grateful. Thank you so very much!

With prayers and best wishes,

Heather M. Rakoczy
Class of '93
Director, Notre Dame Gender Relations Center

Dear Father Ted,

On behalf of all the millions of female Notre Dame fans/alumni/family members, I want to tell you how grateful we are for the gift of coeducation. It was your foresight and vision that allowed little girls, who sat next to their brothers watching the Irish take the field every Saturday, to share in the dream of attending our wonderful university. It was you who eliminated the exclusivity and initiated what we now call the "Notre Dame family."

On a personal note, I want to tell you how much I have appreciated my experience at Notre Dame. As I was sorting through the different scholarship opportunities,

I decided after only visiting the Notre Dame campus that this was the place for me. It was the only university with a special blend of academic and athletic excellence as well as a devoted focus on community and faith. As a female student athlete, it was an honor to wear a uniform that boasted the name of a university I grew to love dearly.

Besides an outstanding education, I learned many valuable life lessons: how to succeed with humility . . . utilizing my resources to help others . . . experiencing my faith on a daily basis.

The beautiful thing about the "Notre Dame experience" is that it keeps on going. My post-collegiate basketball career has taken me across the world, where I have established amazing relationships through my affiliation with Notre Dame. Thank you for opening the doors so women like me (and many others) were given the opportunity to gain the knowledge and experiences from Notre Dame that have allowed us to make a positive and productive influence in the world.

Much love and admiration,

Ruth Riley
Class of '01
Member, San Antonio Silver Stars, WNBA
Olympic Gold Medal Winner
NCAA Irish Women's Basketball Championship Team
Member, Detroit Shock, WNBA Champions 2006

Ruth Riley '01 scores against Purdue University to win the 2001 NCAA Women's Basketball Tournament. The 2001 Associated Press Player of the Year, Riley, a psychology major, was on the dean's list every semester.

ᘓᕕ

Dear Father Ted,

What a pleasure it is to thank you for coeducation at Notre Dame as we near the thirty-fifth year of women on campus.

I am honored to be the first in what I hope will be a long line of Keough women at Notre Dame—my sister, Eileen, my brother Michael's wife, Jinny, and their daughters, Betsy and Katie—all have jumped at the opportunity. I have delighted in seeing my best friends' daughters as Notre Dame student and graduates. Women following their sisters and mothers to Our Lady's university must have been part of your vision, as it is among the finest of Notre Dame traditions.

People often ask if it was hard to be in that first small group of women on campus. For me, the answer is a resounding "No!" We were making history. My female peers were strong, bright, fun, family oriented, and just as excited to be there as I was. You gave us wonderful women mentors—Sister John Miriam, Jane Pitz, and later, Sister Jean Lenz, and so many others. You visited us in our dorms and always let us know you were so clearly determined for us to feel welcome at Notre Dame. Even at eighteen, I knew there couldn't have been many other groups to have had Father Ted Hesburgh as chair of the welcoming committee!

My parents and I still talk about our Mass at the Grotto during orientation weekend in 1972. On a perfectly sparkling Notre Dame morning, you turned to Mary atop the Golden Dome and apologized that it took so long to welcome her daughters to her campus. As a member of that freshman class, that moment reminded me from the outset that Notre Dame is indeed Our Lady's university and, no matter what lay ahead for us, she and you were glad to have us here.

Every time I visit Notre Dame, I remember the first time I set foot on campus with my dad. I knew before I applied that Notre Dame was special. I knew that if I had the opportunity to be in that historic group of women, I couldn't miss it. I had no idea at the time that Notre Dame would be my life's spiritual home—the place where I can always speak freely with Our Lady and come back to center. I am grateful every day that I have had the opportunity to be a part of the university that lives with the example of Mary's great faith, humility, and grace. As a Catholic woman, I cannot imagine having missed that.

You may have done a great thing for Notre Dame, but you also did a wonderful thing for women. This woman, in particular, is forever deeply honored and grateful. Thank you, Father Ted!

With love, gratitude, and admiration,

Shayla Keough Rumley
Class of '76
Trustee, Attorney, Atlanta, Georgia

Dear Father Hesburgh,

Your leadership of the University of Notre Dame, and championship of the decision to alter the admission criteria to allow women, has redefined the future of this great institution.

It has personally enriched the lives of thousands of women and more personally my own. The values-based education offered by the university established a firm foundation and guiding principles that I have relied upon in the practice of my own profession and in my life.

The community of Notre Dame is indeed broad and its inclusion of women among its distinguished members only enhances its strength and value.

Sincerely,

Laura Jonaus Schumacher
Class of '85
General Counsel, Abbott Laboratories Inc., North Chicago, Illinois

Dear Father Hesburgh,

At twenty-two years old, my proudest accomplishments revolve around being a woman at Notre Dame. The opportunity to be here is something for which I am eternally grateful. As a daughter of members of the classes of 1977 and 1979, I followed in the footsteps of my parents in the fall of 2003. I see in them the best of Notre Dame: dedication to faith, family, education, and serving the greater community. I strive to live up to their example.

When I was student body president, I read a note from the first female student body president, Brooke Norton, to the second female president, Libby Bishop. It read, "Notre Dame will be a better place because of you." While this inspired me personally to run for student body president the following year, I find this statement to hold greater importance. Notre Dame is a better place because of its female students.

As the third female student body president in Notre Dame's history, I frequently field questions about being a woman in a leadership position at a traditionally male university. I proudly reply that gender was not an issue during my campaign or during my presidency. Rather, I have been evaluated by my peers based upon my policies and practices in office. Thirty-five years after the introduction of coeducation, I give

## THE OBSERVER

*The Independent Newspaper Serving Notre Dame and Saint Mary's*

VOLUME 40 : ISSUE 87 — TUESDAY, FEBRUARY 14, 2006 — NDSMCOBSERVER.COM

# Shappell-Andrichik secures majority

*General election vote decides race for student body president, vice president*

By MARY KATE MALONE
Assistant News Editor

Juniors Lizzi Shappell and Bill Andrichik ran away with the victory in the student government president and vice president election Monday, winning 51.78 percent of the vote and narrowly escaping a run-off — the first time a ticket has done so since 1999.

The pair will take on its new posts April 1. Shappell will replace current student body president Dave Baron, and Andrichik will replace Shappell, the current vice president.

Typically no ticket wins the majority vote in the general, and that results in a run-off election between the two with the highest number of votes. But this year was different, as Shappell and Andrichik managed to clinch the majority and avoid a week of historically dogged campaigning leading up to the

see ELECTION/page 6

*Losing tickets look toward future, remain supportive of elected administration*

By KATHLEEN MCDONNELL
News Writer

While not all candidates at the national level exhibit graceful concessions, those who campaigned to lead Notre Dame's student body next year did so with humility on Monday evening.

Before the Lizzi Shappell-Bill Andrichik ticket achieved an outright majority — rare for a student body election — some candidates had been counting on having a last shot at campaigning before the assumed run-off election on Thursday.

Despite this, the losing tickets quickly reoriented after the results were announced and were already planning how to positively impact the University next academic year.

Junior Jason Laws and sophomore Bob Costa took special interest in

see FUTURE/page 6

MATTHEW SMEDBERG/The Observer
Vice president-elect Bill Andrichik embraces president-elect Lizzi Shappell after learning of their victory in Monday's general election.

credit for this focus on performance rather than gender to you, Father Hesburgh, and the first classes of women that established female students as equal participants in the undergraduate experience.

In 1842, Father Sorin founded a remarkable university; however, with the introduction of women to the university in 1972, you made this university great. I see women excelling in every college, major, athletic team, and student organization. Thank you, Father Hesburgh, on behalf of the current female members of our student body, for the opportunity to attend Our Lady's university.

In Notre Dame,

Elizabeth S. Shappell
Class of '07
Student Body President 2006–2007

Dear Father Ted,

It was December of my senior year, and I walked into my high school counselor's office with a letter and information brochure from the University of Notre Dame. Mrs. Davis was always supportive of my ambitions to attend college, but she tended to direct most of her students, including me, to schools within our home state of Texas. When I showed her the letter from Notre Dame, she quickly glanced at it, looked up and remarked, "Isn't this an all-boys' school?" I was not sure that she was wrong, but I left the office determined to find out all that I could about this place.

I must admit that I am not an alumna who grew up always knowing she wanted to go to Notre Dame. In fact, up to the time that I received this letter, I had no idea that the university existed. Mind you, this is no criticism of the university's marketing efforts. In this small Texas farm town of a Dairy Queen and one stop light, generations of close-knit families reside in the same neighborhoods and few people speak of colleges beyond the University of Texas or Texas A&M. And even these schools, for many, seemed far away.

With that as a backdrop, I believe it is nothing short of divine providence that Notre Dame came to my attention through a three-fold brochure in my mailbox. It may not sound so providential, since thousands are mailed every year; however, I never had watched a Notre Dame football or basketball game. I did not know a current student or alumnus. I was not even sure where the school was located. For some reason, however, the images on this brochure, among many, and the description of the campus and coursework, grabbed my attention. Within two weeks, I applied.

I waited anxiously as winter changed to spring. Finally, I received a phone call informing me that I was accepted. My father, who expected me to attend West Point, was a little less than pleased. As a retired World War II veteran, he grew up when African-Americans had few choices among colleges and careers. My mother had passed away the year before from breast cancer, and I knew that he was most concerned that I would find a safe and nurturing environment that would provide me with a steady career path. He was also unsure how his small retirement salary would support four years at a private institution.

After a visit to the campus and observing that, in fact, the campus was coed, I realized this is where I wanted to spend four years. With the assistance of financial aid counselors, I convinced my father that it was possible, often saying, "Dad, if you are concerned about my well-being, I think, that from a father's perspective, the next best thing to your daughter going to a military academy is having her attend a Catholic university." He finally surrendered.

I share this story to underscore that Notre Dame was an unexpected gift to me over twenty years ago, and for years since then, it has impacted my life through friendships, faith, and work. I have watched as many other women, and men, pass through this university and leave more knowledgable, more confident, and more connected to their faith and to the Church. Hopefully, we are all more aware of our capabilities, more compassionate of our limitations and mistakes and those of others, and less likely to let fear dictate our choices. With God's grace, we are better leaders, parents, sons, and daughters. Notre Dame has helped so many of us find and stay true to our path.

Father Ted, I could not be more grateful to you for your vision and wisdom in seeing the value of coeducation. I could not be more grateful that my high school counselor was wrong. Thank you.

With gratitude,

Frances L. Shavers
Class of '90
Chief of Staff, Special Assistant to the President, Univerity of Notre Dame

Dear Father Ted,

The year was 1979, and I was sitting in the Grotto with my younger sister Maggie. We were both students at the University of Notre Dame, struggling to achieve in our academic endeavors, working out to maintain our athletic challenges, and praying for our families and friends. One fall evening, you walked by and to our surprise you called us by our first names, Carol and Maggie. We were so impressed that you knew our names, understood who we were, and cared for us. That single moment is one of millions that you have provided to all of your loyal followers.

Thank you for inviting women to attend the University of Notre Dame and thank you for making the transition exciting and fruitful.

Sincerely yours,

Carol Lally Shields, MD
Class of '79, '05 Honorary
Captain, Women's Basketball Team, 1978–1979
Ocular Oncologist, Philadelphia, Pennsylvania

Carol Lally Shields '79, '05 Honorary—captain, Women's Basketball Team 1978-1979 and first ND woman varsity athlete to win the Byron Kaneley Award for Excellence in Academics. She graduated summa cum laude with a 3.91 cumulative grade point average. Today she is a world-renowned ophthalmologist.
Reprinted with the permission of the Notre Dame Sports Information Department.

Dear Father Ted,

The women in my family have a tradition of coming in second. My mother was in the second class of admitted women at Notre Dame, and then I had the honor of being the second female student body president at Notre Dame. I've learned that being second isn't all that bad.

My mother was a math major, and often found herself as one of the few women in her math and science courses during those early years of coeducation. She vividly remembers the anticipation, energy, and charged emotions on campus when in September of 1973 the tennis champion Billie Jean King beat Bobby Riggs in the famous "Battle of the Sexes" match. It was a victory for women's equality all over the world, and on campus it helped to reinforce the status of women as equals, and assert that "they were here to stay."

Almost thirty years later, following in my mother's footsteps (OK, and my father's and grandfather's), I quickly found how much women's equality at Notre Dame had flourished. But yet it was surprising that it wasn't until 2001 did we have our first female student body president. I cherish the several times I got to meet with you when I was student body president. I will always remember staring at the photo you have up on your wall, of you and Martin Luther King Jr. holding crossed hands at a peace rally. In all the previous photos I had ever seen of Martin Luther King Jr., I remember noticing how much he stood out and shone, and everyone else in the photos always faded into the background. What was striking about your photo was how you looked so great and tall standing next to him. It seemed so natural, you and him holding hands.

Recently I was speaking to an internationally known corporate trainer, after a training event, and when talking about the focus and future strategy of training, he stated confidently to me, "women are the future." I can imagine that this is something you said often, back in the late '60s and '70s, when advocating for coeducation at Notre Dame. It's nice to see that the rest of the world is finally catching up with you.

On behalf of my mother and I, just wanted to say thanks Father Ted, for everything. Your vision and leadership has inspired us and I am confident it will continue to inspire others for generations to come.

Libby Bishop Shields
Class of '03
Student Body President 2002–2003, London, England

Dear Father Ted,

I began my journey at Notre Dame in the second class of women in the fall of 1973 at seventeen. I graduated from a Catholic all-girls' high school in St. Paul, Minnesota, with twenty-three girls in my graduating class. I would like to be able to say that going to Notre Dame was my dream from early childhood; that in being in the second class of women at Notre Dame, I felt like a pioneer in a country where estrogen levels were almost as low in that population of students as they are currently in the population of my gracefully aging sister graduates. But that was not the case. The fact of the matter is that my mother filled out my application and sent it in and I was accepted. My brother ('73 BA, '76 JD) and sister ('76 BA, '79 MA, '83 PhD) were students at Notre Dame. Where else would I go? My father and mother—both Irish Catholic—considered it a foregone conclusion and being seventeen without a clue, so did I. Sometimes clueless-ness is a good thing.

My father would talk to me about Father Ted. "Go see him," he would urge. "No way," I thought. I am a seventeen-year-old freshman and have the audacity to try to speak with this man considered by my family to be the single most important American Catholic? I don't think so. But my father was relentless: "Did you go see Father Hes-burgh?" "Would you get your lazy self up and out and go see Father Hesburgh?" Alright already. And so I did—reluctantly. Being seventeen, clueless, and having a father who knew what was important was not just a good thing, it was life altering.

So I went to see Father Hesburgh. I was embarrassed and told him that my brother and sister were students, that I was a freshman and that my father had insisted that I visit him. None of this seemed to interest Father Hesburgh. He wanted to know about me. I had little to tell. He wanted to know why Notre Dame? I was humiliated to ad-mit that I had given it very little independent thought and that I was just following my brother and sister. But that was the truth and God help me, I told him. He smiled and sat me down and told me that I was very lucky and he regaled me with stories of his travels and the poverty and human rights deprivations that he had seen.

I was mesmerized and ashamed, though that is not why Father Hesburgh told me these stories. He asked me what I intended to do with my life and I told him that I, again, was clueless. He told me that I needed to pray; that I needed to thank God for my blessings; that I needed to flourish where I was planted; that I needed to repay God and my parents for my gifts by using them. It was almost like a confessional. I was having a face-to-face confession with Father Hesburgh. For me (as I am sure it would have been for many of you) this was profound. I think I might have been at a kegger the night before; I think I was trying to figure out how to get my homework done so I could get out again that very night. Instead, Father Hesburgh walked with me to the Grotto and we prayed together. It was quiet, cold, and it was dark except for the soft glow of the candles and the stirring of the fall leaves in the wind. We prayed to the Holy Mother and Father Hesburgh told me to ask for guidance in this important year.

I prayed and asked Our Mother to be with me, to direct me, to help me make the most of this gift of Notre Dame and family. Father Hesburgh and I walked back from the Grotto together that night and he told me that he advocated for coeducation at Notre Dame because he thought that women would have a "civilizing" influence on the student population. He told me that he was shocked to be walking behind a group of girls the week before and hearing them use foul language; "cursing like sailors," I think he said. (I was wondering if I had been in that group on the walk home from the kegger.) He told me that we women of Notre Dame have a mission to transform the school; that we came to the school to bring balance to a family. He told me that I needed to know that I could achieve anything that I wanted with the help of God. He told me that I needed to do my part to complete the Notre Dame family. He said goodbye to me and told me to visit often. He wanted to know how women were faring under the Golden Dome. He wanted me to come back and give him reports.

I did not tell my father about this visit, but Father Hesburgh told him. I know because my father said one day "I hear you made a trip to the Grotto." He never nagged me to visit Father Hesburgh after that, but I did. Not frequently, not artificially; but when a need came that required the soothing balm of a man for all students who was filled with love and curiosity. So I stayed at Notre Dame, I studied at Notre Dame, I played at Notre Dame, and I lived at Notre Dame. I went to law school at Notre Dame and continued to visit Father Hesburgh periodically who delighted in my successes and talked with me of my failures. I am quite sure that I was one of hundreds, if not thousands of students that Father Hesburgh touched personally at Notre Dame, but I felt like I was the only one. I never thought myself a leader. Father Hesburgh did. I never thought myself a scholar. Father Hesburgh did. I never thought myself spiritual. Father Hesburgh did. I never thought much about my future. Father Hesburgh made me.

For this, I am eternally grateful. The great experiment of coeducation worked. Father Hesburgh was the cheerleader and manager. Thanks Father Ted. Thanks for making me demand more of myself. Thanks for making me grateful for my blessings. Thanks for making it possible for me to be a Double Domer. Thanks for making me part of the family.

Sincerely,

Carolyn P. Short
Class of '77 BA, '80 JD
Former General Counsel, U.S. Senate Judiciary Committee
Partner, Reed, Smith, Shaw & McClay, Philadelphia, Pennsylvania

In lieu of a letter, I wanted to share with you an excerpt from my conversation with Father Ted, published in my book, *Notre Dame Inspirations* (Doubleday 2006), which exemplifies his spirit and vision.

One of the best things I did at Notre Dame, and this was startling around here given our long history and our male tradition, was saying, "It's rather inconceivable to have a great university named after the mother of God who happens to be a woman and to have all men students. It's masculine. It's like a gym." I said, "It's high time we admitted women as students, professors, administrators, everything." Of course, that came as a bit of a shock to the old boys. But we had a meeting for a whole week and the old boys had a chance to argue. I just sat there and let them talk.

At the end, I just said, "Look we got a university named after a woman who happens to be the greatest human person that ever lived. Jesus was not a human first. He was a divine person with a human nature. She happens to be the greatest human person that ever lived and she happens to be a woman, and this school happens to be named after her. She happens also to be the Mother of God, so I find it a bit inconceivable that in her university she looks down and all she sees is men. I suspect she's interested in women getting this kind of education." I won. The vote on that was, I remember, thirty-nine to six. So I think that was pretty good support. It made a lot of sense. I can tell you that it's a much better place today because half of the people here are women. If you have all men in the place, it gets to be either like a zoo or a gym, and both aren't very civilized. I think women have added a great dimension here.

Thank you, Father Ted, for allowing us to follow our dreams!

Sincerely,

Hannah Storm
Class of '83
Cohost, *The Early Show*, CBS News

Dear Father Ted,

First of all, my sincere best wishes for a Happy 90th Birthday. May I live that long!

I wanted to write this letter to acknowledge the foresight and vision you had for the University of Notre Dame. I guess you could say I am one of the more unique individuals that had the privilege of being at the school under your leadership and before Notre Dame went coed. Coeducation became a part of Notre Dame the year after I left. I will say I enjoyed my experience at an all-male institution but it would have been nice to have had a social environment similar to that of society.

I will be forever indebted to the University of Notre Dame.

Sincerely,

Joe Theismann
Class of '70
Quarterback, Football Team 1968–1970
Super Bowl XVII Champion
1983 NFL Most Valuable Player

Ara Parseghian and ND football team Quarterback Joe Theismann '70

Dear Father Hesburgh,

My father owned one record his entire life, *The Notre Dame Victory March*. It was a forty-five and I can still see the very worn cover with its gold lettering. When I was a baby, every Saturday before the Irish played football, Bill Thompson, Class of 1947, put that record on, scooped me up in his arms, and marched me around the living room. So it should be no surprise that there was only one university I ever wanted to attend. Even when it was all male, I was determined to be the first woman to attend Notre Dame. I was going to talk you into letting me in. But you were the prescient one. You knew Notre Dame needed women and women needed Notre Dame.

I was not the first, but a member of the fourth class of women to attend all four years. And I must admit there were times I had doubts about this dream I wanted so desperately. My first weekend on campus, one of my male classmates dumped his large and smelly bag of laundry at my dorm door, expecting me to wash it. I didn't. In my first class, I was the only woman. I quickly learned not everyone was happy we were here and there were others who thought our biology limited our abilities. And speaking of that biology, who could forget the guys at Sorin Hall who held up ratings cards as we walked to South Dining Hall. Don't ask—I never looked. Yet there were many people who believed in me. Dr. Cornelius Delaney read my Philosophy 101 papers and saw I could think and write. He encouraged and challenged me, continually opening my mind to the expansive possibilities in seeing the world differently. It was a formative experience for someone who still didn't know she wanted to be a journalist. Father Tom Blantz was enormously patient. I would show up late for his U.S. History courses and inevitably take a ten-minute nap during the lecture. Despite my self-inflicted handicaps, Father Blantz's lectures inspired me to dig deeper, learning all I

could about the New Deal and the events that shaped our country after World War II. I found a passion for this nation's history and now I get to help write the first draft.

And there were friends. When I walked on campus all those years ago, I was a scared kid from Brussels, Belgium. In math class, I met someone who looked as scared as I felt, Sarah Devine. She became my best friend and her parents, Dan and Jo, welcomed me as one of their own, even though their lives were filled with six children, grandchildren and the demands of Dan's job, coaching Notre Dame's football team. Watching them deal with the triumphs and challenges of the job, to this day, influence the way I do my job as a reporter. I saw firsthand how important fairness and accuracy are and how rumor masquerading as fact can hurt.

Today, the challenges of coeducation that confronted the first women seem as old and antiquated as a manual typewriter. At this year's meeting of the Advisory Council for the Gallivan Program on Journalism, Ethics, and Democracy, I couldn't help but beam. In talking at length with the students, none of their questions involved gender and its supposed limitations. It never came up as an issue. Their concerns were about internships and jobs, the state of the world, being nervous in front of a camera, and how to get past writer's block. It was what Notre Dame should be: an opportunity for men and women to learn, explore, and achieve—equally and together. It was the kind of scene you must have imagined so long ago.

Notre Dame gave a great education of books and life to my father, myself, and my sister Mary, Class of 1985. And you, Father Ted, gave me my dream. Thank you.

Sincerely,

Anne Thompson
Class of '79
Chief Environmental Correspondent, NBC News, New York, New York

Dear Father Ted,

It has been a wonderful journey with much laughter, intellectual and spiritual growth, lifelong friends, and a deep faith formation along the way. I am so grateful that you decided women had a place at our Our Lady's university.

I absolutely loved my time on campus! As a young girl from Seattle, Washington, who'd never been east of Montana . . . I was fascinated by the nuance of language . . . the way people dressed and the sports they played . . . or didn't play! (Soccer was an unknown sport to women in the Midwest in 1977!) I had one neighbor from Louisville, Kentucky, with the most wonderful drawl! The girl across the hall was from New Jersey and another close friend from Milwaukee. It was a musical menagerie to my ears!

The primary reason I chose Notre Dame was because of the fabulous overseas program sophomore year in Angers, France. I also liked the Irish Catholic heritage and the idea that students came from all over the world to attend was really exciting! Unlike so many of my friends whose mothers attended Saint Mary's and fathers Notre Dame, I was not that familiar with the steeped tradition and lore that my friends in the Midwest had grown up with. I was in for such a treat!

The year in France was one of the best years of my life, rewarding in so many ways. I'm so grateful that the overseas programs continue to flourish for our students and that the global experience remains such a high priority with you and Father John Jenkins. It really opens one's eyes to the fact that there are so many ways to view the world. It was so healthy to attend school with kids from Japan, Germany, Sweden, Holland. We had wonderful late-night debates, just as we did back on campus, but with very healthy and often differing global perspectives from our peer group.

I've been asked to talk a little bit about my experience as the first woman president of the Alumni Association. First and foremost, I have to say that it was such a thrill, and honor to even be elected to the National Alumni Board in the first place. And to be elected by my peers to be president was incredibly humbling. I was surprised to learn, when I joined the board, that there had never been a female president, even though Notre Dame had been coed for decades!

Beth Toomey '81, first woman president of the ND Alumni Association, and Father Ted in fall 2006. They were attending a directors' meeting for the Andean Health and Development Board, meeting in Pedro, Ecuador.
Father Ted is chairman of the board of this sustainable health care project.

I often chuckle at one of the ways Notre Dame inadvertently prepared me for the business world. Just like I was on campus in some situations, many times I've been the only woman in the boardroom. It's never fazed me. But beyond that, the rich sense of the Notre Dame family always lifts my spirits. And every time on campus, it is restorative to my soul.

Notre Dame helped me to learn to be an independent thinker, affirmed and strengthened my faith, and gave me a social conscience that has helped me to be more compassionate to the needs of others in the world. I hope to pass on some of the special gifts Notre Dame du Lac has given me to my girls. . . . to be women of faith and citizens of the world.

Thank you for the extraordinary gift of being a member of the Notre Dame family. Thank you for your vision and sharing your many gifts with so many of us over the years. You are much loved and cherished. Happy 90th Birthday!

Sending a big hug and much love,

Beth Toomey
Class of '81
First Woman President, Notre Dame Alumni Association 1998–1999
Residential Realtor, Seattle Washington

Dear Father Ted,

My education at Notre Dame has made so many things in my life possible. But there's no question what I value most about my connection to Notre Dame. Coeducation allowed a girl from a family of four daughters to connect with our father in a way that would not have been possible in another era. It's a bond that has been strengthened through our shared Notre Dame experience.

Our love of Our Lady's university has connected us in unique ways for more than twenty years. It began with a father/daughter trip to campus when I was looking at schools and continues with our phone calls during every quarter of a football game. (Some from cell phones inside a stadium.) These memories and experiences would not have been the same without coeducation. Some of our best times as a now extended family have taken place on Notre Dame's campus. Generations of our family coming together to enjoy a magical fall Saturday. I can remember when Notre Dame beat Miami in the famous 1988 battle. I rushed the field along with the rest of the student body. When I looked up in the stands, there was my dad waving down to me. He was probably more than a little jealous.

Both of us have been fortunate enough to know you during different eras at Notre Dame. Without coeducation, one of my most treasured memories under the Dome would not have been possible. In September of 2006, you blessed my newborn Cecilia during the Penn

## The Observer announces its 1991-92 General Board

**By MEGAN JUNIUS**
News Writer

The 1991-92 General Board for The Observer has been announced by Editor-in-Chief-elect Kelley Tuthill.

Monica Yant, a sophomore at the University of Notre Dame from Fort Wayne, Ind., has been named News Editor. She is an American Studies major and is currently an Associate News Editor at The Observer.

Joseph Moody, an ND sophomore English major, has been selected as the Viewpoint Editor. He is an Assistant News Editor from South Bend, Ind.

David Dieteman, an ND junior from Erie, Penn., has been named Sports Editor. He is a junior philosophy major with a concentration in Medieval Studies, and currently serves as a Sports Copy Editor.

John O'Brien, an ND junior from Oak Lawn, Ill., has been selected as the Accent Editor. He is an American Studies major and currently serves as The

Observer's Managing Editor.

Eric Bailey will continue to serve as The Observer's Photo Editor, a position he has held since 1989. He is a junior at ND from Crystal Lake, Ill., and an English major.

Emily Willett, a junior at Saint Mary's, will serve as the new Saint Mary's Editor. She carries a double major of economics and business with a concentration in finance and a minor in math. Willett is from Crown Point, Ind., and currently serves a sports writer for The Observer.

Julie Sheridan, a junior accounting major at ND, has been selected as the Advertising Manager. She is from Phoenix, Az., and currently serves as an advertising salesperson.

Alissa Murphy, a Saint Mary's junior from Manchester, Missouri, will serve as the Ad Design Manager. She is a communications major with a minor in professional writing and currently serves as a Day Editor.

State game. I could not wait to call my father and tell him. It's amazing how you continue to touch generations of Domers.

May God continue to bless you and the university we all love so much.

Sincerely,

Kelley Tuthill (daughter of Bruce Tuthill '64)
Class of '92
Anchor/Reporter, WCVB-TV, Boston, Massachusetts

Dear Father Ted,

I wonder what it was like for you to make that decision, one that was far from popular at the time. Did you try to look thirty years into the future and imagine what a generation of Notre Dame women might achieve and how they might bring change to our world? Or did you just know that it was the right thing to do?

Thank you for having the courage and vision to open the university's arms to embrace her daughters as well as her sons. Because of your decision, not only my brother (Class of '76), but also my sister (Class of '79) and I (Class of '82) have had the opportunity to grow in the spirit of Our Lady, and to take that spirit forward in our lives. I hope we made you proud.

Claire J. Twist, MD
Class of '82
Pediatric Hematologist Oncologist, Lucile Packard Children's Hospital at Stanford
    University, Palo Alto, California

Dear Father Hesburgh,

I grew up in South Bend, Indiana, and spent many hours walking, playing, cheering, and praying on Notre Dame's campus. I learned all the great hiding places, ate French fries at the Huddle, fed the ducks stale bread and crackers from my favorite spot on the lake, frequented numerous and various athletic events, and attended Mass at the Basilica. At the time I didn't know that I would or that I even could attend college at Notre Dame. I only knew that I was associated with Notre Dame as a result of my father, Roger's, position in the Athletic Department and because of my family's love for the qualities and spirit of the place. And I also knew that it was special to be part of the Notre Dame family.

Fast forward to June 2004. My dad was on campus celebrating his fiftieth class reunion, I was celebrating my twentieth. Dad has indeed fulfilled an intention he proclaimed to his parents when they dropped him off at school in 1950 to begin his freshman year of studies—"I will never leave this place." Not only has he "not left this place," but his five children, all ND alumni, remain enfolded in the essence of Our Lady du Lac as well. Alongside my dad was my mother, who modeled what it means to have faith even during her battle with cancer that eventually took her from us and rejoined her to Our Lady in 1988.

So it is with great pleasure and enthusiasm that I extend my sincerest thanks to you for seeing and then making real first the vision of coeducation and then later the vision of varsity women's athletics. In April 2007, my sister Kathy and I attended a commemorative weekend honoring Notre Dame female athletes. We were both members and captains of the Notre Dame fencing team during our college tenure. Kathy graduated in 1978 and I graduated in 1984. It was a proud moment for both of us. Your leadership and commitment to create an environment of excellence, diversity, and inclusiveness at Notre Dame gave us the opportunity to excel in the classroom, in athletics, and in life.

My past college experiences along with my present day connection to what Notre Dame stands for continue to inspire me to make real my desire to contribute and positively impact the people and situations I encounter, and to continue following my own spiritual path.

Father Ted, I want to say thank you again for being such an important part of my growth as a spiritual and human being. Your dream of a Notre Dame that included men and women on her campus paved the way for thousands of us to venture out and make a difference in the world.

Sincerely,

Susan M. Valdiserri
Class of '84
Professional and Executive Coach, IBM Corporation, Chicago, Illinois

Dear Father Hesburgh,

In the fall of 1972 I moved into Badin as a sophomore. At the age of nineteen, I was too young to appreciate the magnitude of the journey I was about to begin.

I remember negotiations on coeducation with Saint Mary's had just broken down when Notre Dame opened its doors to women. All the men were "asked" to leave Badin and Walsh halls. Those dorms were designated the new women's dorms. From what we could see, that was the extent of the preparation. There certainly was a shortage of ladies' bathrooms all over campus. Pete, the janitor, complained all year about having the women's hair clog the showers. O'Shaughnessy Hall only had one ladies' bathroom for us to use. The rest of the bathrooms were all urinals. And the ratio of men to women, although one would think exciting for dating, was intimidating in its lopsidedness. To be nineteen and the only girl in most of your classes was tough. To walk into a dining hall alone took guts. There was usually a table full of football players in the South Dining Hall. I had to walk by their table as I left. No one wanted to do that alone. We all tried to get to class on time because if we were late and there were no chairs left, the

Notre Dame men were such gentlemen, they'd all get up to give you their chair—and this, at nineteen, was so embarrassing. During roll call, I'd try so hard to say "present" in my deepest voice so as to call less attention to myself as often I'd be the only female in class. Football games had their scary moments as well, with the women being thrown from row to row all the way up the bleachers.

Father Ted, I was this wide-eyed Mexican American girl who had read all of your publications on education in the Southwest when you were chairman of the U.S. Civil Rights Commission. In a world that was so foreign, your publications made me realize that Notre Dame was headed by someone who understood Mexican kids. I attended all your speeches on campus. I became president of Mecha. I made tostadas for our Mecha stand on football weekends—that was a first at Notre Dame. In the spirit of volunteerism so characteristic of Notre Dame, we started a bilingual tutoring program for the children of migrant workers in South Bend. Things got a little heated when Mecha demanded that you admit more minorities. I was after all, I think, the only Chicana attending that year.

When I graduated in 1975 and was admitted to the Law School, you and Vilma Martinez, president of MALDEF (Mexican American Legal Defense Fund), awarded me a scholarship. You did this for me, despite our differences. In 1993, when I was appointed to the federal bench, I remember so fondly receiving a letter of congratulations from you. I couldn't believe you even remembered me. When I went back to campus and told you I needed your prayers you invited me to stay for Mass with just you and Father Joyce. A Mass with just the three of us. It was very special for me. A truly unforgettable moment.

Father Hesburgh, I was so proud that the president of my university was the chairman of the U.S. Commission on Civil Rights that had accomplished so much. To me, you exemplified the idea of our faith. You were our conscience, and that of our nation. And even when my idealism got away from me and I was impatient with the progress you were making at Notre Dame, your work and accomplishments were the inspiration of my life.

I salute you, Father Ted. I thank you for the example of your life. I thank you for inspiring me. I thank you for the gift of attending this wonderful place and for thinking enough of me, despite our differences to award me a scholarship to Notre Dame Law School. My seven years at Notre Dame changed my life, and in turn, that of my family.

Sincerely,

The Honorable Martha Vazquez
Class of '75, '79 JD
U.S. District Court Judge, District of New Mexico

❧

Father Theodore Hesburgh has played a vital part in Notre Dame becoming one of the most prestigious academic institutions of higher learning. The university has a special place in my heart as two of the most precious people in my life, my daughters, Terri and Sherri, had the opportunity to be recipients of the fine education that Notre Dame provides.

Terri and Sherri both were students and athletes in the mid-1990s as they participated in women's tennis. They were fortunate enough to be able to receive full scholarships to the Golden Dome. Terri graduated in 1994 with a bachelor's degree in business and Sherri graduated in 1996 with a degree in American Studies. They both loved their experience as undergraduates so much that when it came time to pursue a master's degree they both returned to the University of Notre Dame graduating with MBA degrees from the Mendoza College of Business. I can't tell you how proud my wife, Lorraine, and I were at their graduations. Watching them walk down the aisle as Double Domers was a very special moment in our lives.

Over the years, I have fallen in love with the University of Notre Dame. I am very excited about the Dick Vitale Family Scholarship that I have established, which annu-

Sherri Vitale-Krug '96, '98 MBA.

Terri Vitale '94, '95 MBA.
Reprinted with the permission of the Notre Dame Sports Information Department.

ally allocates scholarship assistance to students who participate in activities at the university that do not receive scholarship aid (e.g., cheerleading, mascot, band, etc.).

I am also proud that both of my sons-in-law, Thomas Krug and Christopher Sforzo, were students and athletes at the University of Notre Dame. Thomas participated in football as a quarterback and Christopher was a member of the lacrosse team. Today, Thomas is a prosecutor in Sarasota, Florida, and Christopher is an orthopedic surgeon in Sarasota, Florida. Needless to say, both our daughters and sons-in-law are constantly singing the praises of Notre Dame for helping them grow intellectually and socially.

Father Hesburgh's influence has molded Notre Dame into the unique university that it is today. He is recognized as one of the most influential educators of our time. His passion and wisdom have left an indelible mark on the many administrators, faculty members, and students who have had the privilege of walking the halls of the Lady on the Dome.

My dream is for my five grandchildren to follow the pattern of their parents. I can honestly and truly state that my wife and I have lived vicariously through our children and are envious of the incredible opportunity they had by being students and athletes at a very special university!

Dick Vitale, ESPN Sportscaster, Father of Terri Vitale '94, '95 MBA and Sherri
    Vitale-Krug '96, '98 MBA

Dear Father Hesburgh,

It is with great pleasure that I write this letter to you. I really admire all that you have accomplished in your life and all that you have done. During a time in history when it was not "fashionable" to give opportunities to people of color, you took the lead and opened many doors. In the early '70s when many people were against admitting women to Notre Dame you opened her doors. Just look at what fruit that seed bore! As not only a woman, but a black woman, the opportunities and exposure to different people and cultures I received at Notre Dame is priceless. Your life has been dedicated to the service of others and so has all of your protégées.

I remember the day I first met you. I was a freshman living in Lewis Hall. I was walking toward the back of the Admissions Building when you stopped me. You introduced yourself to me and asked me where I was from. I told you, and then you proceeded to tell me the funny story of how you ran away to Brooklyn when you were a child in New Jersey. You know that you are a "legend" at Notre Dame—but as a student, a legend is sometimes not seen as a real person. However, that day I met a "living legend" who was a real person and down to earth enough to take five minutes to get to know me. Although I don't see you often Father, you still always remember me and that warms my heart. I will always keep you in prayer and hope that my life will reflect, as yours has, the teachings of Christ and the service of Father Sorin as a daughter of Notre Dame.

Love,

Eleanor M. Walker, MD
Class of '84
Radiation Oncologist, Henry Ford Hospital, Detroit, Michigan

Dear Father Ted,

When I first came to Notre Dame as a freshman in the fall of 1974, I think it's fair to say that having women on campus still qualified as something of a novelty. While most of the men's sports programs had been around for a long time, women's sports were just getting started.

I remember the women's tennis team beginning play at the Division III level in the fall of my junior year. Fencing had been a club sport, and that same year it competed as a varsity sport for the first time. I think the men won the NCAA title that year, and the women went something like 13–1 in their first season. My senior year (1977–1978) was the first time we had a varsity basketball team for women. In fact, a few months after I graduated, Missy Conboy, now one of our deputy athletics directors, enrolled as a freshman basketball player.

So, at least when I was in school, women competing at the varsity level was brand-new. There were no scholarships. It was just the beginning.

I didn't have the opportunity to come back to the campus many times after I graduated, but when I returned in 2005 it was amazing to see the progress that had been made in women's athletics while I had been coaching elsewhere.

Soccer has won a couple of national championships. Basketball won an NCAA title. The fencing team competes on a regular basis with the men for national titles. There are Big East Conference championships banners everywhere you look, and any time you see a top twenty listing you find the name Notre Dame.

Just last year there were twenty-two women's All-Americans at Notre Dame, the same number produced by the Irish men's teams. And none of that would be possible if women had never been admitted to the university.

I think of all the intangibles that the members of our football teams take away from their experiences here. Thanks to your decision in relation to coeducation more than thirty years ago, we now have dozens of women's athletes at Notre Dame who have all those same opportunities.

Happy Birthday—and thank you for all that you've done for Notre Dame through the years.

Go Irish!

Charlie Weis
Class of '78
Head Football Coach 2005–
Assistant Coach, New York  Giants and New England Patriots
Four Super Bowl Championships

Dear Father Ted,

I suspect your 90th birthday has come around sooner than you expected. But no one I have ever met has packed more into a life than you have. I still recall those long letters you used to circulate every year detailing your summer break travels—you know, the ones that earned your secretary instant salvation for the hours she spent typing up your copious notes. I always thanked God you were never elected pope because your encyclicals would have been longer than John Paul II's.

As it happens, your 90th year coincided with my fiftieth class reunion. I mention that because ours is one of the few classes left that was exclusively male. And it was you who decided that Notre Dame's days as a males-only university would be numbered. "Best decision I ever made," you said ever after.

As it happens, I wasn't happy when ND went coed. "There goes the neighborhood," I thought at the time. I still think ND lost something it had when it was males only, a form of male camaraderie that shows up still at our class reunions. It may just have been the times, but I persist in thinking that the bonding that took place in that bygone era is stronger and more intense, somehow, than what happens when women are stirred into the mix. So I have always been glad that I experienced Notre Dame when I did. But I do have to admit that Notre Dame has also gained immensely by going coed. Surely the women of Notre Dame have exerted a civilizing effect on the male herd. And they sure have given the men stiff competition—in admissions, in the classroom and, yes, in athletics as well. Only the old timers look back.

I suppose if I could interrogate my undergraduate self he would remind me that it was not easy to scare up a date, especially freshman year, what with the ten-to-one ratio of male ND to female SMC students. Somehow, I did manage to talk one of them into marrying me. But having Betty with me in class, my undergraduate self reminds me, would not only haven been unfair intellectual competition (she still takes better notes) but also terminally distracting. I was never very good at wooing and learning at the same time.

So thanks, Father Ted, for the leadership on this, as on civil rights, academic freedom, and so many, many other issues. And now that you have turned ninety, admit it: You would never have met so many interesting women yourself if you hadn't opened the doors to them at Notre Dame.

Sincerely,

Kenneth L. Woodward
Class of '57
Retired Religion Editor, *Newsweek* Magazine

Dear Father Hesburgh,

I am one of the more obscure coeds—I came to the university by way of a public high school in New York, and found Notre Dame to be a tight fit . . . not only because we were in the gender minority, but also because my working-class background was not reflected in my peers.

I never had time to assess what it was like to be a girl among the traditions of men . . . I entered Notre Dame at seventeen, and was still bathing in the atmosphere that allowed intelligent people (née "women") to be respected for their academic pursuits when my father lost his job. My mother had previously been diagnosed with cancer, a verdict which, in 1973, was almost always terminal. With one parent disabled and the second unemployed, I was headed back to New York before my change-of-address cards were posted. Someone had to pay the bills back home, and that someone was me.

As I was re-packing, and trying to determine how best to return my scholarship and books, I wandered toward the Freshman Resource Center. In 1973, it was located next to the University Employment Office behind the Golden Dome. It was a Friday afternoon in early October, and this area of campus was deserted. I took a wrong turn, and wound up in the Employment Office, in front of a kindly secretary who tried to steer me in the appropriate door. Instead, I took a chance and asked her for a job. "We don't let freshman work" was her reply. Something on my face must have looked quite unsettled, because she handed me an index card that preceded a job inquiry. I wrote that my mother was ill and my father had just lost his job, and handed the card back to the secretary.

There were few people in the office, and no real supervisor, so the secretary read my card. She looked at me, looked again at the message on the card, and motioned me to her desk.

"Can you lift heavy stuff?" she asked. I was a gymnast in high school and quite strong. "Yes," I replied. She looked me over, noting my torn jeans and careless sweatshirt. "Do you care what kind of work it is?" she asked. I had worked every possible job to get to Notre Dame, including factory work and a brief stint as a truck driver. "Not at all," I said.

She nodded and reached into a file drawer in her desk. After scribbling down a note, she handed me an employment form. "Don't designate that you are a current student," she instructed. I filled out the form, returned it to the secretary, and took the name and number on the note. "Report to Al at 7:00 p.m., North Dining Hall," she said. "Wear work clothes." I thanked her and returned to my dorm.

At 7:00 p.m. that evening, I made my way to the North Dining Hall. I lived on South Quad, so I had no idea what was going on in the North Dining Hall. When I got there the entire football team was waiting in the hallway. I squeezed through the crowd to the kitchen to look for Al. I found him at the dishwasher, and quickly figured out what my new job entailed. I was a janitor. I scrubbed floors and bathrooms, washed food machines, and cleaned dishes for the training table. It was the perfect job—no one would suspect I was a coed, and it paid enough for me to pay the mortgage and bills. I started at 7:00 p.m. and ended somewhere around 2:00 a.m. With a seven-day shift, I was making more money than if I had returned to New York. Now, staying in school meant I could do more for my family than if I returned home. I stayed.

During my seven years at Notre Dame, I held many jobs, including a few that actually allowed me to meet you on several occasions. I never got a chance to say thank you; I hope you will now accept my too-belated thanks.

I know, from being on campus in 1973, how much resistance there was to offering a Notre Dame education to women. I am well aware at how much tenacity and courage it took to change the minds and hearts of those who believed that a coed university would be of diminished value. I, along with every other woman who was given the opportunity to belong to the Notre Dame family thank you for your perseverance. But you actually have given me much more.

I am currently a public official, and I've learned that my staff magnifies and reflects my values. The people I hire must be more than competent; they must share my vision. Every person that I worked with or for at the university possessed compassion, patience, and kindness. They all believed that they were a part of something bigger than themselves alone, and that ideal, Father Hesburgh, came from you. It was part of your leadership, and it was mirrored by the people of Notre Dame. I am certain of this, as one of my jobs was to be your mail clerk, and a few years later I assisted Professor Donald Kommers in creating a library to hold the papers from your tenure on the Commission for Civil Rights. Your imprimatur was, and is, evident in the eyes of the people who work for Notre Dame. For this, I am always grateful.

Thank you for your leadership, and for the many lessons I was able to learn while at Notre Dame. And thank you for hiring a compassionate secretary who gave a desperate teenager a chance to stay.

Always,

The Honorable Susan Zwick
Class of '77, '80 JD
Circuit Court Judge, Cook County, Illinois

The Notre Dame Law School Football Team, 1896.

# is Notre Dame
# a place for women?

"Notre Dame men"... that phrase reaches back more than a hundred years and was always tinged somewhat with the pride and ruggedness associated with football.

Football is still an enjoyable autumnal ritual at Notre Dame, but the characterization of the University's students has been changed. Make it "Notre Dame men and women."

Next fall, Notre Dame, for the first time in its history, will directly admit women —both as first-year and as transfer students—to its undergraduate program.

Coeducation has come to Notre Dame's 1,250-acre campus ... and with it a new climate of living and learning at the nation's foremost Catholic university.

Women will like it at Notre Dame.

Men have.

Write: Director of Admissions / University of Notre Dame / Notre Dame, Indiana 46556

1972 recruiting poster for Notre Dame undergraduate women. A copy of this poster may be purchased at www.thankingfatherted.com.

# 3

# ALUMNAE LETTERS— CLASSES OF 1972–1979

# THE OBSERVER

VOL. IV NO. 1 — Serving the Notre Dame and Saint Mary's College Community — FRIDAY, SEPTEMBER 12, 1969

# Co-exchange program affects frosh

Welcome freshmen. You are here.

by Glenn Corso

The most radical innovation to be experienced by the class of '73 will be the expanded co-exchange program with Saint Mary's college. The program, announced last spring by the presidents of both schools, will involve upwards of 245 freshmen from the two institutions. The program will be used in four Arts and Letters courses, including English, Government, History, and Sociology. Notre Dame will admit women to their Humanities program, in place of English.

The second phase of the program will come in the fall of 1971, when both schools will consolidate registration, class schedules, academic calendars and admissions. St. Mary's has doubled its freshman class enrollment to 500, in order to eventually achieve a 1.3 ratio to Notre Dame men.

Rev. Charles E. Sheedy, CSC, appointed head of the program by the presidents of both schools, stated that students would still receive separate diplomas from their respective schools, unless the student became totally involved with their academic program at the other school. Fr. Sheedy went on to say that the eventual goal of the program will be somewhat akin to the Harvard-Radcliffe model.

Dean William Burke, head of the Freshman year of studies, confessed to being "a bit anxious" as to the number of Notre Dame frosh who would volunteer for the program. Surprisingly though, over 600 indicated that they either did not care one way or the other, or would be very willing to participate in such a program. The 250 were chosen by random selection. The courses involved will be basically similar at both schools, though different textbooks may be used. All frosh involved will have the period before and after their co-ex class free, in order to facilitate travel between the two schools.

A radically different approach in frosh counseling will be undertaken this year. Besides meeting with his counselor, a freshman may also have an undergraduate student present at the meeting. He will thus have two opinions available to him on his particular problem.

Dean Burke emphasized that one of the main uses for the undergrads will be to advise those frosh that have especially serious problems in the first few weeks of the school year. The undergrads selected will be those who had the same type of problems at the beginning of their freshman year.

A survey was taken last spring on the freshman counseling system, and as a result freshmen will be allowed to switch their counselor, if they feel they are not getting along with him. Dean Burke also mentioned the prospect of team counseling where 3-4 counselors would sit down with a group of students and discuss any problems they might have.

"One of our biggest jobs is to break down the high school attitude", Burke declared. He went on to explain that many freshmen were reluctant to talk to their counselors about their problems because it had been considered "apple polishing" in high school, and reluctant to talk to him in the role of a principal whom they only saw when they were in trouble.

A black counselor has been added to the Freshman Year office staff, Dr. Robert Seabrooks comes to Notre Dame from Wartburg College in Waverly, Iowa. Dr. Seabrooks will counsel half the black freshmen, along with fifty other students.

# 80 incoming freshmen displaced by incompletion of Grace tower

by Dave Stauffer

Eighty members of Notre Dame's freshman class will report today to temporary residences in the old halls on campus, due to the incompletion of tower "C" in Grace Hall. Freshmen living in towers 'A', 'B', and 'D' will be able to move in today.

All freshmen and upperclassmen affected by the incompletion were notified of the provisions for temporary residence in letters sent August 15 by the Director of Student Residence, Fr. Edgar Whelan. Arrangements were made for those students scheduled to live in tower "C" to move into the newly created three-room, four man suites. Father Whelan noted that in all cases those students would will room with their Grace Hall roommates. This arrangement will keep all freshmen with freshmen roommates, although the freshmen of Grace will not necessarily be sharing their suite with other freshmen.

Because of the incomplete dorm there will also be a slight change in the orientation schedule. Father Whelan, who will also be rector of Grace Hall, will meet with the freshmen of his hall (towers C and D) in the North Dining Hall, from 9 until available to meet the parents of these students from 2 until 5 p.m. on Saturday afternoon. This meeting will be held in the first floor lounge of the LaFortune Student Center. The Grace Hall religious orientation will be held Sunday at 11 p.m. in Sacred Heart Church.

The contractor has informed Father Whelan that the floors of tower "C" will not be turned over to the university individually, as was originally planned in August. Instead, the second floor through the sixth will be available on October 1, while the seventh through eleventh floors are planned to be ready on

# Dissidents plan informal meeting

by Cliff Wintrode

Freshmen and their parents this weekend will be the object of attention from both the Coalition for Political Action and Students Against Racism. The Coalition will present a counter to the ROTC orientation program while Students Against Racism will make efforts to provide a "personal dialogue" with the students and their parents on racism at Notre Dame.

Fred Dedrick, Student Body Vice President and a founder of the Coalition, said that the Coalition will present an informal discussion tomorrow on the second floor of the Student Center at 2:30 to "emphasize the fact that freshmen should look at both sides before deciding".

Brian McInerny, the primary organizer of the Coalition's remarks:

"We are trying to present the other side of the issue to freshmen. We are trying to persuade them to avoid binding commitments at this point in their lives."

The Coalition is also going to pass out literature at the ROTC program inside the Athletic and Convocation Center. The ROTC program is scheduled to be held between the hours of one and two in the afternoon. The Coalition has already prepared a pamphlet for this purpose.

Responding to the question of whether or not the Coalition will be allowed inside of the Convocation Center, McInerny, taking into account the fact that the Convo Center is not being rented but given by the university for use by the ROTC, answered

"I do not see how they can

$\mathcal{H}$ello, Father Ted,

I welcome the opportunity to convey what it has meant to me to be an alumna of Notre Dame.

Growing up in Elkhart, I became enamored with ND from the get-go. My parents took us to the campus for picnics, their friends gave us extra tickets for football games (we took turns going to the games), and when my sister was old enough to drive the family car, she would take me to watch basketball games in the old Field House.

I wanted desperately to attend ND, but did the next best thing by matriculating through Saint Mary's with an ND major—Russian. You cannot imagine how happy I was when the ND-SMC merger talks were on. I have the one-and-only of its kind class ring from my junior year that has the inscription "Saint Mary's of Notre Dame." When the talks fell through, I was crushed. Thank goodness (in your infinite wisdom) that you allowed those of us with ND majors to transfer over for our senior year!

During pregraduation festivities, I vividly remember walking through the reception line with my family and shaking your hand. I'll never forget the graduation

Notre Dame Fencing Team 1972–1973.

ceremony itself, when Father Burtchaell asked those ninety or so of us women to stand and be recognized as the first coeds at ND—what a thrill!

After my first year of grad school at Indiana University at Bloomington, I returned to ND to complete my degree. I was so homesick for the place and I could hardly stand it. It was great to finally get to live on campus in Lewis Hall. I also got to continue with the fencing team, as it was still a club sport for women at the time. (Coach DeCicco was a saint to get a team organized while we were still at SMC!) As a result, I received one of the first ND sweaters issued to female athletes.

Father Ted, I could go on and on. The point is that I am so proud of being a Domer, and I owe that to you. I still get goose bumps when I visit the campus and go to the Main Building, the Basilica, and the Grotto. I remember all of the people and experiences and how that has influenced me. I wouldn't have traded that for anything.

Thanks again, and God bless,

Sally (Fischer) La Plante
Class of '73, '75

Dear Father Hesburgh,

I am so happy to have this opportunity to thank you belatedly for your vision to facilitate coeducation at the University of Notre Dame. I can now appreciate how easy you made it look, but how difficult it actually was. Being in the first class we obviously had our challenges of merger/no-merger, major/no-major, but you quickly and fairly dealt with us that were impacted by the change in plans. I don't ever remember feeling stressed or worried about how I would finish my college years. We actually ended up with the best of both worlds being able to get our education at Notre Dame, but continue to live in the much better dorms at Saint Mary's.

When I think back to the impact this has had on me, as well as my family, it is amazing. My father graduated from Notre Dame in 1942. Needless to say, he was thrilled that the legacy was going to continue. Being a rather progressive male, he was not concerned that females were now going to invade the all male environment. (Unlike my grandfather who had pride in me, but was among the skeptics as to what girls would do to the university of Our Mother). We have continued with the legacy because my daughter is in the Class of 2007. My mother had communication difficulties related to health problems in the last years of her life, but her pride and happiness were clearly evident when my daughter was accepted at Notre Dame.

With my daughter attending Notre Dame I have now had many opportunities to observe the students and the environment and continue to be proud of what I see. It is reassuring to see the social interaction and support the students have for each other. I had gone to a coed high school and I found it allowed me to have males as friends, not just possible date material. Notre Dame has obviously evolved to that. I have many stories I could share on what I have observed, but I am sure you see it every day you are on campus.

Notre Dame is truly a family and it was great that you helped people recognize for a family to be complete there needed to be males and females. I am always proud to say that I was in the first class of women that graduated from the University of Notre Dame.

Thank you,

Patti McNamara McGuire
Class of '73

Dear Father Hesburgh,

Being the oldest child in a family of nine is somewhat unique, but the added fact that my eight siblings are all male is what really catches everyone's attention. "Eight brothers! What was that like?" This question is asked of me again when anyone realizes that I graduated from the University of Notre Dame in the first class that included women, an equally unique position. "Thousands of men and one hundred women at Notre Dame. What was that like?" Teachers and students I encountered in my English and American Studies classes always treated me as an equal and with respect. The '70s at Notre Dame and Saint Mary's was a wonderful experience educationally and socially. Looking back thirty-three years to the beautiful day in May 1973 when I graduated from Notre Dame, I remember how the women graduates were asked to stand and be recognized as Notre Dame's first class of women. I have treasured that designation ever since. Thank you so much for your instrumental role in making Notre Dame a coeducational university.

During my job search senior year, I remember having an extended conversation about topics from Ron Weber's American Studies class, "Prophets of Technology"— interesting issues for a manager at IBM. After the interview and a job offer, I enjoyed a seventeen-year career at IBM before "retiring" to stay home with my children. Recently, I switched gears from technology back to English, earning a master's degree in English. I know that once again as I seek a job, my University of Notre Dame degree will open doors for me.

I was back on campus recently, visiting Notre Dame with my daughter, a senior in high school. It was wonderful to see her accepted to Notre Dame. Thank you again for admitting women, including Saint Mary's students like me who had majors at Notre Dame. It was so disappointing when the merger between Saint Mary's and Notre Dame was halted. Thanks for taking us into your fold and allowing us to become part of Notre Dame. Your efforts have had a very positive impact in my life.

Sincerely,

Mary Beth Caplice Newman
Class of '73

Dear Father Ted,

Without hesitation, I can say that my "total experience" at the University of Notre Dame had a profound influence on me as a person and how I function every day as a member of the larger world campus.

My experience at Notre Dame set the course for the way I have lived my life for the past thirty-five years. And that experience continues to be reflected in the values and morals I practice daily.

It influenced my professional career, my family, my personal relationships, and my strong commitment to giving back through volunteerism. Most importantly, from the day I graduated, ND became the benchmark by which I have continued to measure success. You set the bar high, Father Ted, but I'm glad you did.

As a member of the smallest class of female alumnae (1973), I recall that we had a vast array of experiences that served well to prepare us for our futures. We were exposed to high academic standards. But at the same time we faced several uphill battles; among them some faculty, students, and alumnae who did not support a coed ND. We had to work hard to earn the respect of the faculty and fellow students, but that only made us stronger. And, we worked hard to balance academic pursuit with very active social lives.

Our inspiration to strive for dedication and excellence was the leadership of the university at the time—most exemplified by you, Father Ted. It would have been easy to blame failure on the challenges. But that was not an option. You always expected us to succeed and go on to honor the integrity of the University of Notre Dame.

So it was not a single event, class, professor, or football game that made it a wonderful and memorable experience. Rather, it was the overall experience and role models that laid the permanent foundation for how we would live our lives—the ability to make decisions and accept the consequences, the courage to rise up to meet the most difficult of challenges, the enthusiasm to embrace the goodness in life, and the strength to accept the fate that God has bestowed.

Over the years I have told friends and colleagues that I was fortunate enough to have been at a magical place at that rare moment when the dynamics of change required a leader with vision and wisdom, and I was among a select few women to have benefited.

From the bottom of my heart I want to express my gratitude for your help in shaping the person I am today.

Sincerely,

SMP
Class of '73
PS I'm still sorry for hitting you with a snowball as you exited your office in the winter of 1972.

Dear Father Ted,

From 1969 to 1973, of everyone on campus, my jeans' bottoms had to be the shiniest.

It's impossible to estimate how many hours I spent waiting outside your office door, as well as those of Fathers Jerry Wilson, Tom Blantz, Jim Shilts, and those of Sisters Alma Peter and Basil Anthony at Saint Mary's for interviews for the *Observer* about the ND-SMC proposed merger.

The Sunday after Thanksgiving in 1971—the day after the trustees finished their

# UNFORGETTABLE TEACHERS

*Twenty Educators Whose Lessons Reached Beyond the Classroom*

We recently asked readers to tell us about an unforgettable teacher who changed their life or shook their view of the world. Hundreds of people wrote in, describing teachers of every subject, from English to precalculus. But with few exceptions—including an Indiana woman writing about her mind-blowing introduction to existentialism—it wasn't the subject matter but the person who taught it, who opened the door, that most influenced the students. How creatively teachers conveyed an idea, how much they cared, their high expectations, how all of these things inspired many students to become educators themselves, while others said they became better parents, friends, and citizens. We selected as many excerpts as we could from all the letters we received. We know the world is full of many more unforgettable teachers.

*In loco parentis: H. Ronald Weber, American studies, University of Notre Dame, Notre Dame, Indiana*

Ron Weber, head of the American Studies Program, changed my life.

I was in the first class of women undergraduates who got their degrees from Notre Dame in 1973. It was scary. Some of the profs made it clear they didn't want women on campus, much less in their classes. One of my best friends, a government major, was thrown out of a required class several times by a professor who said he hadn't taught women for twenty-five years and wasn't about to start. The dean kept sending her back. Finally, the prof relented.

Mr. Weber was just the opposite. He represented the best of Notre Dame's philosophy, *in loco parentis*—the school stands in the place of the parent. Ron set the bar very high. He spent considerable time and patience helping me realize the beauty and meaning of the American literature he assigned, while investing considerable time outside class marking up my papers so I'd become a more clear, more imaginative writer.

Like a parent, Ron was protective of me and the other American Studies women majors when we needed it. He regularly went to bat for me and the others when we were put down by a faculty member or an administrator. He always had time to talk, offering encouragement and advice, when the going got tough on the campus newspaper and the other extracurriculars in which I was involved.

Without this nurturing, I would have quit.

Unlike my classmate, because of Ron, I had a phenomenal experience, developing self-confidence, solid writing, and an appreciation of American literature, which continue to enrich my life today.

—Ann Therese Palmer, Lake Forest

Reprinted with permission of the *Chicago Tribune Chicago Tribune Magazine,* cover story, Sunday, August 7, 2005.

**If they have ND majors**

# SMC upperclassmen can win Notre Dame degrees

by Ann Therese Darin

St. Mary's upperclassmen currently enrolled in exclusively Notre Dame major departments will receive Notre Dame degrees, announced Mother Olivette Whelan, SMC Board of Trustee chairman at a student convocation Friday.

Four student representatives and four faculty representatives will be allowed to explain their opinions on the merger stoppage to the Board at its meeting, Dec. 18, Mother Olivette said.

Before introducing the trustee chairman, who flew in from a Boston meeting of the Sisters of the Holy Cross specifically to address the student convocation, Kathy Barlow, student body president, announced an emergency meeting of the Board of Trustees had been requested.

Acknowledging the request, Sr. Alma Peter, acting college president, told Miss Barlow she had notified members Thursday night and was waiting replies Thursday night.

"At Notre Dame there is no opportunity for women," Mother Olivette said, defending the college's position. "They are not yet ready for them."

However, despite the college's feelings, Mother Olivette emphasized, "there will be no change in the coexchange program for next semester."

She expressed disbelief that the St. Mary's Freshman Year Office had denied freshmen the opportunity to schedule Notre Dame classes because the shuttle buses are too crowded. She said that if they wanted to, freshmen could sign up for all of their classes at Notre Dame.

To substantiate this, Mother Olivette quoted Fr. James Burtchaell, university provost, who was unable to accept the chairman's invitation to accompany her to the student convocation.

"While it was impossible for Fr. Burtchaell to be here, " she said, "he did send a message with me: 'There is absolutely no change for next semester. No fees. You can register for any class offered by Notre Dame' ." Burtchaell claimed, she said, that this semester would give the two schools time to reach an equitable solution.

In revealing four students could attend the Trustees meeting, she acknowledged "We always have a time when students and the Board can speak at the other two Holy Cross colleges (Dumbarton in Washington, D.C. and Cardinal Cushing College in Boston.) This has not been done here and I think this was a mistake. I intend to see this will be done in the future."

Before the May ratification of unification by both boards of Trustees, Mother Olivette noted there was much talk about how size and inequality of size, would effect unification.

To stress her point, she illustrated it with an anecdote about a 6'6" man who married a 4'4" woman, who both realize there are going to be problems because of size. The man says, she quoted, "We're going to do things my way."

This would not be the case at St. Mary's and Notre Dame, she stated flatly. "The atmosphere has not been there for the input of women into Notre Dame. Fr. Burtchaell said they wanted such help, but I haven't yet seen it, " she claimed.

Denying financial problems were the major problem, she quoted an article in this week's **Time Magazine**, on coeducation: "Coeducation is a sham unless it has a genuine equality. There must be an opportunity for women."

Most SMC administrators feel, she stated that Notre Dame was reneging on its commitment with SMC for unification, made last spring.

In the spring meetings, both Notre Dame and St. Mary's had agreed that both schools would be re-organized into a new University of Notre Dame encompassing the best of both schools, Sister comment.

"We had this third entity vision in the future," Mother Olivetter reflected, "but what has taken place is something rejected by all of you (students), faculty," and as the Park-Mayhew report predicted, the Board of Trustees have also. "This is absorption," she continued.

"Merger is not possible between two unequal institutions," she emphasized. "It must be incorporation."

For this reason, The Observer learned Friday, St. Mary's alumnae board representatives had refused voting privileges on the Notre Dame Alumni Board last fall. They felt, sources claimed, they would be absorbed into Notre Dame. Instead, they requested a complete reorganization of the Board with equal representation for women.

She implored students to hold off because "we have some work to do as a group of women and as a women's college" before unification could be accelerated again.

SMC students disputed her statement, that "We can show some of the trends of where education can go and we can do this and we can influence Notre Dame, but not too quickly."

Describing Notre Dame as "very traditional" amid much applause from the audience of 1100 students, she said "If we are content to stay in a traditional life, all right, this is a choice we can make."

Exiting off stage to a waiting pool of reporters, Mother Olivette said "they can destroy St. Mary's," refering to the students, "It's within their power."

(Continued on page 12)

fall meeting in Miami Beach—was the heart-stopper. My parents had driven me back to school from Detroit that afternoon. I was unpacking, when the phone rang. It was Frank Devine, assistant news director at WSND (now a *60 Minutes* producer). He'd just heard the merger was off. I was down the road from Saint Mary's to the *Observer*, before Frank was off the phone. Ten hours later, the story was nailed down, thanks to you and the other CSCs, who didn't divulge any embargoed information, but pointed me in a number of valuable directions.

Writing and confirming that story was one of the most exhilarating and frightening reporting experiences of my life. That article and subsequent ones about ND's transition to coeducation won "Best Newswriting Under Press of Deadline for All Midwestern Universities and Colleges" from Sigma Delta Chi, the journalism industry's top society, for 1972 and 1973.

That experience was also scary. Like many of my Saint Mary's classmates, I only had a Notre Dame major—American Studies. With the merger off, nobody knew what would happen to us. It was several long weeks until we were told that we could continue with our majors and receive ND degrees. We didn't need anything else for Christmas that year.

I'm also very grateful, Father Ted, for the patience, encouragement, honesty, and time that you and the other CSCs invested helping me become a reporter. With the coeducation story, you could have blown me off numerous times. Instead you made yourself available and encouraged the other CSCs to do likewise.

Sometimes mistakes happen. Things get reported incorrectly. Instead of being spiteful or vindictive, as some people are, when this happens, you accepted my apologies and said we were moving on. That was an important lesson for my career.

Today the Alumni Directory is one of the first things to which I turn, when I'm given a reporting assignment for *Time, Fortune,* and *Fortune Small Business* magazines, as well as the *Chicago Tribune* Business Section. Trustees, college advisory council members, profs, and alums never fail to come through, no matter the deadline, when I need an interview. Domers I've never met in person have become trusted sources.

Notre Dame's also been the focal point of my family life. I met my husband, Robert, there when he was finishing Notre Dame Law School. I was in the MBA program. As a *Chicago Sun-Times* stringer, I was covering a speech by John Connally, the former Texas governor, when we were introduced. We were married at Sacred Heart, where our sons, Justin and Christian, were baptized. Christian, a 2005 ND graduate in philosophy, is a U.S. Marine Corps Lieutenant, serving in Iraq. Justin, a University of

Chicago graduate and U.S. Marine Corps Lance Corporal, also in Iraq, was accepted into Notre Dame's Law School.

In conclusion, Father Ted, thanks for continuing to be a father, long after your signature dried on my diplomas. And, thanks for keeping the welcome mat out and the light on, when my classmates and I have needed a buck-up and a compass for the road ahead.

Sincerely,

Ann Therese Darin Palmer
Class of '73 AL, '75 MBA

Ann Therese Darin Palmer '73, '75 MBA and Father Ted.

Dear Father Ted,

When A.T. asked me to write a letter thanking you for opening the doors of ND to women, I had to smile, remembering what a thorn in your side the women of the Class of 1973 were. Through no fault of your own, we had become the unwanted stepdaughters of ND, caught in a custody battle between ND and Saint Mary's (or rather, the lack of one), planted firmly on the yellow line dividing U.S. 31, wondering which parent, if either, was going to pick us up after school. Like any child who feels they have been treated unjustly, we were loud, brash, accusing, and angry, and like any father who genuinely cares for his children, you were kind, patient, attentive, and understanding, and eventually it all worked out. For better or for worse, we became the first class of ND women—wait—make that the first of the four Pioneer classes. I think they should just rename our class "The women we didn't know what to do with."

But, the best of endings can come from the most inauspicious of beginnings, and I would have taken an ND degree if I had to swim across Lake St. Joseph in February. You were gracious enough to allow that to happen, (the degree, not the swim) I, for one, will be forever grateful, because it is probably the one thing in my life of which I am most proud. But it is not just the degree I want to thank you for, but the Notre Dame you created for us during those turbulent years of the late '60s and early '70s. All generations face their challenges. Ours was that everything that we knew to be right was now wrong, and everyone we knew to be trustworthy was not. All of the rules we had learned in our Catholic homes and schools were thrown out and in their place were a creed of sex, drugs, and hedonism. The antiwar movement, the women's movement, the black power movement, the Vietnam War, Kent State, the drugs, the riots—it was a lot to absorb without direction, and of course, the movements prohibited taking direction from anyone over thirty. You saw our uncertainty and provided the structure we needed—who will ever forget the famous fifteen-minute rule? You took *"in loco parentis"* to heart, and secretly, we were glad you did, because too much freedom was not what we needed. I have always thought of ND as a sacred place, a holy place, a safe place, where you were free to grow and learn to be yourself, whatever that self might be. So, thank you, Father Ted, for letting us earn our degrees from ND, and giving us such a safe supportive atmosphere in which to grow and learn. You did your job well, and well profited from it.

Have a wonderful birthday, and thank you again.

Sincerely,

Johanna Ryan
Class of '73

Dear Father Hesburgh,

Greetings and Happy Birthday! Thank you for all that you have done for the University of Notre Dame and specifically for the women of Notre Dame. Over the past thirty-plus years, I have been proud to tell people that I graduated from Notre Dame. In the early years, many people were surprised because they really weren't aware that women were attending ND. Being in the first graduating class of women in 1973 was a unique position. The years of "the merger" and then "the nonmerger" made for some interesting times on campus.

I feel blessed to have ties to both Saint Mary's College and the University of Notre Dame. My father graduated from ND in 1942 and it became the only school I wanted to attend. Since ND was not accepting women in 1969, I went on early decision to Saint Mary's and became part of the ND-SMC family. I have many great memories of my years in South Bend. Although my father was not alive to see me graduate, it was still a very special day for me and my family.

Upon graduation, I moved to Chicago and began a career in banking and the young field of systems development. My strong liberal arts and business background led to a successful eighteen-year career from which I "retired" to begin a family in 1991. While my children (a son and two daughters) are still in elementary school, I am happy that my daughters will have the opportunity to apply to both ND and Saint Mary's. I thank you again for your efforts and making it possible for women to attend the University of Notre Dame.

Sincerely,

Peggy Doyle Van Slochem
Class of '73

Dear Father Hesburgh,

Almost thirty-four years ago I received my Notre Dame degree. The women of the Class of 1973, former Saint Mary's students with Notre Dame majors, had lived through the turbulence of the collapse of the proposed merger. At a time when we were concerned about the status of our majors, degrees, financial-aid packages, and dorm accommodations, you and our faculty advisors appreciated our anxiety and made sure that we knew we would be taken care of. You quickly resolved our status issues and informed us that we would receive Notre Dame degrees. To this day I remain grateful and proud to be a member of the first class of Notre Dame women.

My Notre Dame degree has been a door opener both professionally and socially. After graduation I taught American Studies (my undergraduate major) at a Catholic high school in Chicago. A few years later I received a JD degree and spent the bulk of my legal career as an in-house corporate attorney. Along the way, I am sure I was given the time of day and, indeed, recruited because of my Notre Dame credentials. On a personal level, my dear friends include my former Notre Dame and Saint Mary's classmates, and Notre Dame remains an integral part of my life. It has guided my personal growth, what I hold dear, and how I view my world.

Please know that the daughters of Notre Dame are grateful for the courageous decisions you made in building a coeducational university. Your vision and tireless effort enriched the lives of a generation of Notre Dame women. Thank you, Father Ted, for providing the opportunity of a lifetime.

Sincerely,

Julie A. Webb
Class of '73

Dear Father Ted,

One memory I would like to share is the Christmas dinner several of us helped organize in December 1973.

I had started at Saint Mary's my freshman year and then took all my business courses at ND my sophomore year.

My junior year I moved into Walsh, and in December 1973 I was going to graduate with a business degree in management.

I like any excuse to celebrate so I thought we should organize a Christmas dinner. We sent out invitations and Father Ted accepted. It was the eighty-two women from the Class of 1974 and Father Ted. It was a very special night as the dining hall catered the meal for us and we ate in a room above the dining hall. As one would expect, Father

Ted was very gracious and charmed all those in attendance. He has such an aura about him that being in his presence really lifts one spirit.

Being one of eighty-two women we were so scattered . . . I think I was one of twelve management majors and I remember usually being the only woman in my management class. This also meant that I had the opportunity to be the leader of every single project. So this Christmas dinner was very special as it united the eighty-two of us into a wonderful warm evening presided over by Father Ted.

Thank you for allowing me the opportunity to share this memory.

God bless you,

Carole Rechsteiner Adlard
Class of '74

Dear Father Ted,

> "The bigger they are, the harder they fall."
> "A team that won't be beaten, can't be beaten."
> "A winner never quits and a quitter never wins."

Do you recognize the quotes Father Ted? They are from Knute Rockne and ones that I grew up on from the mouth of my father, Joseph Francis Dautrement, (ND Engineering '29). Dad attended Our Lady's university from 1925 through 1929 and was a member of the football team, and as fate would have it, it transferred to the lives of his family members, (i.e., me).

When my sisters came along, they both attended Saint Mary's College, graduating in 1960 and 1968. In addition to our trips to South Bend for the football games, now I had the pleasure of spending more time on campus visiting my sisters and meeting their college friends. This was after all, our home away from home.

When 1969 to 1970 rolled around, it became time for me to choose a college. Needless to say, there was no question in my mind where I wanted to be. Saint Mary's and Notre Dame was the place for me! I am not sure who was more excited with my acceptance, my father or me! The fall of 1970 came and I was off. This was a dream come true for me. I had spent so much time as a little girl walking these campuses and now I was a part of them and the community that brought them alive.

At the end of my freshman year, I had chosen Business Administration as a major and although Saint Mary's didn't offer that, Notre Dame did, and with the co-exchange program it was no problem for me to enroll in those classes there. After all, the two schools were going to merge. By Thanksgiving of my sophomore year that agreement was highly contested and the merger was off. Saint Mary's would remain a women's college, but Notre Dame was now going to be coed.

Where did that leave those of us who were in the middle of this? I had a semester of business classes behind me and was registered for a second one? Off to Dean Raymond's office in the Business College for help. I remember him referring to us as his "Angels" as he said "calm down and apply to Notre Dame as a transfer student. You've taken courses here, we can see your grades. We know you can do the work successfully and you should have a good chance of being accepted." I followed that sage advice. When I went home for spring break, my father met me at the door with tears in his eyes and a letter in his hand. He said, "Welcome home, Notre Dame graduate from the Class of 1974." That was a big day!

In the fall of 1972 I moved into Walsh Hall (my father's dorm his junior year) and a whole new college experience began. The boys weren't always thrilled to have females in class once we lived on campus. I know there was resentment over losing their dorms, rightfully so. And on occasion I can remember hearing, we "only got those good grades because we were girls." I think some professors preferred the all male domain as well.

Campus was not equipped for females in the athletic arena. As I recall, the Rock had no facilities for us to shower or change after playing racquetball. And the JACC (referred to as the ACC when we were there) had converted a men's locker room for our use. Gym classes were waived for us . . . that was a good thing! These nuances are a part of what made us your "pioneers." They were not negatives in my eyes, only challenges that we dealt with that first fall on campus.

As we settled in, the magic of Notre Dame became even more apparent to me. That campus and its community will just envelope you if you allow it. The beauty, the spirituality, the peacefulness, the concern for the less fortunate, the support of the human soul and spirit, it's all there for the taking. Over time, some of those boys whose dorms we usurped became like brothers to me. They still are. The friendships I made, male and female, and have kept over the years are like none I'll ever experience again. Of that I am sure. I think because we were all sharing in this new chapter of living on the same campus our relationships are very special. There is just an unspoken bond that exists between my classmates. We often talk about it at the football games and reunions when we come back to gather. We truly are a part of the "Notre Dame family."

My daughter Meredith graduated this year at Our Lady's university. I am so proud that she chose Notre Dame (and that Notre Dame chose her!). I am certain my father has tears in his eyes in Heaven watching the third generation follow in his footsteps at this university that he so loved. Meredith and her friends have been consummate attendees at our tailgates and so have met many of my classmates over the past four years. They often tell me they hope they can stay in touch with each other the way my friends and I have. That our relationships are "amazing."

We didn't have organized dances. There were no proms or Mardi Gras dances as in my sisters' days or SYRs like today. Somehow they were lost in the '70s. We have to make the boys dance with us at our reunions to make up for that!

Although this note is supposed to be for you, it has been a trip down memory lane for me. There are so many wonderful reflections, Father Griff's Sunday Masses, trips to the Grotto at all times of the day and night, but especially in the winter snow. . . . Is there a place more magical? And what is heartwarming is there were as many young

Chris Kerrigan '74, Joan Dautremont-Gluck '74, Kathy Finke '74, and Anne Cisle Murray '74, all Walsh Hall women's dorm pioneers.

men there as there were young women. Tutoring kids in South Bend, the Pinto project for Ford Motor Co. (Marketing project!!), bookstore basketball, An Tostal weekend, Senior Bar, etc., etc., etc.

Thank you Father Ted for your ever-insightful thinking and perseverance in bringing women to the campus of Notre Dame. You opened the door for us and hopefully we've passed through it and made you proud. Because of you a Notre Dame education has been a gift to me, my niece, and now my daughter, as well as future generations of women to come.

God bless you, Father Ted, on your 90th birthday and always.

Yours in Notre Dame,

Joan Dautremont-Gluck
Class of '74

Dear Father Hesburgh,

I am a proud 1974 graduate of the University of Notre Dame with a BS in mathematics. I fondly remember speaking with you at the thirtieth reunion of coeducation held at Notre Dame in June of 2002. A group of us 1974 women graduates were seated together at the all-class dinner and took the opportunity to greet you.

You shared with us what you considered to be your three greatest accomplishments during your tenure as president of the university—unprecedented growth, lay governance, and the introduction of coeducation. You told us that the admission of women to the university raised the academic bar for the men. Well, it certainly worked in our favor as well. Not only was I academically challenged at Notre Dame (I was one of only four women to earn a degree in mathematics that year) but I learned to work effectively with men and to hold my own. This was invaluable preparation for a career as a systems programmer at IBM where, once again, I was in a small minority of women.

My years at Notre Dame also instilled a thirst for knowledge and accomplishment that led to the pursuit of an MBA and significant career growth. But my years at Notre Dame also instilled a desire to serve my community, which my husband and I take quite seriously and have encouraged in each of our five children.

When I think of my college experience, I have vivid memories of my friends, my professors, and those times when I thought I carried the weight of the world on my shoulders (I've since learned that I never had it so easy!). I also have memories of quiet walks around the lake, prayers at the Grotto, and cheering at the football games. All in all, it was an idyllic time—at the most beautiful and peaceful campus on earth. When I return for football games or class reunions, I still feel that inner peace and overwhelming comfort of returning home.

Thank you so much, Father Hesburgh, for giving me the privilege to be a part of the Notre Dame family. And let me also take the opportunity to wish you a very healthy and Happy 90th Birthday!

With fond regards,

Kathleen Fyda-Turner
Class of '74

Dear Father Hesburgh,

I had the privilege of attending the University of Notre Dame in its first year of coeducation in 1972. What a wonderful experience! It was everything I could have asked for in a college and more. Thank you again and again for the opportunity to attend such a fine institution and to be part of such a fine community.

Notre Dame has impacted my life in so many positive ways. We are a strong stewardship family in the Church, in large part due to the influence of attending Notre Dame. This mustn't be taken for granted however, because I enrolled in ND as a Protestant transfer student. I converted to Catholicism after my children were born and have chosen to educate them in Catholic schools. My conversion to Catholicism was one of the most significant events in my life and in my family's. My husband, Kevin Kopp (ND '74), and I are raising three devout Catholic children. Rok is currently a sophomore at Notre Dame, Hunter is a freshman at Regis Jesuit High School, and Kristen is a senior at USC (we forgive deviance in the family—except on football game days!).

In September of 2004, at the beginning of Rok's freshman year at ND, I asked to see you so that Rok could meet you. We met in your library office. I wanted Rok to meet you so that he could experience firsthand one of the greatest religious and political men of the twentieth century. Father, you have helped the world in so many ways.

You truly have the gift of greatness, and I feel blessed to know you.

I remember being on campus in 1997 for the twenty-fifth reunion for the beginning of coeducation at ND. Father, you attended many of our events that weekend. You said at that time that one of your three greatest achievements in your life was the coeducation of Notre Dame. I am sincerely grateful.

I also remember another reunion story, this one laced with typical Father Ted humor. You told us of the drywall that was placed in front of the urinals in Badin. You let us in on a secret that I'm sure none of us ever knew about. In case coeducation didn't work out, you said the walls would simply have been taken down.

My dad remembers, and was very impressed with your position taken in 1969, when you were the first university president in the United States to come out with a major stand during student unrest on campuses across the United States. You said if force was used on campus, the persons involved would be given fifteen minutes to cease, and if not they would be expelled. My dad thought it was brilliant.

Father, you have touched our lives in so many ways. Every time I have seen you I have thanked you for the opportunity to go to Notre Dame. Once again, thank you and God bless you. You have always had a vision to see outside the box and a gift to make it happen.

The last thing I want to thank you for, Father, is a quote from your book *God, Country, Notre Dame*. It is something that has impacted me greatly. You said you pray it every day, and it covers everything, Father. "No better prayer, no better results: much light and great strength. 'Come, Holy Spirit.'"

Thank you, Father, and God bless.

Sincerely,

Nancy Schoeneman Kopp
Class of '74

Dear Father Hesburgh,

I am privileged to be part of your 90th birthday celebration as I was to be one of the first women at Notre Dame. Entering Saint Mary's as a freshman in 1970, I never envisioned leaving four years later as one of the first female graduates of Notre Dame.

Your vision and efforts made that possible, and I will be forever grateful.

The Notre Dame spirit lives deeply in my family beginning with my father, a 1932 graduate. He was so proud to have his first-born as part of this moment in Notre Dame's history. Given the era in which ND went coed, I suspect that had it not been for his own daughter being among the first group of women, my father would probably not have been particularly supportive of ND going coed. With my husband (also Class of 1974), my sister (1977 graduate of Saint Mary's), my brother (Class of 1979), and two in-laws from Saint Mary's and ND, I am fortunate to be part of a Notre Dame family.

When ND decided to accept women, they published a marketing poster showing a football team from the '30s with their leather helmets with the caption: "Is Notre Dame for Women?" I kept that poster as a symbol of how fortunate I personally was to be part of ND's history and how far women had come. When my husband and I return to the campus, we marvel at the gender equality prevalent there, especially in sports; it is a far cry from the early '70s. Yes, the world and times have changed, but you were instrumental in initiating that change. What a wonderful legacy!

I have my father to thank for igniting the Notre Dame spirit and you for having the foresight to admit women to Notre Dame and providing us an opportunity of a lifetime. To paraphrase the alma mater, "love thee, Father Hesburgh."

Best regards,

Sharon Carey Ryan,
Class of '74

Dear Father Hesburgh,

Not a day goes by that I do not think about the blessings in my life, and my Catholic education (from parochial school through graduate school) is always on the list. And my Notre Dame education is on the list by name.

Notre Dame is a part of who I am. It affects how I do my job, how I deal with people, what I bring to my parish church. It is a part of my marriage (my husband is also a Notre Dame graduate) and the raising of our four children (we visit the campus once a year). It has given me friends who enrich my life to this day. It keeps my daughters wondering what it was like for me to be part of a class that had a five to one ratio of men to women. And it continues to open doors for me wherever I go because people respect it.

Speaking of respect . . . this is where you come in. Thank you, thank you, thank you for your bold move in the fall of 1972 to open Notre Dame to undergraduate women. I was in my first year at Saint Mary's at the time, and I had received a letter before the start of my freshman year that I would receive a Notre Dame degree at the end of my four years. I strongly protested when we returned from Thanksgiving break and learned that the merger was off. In the end I was able to transfer to Notre Dame. But I wonder to this day whether all the women in my freshman class at Saint Mary's who wanted to receive a Notre Dame degree were able to do so.

I know you did not create coeducation alone, and yet clearly without your support it would not have happened when it did. You are an example for all of us. The women of Notre Dame are indebted to you and will always be indebted to you. We will not let our daughters and their daughters forget.

Wishing you many blessings, and with gratitude,

Mary Catherine Dean
Class of '75

Dear Father Ted,

Congratulations on your 90th birthday! You are an inspiration and mentor to all of us who hope to remain active and engaged well into our octogenarian years.

I am Bernard Waldman's daughter, so I have a fairly long history with Notre Dame going back to 1964 when my stepfather, Bernie, married Glenna Frank Ryan while he was on leave from Notre Dame at the Midwest Universities Research Association in Madison, Wisconsin. We came to Notre Dame soon afterward so he could take up his role as assistant dean of the College of Science. As he moved into the position of dean a few years later, I came to my early teen years and considered Notre Dame my home. Your long history with Bernie, dating back to Vetville, was certainly part of that feeling of welcome.

As a young teen, I wanted to go to Notre Dame to college and was patted on the head, by friends of the family who would laugh and say, "Of course you do, my dear," thinking how impossible that would be. But with your foresight and leadership, you made this possible with your announcement of the merger of Notre Dame and Saint Mary's a few years later. Despite the difficulties of that transition and Notre Dame ultimately going coed on its own, you stuck with your principals and gave women a chance.

I had all but two of my freshman classes at Notre Dame that year of 1971–1972, so the transfer to Notre Dame was a natural. It was a dream come true. I became a Notre Dame student that fall of 1972 even though I spent that year abroad in Angers, France. I escaped most of the transitional problems experienced during that first year, since I was off campus, but upon my return, there were still many male students and certainly alumni who felt the change was a mistake and it would destroy the university.

I know there were many difficulties behind the scene those first few years, which made the experience a challenge for the administration.

When I look back these thirty-plus years I am proud to have been among the first of the women at the University of Notre Dame. I see the university has grown dramatically and the bar for admittance has also been raised due to the addition of the female population. Notre Dame is honored not only for her athletic prowess, but now for her academic excellence throughout the world.

Your foresight made this possible and changed the direction of thousands of women and men who had a richer college experience and more fulfilling lives as a result.

Thank you for this gift.

Best regards,

Tawny Ryan Nelb,
Class of '75

Dear Father Ted,

I welcome the opportunity to thank you for coeducation. I transferred from Saint Mary's as a sophomore, and spent that year in Angers. Junior year I opened Farley with Sister Jean, and senior year I opened Lyons, graduating with a bachelor of arts degree, with majors in government and international studies and modern languages. Being a woman student at Notre Dame in those early years of coeducation was an easy transition for me, because the men on both sides of my family had gone to Notre Dame for two generations. My maternal grandparents met at Notre Dame—my grandmother was a "townie"—and my grandfather, Class of 1922, apparently used to ride around South Bend with Father Cavanaugh's driver in Father Cavanaugh's car when he was not in town. One of the people they met on those rides was my grandmother.

My mother met my father outside Alumni Hall when her cousin, a student from New York, fixed her up on a blind date and her parents only allowed her to come out to South Bend because her aunts lived there. That blind date turned out to be my father, and I have a copy of the nice letter you wrote to my father explaining that you could not officiate at their wedding in New York in 1951 because you had to be at the Michigan State game. In clarifying that the game was not as important as getting married, you cautioned my father not to listen to the game on his honeymoon! You also encouraged my parents to say the rosary together every night as a way to keep God close to their marriage and to take turns offering up an intention for each succeeding decade—as good advice then as it is today.

Through the years we would visit South Bend to see the aunts. My father would always excitedly point out to us the first glimpse of the Golden Dome from the tollway. All of us children therefore realized from an early age how magical a place Notre Dame was. We would then all have lunch at the Morris Inn, where on one occasion my then-toddler brother threw a knife and broke a glass, which of course we still laugh about.

Certainly the community living at Notre Dame helped me become a better Christian, and to realize my obligation to help the Lord's less fortunate. All of my stimulating, hardworking professors helped me improve my critical thinking and communication skills, and gave me the confidence to pursue my goals and meet the challenges presented to me. Your vision has been realized, and those of us there in the beginning with you are very grateful to you.

Most appreciatively,

Cathleen Uhl Stock
Class of '75

Dear Father Hesburgh,

As a member of Notre Dame's Class of '76, I am writing to say Happy 90th Birthday and to thank you for bringing coeducation to the University of Notre Dame. It seems an appropriate time to express my appreciation to you, for I have no doubts that my life was immeasurably changed for the better when you had the wisdom and foresight to welcome young women to become full-fledged members of the university community back in 1972. Among the many blessings of my association with ND have been the lifelong friends I made there, including my husband of twenty-six years, Gregory Benz. My year spent in the Rome Studies Program as an architecture student was probably the best year of my life. My husband and I were both thrilled last year when our son Michael chose to enroll at ND (over Princeton, Columbia, and Yale) because we wanted him to have the opportunity of experiencing, as we did, the special qualities of a Notre Dame education. We are all well pleased with Mike's decision and look forward to having his sister Virginia join the ND student body in a couple more years. Because of your courageous decision to move forward with coeducation at the university, both the "sons and daughters" of Notre Dame can share in the blessings of the ND experience. Thank you for making this happen.

Sincerely,

Ann Greenburg Benz
Class of '76

Dear Father Hesburgh,

I would like to thank you for making my dream come true. As a high school junior, I began the college search just like all my classmates, but I did so with a heavy heart. The university that I most wanted to attend, the University of Notre Dame, was not available to me because it was a male-only institution. I looked at other colleges with my parents but none could match the academic excellence and spirit of Notre Dame for me. Having grown up in a household where Notre Dame was a revered institution, I had hoped that I might be a part of it someday and not merely an outsider looking in. My excitement increased as I watched the process of merger talks between Notre Dame and Saint Mary's College unfold in the *Chicago Tribune*. When the *Tribune* eventually reported the University of Notre Dame would become coeducational in 1972, I knew that I had to be a part of the freshman class. Fortunately, the Admissions Office agreed with me and offered me a spot in the Class of 1976 and I was on cloud nine!

Thanks to your foresight, my adult life has been formed by my experiences at Notre Dame. My faith was strengthened by the spiritual presence of men and women religious, such as yourself; I made lasting friendships that I value deeply; my education encouraged me to continue to question and learn about our world; but most importantly, my time at Notre Dame taught me that we serve God through serving others, and I live that mission today through different charity work.

When the university hosted the Women's 25th Reunion in 1997 to commemorate the establishment of coeducation at Notre Dame, we all knew that the struggles we had during the first years of coeducation were well worth the effort. We are eternally grateful to you, Father Hesburgh, for all you did for the equality of women at our beloved university. I feel fortunate that my husband and I have daughters who are members of the Class of 2005 and the Class of 2008. I could never thank you enough for all you have done for women by including them as equal partners in Notre Dame.

Sincerely,

Donna Crowley Campbell
Class of '76

Dear Father Ted,

Thank you for making it possible for me to graduate from Our Lady's university. Attending Notre Dame provided the foundation upon which I've built my life. By living among the women of Walsh and Farley halls and by living and studying at Notre Dame, I incorporated faith, service, and community into the core of my life.

I know that many of my classmates have gone on to achieve great things—they've made a profound impact in the areas of law, science, medicine, the arts, and journalism. I'm not one of those achievers; I've led a very ordinary life since leaving ND. I've had to juggle the demands of family and profession. I've had day-to-day successes and disappointments. However, I believe that attending Notre Dame has enabled me to keep my life in balance. It has allowed me to live my ordinary life in an extraordinary way.

I've been married for twenty-eight years to a man of great faith and integrity. (Not an ND grad, but we won't hold that against him!) My husband practices law and I teach at our local community college. We've served on our town's council, at our parish, and in our children's schools. We will never win awards or national acclaim, but I believe that we've made a difference in our community. Most importantly, we have been blessed with each other and with four sons. We have tried to instill in our sons our faith in God and our love of family and friends. Three of our sons will graduate from Notre Dame over the next three years.

Last week, the women of my class were surveyed by a current ND student who is writing her senior thesis on coeducation at Notre Dame. The spontaneous e-mails that have resulted from our access to this e-mail list have taken me back thirty years!

Without your efforts, Father Ted, I would never have had the opportunity to live among these extraordinary women. Thank you for making so much possible!

With fondest regards and gratitude,

Kathleen Buckley ("KB") Murren
Class of '76

Dear Father Ted,

It is not often in our lives that we can say we were pioneers in anything; but I can say that I was one. That's why it's especially important to thank you for taking a chance and allowing women to attend ND in 1972. It doesn't seem that long ago to me, but the concept of prohibiting one sex from attending a school seems so foreign today. I am sure you had great opposition to this change both from the student body and from ND administration, but you pursued this change, anyway.

I really believe my time at ND changed my life for the better and forever. I had spent my entire life in a small town in northern Indiana. ND, through varied student body and faculty, was my first exposure to life outside the Midwest and the United States. After ND, I moved to Florida, obtained two master's degrees, had (and continue to have) a great career in urban planning, survived cancer (over eighteen years now!), got married at the ripe old age of thirty-six, traveled (and continue to travel) the world, have done long-distance motorcycle rides. I've modeled in fashion shows, moved to Oregon and became a first-time mom at the age of forty-seven. We adopted our daughter Gracie in Nanching, China, and she was placed in our arms on 9/11/01—with CNN on in the background in everyone's hotel room. She is the light of our lives and we are in the process of adopting a second child.

My life has been a real adventure and it started at ND. Thank you for the opportunity to be a pioneer. And I'm not done yet!

Thanks, Father Ted.

Ann M. Pytynia
Class of '76

Dear Father Ted,

I was holding a plate full of scrambled eggs at a recruiting buffet when the conversation turned to my graduation year. The ND professor quickly did the math in her head and realized that I had been graduated with the first class of women to have attended the university for four years. I had to juggle the eggs as she reached to shake my hand saying, "Oh, I always wanted to meet one of you! What was it like?"

The encounter, some fifteen years after I had graduated, helped put into perspective how truly special it was to be one of the first women admitted to Notre Dame. And while the situation itself was unique and could easily have taken on laboratory rat status, I am grateful that we were allowed to live and thrive in as normal an atmosphere as possible.

The education was priceless. It allowed me to pursue a successful accounting career and later, after raising my family, start my own business. The fact that there were so many more men than women on campus, while jolting at first to a girl who attended an all-girl high school, was the best training for me as I entered a male-dominated field.

The people-factor was incomparable, as I still keep in touch with the many friends and professors who helped form the person that I am today. Of course, the best people connection that I made at ND was with the man that I later married. We traveled back to campus to become engaged. An hour later, after placing a random call to your office, we stood on the steps of the Ad Building while you blessed our forthcoming marriage.

The spirituality of the campus is almost tangible. At a time of life when young people are thinking of so many things other than God, the godliness of Notre Dame enfolded me like a misty South Bend afternoon.

For these gifts and so much more, I am grateful to you, Father Ted. It was your vision and courage that touched so many women's lives. Thank you.

Sincerely,

Christie Gallagher Sever
Class of '76

Dear Father Hesburgh,

As a way of introduction, my name is Joanne Toeniskoetter Anderson and I am a member of the Class of 1977. I remember my four years at Notre Dame as happy ones, full of challenge, friendship, laughter, reflection, and opportunity. Living in Chicago has enabled me to maintain an active relationship with the university, and over the past thirty years my family and I have visited often. My oldest son, Ian, graduated last year from Notre Dame and received his master's in accountancy in May. I am the proud mother of a Double Domer!

What an exceptional time it was for me and my classmates to be among the first women to attend and graduate from the university. During those four years, I developed a great deal of self-confidence, learning to hold my own with my predominantly male classmates. I made deep and lasting friendships with both the women and men of Notre Dame. I learned the importance of mutual respect and the value of a healthy sense of humor.

On the occasion of your 90th birthday, it gives me great pleasure to thank you for making coeducation at Notre Dame a reality. Your bold decision in the early '70s has proven to be an absolute, spot-on success. Congratulations!

Thank you for being a man of integrity, vision, and faith, a president and leader of whom we are all proud. May this year be full of blessings and peace. Your loyal daughters of Notre Dame always remember you in our thoughts and prayers.

Sincerely,

Joanne Toeniskoetter Anderson
Class of '77

Dear Father Hesburgh,

As one of the first coeds to attend the University of Notre Dame, I want to thank you for all of your support and tenacity in bringing coeducation to ND. Arriving in South Bend in the autumn of 1973 as a wide-eyed freshman, I did not recognize the challenges that were ahead for all of us—for the administration and the students. It was a time of transition—upset alumni, teachers, and upper classmen. I was fortunate to call Badin

Hall my home, only to discover how many people were upset that Walsh and Badin were women's dorms. However, my experiences at ND prepared me for the male-dominated workforce that I entered after graduation. As a graduate of the then General Program of Liberal Studies, a program offered at only ND and St. John's in Minnesota, I was well equipped to enter the business world, strong in creative writing and thinking skills.

On behalf of my father, Stan Sheeran, who earned a master's and PhD in chemistry at ND, thank you. It was a dream come true for the father of three daughters to hear that coeducation was coming to the university. If accepted, there was no uncertainty that I would attend Notre Dame, as far as my father was concerned. I had a different goal—Duke. I am so glad that my father prevailed. Notre Dame is a magical place that one cannot adequately describe—it is an experience.

If I had attended Duke, I would have never fallen in love with Tom Birsic ('76). Tom was the Student Union president and still fondly recalls great conversations with you late into the evening, when he would see your light on walking across campus.

So thank you on so many fronts—warm memories from the past and a bright future for another generation of ND women. My fourteen-year-old daughter, Kelsey, has every intention on being a member of the ND Class of 2015.

Sincerely,

Patter Sheeran Birsic
Class of '77

Dear Father Hesburgh,

Just look at how lucky I was . . . graduating from Notre Dame and on the steps of the Administration Building with Father Ted!

Little did I realize then just how fortunate I was. Today I know that attending Notre Dame changed my life. Thank you for giving me that opportunity, and for everything that you did to make Notre Dame such a great and special place.

Thank you, and Happy Birthday!

Kristine (Thornton) Brothers
Class of '77

Kristine Thornton Brothers '77 with Father Ted Hesburgh at the doors of the University of Notre Dame Administration Building—Commencement Day, May 15, 1977.

Dear Father Ted,

I can still remember meeting you in the basement of Farley Hall when I was a freshman in 1973. You shared stories of your travels and experiences and wanted to get to know each of us—the first women in Farley.

I was intimidated when I arrived at Notre Dame because my three roommates had gone to Catholic schools—one to a small coed school, one to a small all-girl school and one to a large all-girl school. I went to a large coed public school. It turns out my education was just fine and even though I was very shy, I was more accustomed to being around the opposite sex and handling the freedom college offers you than many of my classmates.

I vividly remember the panty raids, food fights, girls being bussed in for the weekends, drunken parties at the Armory, fake IDs at the Library, Nickie's, Corby's, and Fat Wally's, the editorials in the *Observer* about how the girls went to the guys' parties to drink their beer or whapatoola punch and never talked to them, the Beach Boy parties at Holy Cross Hall, being the only woman in a class, the formals held by every dorm, and the guys being angry and jealous that we did much better in class (we were more serious students!).

By the time I was a freshman counselor for Emil T. in my senior year, there were many more women and a much more normal atmosphere as evidenced by my interviews with the freshmen. My son is currently a junior at ND. The university is evenly split between men and women. The number of campus buildings must have doubled since I attended (with a more amazing building going up almost every year!) and the colleges rank among the best in the world. Even though thirty years have passed and the world has changed in so many ways (hey, we thought we had technology by bringing our Texas Instrument calculator and a TV!), Notre Dame is still the same when I visit my son on a football weekend or attend a reunion or a class. The foundation was laid many years before women entered the university—the Catholic values, the Grotto, the Basilica, the religious in every dorm (such as Sister Jean Lenz), parietals, the polite and friendly students, the caring professors, the students volunteering their time for charities or those less fortunate, the world-class education, the striving for greatness, and the building of lifelong friendships.

Thanks Father Ted, for sharing Notre Dame with women. Every time I return to Our Mother's university, I am reminded what a special place it is.

Gayla Molinelli Bush
Class of '77

Dear Father Hesburgh,

I attribute much of my successes and finding balance in my life to Notre Dame. You have opened many doors indeed, but you gave me more than a door—you offered me an open door whose passage led to an entire new world. As a child of Greek immigrant parents and raised in a small town in Pennsylvania, I never dreamed that my world would become so big. My special place—and space—is Notre Dame. Thank you so much for making the University of Notre Dame a coeducational institution.

Argery Bitchakas Cooke
Class of '77

Dear Father Ted,

I want to thank you for having the wisdom, courage, and insight to challenge years of tradition by inviting women into the halls of Notre Dame. Your decision changed my life. At the age of ten, I decided that I would attend Notre Dame, and I didn't hesitate to tell friends and relatives this when they asked me about my future plans. They all gave me an "Isn't she adorable?" patronizing smile before telling me that Notre Dame was a boys' school. I'm not sure why that didn't deter me from my aspirations to attend du Lac, but it didn't.

When I received my acceptance in December of 1972, I was welcomed into the second class of women at Notre Dame. I still have that letter. My four years there remain some of my warmest in memory. Your personal encouragement of the education of each Notre Dame student was a constant of my experience. When I approached your ever-open office door in the spring of 1976 to ask you to support my efforts to spend my summer in the bush of Kenya, you quickly donated to my cause. Upon my return to ND that fall, you invited me to lunch to discuss my experiences. I will never forget your personal interest in me, one of approximately 8,000 undergraduates attending the university at that time.

Being at Notre Dame in those beginning years of coeducation provided me with a perspective and resourcefulness necessary to achieve and succeed in the male-dominated business world of the early '80s. I am currently an educator, and I hope to instill in my students that same sense of "you can do anything" that you and Notre Dame imparted to all of us.

As time goes on, I am constantly humbled by the achievements of my peers in those early classes of women, and it is certain that Notre Dame breeds an energy and commitment to cause into its graduates. I feel fortunate that my own two daughters, Katie, Class of 2004 and Maggie, Class of 2009, know that being a member of the ND family generates passion for life. You have made this happen for all three of us, and we are all grateful.

Sincerely,

Peg Hornback Culhane
Class of '77

᪤

Happy Birthday, Father Ted!

My name is Eileen O'Grady Daday and I graduated from Notre Dame in 1977. I want to extend all my best wishes for a Happy Birthday, as well as thank you for your vision and courage in converting Our Lady's university into a coed institution.

Way back in 1973, my father—who had always dreamed of going to Notre Dame—convinced me to go through the motions of trying to gain admittance, even though I didn't think I had a prayer. It turned out to be life changing.

I began my college years on the fourth floor of Walsh Hall, with occasional visits by the guys who had lived there just a couple of years before me, and found instant connections with all of the women who lived there with me.

You came regularly to our Walsh Hall chapel to say Sunday evening Masses, and I remember how meaningful they were. Somehow your soft voice and eloquent sermons always lifted us up and filled us with reverence.

It was at Notre Dame that I met my husband, Steve Daday, and you were there to greet us—and our families—at our graduation. We now have six children, two of

# Improved Coaching
# Aids Women's IH

by Eileen O'Grady
ND Women's Sports Editor

Now that the exciting women's interhall football season has ended, many questions arise. Why was there more interest and participation this year? Why did the caliber of the game itself seem to improve?

Why was the race for the championship so much closer?

Although there are many answers to these questions, one is often overlooked, better coaching.

Unknown to many, all six of the women's teams had at least one coach, while Lewis had three, and Farley and Lyons had two. All of the coaches were male.

For the average sports fan, an obvious question comes to mind here: Why would guys take such an active interest in girls' football?

In polling some of the 10 women's coaches, the overriding response was "for the fun of it." But all of them soon took it seriously.

Don Byrne, Badin's coach for two years and Lewis' head coach for two years, stuck with it because he saw real value in the program. "I think it's exciting for girls to have an opportunity to play in sports and not have the social stigma often attached to it."

Byrne stressed the biggest factor in his enthusiasm was the girls themselves. "All these girls really wanted to play," he added. This is evidenced by the fact that Lewis again had 60 girls go out for the team this year.

Out of necessity, Byrne took on an assistant coach last year to help with Lewis, Brian Elpers. Although Elpers was not as experienced in the actual playing of football as some of the other coaches, Byrne saw an advantage in this. He could more easily get across the fundamentals of football to the girls.

Elpers found this the most exciting thing about coaching the women: the challenge of teaching them the fundamentals, all the way to the finer points, and seeing them do so well.

"Out of the more than 60 girls that came out this year, we had only five girls that had ever played before," Elpers explained. "So we had to completely re-do the whole offense and defense from last year."

Most of the coaches had to teach the girls everything. They instructed them how to line up, a count, how to position their feet so they wouldn't lose their balance and throwing and catching the ball. Teaching the backs to spin as they cut up the field, how to run with the flags instead of past them, and handing off were also basics which were taught.

One of Farley's coaches, John Tartaglione, also enjoyed the teaching aspect of the coaching. "A lot of the girls are really talented, and so I got a lot of satisfaction from seeing them do well," he stated.

Fr. Terrence Lally, Asst. Vice-President of Student Affairs, Walsh's only coach, took it up mainly for relaxation from his administrative duties.

He stressed how "bright" the girls are: "I know they were good from the beginning," he stated. "I was really impressed with their discipline and ability to play together."

Lally's philosophy was never to "over-coach." Specifically he'd tell the girls: "Be positive. Don't yell at anybody. Don't push them beyond what they can do and go out there and have some fun."

In general, Lally thought the girls' games to be more interesting than the men's to watch. "They were more patterned, expecially the quarterbacks," he remarked.

"You'd see double reverses, passes out to the corner, and long passes on fourth and long yardage, instead of just barrelling up the middle," Lally continued.

Lyons' head coach, Steve Thomas gained quite a bit of pleasure from the whole thing. His team still refers to him as "coach," or "hon'," and they gave him a "Lyons' hall football coach" jersey. He claims the whole experience "really made my semester. I can't wait till next year."

Thomas specifically noted three things about the girls as compared to many of the men's teams he's played on. "The girls were much smarter in learning plays, had more compassion for their opponents, so they were less anamalistic. Their general attitude was more enthusiastic and more hardworking."

Thomas found a real identity while working with the team. He looked forward to all their practices and actually put on sweats and ran the plays with them in practice. He also enjoyed eating with the team after each practice and game.

"I couldn't study on the day of a game," he claims. "Already I miss those practices."

The coaches all agreed the caliber of the game has improved, even since the beginning of the season.

"We lost our first game to Lewis on one 70 yard run," Thomas explained. "But towards the end of the year, we beat them not by any long play but just by successive drives."

Byrne noticed a drastic shift from a primarily passing attack to a more balanced game. He also commented that the caliber seems to improve when the girls play on the astroturf.

Father Lally commented on the refereeing as a cause. "The officiating was good for the most part. This made for a really sane attitude among the girls."

In any case all these coaches

Better coaching was a major reason for the improved performance in women's interhall this fall.

really found women's interhall a challenge and fun to be a part of. Interested would-be coaches, male or female, might contact these halls next fall, since 7 out of 10 of these present coaches are seniors.

whom already have graduated from Notre Dame and another is at Saint Mary's College right now.

My Notre Dame education has served me well, as I am a freelance writer for the *Daily Herald* newspaper here in the Chicago suburbs, while my husband is an attorney.

Thank you for making that possible. Your milestone decision, going against I'm sure plenty of angry alumni, has empowered thousands of women like myself, with a Notre Dame education and the spiritual experience of attending school there.

All the best, Father Ted, and thank you again for all of your wisdom and courage.

Eileen O'Grady Daday
Class of '77

Dear Father Ted,

As a proud member of the Class of 1977, I was thrilled and honored to be a part of the ND family. You see, my dad was a 1949 grad, and as a little girl I would always insist that I would go to Notre Dame, too. In 1972, just as I was thinking of college choices, I saw that infamous advertisement of the 1908 Law School Football Team with the headline "Is Notre Dame a Place for Women?" Thank you, Father Hesburgh, for bringing us to ND and for giving me this special bond with my dad.

Susan Fitzpatrick Drago
Class of '77

Dear Father Hesburgh,

It was 1973 as I exuberantly read my acceptance letter to the University of Notre Dame. I quickly relinquished my Benedictine College scholarship and headed off the Notre Dame making Walsh Hall my college home. We girls immediately wore our Kelly green Walsh shirts with pride and we too were ND! But in 1973 our male classmates did not always share our enthusiasm for coeducation. We were breaking Notre Dame tradition along with displacing the guys who lived in Walsh, Badin, and Breen-Phillips.

Eventually we were accepted as we too were challenged by the academic rigor and the likes of the "Emil" seven-point quizzes. We prepared for careers while developing lifelong friendships and some, like myself, meeting our future husbands. We were surrounded by the tradition and values that helped shape us.

Today, we celebrate and thank you for bringing coeducation to Notre Dame thirty-five years ago. You have helped shape the role of American women. We are grateful for the Notre Dame experience and equal opportunities. We are appreciative of the education that was extended to us and that has been instrumental in our roles as wives, mothers, and career women.

At my Notre Dame commencement in 1977 your parting words were to live our lives with compassion, commitment, and consecration. You'll be proud to know that I have remembered the three "Cs" in both joyful and challenging times.

In conclusion, the Notre Dame experience was much more than classroom learning. It was preparation for life and God's consecration was with me when our paths crossed at the Grotto in 2003. My family and I were praying at the Grotto on the occasion of my son's graduation. You said how lucky I was to be a graduate and to have a graduate. It was a joyful occasion to be passing Notre Dame values onto the next generation. Yes, I am lucky but it is with foresight such as yours that has made the luck possible. Thank you for coeducation and for shaping the future of Notre Dame.

Sincerely,

Debra Kenny Ellsworth
Class of '77

Dear Father Hesburgh,

I first saw you at our freshman welcome Mass in 1973. You were at once dynamic and full of peace. As you spoke, I felt the power of the place called Notre Dame. Over the years, I would see you, walking around campus. Or, you would come to our dorm for an ice cream social. Sometimes I would hear stories about people I knew visiting you in your office in the "wee hours"—you never chased them out, that we heard. One of our friends got a little tipsy at one of our graduation festivities and begged you to say his wedding Mass. You smiled and said that you would be honored . . . if you were in town.

Whether you were in town or not, you were legendary. We wanted to see you and read about you and talk to you and hear you. Whether in the political arena, or as a theologian, or as an educator, you made us want to listen. You made us think. You made us proud.

Father Hesburgh, you are as much a part of Notre Dame as the Golden Dome and the Fight Song! It was a privilege to have studied at Notre Dame . . . it was a blessing to have been there, during your tenure.

Very truly yours,

Elizabeth Lavins Fitzgerald
Class of '77

❧

Dear Father Ted,

Thirty-three years ago, the University of Notre Dame welcomed the Class of 1977 to campus. I recall how my dad brought me to Notre Dame and helped me move into my dorm room in Badin. It was an extremely warm August day, and the climb to my fourth-floor room was a memorable one. I was not at all sure, when my family drove away two days later, what to think about my "new life."

Thirty years ago, the University of Notre Dame presented its Class of 1977 in a memorable graduation ceremony. Between those two defining moments, many wonderful young women grew up in the glowing halo of Our Lady's campus. Were it not for you, Father Ted, this would not have come to pass, at least not for my class sisters and me. We are grateful for your historic vision for Notre Dame and the blessings that result from your courage to make it so.

Our world is a better place because of you. Through Our Lady and her Son, the women of Notre Dame have and will continue to contribute in ways that perhaps only you could have anticipated.

With love and thanks,

Margaret Smith Gillespie
Class of '77

PS It was amazing to me that your door was always open to the students. Even years later, when my husband (also Class of 1977) came back to campus for a football weekend visit, you welcomed us and took time to chat when we stopped by the library! Bless you.

Dear Father Ted,

Many thanks for supporting coeducation at the University of Notre Dame. For as long as I can remember, my uncle, Father Leon Mertensotto, has been an advocate for Notre Dame and the education the university provides. I was honored in my high school junior year, when the opportunity was given to me to apply for the fall of 1973.

Notre Dame provided me an excellent education, friendships across the United States, and a foundation as to what it means to be a caring and spiritual individual. I entered ND as a young coed, with a very limited vision as to what I might be, and left a young woman, with a vision as to what I could be. My mom to this day claims that the person that entered ND in the fall of 1973 did not come out of ND—I hope that she believes it was for the best! I sure do. Notre Dame was instrumental in who I am today! I am very proud to be one of the first female graduates!

I will always thank you for your vision as to what the University of Notre Dame could be and now is with women on the campus. Many in our extended family, both male and female, have degrees from Notre Dame and live the ND spirit. I met my husband of twenty-eight years at ND and now our son is a senior with graduation just around the corner.

May God bless you and continue to bless the University of Notre Dame. Birthday greetings to you as well on your 90th year!

Lynn Mertensotto Girouard
Class of '77

Dear Father Hesburgh,

Thank you very much for the wonderful opportunity that you have provided for countless women by making the University of Notre Dame coeducational.

My educational experience at Notre Dame strengthened my values of community, encouraged spiritual growth, and yielded lifelong friendships with my peers and the faculty.

I have always looked forward to my visits to Notre Dame for reunions, football games, and other campus events. They also served as mini-retreats with always times of reflection, spiritual rejuvenation, and celebration. I have shared this spirit over the years with my husband, my children, and my friends.

It has always been difficult to express in words the essence of the Notre Dame spirit, its community, and service to others. However, I am eternally indebted to you that I have this challenge! Thanks again!

Sincerely,

Marianne Morgan Harris
Class of '77

Dear Father Hesburgh,

To paraphrase the inscription at the Grotto, I count myself as a grateful daughter of Notre Dame. As a member of the second class of coeducation at Notre Dame, I often think about the fact that only an accident of timing placed me in such a special place at the most unique of times.

After graduating from a high school of 2,000 girls, attending Notre Dame involved a bit of a transition for me. As a business major, I often found myself in class with only a handful of other women, always difficult to be inconspicuous. I suppose none of us women went to Notre Dame to be inconspicuous. I have so many memories unique to that time and place: food fights, necessitating quick escapes under the dining hall tables; panty raids on football weekends; streakers—on the quad, and even in the dorm, one of whom I had the privilege of encountering in the middle of the night; women flooding out the dorms when Billie Jean King defeated Bobby Riggs in the "Battle of the Sexes"; being unceremoniously transferred to weight lifting (with one other woman) when my phys ed sport of choice filled (the coach was mercifully understanding!); Sorin Hall residents rating coeds with flash cards as we walked past their infamous porch; the great privilege of living in Walsh Hall in the shadow of the Dome—a dorm I often thought the guys must have hated to give up. Of course, lucky timing also allowed our class to be at Notre Dame for a football national championship and the legendary streak-breaking basketball game against UCLA (both in our freshman year), as well as many other great sports moments. Being at Notre Dame quickly transformed me into a true sports fan, not bad for a person who didn't know what a first down was until I started college. You could say I adapted.

Thank you, Father Hesburgh, for the vital role you played in opening the doors of Notre Dame to women. I had a truly unique college experience and I loved every minute of it. As I have learned over the years, alumni remain very much a part of the university and I know it will always be a part of me. I have maintained lifelong friendships with a handful of my college friends, and have renewed my friendship via cyberspace with quite a few others as a result of classmate Judge Sheila O'Brien's "Fiftieth Birthday List." My husband, Mark ('77), and I have attended most of our class reunions that have provided great opportunities to sustain and renew old friendships. And finally, we have come full circle as the blessings of coeducation now extend to our daughter Molly ('06). Thank you for your foresight, courage, and inspiration (and timing!) that gave Molly and me and so many others the opportunity of Notre Dame.

Sincerely,

Janet (Laughlin) Hogan
Class of '77

Dear Father Hesburgh,

Did I ever tell you "thank you" for what you made possible for women at Notre Dame? If not, then this letter is long past due.

The inescapable image I visualize when I consider coeducation at Notre Dame is that of the opening door. It's not a new metaphor by any means. Great explorers and researchers have long been described as opening doors to new frontiers. And not too long ago, we as a Church were invited to "open wide the doors to Christ." It strikes me that one of the most popular of the series of posters produced by *ND Magazine* is that of the doors of Notre Dame. They are portrayed as closed, but we know that to us they are ever open, thanks to you.

You opened the doors of Notre Dame to women, Father, and you gave us the opportunity to learn, to discover, to become . . . to explore ideas, ourselves, and others . . . to deepen our faith, and to forge incredible relationships. For many if not all of us, that experience has been one of the most formative experiences of our lives.

Although the lilacs have bloomed many times since my commencement weekend, Notre Dame seems to be as much a part of my present as it was in my past. This is in reference primarily to the remarkable alums I've been fortunate to meet, although the frequent e-mail updates from the Alumni Association, the College of Arts and Letters, and other ND departments keeps the university close at hand, too. Did I say "hand?" I meant "heart"; "close at heart."

I sincerely hope, Father, that this collection of love letters before you can somehow start to repay you for the deep debt of gratitude we alumnae owe you for your vision, your courage, your strength and commitment to coeducation at the University of Notre Dame. It humbles me to think that, even as you helped shape the events of the world, you helped shape the lives of many young women, myself included.

If you ever happen to find yourself in the small town of Wentzville, Missouri, Father, please stop by. My door is always open to you.

With gratitude, thanks, and prayers,

Patricia M. Klepper
Class of '77

❧

Dear Father Ted,

Not only did I get a great education at a great time (1973–1977) but my father, Thomas J. McCarthy (who was a student in your dorm where you served as resident assistant after World War II) was so pleased his daughter could attend his alma mater.

My dad is eighty-two, has Alzheimer's, but is still watching the ND football games every Saturday afternoon and takes an active interest in all the university mailings.

We practiced law together for twenty-six years, and I couldn't be prouder of him. Best wishes for a wonderful birthday, and many thanks for your strong commitment to coeducation.

Colleen C. McCarthy
Class of '77

❧

Father Hesburgh,

How can I thank you for your role in opening up the doors of ND to women under-graduates. Here's a brief true story.

When I was a small girl in elementary school in Southern California I learned about a university called Notre Dame. I saw pictures and heard that it was one of the best universities in the country. I promised myself that I would go to Notre Dame. That was probably around 1964—I was about ten. A couple of years later when my older brother was starting to think about college my mom, dad, brother, and I took a long summer vacation driving from Orange County, California, to the east—we went as far as Michigan. We stopped at colleges in Arizona, Colorado, Nebraska, Oklahoma, Il-linois, Indiana, and Michigan. Of course we went to Notre Dame—I was awestruck. My brother wasn't interested. He went to Michigan State University with a National Merit Scholarship. I kept my ND dream burning in my heart.

When my turn to apply to college came around in my senior year of high school it was in 1972. I still had ND as a dream, but I had to hedge my bets because the cost was steep. I applied to ND, to Scripps Women's College, to Reed College, to UC Santa Barbara, and even to Cal State Fullerton in my hometown. I was accepted at all five schools and was awarded financial scholarships at four of the five. I was devastated that ND did not offer a scholarship. It didn't look like it was going to happen for me. Here's where you really came into the picture. At that time, the country was still roil-ing from antiwar sentiment, college riots, general unrest among the youth. Of course I was intensely interested in finding out about all of it. My parents were so impressed with your strict approach to student unrest—they believed I would be safer at ND than at another big college.

My parents dug deep; I took out a student loan and got a job at the South Dining Hall. I got my dream. Thanks to you.

All my best wishes,

Debbie McGraw
Class of '77

Dear Father Hesburgh,

I am so sorry that I can't thank you in person for the tremendous impact your leadership has had on my life. I'm a member of the Class of 1977, the second year of women and can't tell you what those four years of college meant to me. My years at ND opened my eyes to the possibilities of life and encouraged me to be a lifelong learner. I had come from South Philadelphia and felt my life had been very contained before arriving at ND. I can actually recall the feeling I had during the fall of freshman year,  walking through the gorgeous fall foliage up Notre Dame Avenue toward the dome. Such profound awareness, appreciation, and completeness. My daughter just graduated from ND last fall and she shares my gratitude.

Currently at almost fifty-one, I am pursuing a doctoral degree in psychology. I know that ND led me on that path.

Thank you from the bottom of my heart and depths of my soul.

Best wishes,

Terry Molony
Class of '77
Breen-Phillips

Dear Father Hesburgh,

I first met you as a small girl, running up the stairs of the Administration Building and almost careening into you. My father laughingly asked me if I knew who I had almost knocked over, and explained to me that you were the president of the university. I was unaware of the personal impact that you and your decisions would have on my life.

I grew up in the shadow of the Golden Dome. My father had attended Notre Dame and my mother was a Saint Mary's girl. I spent many summer days at the lakes feeding ducks, visiting the Grotto, and feeling the peacefulness of the prayer-laden stones. I believed that the drinking fountain at the Grotto was a source of healing water. I used to love the stairs next to the old laundry because there were millions of lilies of the valley releasing their fragrance. I went to Mass at Sacred Heart on special occasions and was in awe of the grand Church that was so different from my home parish. I loved Notre Dame, but I knew I could never be a "Notre Dame man."

And then, miraculously, two years before I was to attend college, Notre Dame opened its doors to women. I was accepted into the Notre Dame Class of 1977. As large as Notre Dame had been in my life until then, Notre Dame then became mine. I was living Notre Dame. It was at Notre Dame that I experienced the best teachers in my life. It was Notre Dame where I met the most brilliant, talented men and women in my life. It was Notre Dame where I questioned and grew intellectually and emotionally. It was Notre Dame that gave me a perspective of a spirituality that I enjoy today.

I want to thank you for being part of that decision to accept women into Notre Dame. Not only am I personally grateful for the experience of attending Notre Dame, but I think that women have enriched Notre Dame. The Notre Dame today is better for the years of women treading her hallowed halls and offering the feminine perspective. The Notre Dame of today is stronger academically, offers a more balanced social environment, and has a broader social conscience because of the women that attend.

Thank you, Father Hesburgh. I am now greeted by my father as "Here's my Notre Dame man." Without your action in the '70s, I could never have the privilege of sharing the experience. My oldest son is now a Notre Dame man, and I am proud to share the Notre Dame legacy with him. Thank you and Happy Birthday. I hope we can celebrate many more with you.

Yours in Notre Dame,

Ann T. Moriarity, MD
Class of '77

Dear Father Ted,

Thank you for the gift of my Notre Dame education. I can still recall the excitement of being on campus and walking past the Dome in the fall of 1973. It was like living a dream. At the same time, I felt that I had been given a tremendous opportunity and it was my responsibility to live up to this gift. I had graduated from an all-girls' high school and here I was in one class as the only female. Could I compare academically with all these guys? I took my studies very seriously and studied more than I ever had in my life. The years at ND gave me the confidence for a career in medicine (a male-dominated profession at that time). The people of Notre Dame were amazing—students from all over the country, inspiring professors, and a great president. I still have many enduring friendships from my days at ND. Here is a special memory of the caring nature of the people of ND.

When Father Ted was visiting the architecture students in Rome, my boyfriend asked him to bring an audiocassette back to me on campus. (This was before e-mail and cheap phone calls and I had not heard Bill's voice in months.) So, one morning, the cassette arrived in my Badin mailbox via campus mail. And to think that the president of Notre Dame hand carried this back from Rome for me! And that boyfriend is now my husband of twenty-eight years!

Attending Notre Dame was a life-changing event in many ways for me. So, thanks Father Ted for my education and that of my daughter, Claire Bula (2001).

Beth Neary, MD
Class of '77

Dear Father Hesburgh,

I grew up loving Notre Dame. Talk about Notre Dame, the sight of campus in the fall, the excitement of seeing those gold helmets entering ND Stadium to the sound of the "Victory March" before a big game, the beauty and mystery of the Grotto—were as much a part of my upbringing as Sunday night family dinners. It never occurred to me that, had I been born just a few years earlier, I would not have had the opportunity to attend such a remarkable institution of higher learning and spiritual grace, and I owe a debt of gratitude not only to you but to the class of women before me who paved the way to coeducation. I didn't have to go to Notre Dame after high school. I'm sure I would have turned out fine if my degree came from another college. But so much of who I am today is a result of those very formative years, when I was not just an observer of the Notre Dame traditions but a true and equal member of the Notre Dame community. When I think of Notre Dame, and all of the men and women who shared those years with me, I think of goodness. We are like those candles in the Grotto. I can assure you, we will continue to carry and spread the light and spirit and goodness unique to

our beloved alma mater. Thank you, Father Hesburgh, for making that possible.

Fondly,

Janet Carney O'Brien
Class of '77

Dear Father Hesburgh,

I had two older brothers attend Notre Dame in the late '60s. There was nowhere else that I wanted to go, but I knew I couldn't since I was a girl. Notre Dame going coed my junior year in high school was a miracle in my life. Thank you for being God's instrument on this earth in this and so many other ways.

Blessings to you always,

Anne Berges Pillai
Class of '77

Dear Father Ted,

I remember how it all began. I was sitting in high school class in 1972, and we had been assigned to read an article in the current edition of *Notre Dame Magazine*. On one of the pages, a young lady was seated in front of a large grainy photo of an early Notre Dame football team. The caption read "Is Notre Dame a Place for Women?" My heart stopped for a moment. The University of Notre Dame accepting undergraduate women? Could it be true? Quickly I showed the magazine to my best friend and classmate, Darlene Palma Connelly (BA '77, '80 JD) We looked at each other and the plan was hatched. We would apply.

On a cold February day the following year, with the infamous wintry winds escorting us across campus, we shuttled from the Morris Inn to the Adminis-

tration Building for our admission interview. We were nervous, eager, and so very young. Later that spring we both received word we had been accepted. It was joyous news. Our personal history would be joined with the history of the University of Notre Dame.

Four years later, May 1977, along with our fellow classmates we received our diplomas with your signature. We had tackled Emil T.; some with more success than others, changed majors, made midnight visits to the Grotto, learned the meaning of true friends, lost our hearts more than once and "grew in wisdom and age and grace."

All of this was possible because you took the bold initiative to move forward with coeducation at Notre Dame. We are forever grateful. Thanks to you, our world and the University of Notre Dame is all the richer for her loyal sons and daughters.

May Our Lady continue to commend you to her Son.

In sincere gratitude,

Bridget O'Donnell Provenzano
Class of '77

Dear Father Hesburgh,

As a member of Notre Dame's Class of 1977, I write to thank you for the many gifts my Notre Dame education has provided me. Of course, without your leadership in bringing coeducation to Notre Dame, I would not have been privileged to receive a Notre Dame education.

I am part of a quintessential "Notre Dame family" which includes my father, a member of "Notre Dame's Finest," Class of 1944, my sister, a Saint Mary's College graduate, Class of 1975, and my brother, Notre Dame, Class of 1980. We all live our lives as spouses, parents, and professionals guided by the values that Notre Dame, and you Father, instilled in us. A Notre Dame education and your guidance greatly influenced my father as a lawyer, judge, and most important, parent. His love for Notre Dame in turn influenced his three children to follow him to South Bend for our undergraduate years. You no doubt will remember Phil Russo of Norfolk, Virginia, who was "rescued" by you one evening from the fire escape at Badin Hall not long after the "boys" returned to South Bend as veterans after World War II.

A Notre Dame education instilled in the Russos a desire to lead exemplary lives, to recognize our obligations to our communities, and to analyze critically the moral issues we confront in our daily lives. As lawyers, my father, brother, and I continually are directed by the guideposts Notre Dame provided us.

On the occasion of your 90th birthday, please accept my best wishes and appreciation for all you have contributed to Our Lady's university. Your stewardship for so many years has in large part made Notre Dame the unique institution that it is today.

With warmest regards,

Lee Ann Russo
Class of '77

Dear Father Ted,

Thank you so much for all you did to implement coeducation at Notre Dame! As a member of the Class of 1977, I was honored to have been in the second coed class. My father went to Notre Dame, graduating in 1951. He has six daughters and one son. Since ND went coed, he was able to send three of us girls there. As he said, coeducation increased the odds for him to get one of the seven of us in! It was a great experience and the women I met in those four years were phenomenal.

Wishing you also a Happy 90th Birthday! May God bless you!

Molly McGuire Sample
Class of '77

Dear Father Hesburgh,

It is a great privilege to be writing you and I want to thank you for offering coeducation at Notre Dame. Throughout the years since my graduation in 1977, I have been proud to say that I was from the second class of women entering Notre Dame as freshmen. That was quite a venture considering that I graduated from a small, all-girls' high school. Some people, including some of my male college classmates, thought that women choosing Notre Dame at that time had only an interest in finding a future husband. That was not the case with any of my college friends and acquaintances there. Of course that is not to say that we did not benefit from the social environment in what I remember to be a seventeen to one ratio of men to women. My choice of Notre Dame was based on the kind of community I felt comfortable living and learning for the next four years. By the end of freshman year, I felt such a strong connection with Notre Dame and my friends there that I cried the entire way driving home for summer vacation. Now looking back, I hope that did not hurt my parents' feelings.

My years at Notre Dame have certainly shaped my life—through an exceptional education, affirming my Catholic faith, and also through the lasting friendships that I formed with my classmates. Although most people can say that their college years were some of the best years of their lives, I feel that a Notre Dame experience offers much more than happy memories. There is something very unique about life at Notre Dame and my time there has a special place in my heart. The nurturing and enriching environment helped me thrive and grow during those formative years and I attribute that to your positive influence on every aspect of the university. I am so grateful to have had that experience and so proud to say that I am a graduate of Notre Dame.

Thank you once again, Father, for bringing coeducation to Notre Dame and for everything you did to make the university that very special place.

Mary Reiner Shutters
Class of '77

Dear Father Ted,

My dad Eddie was a blue-collar guy from the west side of South Bend. He dropped out of high school to support his widowed mother, even after the nuns of St. Adalbert School begged his mother to let him continue because they saw his potential.

He knew that attending Notre Dame was as likely for him as going to the moon, but he loved the campus anyway. He and my mother would often dress up their two daughters in our Sunday best, and we would drive across town to attend Mass at Sacred Heart Church (not yet a basilica). I loved looking at the license plates in the parking lot, from exotic, unknown places like New York and Tennessee.

On one of these Sundays, when I was probably five or six years old, I announced that I was going to Notre Dame. After all, my parents were constantly telling us that we had to save money for college, and I figured that this beautiful place had to be one of the best. Mom and Dad laughed, and Daddy explained that Notre Dame was "only for boys."

My dad died suddenly when I was ten years old. When it came time for me to apply to colleges, I considered Saint Mary's. Then one day I spotted a recruiting poster featuring an old-time football team. The caption went something like; "Men have loved Notre Dame for over one hundred years—you'll love it, too." I asked the guidance counselor if this could be true—Notre Dame accepting women? When she assured me that coeducation had begun that very year, I knew where I wanted to be.

With a contribution of grants, loans, scholarships, and summer work, I managed to come up with tuition. I lived at home and commuted to save money. When I graduated in May of 1977, I felt closer to my dad than I had at any time since he died. I could almost see him next to my mother, ready to burst with pride.

During my freshman year, one of my male classmates had told me that "I didn't belong" at Notre Dame because I was taking up a space that could have been filled by a man. After all (according to him), I was "just going to get married and have babies" anyway; therefore, my Notre Dame education would have been wasted. Contrary to his prediction, I had a twenty-seven year career of public service with the United States Government, of which I'm very proud. I'm now volunteering with St. Adalbert Parish in South Bend, and thinking about what my next career will be.

Father Ted, I'm glad to have this opportunity to thank you for allowing me to fulfill my—and my dad's—dream.

Karen M. Sikorski
Class of '77

⟲

Dear Father Ted,

Thank you for initiating coeducation at Notre Dame in 1972, which allowed me to follow my brothers to "Our" Lady's school in September 1973.

I first wandered the Notre Dame campus on a late June evening in the early '60s, marveling at the spire of Sacred Heart in the moonlight and the magic of the votive candles flickering in the Grotto. "Someday," my dad told the two daughters among the several kids in tow, "you two can go to Saint Mary's." "But I want to go here!" I quickly responded, and Father John Reddington, mom's cousin and our host that night, chortled that I probably would.

We returned to ND in May 1971, for my oldest brother Jim's graduation (the first of six Donovans to graduate from ND). And here is my first confession: I violated parietals before I ever matriculated! My nine siblings and I hid out in Holy Cross Hall the night before commencement as our parents had only a tiny hotel room somewhere near Goshen. Jim thought ours was an empty room, but to our (my three sisters and I) surprise, two inebriated Holy Cross hogs burst into their room at 2:00 a.m. to find three teenage girls screaming "Get out!" If the rector ever knew, he wisely remained mum.

Entering as a freshman, I had another shock when room assignments came in August. My brother, Chuck, was a senior in Cavanaugh and I was assigned to a four-man suite in the same dorm, with roommates named Dave, Bob, and Bill. A quick phone call to Father Kieran Ryan, the head of housing, with the explanation that my parents picked the names before their kids were born, secured me a room in Breen-Phillips. For a moment I thought ND was really ahead of the curve being coed by room! Another confession: I thought that you, Father Ted, never slept. One late February night in 1975, my brother Brian, a freshman, and one of his suite mates and I asked the security guard in the Ad Building if we could go talk to you. It was 1:00 a.m. but the light in your third-floor office was on. We were troubled by the prospect that one of my brother's roommates, a sweet kid from New Mexico, was planning on dropping out of school by hopping on a Greyhound bus the next morning. You invited us in, listened to us, and gathered the important info, and then quickly had our friend in with the freshman counselors. You took the time to speak kindly with us and personally took care of this student. We naively thought the president of this huge school would drop everything and help out one of the students . . . and you did! I don't know if you knew how much your gesture meant to us; we knew ND cared for its own.

I also will not forget that, as we left you that night, you asked our majors and grade points. Good little premed, I rattled off my 3.8; my arkie brother and his English major buddy only said they were doing fine. A year later, we would meet you at the Stepan family's Chicago home after a Northwestern game, and you looked me in the eye and said,

"Still have a 3.8?" I was stunned you remembered.

This is my third and last confession: I never knew Tom Dooley, MD, was a Domer until I read his letter to you that stands near the Grotto. In third grade, I had read Dooley's *Deliver Us from Evil* and wrote a book report concluding that I was going to be a missionary doctor just like Dooley when I grew up. As a freshman facing Emil T. and all those smart guys who went to great high schools like my brothers, I found great solace in Dooley's letter, leading me to think I had indeed come to the right school for my premedical education . . . even after Brother A. anxiously asked me, the only girl in our frosh physics class, to provide him with the "feminine" solution to the problems. I tried not to disappoint him but still come up with the right answer . . . not easy in physics!

There is so much to be grateful for after Notre Dame. It provided a wonderfully solid base for my medical education and continuing support for the moral foundation established so hard by Mary and Jim Donovan. Now, as an internist, mother of three little girls, and teacher of Yale medical students and residents, I can only pray for the grace to live the life Mary, Our Mother, and her beautiful university have taught me.

To you, Father Ted, I offer my appreciation and prayers for your continued health . . . and hope that in a few years, one of my little girls will climb the stairs to your office to say "hello."

God bless,

Keiren Donovan Smith, MD
Class of '77

Dear Father Ted,

This letter is to thank you for teaching me a valuable lesson. It was May 6, 1977. A picnic was planned on the South Quad to mark your twenty-fifth anniversary as president of the University of Notre Dame. After hearing you say Mass, my friends and I headed to the picnic. When I reached the food-line checker I was told that it would cost me $10 because I lived off campus. I was incensed, as only a soon-to-be graduated twenty-two-year-old know-it-all could be. I had to borrow the money so I could stay.

As soon as I got home I wrote you a letter describing the incident. I felt better after having expressed my indignation. Until . . . four days later when I received your reply. You enclosed two $5 bills stating "I would be happy to have you as my guest." I was mortified.

But always the educator, you chose to enclose my original letter with your reply. Reading my self-righteous missive next to your gracious reply was a lesson I would never forget. Thirty years and many moves later the letter is still one of my most valuable possessions. I take it out whenever I am feeling a little too full of myself and am reminded of the humble act of a great man. Thank you, Father.

Best regards,

Kathleen Dickinson Villano
Class of '77

---

University of Notre Dame
Notre Dame, Indiana 46556

Office of the President                 May 10, 1977                 Cable Address "Dulac"

Miss Kathleen Dickinson
820 Notre Dame Avenue
South Bend, Indiana

Dear Kathleen:

I don't know who made the arrangements for the picnic or paid the bills, but in any event I'm glad you came and I would be happy to have you as my guest. Enclosed is $10.00.

Have a pleasant Summer.

Ever devotedly in Notre Dame,

Father Ted H.

(Rev.) Theodore M. Hesburgh, C.S.C.
President

Dear Father Hesburgh,

In 1974, at our brother Bob's graduation from Notre Dame, the female valedictorian ended her speech with these simple but eloquent words, "You never leave Notre Dame, you take it with you." This sentiment has rung true for our brother, for the three of us, who graduated in 1978, 1982, and 1985, and for our mother and father, Mary Ellen and Jack Kelly. Notre Dame is truly a special place that has been an integral part of each of our lives—in our memories and continued relationships with the people we met there, and in who we are today.

While our time at Notre Dame spanned fifteen years, it has been a lifetime experience for all of us. Childhood remembrances include raking leaves to Saturday afternoon radio broadcasts of ND football games, Army-Notre Dame games at West Point, and long, but spirited road trips from New Jersey to South Bend for football weekends. After twelve hours of driving, we would vie to be the first to spot the Golden Dome, arriving on Friday afternoon in time to see the marching band practice on Green Field.

As we grew up, we visited one another during each of our times at Notre Dame, and proudly watched our father contribute as a Science Council member for thirteen years. The highlight of our parents' experience in these years was your presence at their meetings and your warm interactions with them. One of our mother's fondest memories is meeting you at an airport en route to South Bend. You greeted her warmly by name and offered her a ride to campus, a simple but thoughtful gesture she has never forgotten.

Father Hesburgh, your contributions to Notre Dame helped make it a very special place for so many, including our family. Each one of us remembers your presence at freshman orientation, special campus events, dormitory Masses, graduations, and later, at alumni gatherings. We also remember your warmth and personal touch when we met you individually over the years. And we were proud to be part of a university whose president was also making a significant impact beyond our campus, calling attention to global social issues, working for justice and civil rights, and setting an example through public service. Of course, we are thankful to you for moving Notre Dame forward into coeducation, making it possible for three sisters to attend.

Time marches on, and we Kelly kids are now in our forties and fifties. This June, we will celebrate our dad's eightieth birthday and all of us know that the perfect place to celebrate is Notre Dame. Outside of family, few things have given us greater pleasure throughout our lives than Notre Dame, and so we will return to that special place together, along with our children. We may leave Notre Dame and take it with us, but it is also a place to where we want to return time and again. Thank you, Father Hesburgh, for everything you did to make it such a special place.

We send you our warmest wishes for continued health and happiness—

Maureen Kelly Berkley
Class of '78

Nancy Kelly Connolly
Class of '82

Patricia Kelly
Class of '85

Dear Father Hesburgh,

I'm grateful to have this opportunity to thank you for your commitment to providing women full access to the extraordinary educational opportunities at the University of Notre Dame. I am proud to be a member of the Class of 1978. My life has been profoundly impacted by my experience at Notre Dame.

My father, Mike, had the great ambition to attend Notre Dame as a young man. Due to circumstances, however, he chose to work his way through the University of Detroit—both as an undergraduate and a graduate student. He vowed to provide his five children with a great education—including college and postgraduate studies. Since he was (and is) an avid Notre Dame fan, I grew up watching and following Notre Dame football. My oldest brother Joe studied engineering at Notre Dame and was a member of the Class of 1971. I had my sights set on the University of Michigan or

Michigan State, since I grew up in the Detroit area and most of my friends were attending those schools. I will never forget the day my dad enthusiastically informed me that Notre Dame was opening its doors to women! I always say that, from that moment on, I don't really remember making a choice—it was certain that, if I was accepted, I was going to attend Notre Dame.

My time at Notre Dame was, at times, challenging. I struggled to grow up and take responsibility for my life and my education. But with the patience and caring of the professors, administration, and other students, I was successful. I learned a lot about discipline at Notre Dame. Today I am executive director of an organization that funds services for people with developmental disabilities. I learned about making a contribution to my community from my dad and from Notre Dame.

Notre Dame is a special place. My dear brother Joe was diagnosed with mantle cell lymphoma in late 2002. He underwent a stem cell transplant in early 2003 and his constant goal was to be well enough to travel to South Bend for football games. By the fall of 2004, he was well enough to be able to watch Notre Dame play Boston College with many of his ND friends. We lit many candles at the Grotto on his behalf. Unfortunately, Joe's health deteriorated and we lost him in early 2005. "Notre Dame Our Mother" was sung at his funeral.

I tell you this, Father, so that you understand that Notre Dame—its values and ideals—live in my heart. Thank you for making that possible. Know that I carry it forward. Your commitment to me and to all the women who have attended Notre Dame carries forward immeasurably to make the world a better place.

God bless you.

Peg Capo
Class of '78

Dear Father Hesburgh,

When I was a junior in high school, my parents asked me to talk to our neighbor, Gigi Masse, who had transferred from Saint Mary's to Notre Dame when it became coed. I remember our visit vividly. I also remember visiting Notre Dame with my father and brother the following autumn and feeling completely at home. I was lucky enough to call Farley Hall and Notre Dame my home from 1974 to 1978. I still see and love my roommates, Mary Kay Braccio and Melanie Jorgenson. I still feel at home on campus. My son will be applying to colleges in the fall. We have visited some of the best schools in the country, but the benchmark is always Notre Dame. I have not yet seen another school that has everything Notre Dame offers. I still thank my parents for sending me. Thank you, Father Hesburgh, for making a Notre Dame education a possibility.

Sincerely,

Marietta Martin Colianni
Class of '78

Dear Uncle Ted,

As your second alumna niece, it is a pleasure to join the daughters of Notre Dame in celebrating your birthday by thanking you for your vision in changing so many lives for the better through coeducation. Oprah Winfrey was asked why she built her leadership institute in South Africa for young girls. She replied that by changing a girl's life, you change a family, and ultimately, a community. As the daughter of your sister Betty, a single mother who used her GI Bill benefits to trudge to night school to earn three masters degrees to improve our family's lot, I can easily identify with this rationale. I will be forever indebted to you for giving my Notre Dame sisters and me the opportunity to benefit from and contribute to the Notre Dame family.

My four years at ND were life changing. Although a bit intimidated by how incredibly smart everyone was, I found my own ship rising with the tide as I embraced the rich academic life. The passion I developed for reading (a prerequisite for all English majors!) and confidence I gained in learning how to ask the important questions, have immeasurably shaped the course of my life. At Notre Dame, I learned to learn. To this day if I do not learn something new every day, I'm disappointed.

I look back at my undergraduate life with enormous pride, fondness, and gratitude. Whether entranced by the visiting authors at the Sophomore Literary Festival, performing at the Nazz, playing bridge with my roommates, cheering at a pep rally, participating in the neighborhood tutorial program, writing my own poetry, whistling up to your lit office after midnight, learning how to use the kiln in the old field house, lighting a candle at the Grotto, or attending evening Mass in my pj's with my Walsh dorm mates, it was all grand.

My ND years also significantly expanded my horizons from small-town life in upstate New York to sharing those important, formative years with a remarkable group of gifted and generous men and women. Among the most valuable, were those with whom I shared my sophomore year in Innsbruck. Were I allowed only two words to describe my experience there, they would be "broadening" and "humbling." My exposure to other cultures, history, art, architecture, and customs made me grow in ways too many to count. I learned through the kindness of total strangers that my mother's lessons of "gaining through giving" were too true, and that there was much more to life than what existed in my own little circle.

I had no way of knowing at the time that the semester I worked at the front desk of the Morris Inn senior year would germinate into a thirty-year career in the hospitality industry. By training hoteliers in communication and service skills, I have continued our family's legacy as educators, and have hopefully done my alma mater and our family proud. I dare say I would not have had the faith to put out my own shingle, or courage to carve out my own niche were it not for the core values and tradition of "giving back" that my years at Notre Dame instilled in me.

Uncle Ted, I feel particularly blessed to have had you as the head of the clan. Whether a birth, death, wedding, or christening, you have been there for all the important family milestones, have listened, guided, and prayed with us. Your remarkable faith, loyalty, availability, and loving spirit have been an inspiration and guiding light for all of us.

I'll close with a favorite passage from a W. B. Yeats poem I learned at ND:

*"When you are old and grey and full of sleep, And nodding by the fire, take down this book, And slowly read, and dream of the soft look Your eyes had once, and of their shadows deep; How many loved your moments of glad grace, And loved your beauty with love false and true, But one man loved the pilgrim soul in you . . ."*

Happy Birthday, Uncle Ted! Please know how truly grateful I am for all you have been and done for our family and the Notre Dame community. You have made a huge difference in countless lives because you gave girls like me the opportunity to experience and grow from the rich academic, spiritual, social life that is so singular at Notre Dame. Families and communities across the globe are better for having their mothers, daughters, sisters, and friends touched by your vision and efforts to leave the world better than you found it!

Much love,

Lyssa O'Neill MacCaughey
Class of '78

Dear Father Hesburgh,

I would like to add my personal thanks for all you did to create coeducation at Notre Dame. It is almost impossible for me to put into words what my four years at Notre Dame mean to me. At times, my experience there seems as much a part of me as my brown hair and brown eyes.

I came to Notre Dame in the fall of 1974 from a small town in the heart of rural Iowa. I was naive and inexperienced, a product of the loving but protected environment where I was born. Notre Dame opened my eyes both literally and metaphysically to the larger world. I spent my sophomore year in France. I took classes from internationally renowned professors. I read books and was exposed to ideas that shook my curiosity and hunger to learn. I made friends that would last a lifetime.

Beneath it all, I developed a strong sense of right and wrong, of what the "good life" really means and how to go about creating it for myself. I think because women were in such a minority during those early years, I felt especially honored to be there. This sense of importance transferred to the rest of life and created in me a feeling that life itself is a privilege, and we are all obligated to make the most of it.

For so many people, Notre Dame on a football weekend is the image they hold most dear. But for me, the everyday Notre Dame is the "real" Notre Dame. I was fortunate to have the security blanket of having a sister who graduated one year ahead of me. I remember one winter night walking back to Farley from her room in Lyons. The quads were painted white from a light snow that had fallen earlier in the day, and the quiet hush of the cold, still air made me feel as though I were the last one awake on campus. In my mind that very image is the definition of serenity. I often hold it in my heart if I'm feeling anxious or nervous and want to calm myself down.

It sounds a little trite but I do believe Notre Dame was more than four years. It was an experience. When I realize that I was just three years away from not having that experience available to me, "thanks" seems hardy enough for the gratitude I feel for you.

Sincerely,

Peggy McGuire LeBrun
Class of '78

Dear Father Hesburgh,

Words can not express my deep appreciation for your leadership in making Notre Dame coeducational. It was always my dream to attend Our Lady's university, but back in the '60s, many people thought it was just a pipe dream. I always had faith, that when it came time, I would be able to go, but time was starting to grow short. Thankfully, you gave us the news we were waiting for and I was lucky enough to be in the third class of women in the fall of 1974.

Being a part of the Notre Dame family has always been important to me. While I was the first person in my family to attend college, my parents raised me as part of the crazy subway alumni. So, even though no one in my family attended Notre Dame, we still felt it was "ours," too. I was lucky enough to meet my husband there and now our oldest daughter is a graduate. When we moved to our present city, Cincinnati, our family was the Notre Dame family. I believe that feeling of Notre Dame being a family is something that you believe in, appreciate, and perpetuate as one of the university's finer qualities. Through you, this family grew to be worldwide.

Your extraordinary leadership elevated Notre Dame from a small but wonderful Catholic university to a top-notch educational institution. We are so lucky to have had you as president of our university. As I listened to my daughter, Moira, introduce you at the yearbook banquet a few weeks ago, I wondered how she chose which of your remarkable accomplishments to use to introduce you. My greatest memories of you are nights like that . . . when you tell your stories. I could listen to your stories for hours.

So, thank you very much for your wonderful leadership, incredible foresight, and beautiful spirituality. Thank you for letting us become members of the Notre Dame family.

We are truly blessed to have crossed paths with you. May God and Our Lady, Notre Dame, love and care for you, now and forever.

Yours in Notre Dame,

Teri Sullivan Madden
Class of '78

Thank you, Father, for welcoming ladies to Notre Dame.

Happy Birthday from a 1978 graduate . . .

What is the most valuable thing I have learned? Volunteerism. No matter how busy I am with kids, husband, job, house, etc. . . . the most important part of my day is spent trying to make the world better for someone else. While working at my paying job, I multitask, running a fund-raiser.

Did ND teach me? Not really. My parents started it. But my obligation is to continue as best I can. So, whether I am raising money for MS, Alzheimer's, Strong Hospital, Breast Cancer, Commission Project via walkathons, telethons, golf outings, past dinners for Rotary, the list goes on and on, I try to do something every day. Trying to be a good example for my kids is sometimes difficult, but I try.

Prayer is very important for me, too. I pray when I work, walk the dog, sit at the computer (JMJ is one of my favorite passwords). My favorite prayers are singing in the church choir—learned a few tunes in the ND Chapel Choir. Those are fine memories of getting up Sunday mornings, after working at the Senior Bar as a bartender until 2:00 a.m. Some mornings I was a little hoarse. I am a lot better now.

Friendships: keeping in touch with people over the distance. I have moved five times for my husband, but keep my ND friends as close as my current friends. Of course, it is easier with e-mail. We had some crazy moments on campus in the early years. Food fights with girls is just as fun. Breaking parietals sneaking in late with boys. Don't tell my kids I am telling you.

I remember my first week on campus. The kids from far away came early to test on campus. Carolyn and I became lifelong friends. She bought the beer. We had parties in the room. We checked out the boys in Flanner Hall, laughed at our follies, fell in love with many boys. I never felt out of place, always had my friends in tow. Even if the class only had a few girls, we were welcomed by 1978. I remember parties every weekend—and studying hard.

I do not have one bad prof story, I got the best education available.

I have pictures of you standing with my friends, as we always had our cameras ready. Thank you for being such a warm person.

It is an honor to be a grad of Notre Dame. It has helped get in the door on job interviews. Considering that I agreed to be the second breadwinner, I have trailed my husband's career, but never lacked a job. Common sense, integrity, honesty, and doing the right thing keeps me on the right path.

Only one regret: I wish I had taken an art class, because I would like to make this a beautiful card for you. But I send you hearts and flowers from my heart.

Thank you, thank you, thank you, thank you!

MAMP
Class of '78

Dear Father Hesburgh,

I want to join the many Notre Dame alumnae and other Notre Dame family members in wishing you a Happy 90th Birthday. There could be no better time than this, this incredible milestone in your life, to take the opportunity to thank you for bringing co-education to the University of Notre Dame. Many of us who have graduated can look back at perhaps a single moment or a collection of moments that eventually became the defining factor in our decision to attend Notre Dame, but the fact remains that without your foresight and your courage to make this significant policy of coeducation, none of us who are female graduates would be just that—graduates. Your decision to make Notre Dame a coed institution transformed my life and the lives of my contemporaries, and it continues to shape the lives of current students and future students as well. Opportunity provides promise and in order for us to achieve any goal we need the opportunity. When we are empowered, we are able to make the leap from our dream to our reality—to be the person we hope to be, and at the very least to know we had the chance to reach that goal. Your decision to make the University of Notre Dame a coeducational institution empowered all female students and gave them the opportunity to make their own future. Father Hesburgh, while your influence is global, and your accomplishments have changed history, know that you also made significant differences on the most personal level. I would not be the person I am if I had not attended the University of Notre Dame. Your decision to make Notre Dame a coeducational institution changed my life. At Notre Dame I found a strength and a confidence that told me that no matter what I chose to do with my life I could do it, whatever it happened to be, because I had attended the best Catholic university in the world. For this confidence and for this opportunity I thank you. Your positive influence will be felt for generations to come and for all of us who have been the recipient of your greater vision we are most grateful.

May God bless you today and always for your diligence and compassion, and may He continue to shower you with the many blessings in the years ahead.

Sincerely,

Mary White Packer
Class of '78

Dear Father Ted,

I remember meeting you while you were walking along the South Quad one evening. You stopped to chat with me. I was just a lowly underclassman and so impressed by your friendliness.

I still view my life at ND as the "Golden Years" of time. As my 1978 classmates hit their fiftieth birthdays in 2006, I was again reminded of the special bond of Notre Dame. How it was and still is the true concept of a "family" with bonds that will never be broken no matter how much time or distance elapses.

I will always be grateful to the good Lord for this experience. The legacy and vision that you had in pushing this institution to go "coed" was a brilliant one. I for one am very thankful for the opportunities with which you provided me.

Happy 90th Birthday, Father Ted!

Sincerely,

Robin T. Price, MD
Class of '78

Dear Father Hesburgh,

Thanks so much for spearheading the transition to coeducation at Notre Dame back in the '70s. I'm a 1978 graduate and was very excited to be able to go to Notre Dame. My education was challenging for sure—and it has served me well. I was very excited to be a pioneer of coeducation! I have been back to the campus several times over the years and I make a point of visiting the Grotto every time and lighting a candle. I thank God for all my blessings and have on occasion asked for help in dealing with a life challenge. I am so glad I have a special holy place to go to when I can.

Thanks again! Go Irish!

Ann Bennett Schoper
Class of '78

Dear Father Hesburgh,

A heartfelt thank you for your courageous (not to mention brilliant) decision to allow women to attend the University of Notre Dame.

In the summer of 1969, I visited Notre Dame's campus with my family. I was entering eighth grade. My brother, who was a year older, had decided at a young age that he wanted to go to Notre Dame, so we traveled from New Jersey to see the campus with the Golden Dome. By the end of our visit, he was convinced beyond all doubt that Notre Dame was his first choice and secretly it was mine also. It was a beautiful campus with a palpable spirit, rich tradition, academic excellence, warm people, and a great bookstore! It was now MY dream to attend Notre Dame. I saw only one obstacle; they didn't accept women at Notre Dame. Then, in 1972, a very wise man with great vision, courage, and impeccable timing, decided to change that and the rest, as they say, "is history"!

I happily and gratefully entered Notre Dame in August of 1974, the third class of women. My years there were nothing short of wonderful. Living all four years in Walsh Hall, I grew in faith, intellect, and character and looked forward to your Masses said in our chapel. I made lifelong friendships that I treasure. The spirit of Notre Dame captured my heart and will remain there forever.

A simple thank you doesn't seem adequate. Yet sometimes in the simplicity of the words the deepest feelings are conveyed. It is an honor and privilege to know you, to be a part of your university, and in a small way be a part of this celebration.

May God continue to bless you . . .

Yours in Notre Dame,

Lorraine Ehrline Sedlacek
Class of '78

Dear Father Ted,

I am sure that you do not remember meeting me, but I can still recall every detail of the first time I met you. It was my freshman year at Notre Dame (fall 1974), and my dorm, Badin Hall, was looking for a priest to celebrate our Thanksgiving Mass. Whether out of ignorance or boldness, I spoke up and said, "Why don't we ask Father

Hesburgh?" That outburst conjured up the response, "Great, you go ask him." So, I calmly called your secretary, asked for an appointment, and was granted one the next day. Upon arriving at your office, I was warmly greeted by you, I made my request, and you immediately agreed to come! While others were surprised that the president of Our Lady's university would consent so readily to celebrate Mass in the smallest women's dorm, I was just naive enough to expect it. That visit to the Main Building and the subsequent Thanksgiving Mass are experiences that I will always remember. You not only allowed women to enroll at the University of Notre Dame, but you embraced us.

As my son's graduation from Notre Dame approaches at the end of this month, I thank you for being able to share with him forever the special bond that Our Lady has imprinted on our minds, hearts, and souls. God bless you, and Happy Birthday!

Sincerely,

Sheryl (Daigle) Switaj
Class of '78

⚗

Dear Father Ted,

Thank you!

Little did I know back in the fall of 1975 how the rest of my life would be impacted by the years I was about to spend at the University of Notre Dame.

Little did I know that as I struggled through *Principles of Economics* I would end up marrying my economics teaching assistant. After thirty-five remarkable years of marriage and raising three wonderful children, am I ever thankful to you for giving me the opportunity to attend the school.

Little did I know that earning a spot on the Women's Varsity Tennis team would lead me to being recognized as one of the first female Monogram winners. And now thirty years later, I'm being honored as a pioneer of women's sports.

Little did I know that my oldest daughter, Carol, would grow to be as passionate about Notre Dame as I. And as she graduates this year, I realize that many of the things she now loves about the university are the very same things I loved as a student twenty-eight years ago.

Father Ted, what I do know now, is that none of this would have been possible without you. Thank you for making the decision to open Notre Dame's doors to women—a decision for which I will be ever grateful. Go Irish!

Warmest regards,

Mary "Shukis" Behler
Class of '79

Dear Father Ted,

I, like so many alumnae, am a legacy. My grandfather (J. Frank Martin) managed to send three of five sons to Notre Dame (my dad, John "Red" Martin '40, Robert, and Frank Martin '56). I grew up saying I was going to ND and my grandfather would agree with me. Gramps would also tell me "if they did not take women by then he would make sure they at least took me."

Well, thanks to you and many others, my gramps did not have to go back on his word. My brother entered ND in 1972 and is in the picture of the South Dining Hall and the sign welcoming women. That picture hung in my room for three years.

On May 12, 1975—I was accepted to ND off the waiting list—I will forever be grateful that you and the nuns decided to make Lewis Hall a dorm that year!

I was excited and scared when I arrived on campus that August. I met all the girls on my section (3 South) my first night and have been friends with them ever since. Eventually, I also got to know my "upstairs" neighbors—your niece Mary and her roommate Elyse, along with Cindy, Nina, and Fran. Some of the women I have remained very close with; others I may not have been in touch with or seen for years but once we do—it is as if we were together yesterday. To me that says so much about Notre Dame and what we all experience—family always and forever. As a result of some personal issues (and not that Dr. Hofman didn't try to help me), I left Notre Dame that January. I never left my friends of the university and all that it meant to me. I came back to New York and attended Hofstra University. I would fly back to visit the week before school started each semester of my sophomore year. I reapplied and came back to Notre Dame as a transfer student for my junior and senior year. Since I had been away—I did not get the "South Bend doldrums"—being back on campus with my friends was the best. I have since been told I was an alum before I graduated because I would be so sentimental about ND and all that it meant to me.

I learned a great deal about myself as a result of my experience at ND. I have over the last twenty-five-plus years tried to live my life with the lessons I have learned. I attended Fordham Law School and graduated in 1986. I have worked as corporate counsel to several corporations. I was recently laid off but know that I will eventually find a job.

My faith has been so important to me and to the life my husband and I have lived together. We have two beautiful daughters, Claire, sixteen, and Colleen, thirteen. Colleen was diagnosed with juvenile diabetes in 1997 and we have been involved in numerous organizations to find a cure and help her lead a normal life. I was active in the Alumni Association on Long Island when our girls were little. Once the girls started attending school and I continued to work something "had to give," so I was no longer active in the alumni association but carried ND with me in my heart as every alum does.

I have proudly acknowledged in job interviews and social settings that I attended the University of Notre Dame. Some have teased me—did I play linebacker? Some have said "No, you went to Saint Mary's." I have corrected them and tried to explain the aura of Notre Dame as best I could. I have used myself as the example ND has shaped my thoughts, words, and deeds. Who and what I am is thanks to ND.

So thank you, Father Ted, for making ND coed. My daughters talk of going to Notre Dame. Their cousin is there now. Of course, I truly believe there is no better place on earth but will keep quiet as we do the college search and let them decide for themselves.

God bless you and keep you.

Very truly yours,

R.M.C.
Class of '79

Dear Uncle Ted,

Thank you for having the vision to admit women to Notre Dame in the early '70s. Never had I dreamed, while growing up in South Bend, that I would be able to one day, attend the university that was such a big part of our family's life. Never did I think it possible that your signature would be on my graduation diploma and that of my father (James L. Hesburgh '55). You were an inspiration and cheerleader to the first graduating classes of women and continue to be an inspiration to the women of the University of Notre Dame today.

I have such fond memories of our time together while I was a student at Notre Dame. Our dinners at Sunny Italy (or "Rosie's" as you called it), our road trips to dinners at Diamond Lake, our Thanksgivings together with Father Sheedy at the Stephan's beautiful home in Evanston, and our long visits in your office in the Golden Dome. All of the students knew that they could come to visit you at all hours of the night and only had to look up to see your light on in the wee hours of the morning to know that you were still at work answering the piles of mail that accumulated each day. Your wonderful assistant, Helen Hosinski, was an amazing woman who could transcribe countless letters a day, in spite of the crippling arthritis in her hands. She was your "gatekeeper" and kept everyone on schedule at all times!

Nothing could have prepared me for my experience as a member of one of the earlier classes of women at Notre Dame. I came from an all-girls' high school in Southern California to (what seemed like) an all-male institution in Indiana with a ratio of seven males to every female. My freshman year, Student Housing put most of our freshman class of women in Lewis Hall, its first year as a dorm (formerly, a convent). The closets were a bit of a challenge since they had been designed for "habits" (robes and veils) and were therefore, long and narrow. We had two freshman girls to a room with a rolling rack to hold all of our clothes (since these rooms were not designed for teenage girls). Having a dorm of mostly freshman girls was a housing challenge due to the lack of upper-class women as role models. We were encouraged to transfer to other dorms (Breen-Phillips, Lyons, Walsh, or Badin) for our sophomore year. I moved to Lyons Hall where I met many other friends with whom I have remained close to this day.

I vividly remember the challenges that the Notre Dame dining hall faced with the arrival of female students. We had two choices of dinner entrees with the same-sized portions served to both male and female students. Needless to say, the "freshman fifteen" took on a whole new meaning after the first two months since we were being served the same portions as the male athletes and students. Thankfully, the Notre Dame food service came to our rescue in 1976 with the first-ever "salad bar."

The older alumni had difficulty in processing the idea that women not only attended Notre Dame but, actually lived in their "old" dorms. Upon moving into Lyons Hall, my classmates and I discovered that the bathrooms had yet to be converted from

"Mens' Rooms" to "Ladies' Rooms." We had gentlemen touring the dorms on football weekends shaking their heads in dismay over the fact that there were women walking down the halls in their bathrobes with towels in their hair. We had taken over "their dorms."

Yes, there were growing pains and, yes, not all the males on campus were initially happy that we were there. However, it was a fabulous journey made easier by people like you, the wonderful dean of the freshman year of studies, Dr. Emil Hofman, and many of the professors who were delighted that we were now part of the Notre Dame family. Our professors welcomed us with open arms and after several months, we felt that Notre Dame was where each and every one of us belonged. Thank you for setting the shining example of how women were to be welcomed in the early '70s.

It was at Notre Dame in 1975, at a Morrissey Hall formal that I met my future husband Jay (James F. Flaherty III '79). It is hard to believe that twenty-eight years have gone by since you married us just after our graduation in 1979. You have baptized

Mary Hesburgh Flaherty '79 and her uncle, Father Ted, in Punta Mita, Mexico, Easter 2007.

all three of our children. Our two eldest children, Jimmy '06, '07, and Mary Catherine '08, are currently students at Notre Dame and it is our hope that our third child, Maureen, will attend Notre Dame in the future. Your vision to admit women has allowed our daughter to get the same incredible Notre Dame experience that I was able to experience and carry with me each day. Our entire family has been touched by your vision. Thank you, Uncle Ted, for being a wonderful uncle, an incredible visionary, a dedicated priest, and a good friend. Happy 90th Birthday!

With lots of love,

Mary (Mary Hesburgh Flaherty)
Class of '79

Dear Father Hesburgh,

I came to Notre Dame in 1975 with a rich Notre Dame family legacy. My father, Donald J. (Buddy) Romano graduated in 1950 and his brother, Michael, in 1949. They both played football under Frank Leahy, which is how the Notre Dame tradition started in our family.

I was the first female graduate from the Romano family. I have four brothers, Danny '78, Rocky '80, Michael '87, and D.J. '90, and one sister, Tricia, who graduated from Notre Dame. My sister, Florence (Lulu), graduated from the nurses training program at Saint Mary's. My sisters and I all married Notre Dame men.

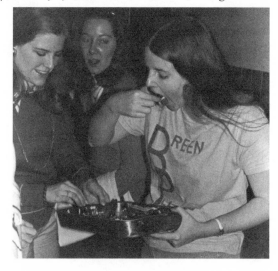

My older brother Danny, Class of 1978, introduced me to his RA in Dillon Hall during his freshman year. Roger Klauer, Class of 1975, has now been my husband for twenty-seven years. We have been blessed with five children. Our three oldest sons have also graduated from Notre Dame. Michael graduated in 2003, Roger in 2004, and Daniel graduated in 2006. We have two daughters at Marian High School, Chrissy and Kathleen. We hope one or both of them might be among the first Klauer women to attend the university.

When I was a student, I had no idea that I'd live here in South Bend as an adult. I've had a number of opportunities to continue close relationships with members of the Notre Dame community. Although I have no official capacity at the university, I love to offer our hospitality to newcomers to the Notre Dame community, whether students, priests, faculty, or new members of academic or athletic administrators. I also enjoy being a trustee at Holy Cross College here in South Bend, as we, trustees, continue to work for avenues of collaboration between the three local Catholic academic communities.

I particularly enjoy my self-described hospitality ministry to the Holy Cross priests. We are so fortunate to have these priests in our local parishes with the rich liturgies they offer on and off campus, and I enjoy inviting them into our home. We've stayed in touch with the work of the Holy Cross Missions through our thirty-year friendship with Father Dave Schlaver. We still keep up with liturgical activities at the Basilica through frequent meals with Father Peter Rocca. My husband takes advantage of spiritual direction from Father Ken Molenaro. Father Ken's Italian heritage helps him understand me, as he gives me spiritual counsel to my German husband. We enjoy the company of the priests at both Christ the King Parish, Father Tom Jones, Father Ron Trippi, and Father Neal Wach, and St. Joseph's Parish, Father John DeRisso and Father Nat Wills. Father Oliver Williams is a good friend of ours and serves as the moral compass of our family and its business ventures. We have watched several deacons grow up over the years—Father John Riley, Father Peter Jarrett, Father Gary Chamberlan, Father Terry Erhman, and Father Andy Sebesta. I enjoy any opportunity I have to support the Holy Cross priests, particularly if they enjoy Italian home cooking.

I'm grateful for all of them and the work that they do to enrich our lives, particularly to you, Father Ted, for all of your personal years of hard work and endless dedication to our university.

With love and admiration,

Christine Romano Klauer
Class of '79

Dear Father Hesburgh,

I will never forget the spring of my senior year in high school when I received my acceptance letter from Notre Dame. I could not believe I would actually be attending college at the school I had seen so many times on TV. A native Californian, I had only traveled outside the West Coast one time in my life before I flew to South Bend for freshman orientation. My excitement was immense!

But as I told people who asked where I was going to college that I would be attending Notre Dame, a funny thing happened. Time after time I was told, "No, you're not—you're going to Saint Mary's. There are no girls at Notre Dame." Well thanks to you, there WERE girls at Notre Dame in the fall of 1975 when I stepped off that plane. And for that, I will be forever grateful.

Not only did your leadership in transforming Notre Dame into a coeducational institution provide me with the opportunity for an excellent education, but it also gave me something much more valuable: lifelong membership in the family that is Notre Dame. At Notre Dame, my faith was enriched and strengthened. From High Mass in the Basilica to quiet prayer and candle-lighting at the Grotto, to midnight dorm Masses, to prayer services when our friends lay dying, faith flourished at Notre Dame. It was such a blessing to me to attend a school where I could go to church with my friends, and then try to put my faith into action. The faith that was nurtured so well at Notre Dame has been the foundation of my life as an adult. My faith gives me a framework with which to measure my life, and is a constant source of help, comfort, and inspiration.

The many opportunities provided at Notre Dame for service to the wider community gave me a chance to expand my learning beyond the classroom and to appreciate the joy of sharing my time with others. In fact, whenever I return to campus (which has been more often the past two years now that my son is a student at ND), I call or visit the woman who I was matched up with as an undergraduate in the "Adopt-a-Grandparent" program. She and I write to each other at least annually, as well. The love of community service that was fostered at Notre Dame has stayed with me, so that service is an integral part of my life.

At Notre Dame, I was treated as a unique individual by my professors. Over the years, I have kept in contact with and visited with some of them, which has been a joy. Father George Wiskirchen concelebrated my nuptial Mass, and it was a privilege to be able to introduce him to my children just a few years before he died. Professor Bill Nichols is another special professor to me, and he, too, has met my husband and some of my children.

By far the greatest gift I received at Notre Dame, though, was the gift of friendship. Notre Dame friendships are lasting and true. With my Notre Dame friends, even if it has been twenty years since we have seen each other, the time melts away and we are instantly at ease with one another. The girl I met on my first day in Lewis Hall freshman year is still one of my dearest friends—more like a sister to me, even though we live far apart and have not seen each other more than a dozen times since graduation. The friends I made as a member of the marching band, varsity band, and concert

band are very special to me as well. I cannot adequately express how much their friendship has meant to me, and how rich my life is because of all the wonderful friends I made at Notre Dame.

So, Father Hesburgh, THANK YOU! Thank you for disregarding the people who wanted to maintain the status quo. Thank you for taking a bold step with an unknown outcome. Thank you for trusting that your experiment in coeducation would succeed. Most of all, thank you for ensuring that the daughters of Our Lady would be able to live, love, and learn at the university which bears her name.

And our hearts forever LOVE THEE NOTRE DAME!

God bless you, Father Ted.
With love and gratitude,

Judy (Cole) Manza
Class of '79

Dear Father Hesburgh,

Thank you for having the vision of coeducation at Notre Dame. That one decision made the difference in my life—the cementing of my faith, the selecting of my ND spouse, and the working of my professional business education that led to my vocation as a college professor, and my continuing lifelong friendships.

All my prayers,

Joan Chobrek Mileski
Class of '79

Dear Father Ted,

Although twenty-seven years have passed since we last talked, I'm hoping that you remember me as the student who had the good fortune of being the roommate of your niece, Mary, for three years at Notre Dame. Words cannot express how much FUN we had back in those days . . . as you know, Mary is quite the mischief maker. There's no doubt that we owe our experiences at Notre Dame to you, and I thank you from the bottom of my heart for accepting women into this very special place.

Honestly, I don't think I had any clue of what to expect at Notre Dame. I applied because my dad was a huge fan of the school. He went to Holy Cross College, so he valued a Catholic education. The ratio of boys to girls was very fashionable for the girls in those days. I remember thinking how grateful I was to have attended a big public, coed high school, because I knew how to act around boys (a lot of girls from girls-only schools did not). We were always "competing" with the Saint Mary's College students for the guys' attention, so social etiquette was important. The Saint Mary's girls were, for the most part, better-looking than the ND women, but they spent a LOT more time dolling themselves up before crossing the road.

The dorm was the nucleus of our friendships and fun. Mary and I lived in Lewis Hall our freshman year, and then we transferred to Lyons Hall for the other three years. We made friends fast, and we enjoyed hitting the party/dance scene, too. My funniest memory of freshman year was the night Mary talked me into stealing a seven-foot-high statue of the Virgin Mary from the basement of Lewis Hall. We somehow got the statue into a laundry cart, and wheeled it out of the dorm, down the road along the lake, and into Morrissey Hall. We managed to put the statue in Mary's boyfriend's bed under the covers in the praying position. Her boyfriend didn't find this prank to be funny, but he ended up marrying Mary anyway. At least he had some indication of what he was getting into!

The dances were fun. There were always plenty of guys to choose from, and we had a blast dressing up and dancing the nights away. The football games were fun. The student section rocked in those days, as it does today. The nights at Senior Bar were fun. We danced to disco until we wore ourselves out. Most of all, our senior trip to Southern Cal for the USC game was fun. I still can't believe we chartered a jet to fly us to LA for the long weekend. . . . Donna Summer and Billy Joel blaring in the background.

The funniest story I have about the coed thing was from my first reunion, five years after graduating. A fellow alumnus who graduated in the '60s came up to me and asked me what it was like to be a female on the campus. He even wanted to know where we went to the bathroom, because his only memory of a "Ladies' Room" was in the basement of the South Dining Hall!

The greatest gifts of a Notre Dame education are the friends you make while you're there, who become lifelong friends, and the special bond that you have for the rest of your life when you meet another graduate, whether it's in a business or personal situation. Now that it's been twenty-eight years since I graduated, I'm getting this question more frequently: "Were you in the first class of women at Notre Dame?" I guess I'm looking my age!

Father Ted, thank you for opening the university to females at a time when the decision was a tough one. There are still male graduates who think that the school was "ruined" when females were accepted, but nothing could be further from the truth. Everyone deserves a shot at a Notre Dame education, regardless of gender, because it's the most special place on Earth. Go Irish!

Elyse (Bonahoom) Newman
Class of '79

Dear Father Hesburgh,

I would like to add my thanks for your efforts to bring coeducation to the University of Notre Dame. The experiences I had and the friends I made during the four years

I spent on the "du Lac" campus are the best of my life—I couldn't imagine any other university being so right for me.

My father, Joe Sommers, was a triple Domer, earning a bachelor's, master's, and PhD in chemistry during the '40s. He was disappointed, three times, when none of my older brothers chose to go to Notre Dame, but I kept telling him, "Don't worry, Dad, I'll be going to Notre Dame!"—even though coeducation had not yet been initiated. Luckily, for both of us, I was admitted into the Class of '79.

My time at Notre Dame was filled with learning, exploring, camaraderie, love, and growth. When I graduated, I got a great job as an accountant at Abbott Laboratories, and am just about to celebrate my twenty-eighth anniversary there. I met my husband-to-be at an inter-dorm party freshman year, and we just celebrated our twenty-fifth wedding anniversary. The older of our two daughters, a Reilly scholar and member of the inaugural Engineering Honors Program, is a proud member of the ND Class of 2009.

My neighbor, John Smith, has told me many stories of life in Notre Dame's post–World War II married student housing, where you served as a young rector. He describes you as a very dedicated, caring, and inspirational person. As a student in the '70s, I remember walking across the Main Quad late at night and looking up to see the light still shining from your office window. I am truly thankful for your life's effort to make Notre Dame the premier university and blessed place that it is today for my daughter to experience.

Yours in Notre Dame,

Betty Pierret
Class of '79

Dear Father Hesburgh,

I would like to thank you for the gift of Notre Dame. When I was a junior in high school, I was looking for a college and we went to watch our local college crew team race Notre Dame's crew team. When Mercyhurst won the race, Notre Dame's boat was still about half a mile out in the bay. It didn't faze the ND kids at all. When their boat finished, they cheered their team on as if they had just won the Olympics! Dad suggested I talk with the students about ND. When I spoke to the crew team, they all loved Notre Dame and none of the students had a negative thing to say about the university. I applied, was accepted, and saw the university for the first time my first day of freshman orientation. I have never regretted my decision to attend Notre Dame. As a member of Notre Dame's tennis team, I was always aware of the impact we could have representing the university to the public.

I received an excellent education at Notre Dame and was accepted into a very competitive Physical Therapy program at the University of Pennsylvania. More than education, I received the gifts of faith, family, and friendship at Notre Dame. Throughout our four years we laughed, cried, prayed, studied, played, served, and worked hard together. Notre Dame is a very special place! I met many dear friends at Notre Dame including my soul mate for life, Chris Schenkel.

You have played a very important role in our family. I met you in person my sophomore year one rainy Saturday night in October while you were working late in your office. You dropped your work to talk with a small group of us from Lewis Hall. I will always remember how kind to us you were that evening!

Chris and I had several miscarriages before spending the day with you before Universal Notre Dame Night in Fort Wayne several years ago. You blessed Christopher Jr. while I was pregnant, and then Patrick, Katie, and Danny as the years went on. We have four beautiful miracle babies. They are gifts from God. Thanks for your faith! The kids met you last summer and were so grateful for the time you spent with them. Chris and Pat are current students, and Katie and Danny are aspiring to attend Notre Dame in the future. Thanks for all of the gifts you have given me through the gift of coeducation at Notre Dame.

Fondly,

Anne Kelly Schenkel
Class of '79

c⤴

Dear Father Hesburgh,

One thing is certain, time really does fly. Is it possible that you have turned ninety? I still see you through the eyes of an eighteen-year-old coed. The year is 1975. I'll be turning eighteen in November, and you are in your fifties and are the president of the University of Notre Dame. An acceptance letter from John T. Goldrick, director of admissions, arrived at my home in New Jersey in November of the previous year. That was a letter allowing me to come to Notre Dame, a letter that altered the course of my life.

Of course I knew about Notre Dame . . . or at least I thought I did. I grew up with little brothers who wore Notre Dame sweatshirts because of the legacy that came before us. My father, like his father before him, shared a love of the law, and a love for Our Lady's university. My grandfather graduated from Notre Dame in 1927, from the Hoynes College of Law with Red Smith, Joe Boland, and Paul Butler. My father, Ed Broderick Jr., was a Double Domer, Class of 1954 and JD 1956. His three younger brothers followed suit and graduated in the late '50s and early '60s. When the acceptance letter arrived in the fall of 1974, Notre Dame was still the school that the men in my father's family attended. Yes, I was very excited about my acceptance but I truly underestimated the impact of that decision.

In the fall of 1975, the opportunity for women to attend Notre Dame was still relatively new. The women who were seniors the year I was a freshman comprised the first class of women to graduate after attending four consecutive years. At that time, the ratio of men to women was about seven to one. If you didn't come from a family with at least one brother, it could be a little daunting.

It seemed as if we were aware of your travel schedule! The students knew when you were on campus and when you were out of town, serving as an ambassador for Notre Dame and for Catholic education. It was a comforting feeling . . . far away from our own homes and our own fathers, to know that you really were there for us at any time of the day and night.

Aside from a business degree, for me, the greatest gift of attending Notre Dame was the gift of lifelong friendship. By allowing women to come to Notre Dame, that decision not only altered the history of the university, it altered the paths of many people's lives. Some of us met our future spouses. Many of us forged lifelong friendships. Thirty years have passed in the blink of an eye and yet the bonds of friendship that we formed as undergraduate women have survived the test of time. The friends we made at Notre Dame represent the family of friends who have been with us on life's happiest days and who stand by our side on some of the saddest days. I feel blessed to count your niece, Mary Hesburgh Flaherty, as  one of the friends that I will cherish for a lifetime.

In a letter I received from Sister John Miriam Jones, assistant to the provost, dated August 2, 1975, Sister John Miriam wrote, "My hope—and prayer—for you is that you will be among those many whose lives become gripped by Notre Dame and never again quite the same because of it."

Thank you, Father Hesburgh, for giving women the opportunity to come to Notre Dame. I'd like to think that Notre Dame changed for the better because we came. I know that I was gripped by the spirit of a very special place and changed for the better when I was a younger woman. I think I speak for many of my fellow alumnae when I say that our lives have never been quite the same because of Notre Dame.

Gratefully,

Karen Broderick Tourville
Class of '79

# 4

# ALUMNAE LETTERS— CLASSES OF 1980–1989

ear Father Hesburgh,

In third grade, 1966 to be exact, I had a teacher who went to Saint Mary's and she told us how the students at ND climbed the water tower and painted a big shamrock there. I asked her if she went up the tower and she said, "Oh no, only the Notre Dame students did." That sealed it for me, that was where I wanted to go to college; the place where the students climb towers. When I was in seventh grade in 1970 and developing a crush on Joe Theismann and a love for football (it got me out of doing the Sunday dishes), I still had that one desire, to go to Notre Dame. By then I had an understanding that Notre Dame was not coeducational, but the world was changing and I could hope and pray. Going to college at the University of Notre Dame was still my dream. By 1976 and my high school graduation, I was prepared and ready to accomplish my dream. No one in my family had ever gone to college and the tuition was certainly a struggle even back then, but I could not go anywhere else.

I majored in civil engineering and had the great pleasure of interviewing you for the *Tech Review*. Funny how I was the one in a hurry and you played classical music and calmed things down. Freshman year our quad sent a silly Valentine card to you and received a much appreciated thank-you note. I cannot thank you enough for making my dream come true. You are an inspiration to us all. Your life, your vocation and faith have made a difference to so many in the world and I am fortunate to have been touched by a part of that experience. Thank you.

Debra A. Bieber
Class of '80

Those of us who entered in the fall of 1976 probably didn't realize that in the following spring, the first class of women to matriculate through Notre Dame would graduate. Living in Lewis at the time, a "new dorm," with mostly just sophomores and freshmen, we were ignorant. And ignorance was bliss.

We were a confident class of women who did not see impediments to our academic or professional choices while at Notre Dame. Our professors treated us, men and women, the same, harshly or fairly. Of course we all thought the discipline in the boys' dorms was lax, but they also smelled like it. Eventually we did hear some of the early horror stories from some of the trailblazers, but we did not experience it; we participated fully in football tailgaters, An Tostal, bookstore basketball, SYRs, and all other aspects of Notre Dame social life, except perhaps the annual panty raid and St. Michael's laundry.

But I'd be remiss not to mention our male counterparts. Maybe because our fellow classmates were not burdened by watching a bastion of male tradition end, but they treated us as equals. Our male peers were our study partners, SYR dates, best buddies, boyfriends and, for some, our husbands. I don't know if we were all enlightened enough or liberated enough to make such a smooth transition on our own, but I do know that Notre Dame, and specifically Father Ted, made sure we were welcomed and appreciated. I think that that is the beauty of a Catholic education, because ultimately underlying the process and implementation of bringing coeducation to Notre Dame, were the principles of our Catholic faith. And, for that, I am forever grateful.

Elizabeth Bathon Brown
Class of '80

Father Ted,

Although I never met you, you were for me the face of ND. I had fallen in love with ND as a young girl revisiting my dad's campus (he graduated in 1959, when I was two months old!), and was always wistful that I would never get to go to ND. But then when I was older, you changed things for me—when my dad brought me to ND for my visit and "interview," I knew that I had found my home. This, despite my dad's horror to see feminine products in "his" bookstore!

Thanks for helping make my dreams come true, and my daughter's (Class of 2008) as well. We are truly blessed that your work in fostering coeducation made it possible for women to say "WE ARE ND."

Mary Blachowicz Lewis, MD
Class of '80

Dear Father Hesburgh,

I was a senior back in 1980 when I recall walking to Dillon Hall for Mass on a beautiful spring evening. I was uncharacteristically spouting off about women and their lack of place in the Church to my roommate. My recollections are fuzzy now but I clearly recall an unmistakable voice behind us say "Good evening, boys" as a couple of students walked past us. My face probably flushed red. Without turning around, I asked my roommate if she thought "he" had heard me. Well, I decided that Father Hesburgh had most likely heard me if I could hear him but that he probably wouldn't think much of me or spend any time considering my complaints. After all, he is the president and I am just a no-name student, or so I thought at the time.

I was, of course, very wrong. During the homily, you spoke to the gathered students about the perfect role model women have in Our Lady and how women should feel comfortable praying for Mary's intercession and guidance as we walk our life's journey. Well, twenty-seven years later, I have never forgotten those wise and comforting words. While my prayer life can still be improved upon today, I do start and end most days with thoughts and prayers focused on Our Lady.

I am now a successful civil engineer, running a consulting firm and I am able to afford to send my daughter to Notre Dame. So, while I am most definitely thankful for the wonderful education I received, I am truly grateful for the strong faith my Notre Dame experience gave me.

Thank you, Father. May God continue to bless you.

Mary Catherine McBride
Class of '80

❧

Dear Father Ted,

It has taken some time for me to properly reflect on the gift you have given so many women by opening the university's heart and soul to us so many years ago.

Clearly, a coed Notre Dame has been pivotal in forging a path for women to have choices and opportunities in work and in life that would not have been in such abundance without you. Recently, I started a company, Ortho Discovery Parnters. I am president and chief executive officer. But, as I sit on this airplane what resonates with me most about having been able to attend Notre Dame has nothing to do with "profession" and everything to do with "people." These graduates, my sisters, my friends, my roommates add a texture to my life that is profound. They define me. Challenge me. Inspire me.

The essence of Notre Dame never leaves you and comes looking for you when you need it most. Its people continue to make their way toward you. My business partner, the most exceptional gentle man you will ever meet attended ND eight years ahead of me and randomly appeared in my office one rainy New York day. He has been a guiding light ever since.

Also, by happenstance, did another Domer—who is now snoring next to me on this flight to Paris—meander into my world. He is the great love of my life (although if we tell him that he will jump out of the plane).

Father Ted, these Notre Dame people that I know and those I will come to meet have been your greatest gift. We are so very grateful that you listened to Our Lady when she whispered in your ear to let us join her at such a very special place.

Thank you.

Sincerely,

Paddy Mullen
Class of '80
Walsh Hall

Dear Father Ted,

Happy Birthday! You have been such an inspiration to so many of us, and I am blessed to know you. Your decision to admit women to Notre Dame, AND your continued support of us, has changed many lives for the better, in monumental ways. Here's how coeducation affected me. . . .

I arrived on campus in August 1976, when there weren't too many females filling the quad. I came from a female-dominated family (one son, five daughters), attended an all-female high school, and had always thought I'd be headed to the beautiful campus across the street! Those early days were filled with much trepidation, as my classes were often all-male expect for me. I was asked for the "female point of view" by professors who may have not been completely on board with coeducation (Precalculus 101 isn't gender-specific!). The curriculum was extremely demanding, and I was a long way from home. I remember walking across the campus, never having lived in the Midwest, hearing different accents, seeing different styles of dress, and MEN everywhere, and wondering how I was going to fit in. . . .

I needn't have worried. The women accepted into that Class of 1980 are some of the most amazing people I have ever been fortunate enough to meet. An intelligent, compassionate, articulate group who had a strong sense of who they were, and didn't worry about conforming to the hallowed halls of the Notre Dame mystique—my female colleagues were going to fill the dorms, classrooms, and fields of Notre Dame with their unique personalities. We stood out on campus, and stuck up for one another—making sure our dorm mates had a friendly face to eat with in the massive South Dining Hall, borrowing one another's formal dresses during frenzied weekends when the male dorms held their dances, forming impromptu study sessions in our dorm hallways late into the night. A strong camaraderie developed during those early years, and still exists today, among my female classmates of 1980—we take care of one another.

My male classmates in 1976 were extremely supportive of their female colleagues as well. They may have been a little confused about how to treat us—I think they looked at us as an "experiment" and weren't too sure how to relate to us in class. Many of them had attended all-male high schools, so we both had a lot of learning to do! For the first time in my life, and like no time since, I developed very strong male friendships—and those relationships helped me navigate the male-dominated workforce in 1980. I had teased and been teased for four years, had been engaged in discussions that broke down stereotypes. "Do you go to Saint Mary's or Notre Dame?" was a frequent question I was asked at a dorm party. This often provoked a spirited discussion on the ability to be intelligent and attractive at the same time! I developed a strong sense of my own personal value, as measured by male standards. I graduated from Notre Dame a feminist—both from my female and male friends. And we had so much fun together! When I returned for my twenty-fifth class reunion, it struck me forcibly how much I missed male companionship, and how much we simply enjoyed one another, whether over a meal, walking to class, at a basketball game or party, or at a dorm Mass. Male and female, we were especially bonded to one another those four years.

Your support of coeducation has been the most important force in making it a success. Because of your devotion to Our Lady, you empowered us to stand apart, to view ourselves as wonderful, and asked us to share our femaleness with the world. Just last year I attended a Mass after a football game in your office, when you honored the women in the room, and exalted our roles as mothers as something so vital and important. I don't hear that, except once a year on Mother's Day—our society either takes it for granted or has forgotten the value of motherhood. So thirty years after I arrived on campus, you are still reminding all of us to honor Our Lady, and that we can do so through the simple acts of daily family life.

I am so proud to be a member of one of the early coeducation classes at Notre Dame. I found my female voice there, and it has served me well. God bless you, Father Ted, and may the blessings of Mary continue to fill you with love, peace, health, and wisdom.

With love and gratitude,

Laura Flaherty Palmer
Class of '80

President Johnson gives Father Ted the Medal of Freedom—September 14, 1964.

President George H. W. Bush and Father Ted.

President Jimmy Carter and Father Ted.

Father Ted and President Dwight Eisenhower.

Dear Father Hesburgh,

I am very grateful for your leadership and wisdom. I, and all the women of Notre Dame, share a deep debt of gratitude to you and your board of trustees who decided to admit women to Our Lady's university. I know that my life would not be the same without her Lady's gift, and I dare say, most of the women of ND feel the same.

In my family, we are the first generation to enjoy a college education. On my father's side, his parents emigrated from Ireland to be a cabby (my grandfather) and a house servant in New York City (my grandmother). On my mother's side, her father was a coal miner who died in a mining accident in his early forties leaving my grandmother with eight young children to raise.

Though I never knew either grandfather, I was blessed with two great godparents: my favorite aunt, who inherited the family business when my uncle died and my godfather, who is a mentor and role model in so many ways. Dan McGinnis, ND '61, is my godfather though he's only nineteen years my senior.

Dan came home once with a gift for me, a blue stuffed animal with a gold ND on the ears. According to family legend, I announced that I would go to ND like Dan. Some "wise" adult told me that I couldn't as ND was for men only. Legend continues with me announcing that I would then be among the first women to go to ND.

As a member of the Class of 1980, I can truly say that I realized my dream.

This fall marks the thirty-first anniversary of my first days on campus. I am also grateful to the two women who were responsible for freshman orientation in Breen-Phillips. Robin Lavender '78 and Amy Thornton Wills '78 adopted me my first day on campus and remain dear friends to this day.

For these stories and all that is Notre Dame, I am thankful to you.

Yours in Notre Dame,

Mary Ellen Woods
Class of '80

Dear Father Hesburgh,

Hardly a day passes that I am not somehow reminded of my ties to Notre Dame, because I have regular correspondence with my former classmates, because the university
is prominent in the sports and world news, because the outstanding Alumni Association keeps me in the loop as to events on campus and beyond, or merely because I am
the proud owner of a vanity license plate. Now as a twenty-five-year alumna, fond and
vivid memories of my years on campus resurface on a constant basis.

I have felt so fortunate to have had the first-class education in academics, spirituality, and life that Notre Dame provided. That education is an ongoing challenge, a
very high standard against which the days of my postgraduation life are measured, and
always will be.

Being a member of the fourth class of women who attended a full four years at
Notre Dame carried a special thrill, that we were part of a wave of change in the university toward inclusion and recognition of the virtues of coeducation. In the years
since my graduation I have seen the women of Notre Dame justify the decision to welcome them, as they have enhanced the achievements and the reputation of the student
body and alumni.

We were honored to have you as our university president and a leader in the national and international community. We wish you a very Happy Birthday, and thank
you for all of your contributions to the success of our university.

As a female graduate, I want to thank you for welcoming me to be a part of the
legend. It has made all the difference.

With very best wishes,

Tracy Blake DeVlieger
Class of '81

Dear Father Ted,

Starting at Notre Dame as a scared freshman, I was welcomed immediately to my new family. I remember orientation with you and many others who, while at first were strangers, soon
became friends and colleagues. You were a big reason I felt at home in a very short time.

Notre Dame is a family, a big, noisy, contentious Catholic family much like the ones many of us grew up with. I feel it every time one of us is honored for our accomplishments, whenever we lose a family member, when our university is mentioned for praise or criticism. I get a little glow inside whenever I can say, "That's my school." I hope you do, too.

When I was at Notre Dame, I made a habit of visiting the Grotto every night before I went to bed. It was a favorite part of my day and it allowed me to put aside the worries about class assignments, tests, and social woes and reflect for a brief time on Our Lady and my good fortune to be right where I was at that exact moment in time. As with most college students, my day often ended in the wee hours of the morning, and I regularly found myself at the Grotto between 1:30 and 2:00 a.m. There was a group of us who had the same nighttime habits and we began to extend our Grotto moments with conversation and fellowship. Those nights are still precious to me.

If I was lucky, I would see you, making the same visit to the Grotto, or crossing the campus from your office to Corby Hall. Your late-night hours were legendary among us students and often we would look up to your office windows in the Administration Building and find them as brightly lit at midnight as at 6:00 p.m. We would stop and talk for a minute or two, then continue to our separate destinations. I treasured those moments of affirmation that the Notre Dame family included all of us.

My life is forever changed for the better because I attended Notre Dame. Casual conversations with new acquaintances always have that moment when someone asks "Where did you go to college?" and I respond "Notre Dame." With any other school, I'll hear some variation of "Oh, that's nice," but when I say Notre Dame everyone has a reaction—most are positive, and I do get the occasional negative. Notre Dame is meaningful to so many people who don't have a direct connection to the university, and I'm lucky enough to be connected and part of the family. My parents, who are gone now, were thrilled to tell people they had a daughter who graduated from Notre Dame and I'm grateful I could give them that moment.

I know it's really difficult to accept thanks, but I would like to thank you, Father, for the love you have for Our Lady and our university. Your efforts are a big reason I'm proud to tell people about my school and so many people react positively to it.

Sincerely,

Anne Giffels
Class of '81

Dear Father Ted,

Thank you for giving all of us the opportunity to develop and grow within the Notre Dame community. Every time I connect with my dorm mates, or run into other women who attended Notre Dame, I am awed by their completeness, spiritually, morally, and intellectually. I am also humbled by their accomplishments, both in a family and corporate setting. My daughter is a fourth-generation Domer (Class of 2010), who is just beginning to understand the power of the gift you gave her. I look forward to her thank-you note to you for your 95th birthday.

When I was a child, my goals were to go to Notre Dame and be a priest. Thank you for clearing the path for goal number one. How much energy do you have for goal number two?

Mary McCarthy Logue
Class of '81

Dear Father Hesburgh,

Happy 90th birthday!

I am a 1981 graduate of Notre Dame with a BS in mechanical engineering and a BA in modern languages. Of the many decisions I have made over the years, my decision (and my parents' great support) to apply to and attend Notre Dame was, by far, one of the most significant in my life! My husband attended ND. My Farley Hall friends are still some of my closest friends. My ND affiliation still opens conversations—and doors. Your vision to admit women to ND gave me the opportunity to indulge all of my interests—from engineering studies to studying in Angers, France.

You are probably familiar with the joke that permeated campus in the late '70s and early '80s—What is the difference between God and Father Hesburgh? God is everywhere, but Father Hesburgh is everywhere but Notre Dame. . . . we knew differently, though, as we walked across South Quad, and saw the light in your administration office burning late into the night (and heard the many stories of students who took you up on your "open door policy" for a late night visit!). We had to share you with our government, other world leaders, other academics, but we knew where your heart was! By the way, I never took advantage of that opportunity—if I have one regret from my ND days, that's it!

Now ND has come full circle in our family. Thanks to his hard work (and a few candles and prayers in the Grotto!), my oldest son will attend ND in the fall, Class of 2011. His brother and little sister hope to follow in his (in my!) footsteps—Class of 2018?!?

Thank you, Father Ted, for your vision to include women at Notre Dame. Thank you for your dedication—to our country, to our God, to Notre Dame. You continue to be an inspiration to all Domers—not just the women who attended ND during those first few years of coeducation. Thanks, Father Ted, for giving me the chance to be part of the Notre Dame family. *Bonne Anniversaire!*

Sincerely,

Mary Jean Schmitt
Class of '81

Dear Father Hesburgh,

My father, Jim Tyrrell, an only child from Detroit, returned from abroad after World War II, attended the University of Notre Dame, and graduated in 1949. He met and fell in love with my mother, Gina Reynolds, a student at Saint Mary's. My mother was from Memphis, Tennessee, and the first of her family to attend Saint Mary's College. The rest of her siblings followed in her footsteps attending either Saint Mary's or Notre Dame. Their courtship led to my father proposing to my mother at the Grotto. Given my family's history, Notre Dame holds a special place in my heart.

I applied for admission in the fall of 1976 to only two schools: Notre Dame and Saint Mary's. I proceeded to accept admission to Notre Dame. I was the first female of my extended family to attend the University of Notre Dame as an undergraduate student from 1977 to 1981. I was the fourth of five girls, and my three older sisters all attended Saint Mary's. In addition, I have had many cousins who have attended Saint Mary's. I felt as if I broke from tradition venturing across the street to attend Notre Dame. Little did I know I would only extend my family's tradition in South Bend.

Throughout my entire life my most important value has been my family. I have been married for twenty-two years and chose to be a stay-at-home mother eighteen years ago. My husband and I are proud parents of three beautiful daughters. One of my greatest joys was sending my oldest daughter Kelly off to Notre Dame in the fall of 2005. Because of this, Notre Dame has become an even bigger part of my life. As a mother, it is comforting to know that my daughter has the opportunity to experience the spirit of Notre Dame as I did twenty-five years ago.

It is because of your courage that I have been able to continue my family's tradition at Notre Dame. By allowing women to attend the university you opened a world of opportunities for upcoming generations of women. I would like to thank you for allowing myself, my daughter, and the many other women the opportunity to experience all that Notre Dame has to offer. My eighty-two-year-old father of five daughters and seven granddaughters especially appreciates your decision, as he was able to see his family follow in his footsteps. The tradition, values, and environment of Notre Dame has touched my life in many ways and for this, I am eternally thankful.

Sincerely,

Patricia Tyrrell Short
Class of '81

Dear Father Hesburgh,

I have tried to start this letter many times but words keep failing me. I wanted to be so eloquent to make you/ND proud. Instead, let me just tell you how proud my grand-mother was when I graduated Notre Dame.

It all started with a little girl growing up poor in New Orleans. A Catholic grand-mother who fostered ideas of that little girl going to Notre Dame even though no one in their family had ever graduated high school much less college. We were a hard-working albeit illiterate family and of course not worldly. We had no idea Notre Dame was an all-boys' school. As I grew up and told people I was going to go to Notre Dame I could see either pacification or smirking in some people's faces but thought they were thinking I didn't have what it takes. Those looks made me strive that much harder. Even when my freshman high school counselor laughed, I was still unaware that Notre Dame was a boys-only university. I'd like to say I got the last laugh but that's not what I think of when I think of Notre Dame.

Notre Dame was the only college to which I applied, and thanks to you, I had an opportunity to be accepted. Notre Dame pushed me educationally, challenging me more than I'd ever been challenged. Notre Dame opened me up to new and different people and situations. Notre Dame helped me grow socially and in maturity. My life would be so very different if it were not for you and Notre Dame. Yes, I worked my butt off but you gave me the opportunity.

Notre Dame changed my life and maybe the lives of all my family. After me, my cousins also attended college. College became a part of our way of thinking. I have a great business and a wonderful family living the American dream. I know anything is possible but only when people of all races, religions, and genders are allowed the oppor-tunity. Thank you. Thank you for giving me the opportunity. I hope I make you proud.

Sincerely,

A.T.

Class of '81

PS When I drove my car all the way from New Orleans to Notre Dame and saw that Angela Avenue lead to Notre Dame, I knew it was kismet! I still chuckle at that!

Father Ted,

You mean so much to Notre Dame, and the women of ND, more than you can ever imagine. We were so thrilled when you officiated over the validation of our marriage vows on October 30, 1998. All my years at Notre Dame, you were like the Wizard of Oz—behind the curtain, pulling the strings. You are so approachable and so good with students, I don't know how you got that reputation. You are loved by many, and the university has much to be thankful for with your guidance over all the years. Bringing Sister Jean Lenz to ND, to welcome the women on campus in the early '70s—what a fantastic rector Sister Jean was. Those were the days. And then moving Sister Jean on to Student Affairs, and keeping her all these years.... And that's just the tip of the iceberg!

Father Ted—We celebrate your life and all you do for all of us. You've had a major role in making ND what it is today, and all of us who have graced the halls of our beloved Mother. Notre Dame Our Mother. Keep up the great work from your thirteenth floor view of the campus. Cheers, cheers for 'ole Notre Dame.

All the best,

Julie Quagliano Westemeier Esq.
Class of '81

Dear Father Ted,

In 1967, in my perfectly ordered seven-year-old world, Notre Dame was the place boys went. That was the year my young life changed because you invited my father, Phil, an attorney in Chicago, to return to his alma mater as your special assistant and subsequently, your general counsel.

As the oldest of the six Faccenda children, I remember moving to South Bend and enrolling in the now defunct Saint Mary's College Campus Grammar School. There I was surrounded by SMC girls and I looked up to them and began to formulate my view of the future as an SMC student. One day I asked my father, "When I get big, Dad, I'll go to Saint Mary's, right?" And he responded "Not if Father Hesburgh has his way, honey. By the time you go to college, there will be girls at Notre Dame." That seemed like a bizarre idea to me then, exciting but unattainable. And, then it happened.

I remember my father endured countless phone calls and personal encounters with his own classmates and other alumni friends, who felt the need to register their distaste with the state of things at Notre Dame. The "things" were the women and often the root of their complaint was their own son's admission rejection. The friend would say "How could they refuse my son in favor of a girl?!" My father patiently listened, without saying much and eventually the guy would talk himself to the end by saying "You are probably happy about it with all those girls you have!"

Of course Dad was happy. And the four Faccenda girls (and one granddaughter, so far) are forever thankful that you made it possible for us to attend Notre Dame and that you have been an important part of our lives!

Much love on the occasion of your 90th birthday,

Maribeth Faccenda-Hough
Class of '82

Father Hesburgh,

I want to thank you, not only for giving me the invaluable opportunity to be a Notre Dame woman by making Notre Dame coed, but also for your unwavering dedication to our formation as Catholic men and women of integrity. Looking back, I really appreciate that you refused to make the dorms coed, even floor by floor, and that parietals were not just rules on the books but were strictly enforced. Just a couple of weeks ago I was talking with a group of women about my experience at Notre Dame, about how truly abided we were by the sexual moral teachings of our Church—knowing that they were there for our own good. My experience was that I never had to worry about a Notre Dame man date raping me or using me sexually. This is so different from people's experiences even at other Catholic universities. People are amazed when they hear about my experience at Notre Dame because they experienced an atmosphere of sexual license in college; and looking back. They wish their college years had been like mine at Notre Dame. I had good romances, and I have very good, lasting friendships. I attribute that to your unwavering dedication to our formation as Catholic men and women of integrity. Thank you, and thank you for all you have done for us with your entire life. God bless you, and happy, happy 90th.

Sincerely yours,

Mary E. Fala
Class of '82

Dear Father Hesburgh,

I want to take this opportunity to thank you for my Notre Dame education. It has guided me in every decision I've made in the last twenty-four years. I feel like I'm making a difference in the lives of my family, my friends, my coworkers. At this particular time in my life, I'm feeling even more of a desire to give of myself to others less fortunate. My Notre Dame experience is still evolving as I grow closer to God and to the person I have always wanted to be. Thank you, Father Ted! You are so cherished.

Love in Notre Dame,

Martha Frey Hart
Class of '82

Dear Father Ted,

I have three vivid memories of my life prior to Notre Dame: deciding I wanted to go to ND, getting my acceptance to ND, and riding up Notre Dame Avenue for the first time.

In 1970, when I was ten years old I pointed to the TV in the middle of a Notre Dame football game and said to my dad (James Beston Powers '52), "I want to go there." When my dad told me I couldn't, I replied, "Then I'll go to Saint Mary's." Two years later, my dream was possible. All throughout high school, my motivation for getting good grades was to get accepted to ND. My second major memory was finding out I was accepted. The vision of my sister Susan, a freshman home on spring break from Boston College, running down the hall of my high school gesturing wildly with her arms and holding a letter (an open one at that!) in her hands and screaming loudly remains with me until this day. Lastly, I will never forget my first visit to Notre Dame, which did not happen until after I was accepted. Riding up Notre Dame Avenue with my father and seeing the Golden Dome brought tears to my eyes; the thought of it still does today!

Being a part of the Notre Dame family has given me tremendous joy these past twenty-nine years. I have said proudly countless times, "I went to Notre Dame." I only regret that my father is not alive to share our next reunion this June, my twenty-fifth and his fifty-fifth!

Thank you from the bottom of my heart for allowing me to realize my dream and to be able to share Notre Dame with my father!

Sincerely,

Julia Power Killian
Class of '82

Dear Father Hesburgh,

Although your list of accomplishments is tremendous, I especially want to thank you for the decision to change Notre Dame into a coed institution.

When I was twelve, my father came home one day and said, "They let women into Notre Dame—now you can go there for college!" Although we grew up avid Notre Dame fans, it never occurred to me that I was going to college, or that my father wanted me to go to Notre Dame. The seed was planted, however, and Notre Dame was the only school I applied to. I began in 1978. My father was extremely proud of me, and although he died when I was a sophomore, I will always carry the encouragement he gave me.

Being at Notre Dame, though, meant much more to me than pleasing my father. I was able to stretch my intellectual boundaries and relish in learning for its own sake. I learned that women could be whatever they chose to be—not just teachers or nurses. They could also be good mothers and wives. My eyes were opened to the diversity of

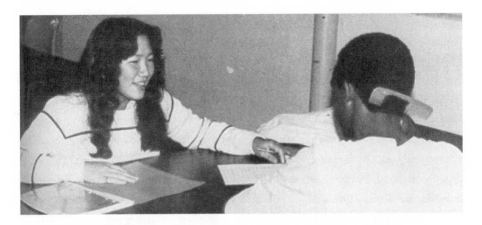

the world and I was challenged to defend my ideas and embrace new ones. I saw social justice in action and grew in my faith.

I also made wonderful friends at Notre Dame—ones I still talk with and laugh with. I saw young people struggle with emotional, financial, and academic issues. I met authors and actors and politicians. My world was awakened.

After I graduated from Notre Dame, I carried the school with me. I spent a year getting a master's at the London School of Economics—a journey I would never have had the guts to make without the support of my ND community. After some graduate work at the University of Texas at Austin, I went to medical school in Houston, and am now a practicing internist.

Many times my connection with Notre Dame has opened doors for me. More importantly, however, is the frame of reference my experiences has given me to confront challenges in my life. I hope that what I give back to society is a small reflection of the life of Christ I learned at Notre Dame.

I am now happily married, and have four children. I hope that one day some of them will want to go to Notre Dame. I have achieved so much in my life, and have much more to do. I know that the opportunity of going away to Notre Dame has allowed me to do so much more in my life. In the words of Isaac Newton, "If I have seen a little further, it is by standing on the shoulders of giants." Thank you so much for that boost! May God continue to bless you on this your 90th birthday!

Sincerely,

Marilyn Mayer, MD
Class of '82

୧ଙ

Dear Father Ted,

"God. Country. Notre Dame." As the fifth of seven children of a proud 1952 Notre Dame graduate, it is a slogan I have embraced all my life. From a very young age, I believed that the University of Notre Dame was a place for those who both excelled academically and were committed to making the world a better place. "That's me," I proudly declared, but my parents quickly informed me that I could never be admitted—because I was a girl.

I am forever grateful to you for changing all that: for giving me, and all women, the opportunity to live four years under the Golden Dome. Those years were years of tremendous intellectual, emotional, and spiritual growth for me. The experiences of my years at Notre Dame and the bonds forged there have enriched my life in countless ways and, twenty-five years later, bless my every day.

Thank you for making it all possible.

God bless you!

Tara Carney Runnals
Class of '82

୧ଙ

Dear Father Hesburgh,

Thank you for opening the enrollment at Notre Dame to women.

You and my father graduated from Notre Dame around the same time—he was in the Class of 1938. He took me to visit the campus when I was a junior in high school and introduced me to you outside the chapel. We have met on several other occasions over the years but that memory remains with me.

My experience at Notre Dame was certainly one of the most important in my life. I am proud to be in the tenth class of women. I spent a wonderful year abroad in Innsbruck, forged many important relationships that endure today, and enjoyed the mixture of excellent academics and unpretentious Catholic spirituality.

Thank you for your foresight in admitting women and leading Notre Dame to the forefront of Catholic universities.

Sincerely,

RHW
Class of '82

꿍

Dear Father Hesburgh,

I will never forget interviewing you for the *Observer* back in the early '80s. Your stories of ongoing peace initiatives with other world leaders, your interest in space, and your unshakeable belief in Notre Dame were inspirational to a nineteen-year-old.

Most importantly though, your ecumenicalism, due to your broad view of the world, left an indelible impression on me. Today as I collaborate with people from different countries and different walks of life, I have found your perspective invaluable.

Your peace initiatives are crucial given the current state of the world. Your words on the library sculpture are so timeless. I am glad they are there for the students who pass by them daily and those who will have the opportunity to read them in the future.

I am certain opening Notre Dame's doors to women was no small task. Thank you for your vision in recognizing the contributions women would make and for your persistence in realizing that vision. As pioneers, we experienced both incredible challenges and phenomenal opportunities, that have profoundly and positively shaped and inspired us. I am grateful.

I enjoyed watching your latest DVD. I cannot believe you are ninety. You really do look much younger!

I wish you all the best.

Sincerely,

Mary Fran Callahan
Class of '83

꿍

Dear Father Hesburgh,

Congratulations on the propitious event of your 90th birthday.

I want to thank you today for your leadership in bringing women into the Notre Dame community. The education and experience that I received at the University of Notre Dame made me a better person. My education at Notre Dame set the groundwork for my future educational endeavors—a Fulbright Scholarship, a master's in development studies and a PhD in economics—and gave me the fortitude and character to participate in the Holy Cross Associate program, to stand for local political office, and to never be shy about speaking out for justice and equality.

Thank you for touching my life. May God bless you with continued good health and longevity.

Best wishes,

Susan Fleck
Class of '83

Dear Father Hesburgh,

One of the greatest benefits of a Notre Dame education lies in the emphasis on family. Not only do generations of students tend to follow alumni parents or relatives to campus, we also become aware of the global connections that bind people together. Of course, every family includes women, and I appreciate your role in admitting women to Notre Dame. That change helped create an atmosphere of inclusion which is so important—and often lacking—in our society.

There are so many ways in which social forces can divide us: Republicans vs. Democrats; Americans vs. foreigners; white vs. black; Christian vs. Muslim. You have worked to unify people of different backgrounds, faiths, and nationalities, and bringing men and women together on the Notre Dame campus was an important step in that direction. When I look at the amazing accomplishments of my fellow alumnae, it's clear that they have become great mothers, as well as successful professionals, strengthening their families while making a difference in society. We might not have come so far without feeling that we belonged, and Notre Dame helped foster that sense of inclusion.

Thank you again for your contributions to Notre Dame, and I wish you many more years of happiness.

Sincerely,

A. H.
Class of '83

Dear Father Ted,

Thank you for making Notre Dame coed. I used my electrical engineering education working at a technical company and now am volunteering at my children's schools.

What I have enjoyed most about having a Notre Dame education is jointly sharing the ND spirit with my father, sisters, and cousins. I am proud to be an ND graduate.

May 2007 was designated "volunteer month" in honor of you. I would like to thank you and Coach Dennis Stark for encouraging me to volunteer as a student because it has made a difference for me.

Thank you, Father Ted, for all your hard work and care all of these years.

Sincerely,

Jean Murtagh Hillman
Class of '83

Dear Father Hesburgh,

This note is to thank you for enabling women to attend the University of Notre Dame. Your vision of a coeducational institution has positively impacted so many lives and created an amazing legacy for the university.

For me personally, my education at ND changed my life. The relationships forged there, the quality educational experience, and the values that were ever present in this unique ND environment provided a foundation and framework for my life's journey. There are no words to express my appreciation and admiration for your perseverance and foresight in opening Notre Dame to women.

Thank you, God bless you, and GO IRISH!

P. K.
Class of '83

Dear Father Hesburgh,

Thank you for the opportunity of a lifetime by leading the University of Notre Dame to coeducation. As my daughter so eloquently stated in a freshman high school English class paper last fall, "My mother dreamed of attending the University of Notre Dame since she was a young girl. In 1972, Notre Dame became a coeducational school, so her dream could become a reality." I was honored to follow in the footsteps of my father, John F. Tuerk, deceased, Class of 1954.

My Notre Dame education has impacted every aspect of my life. My years at Notre Dame under your leadership have guided me through church, family, professional, and community relationships.

May you have a blessed and Happy Birthday. God bless you always!

Yours in Our Lady,

Anne Tuerk Klinepeter
Class of '83

cᴏ⫯

Dear Father Hesburgh,

I began my Notre Dame education on the day I was born. I was born while my father was teaching U.S. Marine Corps ROTC at the university in 1961 and studying for a Masters degree in mathematics education. I was baptized at Sacred Heart. I grew up a Notre Dame fan, although no one in my family had ever attended the university except for my father's master's program. With three older brothers, and with the university still all male during my early years, I was the least likely to attend. Your courage and foresight changed that for me and for many of my peers.

My experience as a woman at Notre Dame helped me to learn to deal with controversy and adversity, and that sometimes it's worth it to challenge the status quo when it's the right thing to do. When I first arrived at Notre Dame as an undergrad, we were well past the first "hump" of struggling to make coeducation the norm. However, we were still a long way from the atmosphere the students enjoy today. I chose engineering as my major, to further cement my status as woefully outnumbered by male students. But our status as women wasn't cause for controversy—we enjoyed positive relationships with the male students and professors—even the ones who thought we shouldn't be there. We often joked about the women of ND—my favorite was that the difference between ND women and garbage was that garbage gets taken out at least once a week. I laugh when I think of the times I heard a knock on my dorm room door on a football weekend, to be greeted by a polite but obviously heartbroken older male alum who proceeded to tell me that was his room when he was at Notre Dame. I was privileged to be a part of some female firsts at Notre Dame too. I was able to play on ND's first interscholastic women's softball and soccer teams. While those rudimentary beginnings of the programs were a far cry from the nationally ranked, scholarship teams of today, I'm proud to be able to say that I was there when it all started.

More importantly, what I gained from my Notre Dame education goes beyond what I experienced as a woman at Notre Dame. It was what I experienced as a person at Notre Dame that made the most difference in my life. I found a sense of belonging to something larger than myself—to a long tradition of the pursuit of truth, excellence, and morality. It is these ideals that have strengthened my faith, and my belief that doing the right thing is always more important than doing the expedient thing. What I first experienced at Notre Dame, (for the first time outside my own family) was a sense that I was connected to something bigger than myself—the Notre Dame community. That alone helped me to better understand and accept my faith as a Catholic. A commitment to excellence and truth is something that is integral to the Notre Dame experience, and I'm tremendously grateful that the opportunity for that experience was opened to women.

The Notre Dame experience for women should teach us all that if something is the right thing to do, no matter how unpopular, difficult, and even despised it may be at the time, eventually it will be accepted, applauded, and become the norm. Thank you for having the courage to make the difficult and controversial decision to allow women into the Notre Dame community. I wouldn't be the woman—or the person—I am today without it.

Sincerely,

Nancy Jackson Patrick
Class of '83

To our dear Father Ted,

Words cannot do justice to the feeling of gratitude I have in having had the opportunity to attend Our Lady's university, Notre Dame du Lac. I graduated with the Class of 1984 (an awesome class, I might add), and in doing so fulfilled a lifelong dream of mine of being part of the Notre Dame family. I am so thankful to you for your vision, which included women and for welcoming us so deeply into the community at Notre Dame. It is an honor to be able to share this note of thanks with you. God bless you, Father Hesburgh. You are loved by many!

Gratefully yours,

Dawn (Robinson) Hennessey
Class of '84

Dear Father Hesburgh,

Thank you for admitting women to Notre Dame. My two uncles graduated from ND in the '40s. I remember the first time they went to an ND home football game after coeducation. They wailed and carried on for hours about "girl cheerleaders on the field!" I can remember it like it was yesterday, even though it was thirty-four years ago!

At any rate, I applied to ND because my dad had always wanted to go here, but didn't get in after World War II. I wanted to make him happy. I made him happy by coming here. I also made my two uncles happier than they ever thought possible when contemplating the concept of "girls at Notre Dame."

Notre Dame has a special place in my heart, as both a loyal alumna and an employee. You have made this a place of which to be proud, and I consider myself fortunate to be able to share in a small part of the legacy you created.

God bless,

C. P.
Class of '84, '95 JD

1977-1978 Women's Engineering Club.

Dear Father Ted,

In 1976, as an eighth grader, I visited Notre Dame for the first time with my parents, who were attending a weekend meeting of the Advisory Council of the School of Business. During my visit, I was awestruck by the beauty of the campus, the spirit and energy of the students and administrators, and the university's devotion to Our Blessed Mother.

Through a mix-up, I found myself without a ticket to the football game that weekend. My parents had entered the stadium ahead of me, and my father had given me tickets for seats in another section of the stadium so that I could sit with the younger daughter of another council member. Much to our dismay, and unbeknownst to my father, the tickets were for the game the following weekend, and we were denied access to the stadium. Fortunately for us, you happened to come along, and when you discovered our dilemma, came to our rescue and invited us to watch the game with you in your box seats. It was a tremendous thrill and honor to be your guest. But it was your kind and gentle manner, your obvious love and commitment to the university, and your faith and dedication to country that convinced me Notre Dame was the place for me. I recall telling you this in a thank-you note, and your letter back to me in which you counseled me that if I hoped to attend Notre Dame someday, I would have to work very hard and devote myself to my schoolwork. I heeded your sound advice, and fulfilled my dream when four years later, I entered Notre Dame as a freshman.

My experience at Notre Dame was all that I hoped it would be and much more. During my four years there, I grew spiritually, personally, and intellectually, and made lifelong friends who are an ongoing source of love and support. The lessons I learned at Notre Dame continue to shape and guide me, and each time I have had the opportunity to return to the campus I feel renewed, inspired, and so incredibly blessed to be part of the Notre Dame community.

Words can never express how grateful I am to you for your commitment to coeducation at Notre Dame. The university has meant so much to me and countless other women, and we so appreciate your vision and persistence to make our dream of attending the university a reality.

God bless you.

Very truly yours,

Neilli Mullen Walsh
Class of '84

Dear Father Ted,

Thanking you for the gift of Notre Dame is thanking you for coeducation, and for so much more. For my family, Notre Dame is part of us in almost every significant way. When my father decided to come to Notre Dame in 1967, it became part of nearly everything we did, and we loved it. The Notre Dame that we came to was the Notre

## FATHER TED'S PRAYER FOR MOTHERS

May the Blessed Mother bless you with her wonderful child, Jesus.

Dame that you created. It was special. There are not words to adequately thank you for that, for that place, for that feeling.

For my three sisters and me, the idea that we would some day attend Notre Dame, seemed, even before women were admitted, like a foregone conclusion. I can remember sitting with you and my dad at the table one summer evening, and you asking us, if we had our choice, where would we go to college. I was probably ten, and Notre Dame had either just begun accepting women or was about to do so. We all knew the right answer. Notre Dame, of course.

The gift of Notre Dame is the gift of a lifetime of relationships with the best individuals that the world has to offer. You gave us that gift, and so many more. Thanks.

Susan Faccenda Walsh
Class of '84

❧

Dear Father Hesburgh,

Many years ago, I remember seeing you interviewed on *60 Minutes*. You told the reporter that the most significant thing that you had done at Notre Dame was to make it a coed school. You said—and I'm paraphrasing, from my recollection—bringing women to ND improved the school significantly. I was very impressed that of all the things that you had done, coeducation was what stood out in your mind as being important. (In the same interview, you also said that you would not have a problem with women priests. I was also impressed by that comment.)

I'm proud to be an alumna of Notre Dame. My wish is for my young daughters to attend ND someday. Much of my wonderful experience is due to your hand in forming the environment that was present while I was there. Thank you for the opportunity to learn and grow in a positive manner, and for your role model as a citizen of the world. You were, and still are, one of my most admired persons.

May God continue to bless you,

Claire C. Yang, MD
Class of '84

Dear Father Ted,

It is a pleasure to honor you and thank you for your insightful decision to turn Notre Dame into a coed university. While your opponents were afraid to change, you embraced it and recognized all the great benefits of bringing women to ND.

I hope you take great pride in seeing these fantastic women lead their communities as doctors, judges, CFOs, consultants, teachers, and moms. Notre Dame gave all of us extraordinary skills and vision to be the best we can be.

On a personal note, my alumni dad was quite opposed to the coed change . . . until, of course, all three of his daughters were accepted to Notre Dame. He's never been happier.

As a Double Domer, CPA, ten-year employee of the university, entrepreneur, and mother, I salute you, Father Ted! You remain forever in our hearts.

Love,

Katie Anthony
Class of '85

Katie Walsh Anthony '85, Father Ted, and Mary Beth Wackowski Wittenauer '85 on the night before Commencement 1985.

PS You'll also forever be one of our favorite clients at Anthony Travel and what a wonderful gift to us! Thank you.

Dear Father Hesburgh,

I didn't want to let the opportunity pass by without offering you many thanks for your great foresight in opening up Notre Dame to women, thus allowing me the great honor and pleasure of acquiring my college education there.

Notre Dame has had a profound impact on my life. Of the more obvious, I met

my husband there, and married him in Sacred Heart Basilica on May 11, 1991. We have four wonderful daughters. We are doing our best to raise them with the love, consideration, and values so evident on the campus at Notre Dame. (Our oldest, eleven, has the aspiration of one day solving the Middle East peace crisis, so we'll stay tuned to see if that happens . . . if it does, your decision had a hand in it!)

I studied business, and my training at Notre Dame was excellent in preparing me for the world of work, as well as to bring the ethics that I learned in the shadow of the Dome to the workplace. Business can be a slippery area, and having a clear sense of where to draw lines was incontrovertible.

Finding a new depth to my religion was another marvelous way in which I benefited from my Notre Dame experience. God and Jesus Christ are so obviously present on the campus, among the faculty and staff, and among the student body. Each time I step on campus, my heart is full of the joy of faith! I carry that back with me into my everyday life, and enjoy a closer walk with God due to the fullness of the spirit there. In 1999, my second daughter (then two and a half) suffered a life-threatening fall in our home, and sustained a severe brain injury. Prayer during this time was of the essence, and we contacted so many of our friends from our Notre Dame circle to join us in prayer. Her survival was in question for nearly two weeks, and once survival was assured, her recovery was expected to be slow and probably incomplete, due to the severity of her injury. We prayed so hard, and our Notre Dame community joined us in prayer; even many we didn't know. I'm delighted to report that my daughter was up and walking inside of a month, and achieved a full recovery! Her doctor declared it a miracle. . . . she is now full of spunk, and in fourth grade, and we are forever grateful for the miracle of faith that has her still with us.

Finally, I'll never forget the great students from all over the world that I had the enormous pleasure and honor to meet and get to know. I now have friends from all over the United States, as well as from a number of different countries! This has helped to expand my mind, and be open, understanding, accepting, and delighting in cultural differences among people from so many walks of life.

Once again, you showed such wonderful foresight in opening up such a traditionally male institution to women. Notre Dame is an amazing and special place . . . beautiful and deep . . . fun, exciting . . . thought-provoking, spiritual, and moral. I will be forever grateful for having had the privilege of attaining my college education there.

Thank you, and may God continue to richly bless you!

Leanne Fellin Burnett
Class of '85

Dear Father Hesburgh,

Thank you for opening the doors of coeducation at Notre Dame. I feel one of my greatest accomplishments was graduating from the University of Notre Dame. It truly is a "family," and I have kept in touch with many friends, male and female, over the years.

By the time I entered Notre Dame in the fall of 1981, coeducation was nothing new. Although the ratio of men to women was still almost three to one, I never felt in the minority. People not associated with the university would always ask, "Oh, you mean Saint Mary's College?" when I told them I went to Notre Dame. I would politely tell them that Notre Dame had been coed since 1972.

My freshman roommate and I are still close friends after twenty-five years. I remember waking up to the band at 8:00 a.m. the first football weekend, and saying to each other, "Isn't this great?" I can still say that, and hope my two boys will attend the university.

Thank you for a job well done!

Sincerely,

Kathleen K. Shannon
Class of '85

Dear Father Hesburgh,

To this day, and I'm certain will always be the case, my education from, and being a part of, the University of Notre Dame are some of the most rewarding and special things in my life. Being a member of the great Notre Dame family continues to positively impact my life daily, as it gives me the drive to strive to do and be the best I can be each and every day in every aspect of my life from being a mother, wife, Catholic, attorney, friend, and American citizen. I am very proud and happy to be a part of Notre Dame, and I strive to make her just as proud and happy of me each and every day.

I thank you for my being able to attend the University of Notre Dame for the aforementioned reasons and also for the great opportunities I have been afforded as a result of being the person Notre Dame has made me. Because of Notre Dame, I have a premier position as a corporate attorney at a Fortune 500 company and am able not only to maximize the time and quality of life I have with my family but also to support my community as well.

Yours in Notre Dame,

Elizabeth Sherman Cox
Class of '86

Dear Father Ted,

Notre Dame has always been, and I am sure always will be, a huge part of my life. It is hard to explain to people I meet now that I didn't just go to Notre Dame for college, but that I grew up with Notre Dame and it is a part of me. You have played such an integral role in bringing Notre Dame into my life.

My niece is a junior at Notre Dame and now my nine-year-old daughter wants to be like her cousin and go to Notre Dame someday. Thank you, Father Ted, for giving all of the Faccenda girls and their daughters, the opportunity to attend Notre Dame.

Most sincerely,

Peggy (Faccenda) Green
Class of '86

Father Ted,

I can't thank you enough for the instrumental role you have played in my life, but I will try!

Attending the University of Notre Dame was a key factor in the course my life has taken. I received an education not only of the mind but of the soul, as well. I had attended Catholic schools from first grade and perhaps was complacent about the role that my faith played in my life. The university gave me the opportunity to not only broaden my mind but to grow independent in my faith through the support and example set by my fellow classmates as well as the faculty and staff. My experiences at Notre Dame taught me that it was not only possible but necessary to keep God first in all things even as I moved out of a sheltered life into a world fraught with many difficult choices. Thank you for giving me the opportunity to grow and learn in an environment that values and instructs the whole person—not only the mind, but the body and soul as well.

I graduated from Notre Dame with a BA in government and computer applications. I believe my strong, liberal arts education taught me that education is not just a step to get a job but the lifelong process of a healthy mind. After graduating from Notre Dame, I attended the University of Virginia where I earned my MA in foreign affairs. My mentor at Virginia was Kenneth Thompson, and I worked for him at the Miller Center of Public Affairs. This public policy institute gathering the oral histories of contemporary presidencies opened my eyes to even more of the world and its possibilities. Thank you for allowing me to step onto the path that led my feet to a future of possibilities that I was previously unaware.

The close-knit family that is Notre Dame is still with me every day. I met my husband, Dave, at Notre Dame and we are blessed with six wonderful children (whom I hope are all future ND alumni!). I made other "friends for life" at the university as well. We live all over the country but keep in touch and try to get together almost every year. I meet other alumni wherever I go, in and out of the local Notre Dame clubs active in the cities where we have lived. The connection felt with fellow alumni is almost tangible.

Thank you for giving me the opportunity to have friends wherever I travel.

On a personal note, I am one of the countless students whom you welcomed into your office on a regular basis. I am so grateful to you for not being just a figurehead

worried about the bottom line of running the university, but a caring person who reached out to the student body at every opportunity. We knew you cared about each and every one of us and wanted us to succeed. Thank you, Father, from the bottom of my heart.

With grateful appreciation and love,

K. R. B.
Class of '87

Dear Father Hesburgh,

I have to say, being able to attend Notre Dame was one of the most rewarding experiences of my life. I gained valuable lessons academically, socially, and spiritually that continue to impact my life today. I will always have the Notre Dame spirit within me and I am fortunate to be able to share it with my family. Thanks, Father Ted, for the great memories, opportunity, and the honor to attend such a wonderful university.

Leslie (Borzilleri) Cullinan
Class of '87

‹❧

Dear Father Hesburgh,

I would like to take this opportunity to personally thank you, not only for your dedicated service to Notre Dame, but for affording women the opportunity to receive a Notre Dame education.

I am honored to be a graduate of the Class of 1987, your last class as president of the University of Notre Dame. Although I have obtained a JD (Duquesne University School of Law, 1998) and am employed as a special agent with the United States Secret Service, these accomplishments pale in comparison to the pride of graduating from Notre Dame.

To me, Notre Dame has always represented a commitment to excellence. You and Father Joyce made this university great, which is why your names are synonymous with Notre Dame. As an ND graduate, I can only promise you that every day I strive for that excellence and try to live up to the Christian ideals that epitomize Notre Dame.

Thanks again for allowing women to be an integral part of Notre Dame.

God Bless,

Sheila A. Horox
Class of '87

‹❧

Dear Father Ted,

Years ago, when you made the decision to open Notre Dame to undergraduate women students you changed my life. I will be forever in your debt. After graduation in 1987

I landed a job in a business that paid well, but when the opportunity presented itself to work for Notre Dame in the Development Department in 1991, I accepted in a heartbeat.

My fund-raising duties with private foundations involved traveling and working with you. Again and again I was able to see, firsthand, the love and respect you command in a room, in cities across America. I was proud to serve alongside you and Father Ned Joyce, and feel privileged to know you as a friend.

Working together to help secure Notre Dame's future we raised over $10 million. This ranks as one of the greatest experiences of my life. Thank you, Father Ted, for your friendship and for the fine example you set for all of us.

Sincerely yours,

Ann Rathburn-Lacopo
Class of '87

Dear Father Hesburgh,

Thank you for making ND coed. When I was a little girl, my dad mentioned that his dream was for me to go to Notre Dame, but that only boys could go. Instead of forgetting about it, the idea stayed with me through the years. By the time I got to high school, ND was accepting girls. I graduated in 1987, with a liberal arts degree, honors concentration. You once signed a keepsake quilt piece I had, and graciously took time to show me the football from a famous game. I had no idea why it was special, but I remember fervently wishing I did. It's a favorite memory.

Ann Michelle (Girten) Porter
Class of '87

Father Ted,

The opportunity to graduate from the University of Notre Dame is definitely one of the top highlights of my life. Rarely a week that goes by that I do not thank God for answering my many prayers and blessing me with an acceptance letter from my dream school. I wear my love for my alma mater on my sleeve, for Notre Dame and what it represents plays a big part of defining me as a person. Notre Dame gave me the academic fortitude and confidence to follow any career aspirations I may have and overcome the many obstacles that I continually encounter along the way. Though I am sure I am not always successful, every day I like to believe that I strive to live my life to the high Notre Dame standards of always doing what is spiritually, ethically, and morally right.

I grew up in a Catholic household in a suburb of Detroit, where cheering for the Irish sports teams was like a second religion to all of us. My father and uncle are 1949 graduates and ever since I was a child, I had my heart set on going to Notre Dame. My dream would never have become a reality without your trailblazing efforts of turning this special place into a coeducational university.

My first home football game as a student on campus in 1984 was when it finally hit me that I had "arrived"—I was living my fantasy. I finished my four classes by early afternoon, tossed my books on my bed, and ran out of my dorm to experience the electrifying atmosphere that arrives each home football weekend. There I was strolling alone around campus with my head held high and tears streaming down my cheeks, as it sank into me that I was actually a student at this spirited place. My heart was bursting with pride as I walked amongst all of the fans and alumni thrilled to simply be back home at the Golden Dome. I cannot begin to explain the sense of fulfillment I was encountering, except to tell you that I will always savor the memory until I pass from this life.

The spirit of Notre Dame and the quality of the people that associate themselves with the place is second to none. I cherish that incredibly special bond that exists between Notre Dame graduates, that small kind of fraternity that strives to take care of their own. Being a woman coming out of Notre Dame reassured me of the pick of which major accounting firm I wanted to accept an offer from upon graduation. Even today as I continue to build my career as a financial advisor, I can appreciate the doors that open for me and the instant respect I get in the business world, because I am a graduate of the University of Notre Dame.

Father Ted, you are the epitome of a Notre Dame man. All of the wonderful things you have done around the world for humanity and charitable causes have helped

build the Notre Dame name into the world renowned, highly respected institution of higher learning it is today. I can remember the first day I actually met you. It was first semester my freshman year and you were making dorm visits to meet your students. When I introduced myself and shook your hand, I was overwhelmed with the warmth that you exuded from that one handshake. I was well informed of your accomplishments and that your reputation was bigger than life itself, but here you were making conversation with me, letting me know that I mattered to you. I am and will always be amazingly proud of having you as a president of my beloved alma mater. I consider you, Father Ted, as best personifying Notre Dame and being the beacon of my faith. It has come to the point that I myself feel a sense of accomplishment when I hear your name quoted on a presidential debate or hear it reported that you have more honorary degrees than anyone else in the world.

In closing, beloved Father Ted, I thank you from the bottom of my heart for opening the door for my admission to Notre Dame and thus making me the person I am today!

Yours truly,

Amy Treder Kelliher
Class of '88

Dear Father Hesburgh,

I would say that I would not be here without Notre Dame. I grew up in a Notre Dame family. My father, after being released from the Japanese internment camps, matriculated into the University of Notre Dame. This was during the formal times of dressing up in a suit and a tie for dinner at the dining halls. Also this was during the times, as my father says, when you just carried two suitcases to college, one full of books and one full of clothes. My father is also what people call a triple Domer, being the first Japanese American to receive all three degrees (bachelor's, master's, and PhD) in mechanical and aerospace engineering from the University of Notre Dame. He loved the place so much he stayed on as a professor of mechanical and aerospace engineering for several years before advancing to be assistant vice president for research and sponsored programs, or as I saw it when I was little, he worked under the Golden Dome where I thought God lived. My mom was also what now Domers call a SMC chick. She was a foreign exchange student from Vietnam and graduated from Saint Mary's

College during the time when the women wore white gloves, heels, and hats when in the public eye. And so, the classic ND-SMC union resulted. Father Hesburgh, you have been a friend of the family since my father joined the Notre Dame family. You have blessed our family. Every year I return home for Midnight Mass at the Basilica, always looking forward to catching even a glimpse of you.

I was six years old when Notre Dame went coed, and I knew I wanted to graduate from Notre Dame since then. I recall family swim day at the Rockne pool, which I called "the Rock" every Sunday, and ice-skating with my family at the ACC, now the Joyce ACC. . . . I use to chitchat with the Notre Dame coeds that I met at these places. Also, I remember thinking it was so neat while growing up to see that several of my father's former students would come back to visit him during either home football games or alumni reunion week—thinking that Notre Dame has such great professors that I would probably want to come back and visit too.

I recall my freshman year in 1984, having lunch with then Freshman Year of Studies Dean Emil T. Hofman, who was also my general chemistry professor, SYRs, my friends at Carroll and Holy Cross halls across St. Mary's Lake, which I used to jog around. I particularly remember one night, worrying about finals. I went out for a very late-night (past midnight) jog around the campus to relieve some stress and ended my run at the Grotto to light a candle and say a prayer. There I saw a man in a black beret and a tan trench coat. I was nervous wondering why someone other than a student would be out there so late. I cautiously kneeled to say a prayer, keeping my eye on the man who was

cloaked in darkness. After I made the sign of the cross and stood up, he commented to me on how beautiful the night was. I did not look at him and nervously said, "Yes it is," and started to move away from him. He sensed my nervousness, so he turned and said, "Let me introduce myself, I'm Father Ted Hesburgh." I'll always remember that meeting with you. You later reported to my parents about the meeting and my mother wondered, off the topic, what I was doing out so late at night instead of studying.

Growing up near and getting my formal education at the University of Notre Dame has kept me grounded during life—even after receiving my bachelor's degree. I have continued with an academic career and have my PhD in biochemistry and molecular biology. I am studying the molecular basis and therapies for muscular dystrophy at the Wellstone Muscular Dystrophy Cooperate Research Center at the University of Iowa Carver College of Medicine. I truly believe that I could not have gotten this far without the guidance I received by being part of the Notre Dame family. There is always something special when I go home to visit my family in South Bend and seeing the Golden Dome as I come off of the I80/90 toll road . . . I always know I'm home when I see the Golden Dome.

Thank you, Father Hesburgh, for allowing me to make the University of Notre Dame a place to call home.

Yvonne M. Kobayashi
Class of '88

Dear Father Ted,

I fell in love with Notre Dame in 1973. My brother was a freshman and I was an impressionable seven-year-old. Bob brought the Notre Dame spirit home with him that Christmas and I was quickly infected. I soon was telling everyone I knew that I wanted to go to Notre Dame. I did not know at the time that my dream was possible only because of your decision the previous year to make Notre Dame a coeducational university. Thank you, Father Ted, for making my dream, and the dreams of so many other women, possible.

Over the years, I learned much about you and your profound impact on Notre Dame. I realized that your leadership made Notre Dame one of the best universities in the world. Your involvement in so many works of public service awed me. Your commitment to God and Our Lady humbled me. Your great work deepened my desire to attend Notre Dame. In my heart, you were Notre Dame. You still are.

Notre Dame's influence on my life is total. I have not only been shaped by my four years there and the education I received, but also by the choices and sacrifices I made to get there. I made those choices and sacrifices because of my intense desire to be a part of a very special place. It is because of you, Father Ted, that Notre Dame is that place.

Your life has been so well lived, and all members of the Notre Dame family are better for it.

With respect and gratitude,

Jeanne Quigley
Class of '88

ᢙ

Dear Father Ted,

We both attended Notre Dame (1984–1988 and 1987–1991) and overlapped during our freshman and senior years. Coming from a small town in Montana, we each arrived at the esteemed university awestruck by its beauty and sheer presence. Like other Notre Dame female students, we were greatly appreciative of your vision of giving women the opportunity to attend Notre Dame.

Our years at Notre Dame were filled with interesting lectures and a lot of library time. But along with our studies, we also participated in sports, volunteered on and off campus, and most importantly, attended Mass, and made frequent trips to the Grotto. We learned to overcome obstacles, dream big, and never be intimidated. Not only were our minds challenged and enriched, but our souls were also nurtured continuously. In four short years, our moral character and religious beliefs were strengthened and cultivated. Instead of leaving with just a diploma in hand, we left as better human beings—aware of our commitment to others and forever aware of the need to give back. The spirit that transcended the Grotto and filled our hearts enlightened our lives and will forever live within us and our families.

Kerry and Amy Regan

Father Hesburgh,

Life is full of decisions and the right decision is usually the harder one to make. My parents and my experience at Notre Dame have helped me make the harder decisions. Thank you for making the school coed.

Megan Keane DeSantis
Class of '89

Thanks Father Hesburgh!

I graduated in 1989. My Notre Dame education taught me to see the world through caring eyes. I know the sense of community drew me to Notre Dame in the first place. Participating in activities at the Center for Social Concerns also influenced my

decision to join the Peace Corps. I taught in Nepal for two years. That experience has colored my world ever since. Now that it's been a while since I graduated, I still feel connected to Notre Dame through football games! It's wonderful to get together with old friends and our families and watch a game! Go Irish!

Thank you so much for making the opportunity for women to attend Notre Dame possible!

Sincerely,

Chrissy Rivaldo Kohrt
Class of '89

Father Ted Hesburgh,

Thank you for helping women have the opportunity to go to Notre Dame! My experience was tremendous—my education was excellent, but most importantly I went to a Catholic university where I met many spiritual people. These people I still keep in contact with—friends for the journey of life.

Thank you!

Cecelia A. Novitt, MD
Class of '89

Dear Father Hesburgh,

I wanted to thank you for the role that you played in encouraging the university of Our Lady to open itself to female enrollment. I hope that the campus is richer for the presence of women in its student population. I know that I was utterly blessed to have had the privilege to be treated to a level playing field where it was assumed that women did make intellectual contributions to academic life that were equal to men's. Not necessarily always identical kinds of contributions, but equally valued ones. As a member of the Program of Liberal Studies, I know that the world wasn't always this way. The scar-

city of women authors in that program reflects this. In so much of past human history women have been relegated to the "practical sphere" and thought of especially in terms of their capacities to nurture and mother. While I fully believe that this aspect of femininity must be respected, I feel it is the contribution of twentieth century theology to see that, because women are fully persons, and personhood includes spirit and mind, it is not reasonable to exclude women from intellectual life. I think that this century has reaped the benefits of promoting female education. As a woman who went on from Notre Dame to complete a PhD in medieval studies, I can appreciate how my own field of intellectual history has been enriched by feminine interest in domestic history, an area largely unexplored in previous centuries, as well as the history of the body, female piety, and community. And I can think of many women contributing solidly in traditionally male-dominated fields of medieval studies such as ecclesiastical history and philosophy. As history continues to unfold, I expect that the canon of great books will include more and more women and that women will be found teaching them. I appreciate the way that female gifts, moreover, can be channeled into the intellectual nurturing of students' minds, careers, and lives.

As a mother of four children, I understand that the demands of the "practical sphere" will probably always weigh heavier for women. The deferment of our own career goals in favor of the nurturing of little ones will probably always be a greater reality for women. The challenge of the next century is to help women balance career and family in the way that is best for each family. For your part in bringing us this far, I remain eternally grateful.

With sincere appreciation,

Teresa Pierre
Class of '89

Father Hesburgh,

Words can't begin to describe how thankful I am for your efforts for the women of Notre Dame so many years ago. Like the hundreds of other notes I'm sure you'll receive, my days in South Bend most certainly changed my life and continue to play an important role for me each day. The people I met while there were tremendous and the academic education I received was exceptional. Even more than that though, the way Notre Dame enhanced my faith was by far the most profound difference. Being in such a strong Catholic environment, I was able to better understand that true sense of God as *"Agape."* I've tried to live that faith ever since and pass those ideals to my children as well. My hope is that one day they too will get to be a part of such a special place . . . and thanks to you, both my sons AND my daughters will have that opportunity.

Melissa Hock Porter
Class of '89

Dear Father Ted,

My father graduated from Notre Dame in 1954. He was my hero. As a little girl I would trace pictures of my hands and then painstakingly draw a special ring on the right hand to resemble my dad's Notre Dame class ring. It was, I thought, magic.

My dad was a man of tremendous grace. He was a man of integrity, faith, deep, deep love for his family, and above all, a man of honor. He was smart and funny and incredibly kind and always had a gentle and kind word to say to anybody he met.

My dad loved my mom more than I ever realized. Their marriage was one of love and faith and trust and joy. My sister and I watched as Dad lovingly held her in his arms as she battled colon cancer. I was there when he kissed her good-bye and told me to pray to God that he would someday be with her again in Heaven.

I was also there two years ago, cradling my dad in my arms as he died. I felt at once that my life was over and that I was also supposed to be profoundly happy that he was at last with the true love of his life.

Why would the character of my dad be at all in keeping with the spirit of this exercise honoring Father Ted's influence on coeducation at Notre Dame? Well, I am convinced that Father Ted Hesburgh is the reason why my father was the man he was. I am convinced that my dad's time at Notre Dame groomed him to be the perfect dad, husband, brother, member of community, leader, and above all, loving tribute to Our Lady and her university. For me to have been given the opportunity then also to come to Notre Dame meant that I too would have the chance to grow into a woman much like my father.

I could speak to the fine education or job opportunities that came my way as a result of attending Notre Dame, but it's not enough. Instead I would like to think that I am a smart, funny, kind, independent, capable woman because I had the opportunity to walk in my dad's footsteps on his beloved campus. When I go to the Grotto I am reminded of the many, many nights my dad must have spent there praying for guidance or in thanks. When I attend Mass with other members of the Notre Dame family, I am reminded that without Father Ted's foresight, I would not have had the chance to call myself an alumna.

Thank you, Father Ted. You nurtured a very special man in my life and made him the perfect father. And, because of your vision to allow women to come to Notre Dame, I am happy and very, very proud to say that I am truly that man's daughter and will always love Our Lady and her university family worldwide.

God bless and keep,

Coni Rich
Class of '89

Dear Father Ted,

Thank you, Father Hesburgh, for your vision of a coeducational Notre Dame. I treasure the years I spent at Notre Dame as an undergraduate. I think of my years there often and the extraordinary people I met and befriended. Notre Dame changed my life in so many ways. It gave me a deeper sense of spirituality, peace, and a sense of purpose. I am a high school teacher now and students often ask me about the university. I have encouraged many students in their applications to Notre Dame, especially those students who are seeking an environment that is challenging and nurturing in so many ways. Thank you for making it possible for me and other women to attend such a wonderful university. I have been truly blessed to have been a Notre Dame graduate.

Sincerely,

Marissa M. Sarabando
Class of '89

# 5

# ALUMNAE LETTERS— CLASSES OF 1990–1999

ear Father Ted,

I just wanted to take this opportunity to thank you from the bottom of my heart for your amazing decision to allow women to attend Notre Dame as undergrads.

Without that courageous decision, my family and I would not be who we are to-day—the values we were taught, the traditions, the reinforcement of our Catholic faith.

I am so blessed to have had an opportunity to attend Notre Dame and not only obtain a first-rate education, but also solidify my core beliefs in God, our Church, and myself.

I am proud to say that both my father (Terry Desmond '63) and grandfather (John Breen '33) graduated from ND.

I am one of five siblings to have graduated from the Golden Dome. My two sisters are Margaret Desmond '87, '96 MA, and Anne Desmond-Zilvitis '97. My two brothers are Tom '88 and Matt '91. Kevin will graduate next year.

Not only am I a third-generation legacy but I am convinced it runs in my blood. I could not be more proud!

None of this could have happened without you, Father Ted.

Thank you very, very much.

Kathy Desmond Barr
Class of '90

Dear Father Ted,

When I was four years old, you made a decision that would later direct the course of my life. You admitted women into the university of Our Lady.

Now, as a grown woman raising children on my own, I believe that adage that says, "If you educate a boy, you educate a man. If you educate a woman, you educate a family." Due to your decision thirty-five years ago, my two daughters, Lillie and Lucy, are touched every day by a Notre Dame education because the mother raising them was educated beneath the Golden Dome. It is an opportunity you gave me that will affect my family for generations.

I will never know how it came to be that you reached your decision—whether you knew the answer suddenly in your heart or if you agonized over it. I do know now that, as thanks for a Notre Dame education, I strive to live each day as testament to the wisdom of your decision. It has been one of the greatest joys in my life to be a representative of the University of Notre Dame. I thank you from the bottom of my heart for that opportunity.

With love and gratitude and a big Happy Birthday to you on May 25,

Mollie Boylan
Class of '90

⌒⭑

Father Hesburgh!

Thanks for making Notre Dame coed and thanks for all your work with civil rights. If you had done neither, I would not be a medical doctor today, being both African-American and female.

Thanks for believing in a future that could be different!

Lena Jefferson, MD
Class of '90

⌒⭑

Dear Father Hesburgh,

I would like to express my sincere gratitude to you for your efforts in bringing coeducation to the University of Notre Dame. But for that pivotal decision, the history of my life would have a much different telling. I still remember the day I received my acceptance letter in December of 1986! It was one of my proudest days and I was blessed to have been able to actually enroll to attend the university. My decision to take the path was the start of a rewarding and enriching journey. I was in the first group of freshman girls to live in Howard Hall on South Quad when it converted to a female dormitory in 1987. I specifically selected the dorm because I wanted to be a part of starting something new. It was thrilling to be a part of history—albeit on a much smaller scale than the women who were among the first to enroll as students at Notre Dame in the '70s.

Thank you for your vision and guiding hand in ushering in a new era for the university with the admission of women. Generations of women across the country have been affected, and will continue to be affected, in immeasurable ways as a result of this accomplishment. I, myself, am among the privileged group of women to have been enriched in countless ways by my attendance. It was a once-in-a-lifetime experience that I will forever cherish!

Have a fantastic birthday on May 25!

Best regards and *Wake Up the Echoes,*

Melissa (Smith) Drennan
Class of '91

Dear Father Hesburgh,

Thank you for my Notre Dame education. I am a 1991 graduate, born in 1969. There-fore, I have no memory of the time prior to the coeducational opportunity at the uni-versity. Although I rarely think about the time that ND wasn't coed, I know that the change allowed me the experiences that I had. I know that Notre Dame has always been and will continue to be an excellent place for higher education.

Thank you for all of your contributions to the University of Notre Dame. May God bless you and keep you.

Sincerely,

Brigid C. Greening
Class of '91

Dear Father Hesburgh,

I have been reflecting recently on my Notre Dame experience and the direction it gave my life. In honor of your 90th birthday, I am sending you this little note of thanks for giv-ing me, and so many other women, the opportunity to become a Notre Dame alumna.

I received a wonderful academic education at Notre Dame that opened many doors for my professional career in engineering. However, my experience extends be-yond the classroom education. The friends I made at Notre Dame are still friends today. My Howard Hall roommate is the godmother of my son! But even more important than those friends, is the fact that I am a Catholic growing in my faith. Attending Notre Dame helped me remain Catholic through a time in my life when it would have been easy to stray from the Church. I am thankful for Our Blessed Mother watching over us, the bells of Sacred Heart ringing every fifteen minutes, the dorm chapels with Sunday evening Mass, the prayers at the start of classes, the crucifix in every classroom, lighting candles at the Grotto, single-sex dorms with parietals, the solitude of the lakes. These ever present reminders of our Church allowed Catholicism to be a part of my daily life even though my faith formation was still so immature. I was not the Catholic then that

I am now and I still have far to go, but then again, faith is a life journey today. I share that journey with my husband, Chris, as we strive to raise our three beautiful children, Emma, Anderson, and Charlotte in the Catholic faith.

Thank you for making the decision to allow women to attend Notre Dame! Happy Birthday, Father Ted!

In Christ,

Christina Mueller Taurence
Class of '91

Dear Father Hesburgh,

You have touched my life in a profound way even though I have only met you twice. You said Mass for a small group of us in the log chapel as we started the Native American Alumni Board and then you said another Mass for the Minority Alumni Network in your apartment. You shared inspiring words and I could clearly see and feel the passion you have for Notre Dame.

Notre Dame is an integral part of my life. There are not many instances in my life that I can think of where Notre Dame and its family have not been involved or affected me in some way. Notre Dame, its family, and its venues (the Grotto, in particular) have been there in the very worst and best times of my life.

I do not find it ironic that I write this note on the anniversary of my father's death. He loved the university and never doubted my statement as a five-year-old that I would one day be a student. Notre Dame was there for me when he died. I was a junior in the middle of finals at the library when my roommate found me and gave me the news. In a matter of one night, my finals were rescheduled, my belongings were packed, my flight was changed, and the dorm staff and friends helped me to feel like I was not alone. I do not believe any other school would have been so attentive and compassionate.

It is for reasons like this that I love the university and why I am so thankful to you. So much in my life would not be the way it is if it were not for your efforts to make Notre Dame a coeducational institution. I cannot imagine my life without having attended Notre Dame. It brings me peace and guides me to live life at the highest common denominator.

Notre Dame has been a blessing to me and my family. I was the first in my family to go to college. Since then, five cousins have received degrees, including one who also attended Notre Dame a few years ago. Because of your passion to grow the university and make it the best place it can be, you inadvertently helped to create a legacy in a family from a village of five hundred people in the middle of New Mexico.

Notre Dame is truly blessed to have you as one of its leaders.

Sincerely,

Elaine J. C. DeBassige D'Amato
Class of '92 (Ojibwe Chicana)

❧

Dear Father Hesburgh,

Thanks for making ND coeducational. If you hadn't, I would not have gone to ND, or met my husband there (we're both Class of 1992), and we would not have our baby.

Also wishing you a very Happy Birthday and all good things. My ND education has made a huge difference in my life. I learned a great deal and more importantly met very special people—many lifetime friends.

All the best,

Laura LaVelle
Class of '92

❧

Dear Father Ted Hesburgh,

I wanted to thank you for the decision to make Notre Dame coed. I graduated from Notre Dame in 1992, twenty years after the first class of women entered the university.

Notre Dame has and always will continue to be a special place for me. Its sense of place and spirit are unique.

Over the past ten years I have lived in Seattle and have been in high-tech at

Microsoft. While my graduate studies helped prepare me for a specific job and career in business, my education at Notre Dame helped prepare me for life.

My experiences there and learning from living in the dorms, my professors and the lifelong friends I made there have shaped the way I think about my role in the broader community. I was always inspired at how the focus on impacting and serving the community imbued life at Notre Dame. I believe some of that was influenced by you and the other leaders of the university who have focused on social justice, teaching, and action.

My grandmother has made two trips to visit me in my life. Once, when I was born and the second was to visit me while I was a student at Notre Dame. She loved visiting the peaceful Grotto and equally loved cheering on the football team at a game. It was wonderful to share the weekend there with her and she still talks about the trip.

The opportunities for women in education have changed significantly from my grandmother's generation (who did not go to college) to my mother's (who attended a two-year nursing school) to mine. And for that I wanted to thank you for the experience to attend Notre Dame.

Best regards,

Laura Garcia Pendergrast
Class of '92

Dear Father Hesburgh,

Thank you for opening the doors to women at Notre Dame. My great uncle was Father Ted Mehling. While he passed away long before I was born, I grew up hearing the stories from my grandparents, Norbert and Jean Mehling ("Gramps" and "Nana" to me) about his time at ND and their visits with him on the beautiful campus.

Still, my first visit was not until after I was accepted, and I was instantly smitten with the campus and the people I met. I loved every minute at Notre Dame and my only disappointment is how quickly my four years there passed. I forged dozens of friendships, many of whom remain my dearest friends and confidants. Of course, I was challenged by my coursework and the professors, which prepared me well for law school and life, but, admittedly, it was the late-night conversations and debates (about current events, goals, and dreams) with friends and classmates that left a lasting impression.

I am now a practicing attorney in Cleveland, Ohio, and just made partner in my firm. I married an ND classmate and we have two beautiful sons (ages five and three). My husband, Don, is a proud "stay-at-home dad" and, I think I'm safe to say, he thanks you, too.

You have touched thousands and thousands of lives and I wanted to let you know how appreciative I am for touching mine.

Sincerely yours,

Darcy Mehling Good
Class of '93

 ᘓ

Dear Father Ted,

I suppose that, for most people, the college experience is life-shaping, if not life-transforming. Notre Dame was both to me. Of course there are the integral parts of dorm life: SYRs, intramurals, Sunday Mass, and the often cursed parietals. Not only are these dorm-centric experiences unique to Notre Dame, but with over 80 percent of students staying on campus all four years, these experiences are at the core of ND student life. Also striking is the academic rigor of both the faculty and student bodies. The pursuit of a university degree in the midst of the talented individuals that Notre Dame draws is certainly sufficient to have a lifelong impact on anyone. Yet my own defining moment crystallized during a week of RA orientation in the fall of 1992.

I was in a classroom with about forty others (some were there to orient, though most of us were there to be oriented). One of the speakers said that being an RA is a ministry. When asked why, he said that RAs were ministers to the dorm community. We were to become confidants, counselors, friends and, when needed, disciplinarians. Our own time would now, to a large extent, become the time of others. We would work where we lived. This was, he said, a calling to serve. I had never before thought of RAs as ministers. Then the lightbulb went on.

That characterization was so correct. It was so simple and yet so powerful. My year as an RA was a ministry. Yet, I don't think I ever would have recognized it as succinctly had someone else not identified it for me. And once I lived with that word and that service for a year, it occurred to me that, for most people at Notre Dame, ministry is a way of life. That is one of the great values that Notre Dame evokes in those that comprise it.

For some students, ministry lies in the social service they perform either during school breaks, during the school year, or after graduation. For others, it lies in serving their dorm, whether as part of the residential staff or of the many committees that drive dorm activities. The ministry of rectors and the clergy who live in the university is palpable in everything they do. Their ministry is evidenced in the little things like having meals with the students, barbequing food during football weekends to help raise money for various causes, cheerleading on the sidelines of intramural events, and simply being available to talk. That same ministry is, in so many ways, the essence of Notre Dame. It permeates life at ND and it belies most of the meaningful experiences

Father Ted celebrates the wedding of Zulfiqar Bokhari '93, '96 JD and Paulita Llopsis Pike '93, '96 JD in a coffee plantation in Santa Tecla, El Salvador, August 10, 1996.

on campus. Above all, Notre Dame is a place where people care. They care about each other's development, happiness, and spirit.

I have been fortunate to know Father Hesburgh during many stages of my life. I knew him when I was a child, an adolescent, a student, a bride, and now as a mother and a professional. Father Ted, through his life, his actions, his leadership and love personifies Notre Dame. Or is it that Notre Dame reflects Father Ted? For sure, the place is a reflection of him. And, while there are many individuals who have helped shape the university and contributed to what it is today, no single person has been more instrumental in defining Notre Dame than Father Hesburgh. For that, all of us who have been blessed enough to walk under the Golden Dome and to grow among those who truly care, must give thanks to Father Ted.

Paulita Pike
Class of '93, '96 JD

Dear Father Hesburgh,

Thank you for extending the opportunity for admission to women at the University of Our Lady. From the moment I received and read the "Dear Prospective Student" letter in the fall of 1988, I knew that Notre Dame was where I belonged, where I would always belong. In fact, I was absolutely convinced that that general letter had been written specifically and personally to me, it spoke to me so intimately. It was one of those instances when I was keenly aware of the presence of the Holy Spirit for it was the Holy Spirit at work, introducing me to the place that would become my home-away-from-home for the next four years and my beloved alma mater and heart's home for life. Like my faith, Notre Dame is a part of who I am down to the very fiber of my being. The relationships forged, the experiences enjoyed, the education earned, and all that being part of the Notre Dame family encompasses have shaped my life. We are each the sum total of our experiences, and being part of Notre Dame has brought me closer to the fulfillment of God's plan for me. For the blessing of being a student at, graduating from, and being ever-associated with the University of Notre Dame, I will be forever grateful.

Yours in Notre Dame,

Jean C. (DiTullio) Ryan
Class of '93

Father Hesburgh,

I can't imagine how many women are sharing their appreciation with you, but I'm happy to be one of the many. I could go on about how much ND helped me as I've grown throughout my career, but that is secondary to what it gave to my family . . .

My father was a Domer. He was lucky enough to have four beautiful daughters, but no sons. I am the eldest and was born the same year that the school opened to women. Dad's dream was to have one of his daughters attend his alma mater, and I was the chosen one. Had Notre Dame not opened up its doors to women, I would not have been there. Like many fathers and daughters, he and I had a hard time finding common ground. Notre Dame was the exclusive bond that we shared, no one could take that away from us.

We lost Dad to cancer six months ago. I will always look to Notre Dame as the one thing we had that was exclusively ours. The school is even more special to me now that he's gone. Thank you for giving me the opportunity to fulfill my daddy's dream. Thank you for all the daughters whose fathers had that dream for them.

Shannon O'Connor
Class of '94

 махровый

Dear Father Ted,

Thank you, Father, Notre Dame changed my life. I met wonderful people, a lot of them are still a very important part of my life.

My education was tremendous—I am so fortunate to have been able to take part in such a wonderful tradition. My love for ND grows each year even more and more.

Thanks again to a wonderful man.

Go Irish!

Becky Alfieri
Class of '95

Father Hesburgh,

As a proud alumnae (Theology '95) I would like to take this opportunity to express gratitude for the coeducational vision that allowed me to attend the University of Notre Dame. With compassion, justice, equality, faith, and service as the foundation, the University of Notre Dame opened its doors to create a coeducational environment that has helped to spread our university's message to every corner of the globe.

After graduating in 1995, I served as a Holy Cross Associate in Chile. I remain one of only two African-Americans to have served in this program to date. The lessons I learned at ND, living in Walsh Hall, playing interhall sports, working at the South Bend Center for the Homeless, and ultimately serving as an associate in Chile are all blessings that came from one. The university took a grand chance on coeducation and in the face of adversity, as is so often the case—spread the message of peace, faith, compassion, and understanding . . . creating, for me at least, a continuation of blessings and an ability to reflect that I just don't believe that I would have found elsewhere.

Today I serve the Fillmore Leroy Community in the City of Buffalo, New York. A proud Buffalo native, I am the executive director of the Fillmore Leroy Area Residents Inc., (FLARE) a nonprofit housing and human services agency. We serve the poor and disenfranchised, working to improve the quality of life of those who are of low to moderate income. I credit my opportunities at ND, in Chile, and in my home as a youth for the way in which I serve today. Coeducation has opened doors and created realities that may have not been realized for me at another college or university. As we rehabilitate houses in our service area, conduct after school programs for school-aged children, house women escaping domestic violence and prostitution, provide affordable rental and homeownership opportunities—I give thanks for Father Don McNeill, Lou Nanni, Kathleen Maas Weigert, Sue Cunningham, Mary Ann Roemer, Padre Ahumada, Poppin, Padre Don K., Chris Johnson and every CSC, ND grad, and future Domer I meet. I am a part of something great, with that I carry my responsibility and continue on in faith.

I thank you again for all that you have done for Our Lady, our friends, and our hope. Be blessed and go Irish!

Yvonne C. McCray
Class of '95

Dear Father Hesburgh,

I wanted to take this quick moment to thank you for the opportunity to attend Notre Dame—the school of my father, uncles, and grandfather. I know they felt the full appreciation of the switch to coeducation when I received my admittance in 1992. And they continue to be thankful as my sister begins her freshman year next fall.

Being a part of Notre Dame was, and continues to be, a defining part of my life. My four years on campus gave me a fantastic education that has served as a foundation for great things in my career. It has created lifelong friendships that I continue to cherish and rely on. And finally, it inspired a greater belief in God and the Catholic Church that I strive to follow every day.

Notre Dame has also helped me to make new friends and find my place in new communities since graduation. ND alums are such a fantastic family; I could always count on the local clubs for direction, activities, and a welcoming that cannot be found from any other group in the country (and probably the world). With each new place I have lived, I have made an effort to find those new family members to make me feel instantly at home.

I cannot imagine having spent my four years anywhere other than Notre Dame. They were four of the best in my life. Every year I make my way back to campus, most recently with my fiancé. While he is a Ball State grad, I am making every effort to "convert" him. My dream is that any future children we have will have the opportunity to love Notre Dame, not only through my eyes, but through their own, as students and ND alums.

Again, thank you for making the leap of faith in admitting women to Our Lady's university. It has made me who I am, and for that I am forever grateful.

With appreciation and devotion to Our Lady,

Amanda Marie Bruntrager
Class of '96

Dear Father Hesburgh,

I have searched my current social circles for the quality of friendship I grew to expect at Notre Dame. The women in my dorms, Knott and Cavanaugh, were exceptional souls. The bonds we formed with one another are as solid as any you will find the world over. Our relationships were honest, nurturing, and mutually rewarding. I never knew a

Domer to be anything but interesting, energetic, and committed to the greater good, be it of her friends, her dorm, or society. I will always be a proud and loyal daughter of Notre Dame.

When I first began to date my husband, early in the summer of 1999, we attended many family barbecues, and other social events. His sisters, female cousins, and friends commented to him on how "together" I appeared, and at a relatively young age. My husband and I are separated by eighteen years, so many of the guests we encountered were older than I was, and well established in their careers and relationships. One woman asked about my background, which my husband proudly proclaimed, including the details of my Notre Dame experience. She responded, "Well, now, THAT makes sense! Notre Dame will open many doors for her." How could she have known! In the few short years since graduation, I have risen to the position of assistant superintendent of schools in a fairly large regional district in Massachusetts. Each time I interviewed for a new administrative position, my Notre Dame education became a focal point in the conversation. I owe you a considerable amount of appreciation for your work to make Our Lady's university available to me, and to my friends. My Notre Dame "sisters," I am certain, join me in my expression of thanks to you, Father Hesburgh, for all your efforts.

My prayers for continued success and happiness! May God bless you, Father Hesburgh, and may God bless Notre Dame!

Sincerely,

Melissa Pirelli Earls
Class of '96

Dear Father Hesburgh,

I remember many of my final nights at Notre Dame, lying in bed thanking God for the opportunity to be a part of the community at ND. I felt so blessed then, and still, now. I also remember during that year, realizing the commitment my family made to my being able to attend and how I constantly thanked my parents for that. Never did I think to give thanks to you! So, Father Hesburgh, thank you for making ND coed! My life would be starkly different had I not been a student at Notre Dame.

I fondly remember dining with you and my other Breen-Phillips friends at the Morris Inn in 1996. We had the highest bid for a meal with you from the BP Meal Auction. You gave us a tour of your office as well. After that, I always used to look up in your window as I made the trek from BP to a night of studying at the library.

As an ACE teacher, I will never forget one of your homilies you gave in the Stanford-Keenan Chapel. Your "Come, Holy Spirit" homily. "Come, Holy Spirit" became my mantra, especially as my ACE experience became more challenging and I endured that first year of teaching. I still use this simple prayer today. Thank you.

You have made the world a better place. You made my life better as you opened the doors at Notre Dame to women. Countless "thank yous!!"

Warmest regards,

Stacy Carel Flieller
Class of '97

Dear Father Ted,

I remember being a freshman in the fall of 1993 and sitting on a bench at the Grotto. I was contemplating the usual student things when an older gentleman came down the right staircase. He stood at the side of the Grotto, closed his eyes, said a prayer, and then continued on his way. It was only as he departed that I realized he was you. That always stayed with me, your (and our) humility before God. Thank you.

As for my Notre Dame education, besides my family, it is the greatest gift that I could have ever received. What I learned both in and out of the classroom has shaped my life forever. The friends I made there are the best ones I have in the world. I am also proud that my ROTC experience on campus led me to be a fighter pilot in the U.S. Air Force. Now, as I eagerly await the arrival of my baby girl, I look forward to passing on the lessons I learned under the Golden Dome. Thank you for the opportunity to be part of Notre Dame. I will treasure it always.

Capt. Kate Lowe (Wildasin)
Class of '97

Dear Father Hesburgh,

I am one of the many women who have been lucky enough to have attended Notre Dame. I transferred in my sophomore year and the difference in the quality of education was extraordinary. However, the education did not stop at the academics, as I learned more about faith, living and giving in a community, spirit, making lifelong friends, and that special something you just can't explain, but you feel deep down in your heart. In our hearts forever. . . . Thank you for making Notre Dame available for women and such a great university!

Jennifer Rockwell
Class of '97

⌒

Dear Father Hesburgh,

I am thankful that you had the vision to turn Notre Dame coed for many reasons. The most important reason is I found my closest friends and made deeper connections with my father, brothers, and sister (who all attended Notre Dame). My husband is a '91 grad and I am a '97 grad. Thanks to your wisdom, we can look forward to sending both our son and daughter to Notre Dame. I value my education but I most value the Notre Dame family the university gave me.

Sincerely,

Kate Rosenbach York
Class of '97

⌒

Thank you Father Ted,

Being a part of the Notre Dame family has been invaluable to me as I have moved across the country. My brothers and sisters are always there to welcome me with open arms. Without coeducation at Notre Dame I would have missed out on much love, laughter, and learning.

Kathryn Bokowy
Class of '98

Dear Father Hesburgh,

As clichéd as it may sound, I would not be the person I am today if I had gone to college somewhere other than Notre Dame. Having grown up in Massachusetts and attended a Jesuit high school, there was plenty of incentive for me to go to Boston College. I would like to think that I have always done things my own way, so I applied to Notre Dame instead. Coming from a close family, the idea of going to a school a thousand miles from home was tough to swallow. However, once I arrived on campus in August of 1994, I moved into Lyons and never looked back. That very first weekend I met people who have remained some of my closest friends to this day. While my classes were challenging and there were more opportunities to attend arts and cultural events or hear expert speakers from all over the world than I can count, the people that I met during my four years at Notre Dame really stand out in my mind. Fellow students from all over and professors with varying backgrounds all challenged me to think

and develop and strengthen my own ideas. Several of my dorm mates stand out in my mind as having been especially fantastic at expressing their views and challenging me to examine my own thinking. At the tender age of eighteen, I must confess that I was fairly self-centered and unused to rationalizing my beliefs. Socrates said "the unexamined life is not worth living." I truly believe that if I had not been fortunate enough to attend Notre Dame and make the friends that I have, I would not be quite the person I am today.

Thank you and God bless,

Lauren Mack
Class of '98

Dear Father Hesburgh,

I welcome this opportunity to thank you for all you have done for the university, but most importantly your efforts supporting coeducation.

It is thanks to you that I was able to experience firsthand the deeply rooted ties that both sides of my family share with Notre Dame. Ties that influenced the person I am, well before I moved into Lyons Hall and ties that were strengthened by my experiences in and out of the classroom in my four years there.

One of the biggest lessons I had reinforced is that in addition to faith and love, education is one of the most powerful forces we have at our disposal to effect personal as well as global change. In the nine years since I graduated (where does the time go?) I now see just how blessed I was to receive the caliber of education I did at Notre Dame. My four years without a doubt prepared me for success in business and have helped me get where I am professionally. As a marketing major I was quite pleased when *Business Week* finally realized what any business major could have told you—our undergraduate program is among the best in the world. From my very first day on my first job, I was grateful to draw on the lessons of such excellent professors as Murphy, O'Rourke, and Father Ross. I soon realized that I had an edge on individuals from other universities because I was not only taught about my area of expertise but also how to truly learn about the world around me. Notre Dame's "liberal education" that mixed business with philosophy, theology, language, and the arts is an approach that makes for a much more balanced education and gives graduates the tools to not only perform on the job, but to truly excel at work as well as in our community. Our world view was not to just learn about how to correctly balance or analyze a company's books but to see past the bottom line to the company's place in the community and how its social impact was just as important as its economic impact. This difference is recognized by other Domers and non-Domers alike.

To think that I may have been denied this unique environment because I am a woman is something that, thanks to you, is unfathomable. Thank you for your vision and faith in women and for opening Notre Dame's opportunities and traditions to us.

One last special thank you. One of my most unique memories of my four years at ND was a private meeting I had with you and Father Joyce. I am a third-generation Domer on both sides of my family (Grandpa played for Knute, my parents were married at the Basilica, I have lost track of the total number of Notre Dame grads we have in our family. . . . You get the picture) but it was because of one particular relative I had the pleasure of your company. My great-uncle was your predecessor, Father John Cavanaugh. Father Joyce found out about the connection when I was a sophomore and before I knew it I was meeting with both of you in your office. That visit was such a pleasure for many reasons—but most importantly your stories gave me a sense of who my great-uncle was in a very unique way. I also remember you turning the conversation from the past to my future and how you subtly challenged me to live up to the ideals we were discussing—ideals started by "Uncle John" and carried through by you in your tenure at Notre Dame. I just wanted to say I got the message loud and clear. I continue to draw on that conversation ten years later. Hopefully, I am holding up my end of the bargain for the opportunity you gave me and all Notre Dame alumnae.

With warmest regards,

Colleen Ryan
Class of '98

❧

Dear Father Hesburgh,

One of my fondest memories of Notre Dame is a conversation we had in the Hesburgh Library.

It was with great apprehension that I left my well-worn wooden study carrel full of used books, highlighters, pens, and tattered papers, to approach your office on the thirteenth floor. My thoughts traveled to my mother's recollections of a conversation with the young priest outside her childhood home on Juday Creek (South Bend) that left a lasting impression, my father's words of admiration for the man who had served in facets of public life and shaped politics of his generation in many ways, and the namesake of the Hesburgh Program in Public Service to which I was enrolled. The feeling of intimidation quickly faded as you welcomed me into your office with a warm smile and showed me a memento commemorating the admission of women to Notre Dame in 1972.

During our conversation, you asked me among other things about my impressions of being a woman at the university—at that time my impressions were limited to positive experiences in the classroom and in the dorms, some complaints from former male alumni of Pangborn that the dorm was converted to a female residence, and a hope for greater female leadership in the student government (that I participated in). It was only with later reflection that I could see how the role of women at Notre Dame was still evolving given the relatively recent admission of women to the university. The election of the first female student body president a few years ago was a signal to me that the role of women on campus is still evolving, and the positive influence of women on the Notre Dame community continues.

Later, during the week of my graduation ceremonies and events, I had the pleasure of meeting you again—but as part of a larger forum where you spoke to the outgoing class of Hesburgh Program students. Among the many pieces of advice you gave to us, stressing the call to service in local and global-minded ways, I found your advice on relationships the most memorable. I was struck by how in tune you were with the issues facing my generation—and how you used your experiences and spirituality to offer us practical advice to face the next steps and challenges in our lives. I was truly inspired.

Recalling all of these things, it is apparent to me that you continually reach out to the local community, the Notre Dame community, and the global community—playing an important role in the issues they face both past and present—and are truly an inspiration to many.

In short, thank you, Father Ted—your influence spans many generations.

Warmest regards,

Michele R. Costello
Class of '99

Dear Father Ted,

There are some situations in life where even the most heartfelt thank you will never do the situation at hand justice, and this is truly one of those. There are so many things that go along with my Notre Dame experience, which I could thank you for—the foundation for a successful career, having the opportunity to meet others and make friendships that will last our lifetimes, a deeper understanding of my faith, and how my beliefs shape my values within my life and my community . . . the list could go on and on. But in retrospect, if there was only one thing which I could say thanks for, it would have to be a chance. You provided me with a chance to attend the university, and for that I will be forever grateful.

The best gift that one human can give another is a chance—be it in life, love, career, or whatever the person desires—because with a chance comes opportunity, and with opportunity comes the ability to truly see and grow an individual's potential. I

cannot begin to imagine how my life would be different now had I not become a part of the Notre Dame family and been blessed with the possibility to thrive for four years on the campus of the university. That chance provided me with the insight needed to have not only a successful professional career, but also to become successful in my life and aware of the needs of my community and those around me. The ability to have a top-notch education while refining and enforcing my life values is something that has been invaluable to me as I have gone through life, and is something, which I doubt I would have found elsewhere. Other universities do have excellent credentials and wonderful academic programs, but what truly makes Notre Dame unique are all of the life lessons which a student learns, embodies, and carries with them after leaving. These values set Domers apart from their colleagues as a sense of humanity seems to be carried through whatever we do, and instills in us a sense of both leadership and stewardship as we move through life and interact with our communities.

So, thank you, Father Ted, for my chance, and for the chances that you have given to all of the women who have been fortunate enough to attend the university. I would not be the person who I am today—someone who feels fulfilled to know that they are reaching beyond what they thought possible of themselves—had it not been for this opportunity.

Happy 90th Birthday!

Best regards,

Annie Fitzpatrick
Class of '99

Dear Father Hesburgh,

I am a proud 1999 graduate of Notre Dame's Biology program. I can't tell you how much my Notre Dame experience has changed my life.

I fondly remember some late-night study breaks when my friends and I would come to visit you in your office on the thirteenth floor of the library. I specifically remember one evening when you and Father Joyce invited us in to share an apple with you over some good conversation. These are the memories that will stick with me forever. This is when I had the opportunity to learn about your human spirit, and learn how you were able to do so many amazing things, and learn so many languages in your lifetime. You are truly an inspiration!

Your commitment to making the university a better place is quite evident on campus today. Your decision to allow women to attend Notre Dame has changed so many lives, including my own. I am grateful for the opportunity to grow academically and spiritually at the University of Notre Dame.

Respectfully,

Sara Rathman Zwart
Class of '99

# 6

## ALUMNAE LETTERS—
## CLASSES OF
## 2000–2011

Dear Father Hesburgh,

We thank you, belatedly but sincerely, for creating the changes that allowed women to attend Notre Dame. Five of the seven women in our family graduated from Notre Dame. Three of us, including me, met our husbands during our time there. My husband Chad (1999) and I have since been blessed with two beautiful children. At the time you opened the university to women, it might well have seemed a policy decision, possibly a social one, but not a decision that would matter into eternity. But as I look at our two sleeping children tonight, whose souls God created in love and who will exist with Him in Heaven for all time, I know your decision to open Notre Dame to women did indeed have a lasting impact. Without you and without that decision, we would never have met, and these two amazing children would not exist. How many other children exist because of similar "Notre Dame marriages"? Please know that we thank God every day that we were able to meet at Our Lady's university and to have the privilege of bringing a new family into the world in partnership with Him.

Notre Dame has made a difference in my life in so many other ways as well . . . taught me to think, made me more conscious of my relationship with God, given me lasting relationships and an appreciation of football that I never would have ex-

pected to gain . . . and for all of these, please know that I and countless other women will remain grateful to you forever for making all of these opportunities available to us.

Thank you, and God bless.
Sincerely in Our Lady,

Patty Rice Doran
Class of '00

Father Hesburgh,

We have the same birthday! I guess that makes us both twenty-one again!

Thank you for the leadership and support making Notre Dame a coed university in the '70s. It was your decision that gave my father, Ernie Hughes ('78) the opportunity to meet my mother, but also for me to meet my husband Matthew Thompson. We are both 2000 graduates and married in 2005 in the San Francisco Bay Area. We

have over twelve sets of friends who also met their spouse while being students at ND and at our wedding, we had over forty Notre Dame alumni, both male and female, who have become not only our close friends but also our mentors in life. Your decision has given me the most precious gift of my life, my husband Matthew and I am forever grateful to you for being such a humanitarian and friend.

God bless you always,

Christine (Hughes) Thompson
Class of '00

Father Hesburgh,

Thanks to you, I never had to wish I could go to Notre Dame and know I couldn't because I was a woman. A lot of my relatives went to Notre Dame, my dad ('77), his two brothers ('79 and '80), and my mother's brother ('73), so of course ND was a big part of my life growing up. My mom went to Notre Dame, too (Class of 1977), and was in the second class that accepted women as freshman. Because she went there I never had to think that Notre Dame wasn't an option. She actually told me about you when I was little, about how you made ND a coeducational university and what a great president you were. My grandmother loved you and my mom told me that she bought a book of yours for her for Mother's Day. She decided to take the elevator to the thirteenth floor of the library and you welcomed her into your office and signed the book for my grandmother, who was very excited to receive it. Our family still has that book. The thing that I find amazing is that my grandmother couldn't go to college, but my mother dreamed about going to Notre Dame when it wasn't coed. She felt so lucky that the policy changed in time for her to be in one of the first classes of women there. I, on the other hand, always had Notre Dame as an option available to me, all I had to do was work hard to get there, but it was always there. I was on the women's crew team at Notre Dame (1997–2001) and became captain my senior year. That year, 2001, we named one of our crew racing shells after you and had it "christened" at half-time of a men's basketball game. I got to shake your hand that day and have my picture taken with you as we christened the boat. The man that made it possible for me to be there and a man of legend in my mind. I still have the picture and show it off with pride.

My life has since moved on, I went to law school and am now a prosecutor, but Notre Dame is still a huge part of my life, maybe not so much overtly, but I carry the things that I learned there with me every day. For me, it was the only place I wanted to go to college and will always hold a special place in my heart for the memories I made there, even since I was a very little girl going there with my parents. So, thank you. Thank you that I never had to wish I could go to Notre Dame and know I couldn't because I was a girl. Thank you for providing a university that respects, supports, and applauds women.

Thank you for Notre Dame.

With sincere respect and love,

Claire Elizabeth Bula
Class of '01

᷂

Dear Father Hesburgh,

It would be near impossible for me to summarize in one note what my four years at the University of Notre Dame meant to me. Simply put, those four years were the fulfillment of my childhood dream and enabled me to launch a successful career in the commercial real estate industry. However, my four years at Notre Dame meant so much more. Each day at the university was a gift that I tried to enjoy to the fullest extent: meeting lifelong friends from all corners of the United States; learning from my professors and peers through my studies; developing my spiritual side at Notre Dame encounter retreats; cheering on our athletic programs including football, baseball, basketball, soccer, and lacrosse; enjoying the community in the dorms; appreciating the beauty of the

campus and taking time to reflect on my experiences at the Grotto. There truly is something special about the University of Notre Dame. Ultimately, Notre Dame feels like HOME to me.

Thank you for making it possible for women like me to attend such a prestigious university. It truly is a life-changing event, one that I will cherish for all of my life.

Best regards,

Kerry Doolin
Class of '01

᠑

Dear Father Hesburgh,

Thank you for making it possible for me to be a proud alumna of Notre Dame! I love being part of the Notre Dame family.

Love and prayers,

Elizabeth
Class of '02

᠑

Dear Father Ted,

There is no real way to thank you for the opportunity you made available to me by making Notre Dame a coeducational university. When I was growing up, it was always my father's school, but as I began to plan for college, there was really no other place I would imagine myself. Notre Dame quickly became not only my father's school, but my school and sanctuary. Once I was accepted, there was no question, I had found my place on this earth.

There was no way for me to know the extraordinary relationships I was about to develop, once I arrived. Coeducation at Notre Dame has given the university a different feeling. After listening to my father's stories about his time there, I am certain that it has changed the university in a way that no other decision could have. It is a place where both sexes can live, work, study, and play in a way that creates lifelong friendships.

I know that my friendships that were forged in my days at the university are much stronger than any relationship I have made away from the university. Without coeducation at Notre Dame, I never would have met my best friends or my husband, Kevin Friedman ('00). There is no doubt in my mind that God was watching over the two of us. If we had not met that first week my freshman year, we would have eventually. There were too many coincidences.

I am not sure where I would be now, if Notre Dame had not been a possibility for me. It is an amazing school. It is a school that has shaped so many lives. Without your effort to have women come to the university, so many thousands of women would not have the same purpose and dedication in their lives. I count myself as one of those very fortunate women.

Sincerely,

Catherine (Casey) O'Neill Friedman
Class of '02

Dear Father Ted,

A question I am asked frequently is why I wanted to attend Notre Dame. My succinct response is "because I used to watch Notre Dame football games with my Irish grandfather." I have a passion for the university and for the football team that surprises many, but really my love for Notre Dame runs much deeper than football. I share my love with countless fellow Domers—inspired by the sense of tradition, the true meaning of the Notre Dame family, the Catholic presence, the friendships forged during my undergraduate years, the sense of identity and service to society that are instilled in students, the sincere commitment to academic discussion and reflection, and the beautiful campus, among many other reasons. However, my passion is also deeply rooted in the memory of my grandfather. Although he never visited Notre Dame, I feel a strong connection to him on the campus. When, at a young age, I declared that I was going to Notre Dame, many of the adults in my life just nodded their heads to appease me. Not my grandfather. He listened to me and believed me. Notre Dame is something I first shared with him, and it was a way that I keep him close to my heart—now and forever.

Since I graduated in 2002, my Notre Dame degree has proved invaluable to me on many occasions. It has prepared me to make contributions to the world both through my career and through service, it has won me instant friends in fellow Domers; it has guided my life's decisions. Attending Notre Dame was always my dream, and I look back with fondness on the memories created there. Thank you, Father Hesburgh, for opening the doors to coeducation and welcoming me to the Notre Dame family. I am forever appreciative.

Carianne Johnson
Class of '02

Dear Father Hesburgh,

At first, I thought I was just writing to thank you for implementing coeducation at Notre Dame. Then when I sat down and really gave it some thought, I realized I had to thank you not just for a large part of my identity, but also for my very existence as a person! Let me explain.

Because of your efforts to bring women into the Notre Dame family, my mom, Ann (Timm) Rimkus ('77) had the honor of being one of the first women to attend the university. It was there that she met my dad, Charles Rimkus ('77), as they were both math majors and enrolled in many of the same classes. Seeing as how they met, dated, and fell in love under the Golden Dome, I am not sure I would be here today if my mother had not had the opportunity to attend!

My parents raised me and my siblings as true Irish fans. Every year, we visited Notre Dame's campus, and by the time I was in fifth grade it was evident—I was meant to attend no other school but Notre Dame. I worked incredibly hard in school, and just a year after my sister Kathleen (Rimkus) Graziano ('01) was accepted, I too, received my acceptance at Notre Dame! This was easily one of the happiest days of my life. Two years later, my younger sister, Laura Rimkus ('04) was accepted into the university as well. It was truly a remarkable experience to attend college with both my sisters, and a true testament to the influence you have had on my family!

I am so grateful for the opportunity I had to receive a Notre Dame education. With every person I have encountered in graduate school and the workplace, I have not met even one who feels about their college the way I feel about Notre Dame. As you know, it is a truly special place, and I feel infinitely fortunate to be a part of the Notre Dame family. Notre Dame not only gave me a quality education, but also taught me the values of service and selflessness that I bring to my teaching job every day. Notre Dame has truly shaped the individual I am today. Thank you, Father Hesburgh, for making that possible.

Gratefully,

Elizabeth Rimkus
Class of '02

Dear Father Hesburgh,

I count myself blessed to have enjoyed seven years of my life under the Dome while earning two degrees from the university. With my first view of campus, from a shuttle bus traveling down Notre Dame Avenue taking my mom and me to the Morris Inn on a snowy December evening, I knew it was a place I could call "home." Eight months later, Notre Dame became my home, and in many ways, it will always remain my home.

To call the seven years I spent at Notre Dame (nearly one quarter of my life to date) life-shaping seems like an understatement. I arrived on campus a shy, timid freshman, unsure of my future and unsure of how I would incorporate my Catholic faith into that unknown future. During my undergraduate experience, and again during my law school experience, I found first-rate professors who encouraged and expected students to think on their own and develop their own ideas. Faculty and students alike exhibited a strong commitment to faith and service, and spirituality was easily incorporated into every aspect of life. Perhaps most importantly, I found the Notre Dame family. During my seven years at Notre Dame, I developed lifelong friendships with men and women who are more like family than friends. My husband and I met in history class during our sophomore year. I feel fortunate that we are able to share much of our Notre Dame experiences, first as friends, then as a couple, throughout our engagement, and after celebrating our wedding at the Basilica of the Sacred Heart.

During those seven years, I received a world-class education, and was instilled with the same commitment to excellence that the university exhibits on every front. The "Play Like a Champion Today" sign that hangs in my office reminds me, as a second-year attorney I can make this world a better place by striving for both excellence and justice in everything that I do.

I extend my deepest heartfelt thanks to you, Father Ted, for making the Notre Dame experience available to women, and for all of your contributions to the Notre Dame community. On May 25 of this year, and of every year, knowing that words cannot adequately thank you for all that my Notre Dame education and experience continue to give to me, I will think of you with gratitude, and pray that God may bless and keep Our Lady's university and all her family.

Yours in Notre Dame,

Beth (Sheehan) Silker
Class of '02, '05 JD

Dear Father,

Thank you so much for your efforts to ensure that women are able to participate fully in the Notre Dame experience. As a Double Domer I can tell you that my attendance to Notre Dame has had a positive effect on every aspect of my life.

Yours in faith,

Sharon Theisman
Class of '02

Dear Father Ted,

I was lucky enough to live with your great-niece Susan throughout my time at Notre Dame. I will never forget the first time I walked into your office freshman year and

saw all of your books, pictures, and awards—the whole space is a true testament to how much your influence and intellect is respected, both inside and out of the Notre Dame community. Needless to say, I was slightly intimidated to meet the man I had heard so much about; however, any feelings of intimidation immediately disappeared when you entered the room and gave us all bear hugs. We sat in your office overlooking the campus and you told us numerous stories and put a huge emerald ring on my hand that had been given to you by one of the popes—talk about knowing how to put a girl at ease, cover her in jewels!

Throughout my four years at Notre Dame, there were a million things that I was thankful for—the beautiful campus, the stimulating classes, and the lifelong friends I made to name a few. Without you making ND coed, I never would have had the opportunity to experience any of those things. I truly believe that Notre Dame is a special place where there is a real feeling of spirituality and, though it sounds clichéd, a feeling of belonging to a family. We used to go to your office after home football games to celebrate Mass—how many other schools can say that their students come together around the Eucharist as often as they come together in the stands of a football game?

I still look back fondly on my memories as a student and try to get back to campus as much as possible, whether it be for a recruiting event or a football game. Working as a financial analyst in New York City, I use the education that I received at Notre Dame on a regular basis. More importantly, I am able to utilize the education I received outside of classroom walls. Having role models like you on campus highlighted the importance of Christian service and I continue to do the volunteer work I so enjoyed doing in the South Bend community here in New York.

Father Ted, thank you so much for all you have done for our great university. You truly are a role model to so many and I wish you nothing but continued success. Best wishes and thank you!

Meredith Holt
Class of '03

෧෬

Dear Father Ted,

I am writing to you to thank you for all the great work you have done for Notre Dame on a grand scale, and for all the great work you have done for my family and me on a small scale.

I graduated from Notre Dame in May 2003, a four-year resident of Farley Hall. You always would say our special Sunday Mass in celebration of Pop Farley week ... even if we had to move Mass from the normal 10:00 p.m. time to 3:00 p.m. to allow for Super Bowl watching! You were always willing to give of yourself. You signed your book for my dad, and he still keeps it on the shelf by his bedside. Another lucky day, you even invited us Farley women up to your office to see the view and the special carpet. Father

Joyce took this picture. I am standing next to you, second from the right.

Being part of dorm Mass, and later working as a liturgical commissioner with Sister Carrine Etheridge my next three years at school made Notre Dame more than a place—it became home, with people, with family. Our traditions, even Pop Farley Mass

with you in the dorm, became part of my character. Thank you for helping me to develop that character.

I am the oldest of two, and though I asked Santa for a sister, I got Brian. I love my brother dearly, but I still always wanted a sister. I met wonderful sisters in the halls of Farley who still are with me today. We once worked through accounting exams and cockroaches in the halls. Now we work through wedding plans and decisions to move across the county, take new jobs, or enter graduate school. I have stood up with these women during their weddings, and now they stand up for mine. Thank you for giving me my sisters.

Last June I married a wonderful man I met studying abroad in London. He, too, is an ND graduate. We are very different. Chris is from Texas, likes country music, and cheers for the Astros. I am from Chicago, like the oldies, and cheer for the Cubbies. With all our differences, our paths still crossed. Notre Dame, our common faith, and love of football, brought us together and helped our friendship to develop and blossom into joyful love. Father Pat Neary (who would say our weekday Mass Monday nights in Farley) said our nuptial Mass. We have another link to the beginning of our relationship. Thank you for giving me my future husband.

Finally, I am putting my dual finance and Spanish degrees to great use. I am a junior broker at the number-two global insurance broker, servicing Fortune 500 clients. I have been working there since graduation. I chose Aon not only for business purposes, but because Aon has a strong sense of community and philanthropy. Every Tuesday, I take a chauffeured bus with other employees to a west side Chicago school and tutor second and fourth graders in Math and Language Arts. We participate in this service during business hours with full support of our managers and senior executives. It is the most fulfilling and tangible part of my job. Thank you for preparing me with a wonderful education, a nimble brain, and a generous spirit.

I wish you all the best on your 90th birthday. I still often think of your simple but effective prayer when I need to feel centered: "Come, Holy Spirit."

Thank you for everything and for all the good you did in making Notre Dame a special place for coeducation. May God continue to bless you every day. I will keep you in my thoughts and prayers. I feel my many blessings of friends, family, and spirit every day.

In Notre Dame,

Christina Lindemann
Class of '03

Dear Father Hesburgh,

It is hard to put the Notre Dame experience into words, though a few come immediately to my mind: integrity, tradition, friendship, spirituality, knowledge. These are all, without a doubt, among the founding principles of the university that Father Sorin built in 1842. But as a student in the late '90s and early '00s, I was struck to learn just how great a role you and your administration played in preserving these values and shaping them into the campus that I knew and loved for the four years that I attended Our Lady's university. And so it is with deep gratitude and admiration that I write to thank you, not just for coeducation, but for all that you have done to ensure that Notre Dame remains at once among the most rigorous and most compassionate of college campuses in the nation.

I am, perhaps a bit selfishly, grateful for coeducation quite simply because without it I would never have had the college experience that I did. I would not count among the greatest benefits of living in Chicago today that I am only ninety miles from campus at any given moment. I would not have the joy of returning each fall to watch the Irish battle on the football field, to pester the poor girls who currently live in

123 Walsh Hall, and to revisit all the iconic sites of my emotional and academic maturation—moments of spiritual clarity at the Grotto, friendships cemented over quarter dogs, bolts of inspiration that hit after being jerked awake (again) by the closing bell of your library. Most importantly to me, I would not have four best friends to whom I am so close that they might as well be my sisters, even though jobs and husbands now make it regrettably impractical for us to share a two-bedroom suite with a mini-fridge and a disco ball.

One might say that this is all well and good, thanks to coeducation, but that under any other circumstance, had Notre Dame not begun enrolling women in the fall of 1972, I would have made myself just as easily at home at any other university. But clearly then one does not understand the Notre Dame experience—or the struggles that the first classes of women endured a generation before me to see this historic integration of genders though. I feel that a great deal of thanks is also owed to these women, as is a promise from current students to continue advocating for gender equality on campus (thirty years later the "old boys' club" sentiment is still felt in many aspects of student life).

Nevertheless, while the sentimentality of my experience and the compassion of so many inspired individuals that I met at Notre Dame remain closest to my heart, it is the academic character of the university for which I am most grateful to you. In my mind, a university cannot truly boast intellectual integrity without coeducation; it cannot teach and solicit world-changing ideas without input from men and women alike; and it cannot continue to attract leading faculty without being able to offer them the best and the brightest students from both halves of the world's population.

It's impossible to isolate coeducation from the myriad of measures you took during your presidency to ensure academic freedom and promote intellectual excellence on our campus, and I want to thank you most sincerely for preserving this core mission of our university.

In my very short career in university administration, I have learned above all that change, even in the most progressive of institutions, does not come easily. It takes courage, fearlessness, and conviction to see even the most necessary of reforms through. I am continuously humbled by your command of these traits in all that you have done on and off our campus, and I remain deeply, deeply grateful for the opportunity that you have given me to become a part of the Notre Dame family.

Sincerely yours,

Katie Malmquist
Class of '03

Dear Father Hesburgh,

I write this letter to you from my assistant rector's apartment in Farley Hall. As one of the female Double Domers, I am doubly grateful to you for giving me the chance to attend Notre Dame, the setting for the last seven years of my life, the place where I found my future, my closest friends, and my faith. I am so honored to have met you during my time here and to have the opportunity to contribute this tribute to you. Your indelible mark on Notre Dame's history will never be forgotten.

In Notre Dame,

Katherine Margaret Mosesso
Class of '03, '07 Law

❧

Father Hesburgh,

I can't thank you enough for giving me the opportunity to attend (in my opinion), the greatest university of all time. My experience at Notre Dame will remain the best four years of my life. I found forever friends, I found God, and I found myself. I am a 2003 graduate and I just graduated from veterinary school at the University of Illinois. I plan to pursue a specialty in small animal oncology. I truly believe I would not have had these opportunities without a Notre Dame education.

Thank you again for allowing myself and all the other women of Notre Dame to reach our fullest potential and achieve all of our dreams.

Kerry Rissetto
Class of '03

❧

Dear Father Hesburgh,

Thank you for bringing coeducation to Notre Dame. I cannot imagine where I would be today, had it not been possible for me to attend the University of Our Lady.

Notre Dame made it possible for me to meet some of the most incredible people in the world—caring, intelligent, passionate individuals who have their lives focused on living their faith. These people helped my faith to grow stronger, by encouraging me to live a life that follows the Gospel. These people will always be some of my best friends, no matter the distance between us.

Notre Dame gave me a greater love of liturgical music, through my involvement in the Liturgical Choir. For five years I had the privilege of singing praises to God from the choir loft of the Basilica. I cannot imagine a more wonderful way to partake in the Mass week after week, than by singing with an outstanding group of musicians and having a bird's-eye view of the Liturgy in one of the most beautiful churches I have ever laid eyes on.

Notre Dame gave me the academic challenges I needed to be successful upon venturing into the "real world." Many classes tested my intellectual stamina. I had to learn to assess how much I could on my own, and then realize it was OK to ask others for help when the work was over my head. I learned that teamwork can make all the difference between success and failure in many situations. My Notre Dame peers willingly worked with me on those assignments I found difficult, and in return I helped others when they were struggling.

Notre Dame showed me why "Catholic" means "universal." I saw our Notre Dame family unite for so many events, and continue to see its strength as an alumna. It is always incredible to see alumni return to their alma mater from all corners of the globe for various occasions—football games, Masses, graduation, alumni reunions. In my move from Notre Dame to Milwaukee, I sought out Notre Dame graduates through the local alumni club, and have become close friends with many of them over the past year. I still remember the student body gathering on South Quad for the 9/11 Mass, and being so impressed by the way we came together as one to support each other. We really are a model of the Body of Christ.

Notre Dame brought me my ultimate calling—a call to marriage. I met my husband at Notre Dame. Through our singing in the Liturgical Choir, spending a semester abroad in Spain, and sharing numerous wonderful experiences together on campus, we learned to grow in our friendship, our faith, and our love for one another. We were married at the Basilica on May 13 this year, with the Liturgical Choir singing from the loft—we couldn't have imagined a more beautiful ceremony or a more appropriate place to celebrate our marriage. Notre Dame will always be home to us, and getting married anywhere else just wouldn't have been the same.

Thank you for making it possible for me to attend Notre Dame. . . . for making it possible for me to meet my best friends, grow in my faith, and find my husband. My life has been filled with many tremendous blessings because of coeducation at Notre Dame. I will always be a loyal daughter of Our Lady's university.

Love,

Teresa (Bloemker) Mitchell
Class of '04/'05, EG/AL, Five-Year Dual Degree Program

Dear Father Ted,

I remember vividly driving down the tree-lined avenue up to the Golden Dome for freshman orientation at Notre Dame in August of 1998. While introducing myself to several of the girls I would live with, I learned that I was not the only legacy in Badin Hall. In fact, many of the girls were attending Our Lady's university—the university of their fathers.

Within a few weeks, my close friends and I shared a conversation that only occurred because of you, Father Ted. We were discussing how exciting it would be if our children also attended Notre Dame. "Won't it be cool," we exclaimed, "that our sons and daughters will be able to say their mom went here—instead of just Dad?" For the first time we realized what a gift it was to be able to attend Notre Dame, a gift that wasn't available to our mothers.

Growing up my father told me stories of how crazy Notre Dame was before women—the food fights in the dining hall, the wrestling at "the Rock." He always said, smiling, "women probably have made things better—or at least more civilized." I agree with my dad. Notre Dame is better because of the influence of women, and that is all thanks to you, Father Ted. Thank you for opening the door to me. Thank you for allowing me to be a Domer. Thank you for allowing thousands in future generations of Notre Dame students to tell people at their freshman orientation: "Yes, I am a legacy. My MOM went here."

Sincerely,

Laura Rompf Soldato
Class of '04, ACE Graduate
2002 Senior Class Vice President
*Observer* News Editor

Dear Father Ted,

While attending Notre Dame between 2001 and 2005, occasionally I wondered about the university's past and how much it must have changed over the years. I only knew it as a place that embraced diversity of all kinds. Intellectually, I found my classes extremely stimulating because of the variety of perspectives among my peers. Socially, I found mature men and women who enjoyed interacting with one another. Due to your perseverance, Notre Dame is truly a community that welcomes anyone, and every graduate has benefited from this atmosphere. Thank you for your foresight and determination.

Coeducation allowed for a Notre Dame experience that has enriched my life and offered me unique opportunities. I participated in the fortieth year of the Innsbruck study abroad program and was able to travel all over Europe. That year broadened my horizons and deepened my interest in international affairs, which is why I moved to Washington, D.C., after graduation to work for Congress.

I am still in close touch with many of my friends from my four years at Notre Dame. Living in Washington I have met many other Notre Dame graduates and this has given me both friendships and career opportunities.

I am so grateful for my Notre Dame education. It has made me an inquisitive, motivated, and more thoughtful person. Thank you, Father Ted, for the opportunity to spend four years at such a wonderful place.

Sincerely,

Emily Anderson
Class of '05

## For . . . thanks
### (2005)

*Annamarie Bindenagel*
Notre Dame, 2003
Washington, D.C.

For the rustle of colourful autumn leaves
For the chorus of voices in an uproarious debate

For the sleek pull of a swimming stroke
For the splash—interrupted!

For the soaring sopranos resonating—
For the booming basses resounding in the sanctuary

For stealthy climbs into tree branches on the island, perches for professions of "I love you"
For rafts hastily grafted and rafted, raced across the lakes

For midnight strolls under moonlight skies, stars reflecting in shining eyes
For a sacred safe space for tears and laughter, learning and living and losing and loving

For the privilege to be there, men and women—under God, in country, at Notre Dame
For this, thank you.

Dear Father Hesburgh,

I want to express my gratitude to you for making Notre Dame coed so that I had the opportunity to attend Our Lady's wonderful university. In addition to meeting some amazing people and friends in my four years there and learning so much in and out of the classroom about myself and others, I think the thing of most impact about my Notre Dame education was the renewal of my faith. It had always been there, but got slightly pushed aside during my years at a public high school. The strong sense of God, community, and faith that I found at Notre Dame helped revive religion and God in my life. Not only were dorm Masses an amazing way to bond with your dorm mates and classmates, but also the endless amounts of service projects available made it so easy to help others while infusing that desire to serve those less fortunate in any way and time possible. I would be lying if I said that attending Notre Dame had no effect whatsoever on my life now. It has definitely changed me for the better, and continues to influence my life and its decisions. So thank you again, Father Hesburgh, even though thanks seems like such a small and insignificant thing to say for a gift that means so much.

Laura Fraczek
Class of '05

Dear Father Ted,

Many thanks to you for all that you have done to promote excellence in education for women, and most importantly for making the decision to allow women to attend the University of Notre Dame.

Much has changed since 1972. The last three decades have unfolded with many "female firsts," with women assuming new leadership roles in business and politics. As it has become increasingly common to see women participating in positions of authority, the Notre Dame community cannot forget what it was like a generation ago. Your

Christina Dehan, Jill Joehl, Rachel Kelley, Jennifer Liebenauer.

decision to open the doors of America's premier Catholic university to women has enhanced our lives and American society in general by preparing women to be much-needed leaders for our world.

As a 2005 graduate, I have been blessed with countless opportunities available to me by way of my Notre Dame education. My friends and I from Lewis Hall have broken into careers traditionally dominated by men, myself in investment banking, with others in engineering and medicine—and I look back with appreciation for the respect and acknowledgment you granted to Notre Dame's daughters. I know none of us will ever forget your landmark decision. Wherever life leads us we will always make you proud.

Jennifer Liebenauer
Class of '05

Dear Father Hesburgh,

I often tell my grandparents that the best gift they have ever given me was a Notre Dame education. They paid my way for the best four years of my life. I thank my parents, too, for giving me countless opportunities through their love and support that ultimately enabled me to live, learn, and eventually live at Notre Dame. The many friends I made while at ND deserve credit, too, for helping me to become who God intended me to be through love and fellowship. It seems that I am in debt to these people who

allowed me to grow in love, faith, and learning. So thank you, too, for coeducation at Notre Dame. My Notre Dame education, the friends that I made, and the person I've become will no doubt serve me in good stead.

For Our Lady,

Whitney Marie March
Class of '05

᎐ᨤᨦ

Dear Father Hesburgh,

I wish I had the words to explain how changed, strengthened, and blessed my Notre Dame experience has made me, and I wish I had the words to show you how deeply I thank you for allowing me as a woman to have that opportunity. I have been sitting in front of this blank screen . . . and I am starting to realize that I absolutely do not have the words. While I am fortunate to feel so deeply blessed, it is also amazingly frustrating not to feel like I can communicate it to you as a person that made it happen for me.

I grew up in the typical Notre Dame family—my dad went to law school at ND and I have a brother, two years older, who also attended. My lifelong dream was to go there, and yet I was not admitted the first two times I applied. To this day I cannot figure that out, but I am actually extremely grateful for those rejections because they made me realize that I have the strength and persistence to realize dreams that are initially denied to me. Going to Notre Dame was everything and more than I ever hoped for—and that's saying a lot when it's your whole being's dream just to go. To this day it is the closest experience I have ever had with God, and it has just made me believe.

I actually bumped into you in an elevator in the library once. You asked me to push the button for a certain floor because you could not see them so well. I don't remember what I said, but I do remember that you responded by saying you were lucky just to have over eighty years of good vision. You are really blessed to have that kind of attitude, and luckily Notre Dame is full of people who can not only keep things in perspective, but also be happy with what God has given them.

I wish I had forced you to have a conversation with me. Sounds strange, I'm sure, but I know you have lead an incredibly full life, and I just would have liked to hear from you how you did it, and what kept you going during the hard times. I particularly think your involvement with the civil rights movement is inspirational; I am a white woman in an African-American Studies master's program at UCLA (I graduated from ND in 2005). It can be frustrating to have white peers imagine that it's crazy for me to be in the program, and that they as whites are somehow not affected by racial problems throughout the United States. But, if ND taught me anything, it's that doing something hard for the good of people you'll never know is better than doing something easy for the good of yourself.

Please know that all the good I am able to do in my life (my little sister and I have plans to be at least one hundred years old) comes from my time at Notre Dame. For that, you are responsible.

THANK YOU.

C. R.
Class of '05

Father Hesburgh,

I was allowed to attend Notre Dame because of support, yours in particular, for coeducation at the university. I will value my Notre Dame education for the rest of my life. It has helped to shape the person I am today, and I truly thank you for allowing me the opportunity. Thank you.

Jessica Smith, 2Lt, USAF
Class of '05

Dear Father Hesburgh,

Congratulations on the celebration of your 90th birthday and happy thirty-fifth anniversary of coeducation at the University of Notre Dame.

I would like to take this chance to say thank you, on behalf of all the women that graduated in my Class of 2006. Standing true to the mission statement of this university, you saw the need to expand and challenge the social norm. In order to foster an environment that enriched learning, you provided the opportunity for a new voice with diverse opinions to participate at a prestigious university. By inviting women onto Notre Dame's campus, you encouraged thoughtful, intelligent discussions, respect for the opposite sex, a positive intellectual learning environment, an assertive drive within the classroom and in campus activities, ambition for career goals, and much more.

How has your decision impacted me? Taking on the responsibility as a female student leader was one of the best experiences and memories I had at Notre Dame. With great mentoring, support from resources, and peers (both male and female), I was able to grow and develop myself into a better person and leader, which ultimately prepared me for the real world. This opportunity also laid a path for future female student leaders to unite our campus toward carrying out the mission of our university.

I hope you know that your efforts to make the Notre Dame community a successful place are truly appreciated.

Thank you again and congratulations,

Emily Chin
Class of '06, President

Father Hesburgh,

I have a shirt from my involvement in Notre Dame Student Government that reads, "The very essence of Leadership is that you have to have vision—Theodore M. Hesburgh." I can think of no better way to describe a man of such humility and character, and most certainly vision—as I write to congratulate you on your 90th birthday and the thirty-fifth anniversary of coeducation at Notre Dame, both incredible achievements.

One may think that as a recent graduate of Notre Dame, I would have less of a connection to your Notre Dame and the leadership you provided during your tenure as president of our great university and after. However, as I reflect on my time at the university, each milestone during my four years was marked by your presence. Whether it was freshman orientation, a Badin Hall Mass, junior parents weekend, lectures in the Hesburgh

series, or senior graduation this past May, you were there each step of the way offering your wisdom. Each time I heard you speak, I was more amazed by the profound influence your decisions have had on thousands of Notre Dame students as well as those who have not have the opportunity to attend the University of Our Lady.

I must confess that it is impossible for me to imagine a Notre Dame without women.

Your vision of a community, focused on faith and academics, composed of both women and men, is now a reality. And I believe I can speak for my classmates when I say our academic and spiritual experiences were only enriched by the presence of both women and men. I can imagine that thirty-five years ago your decision was not easy, was probably controversial, and was undoubtedly questioned by many in the Notre Dame community. I hope today, when you walk our beautiful campus, you see the realization of your vision. I thank you for that vision, because it if were not for you, I would not be a proud alumna of the University of Notre Dame.

Yours in Notre Dame,

Laura Feeney
Class of '06

Dear Father Hesburgh,

I feel honored to have the opportunity to wish you a very Happy 90th Birthday this year. Your life has been a gift to the world and I thank God for blessing us with you! Likewise, I would like to express my profound gratitude for a particularly precious gift that you first gave to my mother Ceyl Prinster ('76) and then to me: the opportunity to experience a college education at the University of Notre Dame.

You taught me one of the shortest, most powerful prayers I have ever known: "Come, Holy Spirit." Father Ted, because you enabled women to attend the university, the Holy Spirit has influenced my life in beautiful ways since the day I was born, literally. My mother graduated from Notre Dame with the first class of women and her spirit has inspired me in countless ways. Not only has she shown me how to love her children, her husband, and her own parents, she instilled in me a love for learning and a confidence that dreams can be achieved through prayer, and hard work with love.

You opened a path to Notre Dame for my mother thirty years ago and grace allowed me to follow in her footsteps. From there, the phenomenal service-learning and international study programs of Our Lady's university revealed to me the critical importance of working toward improved access to basic education in the United States and worldwide along with gender-equity initiatives in underdeveloped nations.

I only recently graduated in 2006, but I am already proud to have been shaped by Notre Dame. Though I do not know exactly where I am going, I feel a sense of purpose. I thank you for awakening in me the spirit to love my family and to work for justice for the world's most disadvantaged groups for the rest of my life, just as you, my mother, and members of the extended Notre Dame family have done.

Most sincerely,

Megan Prinster Sheehan
Class of '06

Father Ted and Father Ned Joyce, executive vice president, "retiring" into private life, 1987.

Dear Father Hesburgh,

"I give thanks to my God in every remembrance of you, praying always with joy in my every prayer for you [. . .] you, because of your partnership for the gospel from the first day until now. I am confident of this, that the one who began a good work in you will continue to complete it until the day of Christ Jesus." Philippians 1:3–6

I thank my God for that trip we shared in the library elevator during the fall of my freshman year. . . . when I did not realize who you were until after I had gotten off the elevator.

I thank my God for the Mass we shared, crammed into your office at the top of the library (sitting on the floor), after the 2004 Purdue game. After such a wounding defeat, what better way was there to remind us of life's truest priorities? Even if Irish football fails us, God never will.

I thank my God for every tour I gave through the Admissions Office when I was able to share the story of your so very wise decision to admit women in 1972, thirty years prior to the year I entered Our Lady's university.

I thank my God for being able to represent Lewis Hall, the largest female residence, as well as St. Cecilia Academy in Nashville, Tennessee, which hailed the first female valedictorian at Notre Dame.

"I give thanks to my God at every remembrance of you" and of the four-year Notre Dame chapter of my life, which—without you—would have been merely a dream.

In peace and gratitude,

Aimee A. Shelide
Class of '06, '08, MA

Dear Father Hesburgh,

I met you last spring at a ceremony for the hanging of the famous photograph of you with Dr. Martin Luther King Jr. in the LaFortune Student Center. Student government had decided it was time that this long talked-about image be commemorated and placed in a high-profile location not only for the students and other members of the community to admire, but also as a symbolic testament to Notre Dame's newest tradition, one that you strove so vehemently toward, a commitment to diversity.

My committee, the Student Senate Committee on Multicultural Affairs, had arranged the ceremony which included speeches by student government leaders as well as by you, Father Hesburgh. When you entered the room and sat down next to me, you casually told me about an award the NAACP had honored you with that you did not think you deserved. I must say that in reflecting in all you have done for traditionally underrepresented groups, I and others owe you the utmost gratitude.

For inspiration for this letter, I recently perused old copies of the *Dome*, the Notre Dame yearbook. I imagined what the experience for women of color must have been like in the early '70s at Notre Dame. Doubly marginalized in an environment that was largely white and male, they must have had some monstrous hurdles to climb. I, on the other hand, am a minority female at the end of that legacy, benefiting from their sacrifices and from yours. In admitting all women and particularly women of color, Notre Dame demonstrated equality and justice, in a time when those very values that are said to define our nation were so greatly lacking in similar institutions. When I look at Notre Dame today I can see progress toward your vision for a truly diverse Notre Dame. While there are plenty of improvements to be made, I feel that Notre Dame is slowly becoming the kind of Catholic institution you had envisioned, one that is truly all-encompassing.

At the end of the photo-hanging ceremony, you kissed my cheek in celebration of the day. Someone from the *Observer* captured that moment in a photograph, which I now preciously keep in a photo album. There's something magically symbolic about that moment of Father Hesburgh kissing the cheek of a minority female in front of a photograph of himself with Martin Luther King in the '60s. Martin Luther King would have been proud of where we've come, Father Hesburgh.

But Martin Luther King would also look to the future. I hope that the path that you've paved for women of color at Notre Dame will be continued by your successors at Our Lady's university. You have shown us the leadership necessary to enact meaningful change in unjust and inequitable situations. My hope is that Notre Dame's future leaders and administrators will continue to examine the issues facing minorities and women within the Notre Dame community and show similar dedication to the values of equality and social justice by working toward change.

Sincerely,

Destinée DeLemos
Class of '07

᥈ᢒᡱ

To Father Hesburgh,

In trying to think of what Notre Dame has meant to my development, I am coming to a roadblock, because despite innumerable attempts at escaping it, the force within Notre Dame has always pulled me in a direction beyond my control. The Notre Dame family is an intoxicatingly attractive group of talented, value-grounded, and always searching men and women. From the outside, I have every reason to believe that I have a seat at the family table. Still, like in any family, I never quite felt worthy of all the responsibility and richness of mind and spirit I sensed all around me.

I unsuccessfully tried to attend the football games. The cheers and chants bored me, as well as the incessant talks with alumni and hometown acquaintances who only seemed to care about bowl possibilities or the running back I had never even heard of. The library always seemed so intimidating with the mounds of dusty and mold-ridden books—like all the knowledge I could conquer if I had the time. The women always seemed too perfect, and the men just beyond date-ability with all they had going for them. Seeing the priests walking around and the students who regularly attended Mass seemed so admirable and made me jealous for the faith I yearned to possess. No, I did not feel I deserved to be walking by the Basilica or the library or the stadium. Who was I to belong with such a group of scholars and believers?

As a senior now, I see no need to lament over my membership in the institution of Notre Dame. I know that all the time spent wanting, planning, and rehearsing to be part of the family is precisely what marks my membership in the family. There is no need for a card or invitation—nothing beyond a readiness to act within the spirit of that family. Before we came here we were already together. It is precisely that vulnerability and honesty of heart that we come in with and is never allowed to harden that makes us so paradoxically strong. The self-awareness and knowledge of human fragility opens us to all people and all circumstances, especially to the oppressed and weak. We are never really ourselves so strong, but with each other to support and inspire us, who knows what we could not do.

I have twice had the gift of talking with Father Hesburgh, once with a class and another on an errand. After responding to his questions, he both times gave me blessings to go on and lead my life in service. Knowing that my head was one of the thousands he has touched, I never felt as if I did not belong at Notre Dame. The mini-ceremonies instead imbued me with the sense of obligatory citizenship to all people. For just as I am one of the billions sharing this creation, so too am I one of the billions made to do the best I can with my time in it. I may not have a special calling, or have a head seat at the table, but as one of the crowd I have a much better view of the spectacular myriad of tiny moments of joy.

I am a loyal daughter, and following the advice given to me atop the thirteenth floor of the library, overlooking all of the campus, I will leave the Dome to try to create a world that triumphs compassion and undoes wrongs.

Teresa Hagan
Class of '07

Father Hesburgh,

Of all your accomplishments, I am most grateful for your efforts to admit women to the University of Notre Dame. Without this, I likely would not exist or be a third-generation Domer. My mother, Patti McNamara McGwire '73, was in the first graduating class of women. Though my father, Michael Paul McGwire '74, is also an alumnus, my mother was essential in imparting in me the spirit, tradition, and love that is Notre Dame, as her appreciation increased with the fact her father was the first generation of my family to attend this great university.

I write this letter because your decision to admit women affects more than the first few classes of women graduating from the University of Notre Dame. It affects more than the women that continue to graduate from this university. As a prominent president at a prestigious university, you helped the United States step into the future. Essentially, without you, the lives of most women would be vastly different: much less successful and even less satisfying.

Your decision is similarly admirable simply because of its progressive nature. Then, and even today, men of influence and prestige affiliated with the university question the decision and wonder what Notre Dame would be like had it not been made. I am comfortable asserting that the university would not be what we know it to be today; the home we hold close to our hearts would not be the place of warmth, love, and camaraderie that we know it to be.

In closing, thank you. Thank you for your foresight. Thank you for your trust, your compassion, for women. Thank you for changing my mother's life, my life, and the lives of all of those people we have been able to touch as a result of our time at Notre Dame. Finally, I thank you for providing me the opportunity to look to a future of success, love, compassion, and faith that I would not be able to look forward to without my time at Notre Dame.

With love and many thanks,

Megan McGuire
Class of '07

Dear Father Hesburgh,

I have so many things to thank you for I don't know where to start. First, the admission of women to Notre Dame has to top my list. As a member of the Class of 2007, I realize that I have changed in so many ways in my four years here because of what Notre Dame is and makes its students strive to be.

However, I must also thank you for a deeper experience: the chance to share Notre Dame. I am the daughter of two Notre Dame graduates, John and Jan (Reedy) Thornton, Class of 1977. Without the admission of women, I would literally never have been born. My parents met while at school and started a family that continues to tie itself to the university. While I recently graduated, my sister recently started her freshman year as a member of the Class of 2010. Notre Dame has always been a part of our family from the moments growing up when my dad yelled at the TV during Irish football games to the family trips to the Grotto during football weekends and now move-in. Together we have been able to share these experiences and wait for my youngest sister to decide if she too will join the extended Notre Dame family.

As a senior this past year, I had to reflect on what I plan to do in the future and what has happened over the last four years. I still stop sometimes walking across campus and take a moment to realize how fortunate I have been to be a student at Notre Dame. When I talk to other college students, they never seem to have that connection that so many Notre Dame students feel toward Our Lady's university. Their college experience isn't about the amazing people they met, the faith they developed, or the life lessons they learned.

As graduation approached, I knew that I was ready to take on the world and to make my place in it. I was ready because Notre Dame has prepared me. It has made me a person that understands how faith must play a role in our everyday lives. It has made me appreciate others for their strengths and weaknesses; it has made me appreciate myself for my own strengths and weaknesses. I have learned that we can all make a difference but must also let others make a difference in us.

For my senior history project, I wrote a thesis on coeducation at Notre Dame. It was amazing to hear the struggles and successes of those first classes of women. They were able to pave the way for so many years of women in the future. They have helped to change Notre Dame just as your decision to admit women changed Notre Dame.

So, Father Hesburgh, thank you. Thank you for the chance to have attended Notre Dame and to have been a part of what happens every day on campus. Thank you for letting my family share those moments together growing. Thank you for helping to create a place like Notre Dame, a place that you can't understand until you've experienced it for yourself.

Thank you and Happy Birthday,

Erin Thornton
Class of '07

Dear Father Ted,

Every time I tell someone that I'm the daughter of a Notre Dame graduate, they ask me what year my "father" graduated. Immediately, I am proud to announce that my mother, Mary Beth Faccenda Hough, graduated in 1982. Without you, Father, my mother, my aunts, and I would not have been able to attend this great university. I would like to thank you much for this opportunity and your endless dedication to the development of young men and women throughout the years.

Love,

Kayleigh Hough
Class of '08

Dear Father Hesburgh,

You are to be credited for where I am today and who I will grow into tomorrow. Thank you for allowing me to take "being a girl" at the University of Notre Dame for granted. I have never once felt that I did not have the opportunity to step up and lead at our fine university. If I wanted to lead a group or get involved, it was a matter of raising a hand, speaking up, or just arriving at an open meeting rather than overcoming adversity and major hurdles as so many women before me did. "Yes, I want to join your club." "Sure, I would love to take a leadership role." "My name is Bridget Keating and I am proud to serve as junior class president."

It is no accident that I have enjoyed a level playing field in student leadership and academics at Notre Dame studying accountancy and in the Hesburgh Program in Public Service. In receiving praise for your accomplishments in coeducation, you would be swift to credit the first females who carried the torch—therefore, I will do the same. Strong female leaders are woven through the blue and gold fabric as administrators and professors. The Class of 2008, which I am so blessed to lead, is presently under its third female class president in as many years; three of the four classes have females at the helm—as well as our student body.

Your vision has guided Our Lady's university and has established it as an international beacon of faith and education. Your work for the Fighting Irish is only one of countless fights you have fought for people everywhere. Your national servant leadership to the United States, especially with civil rights, gave the world the chance to see your heroic ways.

As an admissions tour guide, I spend a significant amount of time discussing your contributions and leadership roles. I profess to everyone and believe with every ounce of my being that you, Father Ted, will be canonized a saint. If not you, then who can the present and future Church look to? Meeting you laid the foundation of my Notre Dame experience that has been full of endless blessings, many for which you are directly responsible. Your forward vision, expression that Notre Dame is a better place because of coeducation, and such progressive views, such as women entering the priesthood someday and serving as president of the University of Notre Dame invigorate me and all believers.

You have been sent to us by the grace of God to hold the hand of Our Lady's university and take it to unparalleled heights. Notre Dame is so much more than the bright students currently receiving the finest education possible. It is about the Notre

Dame family, which began in 1842 and has cared for each of its members ever since. Of course, I do not want graduation in 2008 to come any more quickly than it already will, but I know that when I leave Notre Dame, Notre Dame will never leave me. With Mary at her grand height looking over us, why wouldn't women be leading? You made this possible. God bless you and God bless Notre Dame.

In Notre Dame,

Bridget Keating
Class of '08, President

Dear Father Hesburgh,

I just finished my third year here at Notre Dame, but ever since my first day as a freshman on the campus, I have come to realize how truly blessed I am to be a student at this university. Every time I go back home I come to appreciate more how Our Mother has touched my life in ways that others cannot begin to understand. I am constantly reminded that I was meant to be at Notre Dame. The sense of community, family, and friendship are values that prevail at this university and are dear to my heart as both a first-generation Domer, as well as a first-generation American because there is nowhere else that I would have felt as though I truly belonged except at Notre Dame.

I joke around with my parents that Notre Dame has been the best money they have ever spent on anything, and in all honesty this is true. In my time here, I have come to find that my education as a science preprofessional and Italian double major is one that will provide not only the flexibility, but also a myriad of options for further education or career plans long after graduation. However, my education at Notre Dame has gone beyond mere academics. At Notre Dame, I have been encouraged by friends, mentors, rectors, and professors to pursue my interests, hobbies, and intellectual curiosities, and as a result I have blossomed into what I believe is the well-grounded, holistic person I want to be. Notre Dame has given me the chance to not only challenge myself academically and spiritually, but also find balance in all aspects of my life. In the spirit of Notre Dame, I have learned to cultivate my relationships with the people who will be my best friends for the rest of my life, to continue to learn about my Catholic identity at weekly Mass and visits at the Grotto, and I have come to learn that football

Saturdays are almost as important as Sundays for the Irish. Notre Dame is not just my school—Notre Dame is truly my life.

I am so thankful for each and every person, event, or memory that has positively impacted my time here at Notre Dame thus far, and that will continue to shape my future long after I leave ND. I will forever carry what I have learned here at Notre Dame into every aspect of my life, and I know that when my children attend Notre Dame, they will have an experience that cannot compare. I am grateful for all of the women who will continue to have the opportunity to contribute to the traditions of academic excellence and Catholic heritage that are the ideals of Notre Dame. Thank you, Father Hesburgh.

In Notre Dame,

Marianna Montes
Class of '08

Dear Father Hesburgh,

I recently had the pleasure and honor of meeting you during Junior Parent Weekend Committee breakfast. It was a particular thrill for me, as I grew up on the story of your generosity, kindness, and uncanny insight. Please let me explain.

Nearly twenty-one years ago, in April of 1986, my parents attended a Notre Dame Chicago Club dinner, specifically to hear you address the crowd. My dad, John Mulvaney, is a 1972 graduate. My mom, Mary Kay Davy, is a 1973 Saint Mary's grad. Having been huge fans of yours from their days under the Golden Dome in the early '70s, they were particularly anxious to hear from you in your early retirement days.

At that time, my mother was about eight months pregnant with me, her fourth child (of their eventual five). My mother, then in her mid-thirties, was for some reason extremely apprehensive throughout the pregnancy—constantly fearing that something was going to go wrong. She worried about it almost continually, spent sleepless nights, and prayed fervently to be blessed with another healthy child.

When she arrived for the ND dinner that April night, she recalls that for once she was not feeling especially apprehensive, but in fact, was pleasantly distracted by the festivities of the evening. Upon entering and traveling up the escalator of the International Ballroom of the Hilton, she immediately encountered you conducting a receiving line. Without her having said anything at all to you other than "Good evening, Father," she told me that you immediately stared at her with those incredibly piercing and perceptive brown eyes, saying, "That baby is going to be all right. Please let me give you my blessing." My mother often says she nearly fell back down the escalator; she was so shocked at the way you literally read her mind and instantly calmed her fears.

Indeed, you were exactly right. Three months later, I was born a healthy child. Now as a junior civil engineering major at Notre Dame, I am living my dream of studying at one of the greatest educational institutions in the world—a very special one indeed, because of your courageous insight to admit women to share in and contribute to its incredible resources and traditions. I truly believe my experiences here could not be matched at any other university. Notre Dame has become my home away from home and for this I am forever grateful. Because of your blessing and your insightful leadership, I look forward to becoming a Notre Dame alumna in May 2008. Thank you for everything.

Sincerely,

Katelyn Mary Mulvaney
Class of '08

Mary Kay Davy Mulvaney (Saint Mary's College '73), Father Ted, Katelyn Mulvaney '08, John Mulvaney '72 at ND Junior Parents Weekend 2007.

Dear Father Hesburgh,

First and foremost, I would like to wish you a wonderful 90th birthday.

I would also like to thank you for your devotion and services to Notre Dame. Your dedication to social justice has been a continual inspiration to the student body. The guidance you have given us, as a role model and as a mentor, fosters a philosophy within the student body that stresses both social and cultural awareness of the world. You have shown us what it means to truly be committed to social progress.

I would also like to convey my gratitude for your decision to make the Notre Dame education available for women. I have dreamed about attending this university since I was a little girl and now I am a double major in political science and economics with a minor in Middle East and Mediterranean Studies.

Your accomplishments and dedication to social progress has impacted countless lives and will be remembered within the students' lives you have touched. Your continual guidance has made this university the amazing institution it is today. Therefore on behalf of the Class of 2009 and all the women attending this university, thank you, Father Hesburgh, and Happy Birthday!

Sincerely,

Sarah Burch
Class of '09

Dear Father Hesburgh,

The first day I ever set foot on this campus was during the spring of 2005, on a day with warmer weather than my Southern hometown. After spending just one afternoon touring, talking, and trying to find out what this place was all about, I had been here long enough to know that the people that comprise this institution are unlike those anywhere else in the world. That day, it was not the fact that everyone here dedicates their intelligence to their studies or gets involved in sports and extracurriculars or takes time out of their busy schedules to perform volunteer work in the local community—on top of all that, the people that comprise the University of Notre Dame are a family.

Now today I am able, because of your gift of coeducation, to be part of this family. Whether studying bio in the library until 2:00 a.m., having a snowball fight after the first snowfall, or simply walking across the quad, I am surrounded by incredible people. No matter how cold it gets here in South Bend, I remain embraced in the warm character of the company exemplified in my roommates, professors, classmates, and even mere acquaintances.

Everything about Notre Dame that I love, especially the people, I would have been unable to experience in the same way that I do now, were it not for the profound risk you took to establish coeducation at this university.

I am so glad I have had the opportunity to thank you properly for such an incredible gift. We're so blessed to call you our own!

Sincerely,

Carrie Elstad
Class of '09

Dear Father Hesburgh,

When I first arrived at the University of Notre Dame, there was always talk about the Golden Dome, the football stadium and games, Touchdown Jesus, the Grotto, and every other famous monument and event that makes this university. But there was much talk about a Living Legend—someone who redefined not just this university, but the entire nation. They talked about you, Father Hesburgh: a man of God, a man of love, a man of hope. What is even more extraordinary about you is that you are a man of redefining sight. You constantly seek for the betterment of tomorrow, by doing so today. You take risks without any fear in order for those to have an opportunity to make something of themselves, to make their lives rich, and to be truly happy. Father Hesburgh, in 1972 you opened the door for women to redefine standards, and show the world what we can do. There are women making small and big differences in this world every single day. Because of you, there are numerous intelligent, strong, confident, spiritual women across this nation and the world, enriching their lives and pursuing their dreams.

I remember distinctly the day we first met. December brought its coldest and rainiest Tuesday. You were smoking a rich cigar that filled the room with a sweet scent, and I wore bright orange rain boots splashed with water drops. The first thing you asked was, "Are you Latina?" I responded, "Yes, I am. I am Mexican American." Immediately you noticed my ethnicity. You acknowledged me, and everything that has made me the person that I am today. And because of Notre Dame, I am continuing to develop and reinforce who I am, and who I want to be. This would have never been possible if you did not help make Notre Dame coed. Further, I, a first-generation Mexican American from Southern California, am able to receive an excellent education at one of the top universities in the nation. Not only have you provided me and numerous women of all ethnicities an opportunity to do something great, but also to live a life of meaning, understanding, and hope. Thank you for making thousands of dreams a reality, and deepening the hope and faith of numerous individuals. Thank you, Father Hesburgh, for making my life journey truly special. I hold you very close to my heart.

Happy 90th Birthday, Father Hesburgh. May God continue to bless you.

In Notre Dame,

Lourdes Meraz
Class of '09, Sophomore Class President 2006–2007

Dear Father Hesburgh,

As members of the Class of 2010, although we have not been on campus long, your legacy has already been an inspiration to us all. I especially want to say a big THANK YOU from the women of my class. You not only opened doors for us to become equals at this great university, but also give us the courage to lead. Notre Dame has four female class presidents this year—without your perseverance that never would have been possible. Thank you again.

Have a very Happy Birthday.

Charlotte "Charlie" Buhler
Class of '10, Freshman Class President

Dear Father Hesburgh,

Happy Birthday! I just finished my first year at Notre Dame, but I can already appreciate everything you have done to permit me to attend such a prestigious university. This school has opened up so many opportunities for me. The diversity of interests in my roommates, the ability to give back of my talents, and especially the chance to join up with others in support of my beliefs has far exceeded my expectation of what I envisioned my college experience to be. And it's only just started! I thank you for giving me the chance to succeed academically and spiritually.

You have also allowed me to make a special connection with my mother by following in her footsteps as an undergraduate. Hopefully one day the Notre Dame family will extend to include my own daughters.

Thank you and Happy Birthday.

Elizabeth Grace
Class of '10

Dear Father Hesburgh,

Though I have only met you in person twice, I feel compelled to write you and express my many thanks to you. I just finished my first year at Notre Dame and I can't even begin to tell you how much I love it. It wasn't until the summer before my senior year of high school that I really thought about Notre Dame—when I experienced the leadership program that was directed toward African-American students. With the knowledge that I would be venturing to South Bend to go to the university, a teacher at my school recommended that I schedule a meeting with you. Without any knowledge of your amazing life and accomplishments, I agreed. I was given the opportunity to get a preview of the wonderful person that is Father Ted when presented with your book *God, Country, Notre Dame.*

　　I have been asked the question "So why Notre Dame?" about a million times and I usually reply enthusiastically about the leadership program—but in all honesty, my choice was the product of getting to know you through your book and meeting you briefly (about fifteen minutes). I know that Notre Dame is the place where I am meant to be. I would have never been exposed to this place, however, if it wasn't for you and the efforts you have made in coeducation and diversity recruitment. I will venture to say that my mention of you in my personal statement is what sealed the deal for my acceptance. When I met you the first time, you said that you wanted to see me next

year (this year) as a student at Notre Dame. As I traveled up to the thirteenth floor to see you the second time, I was overwhelmed with gratitude. I made it, Father Ted, and I want you to know that I couldn't and probably wouldn't have done it if it wasn't for you. Thank you so much for giving me this incredible opportunity. God bless and go Irish!

Sincerely,

Amber Herkey
Class of '10

Dear Father Hesburgh,

Thank you for making it possible for me to apply and to attend Notre Dame. The university has always been a huge part of my life. I was baptized in the Log Chapel on campus, and my parents brought me to football games every year thereafter. My family is very important to me, and Notre Dame has been a very important part of my family. Since I will be attending Notre Dame in the fall, I will be a fifth-generation student from my dad's side of the family, following the footsteps of my great-great-grandfather, my great-grandfather, my grandfather's brothers, and my dad, Frank J. Oelerich III '82. Being the eldest of five girls, and watching all my sisters as they were baptized in the log chapel, and visiting the campus numerous times, Notre Dame became a place where I felt comfortable, happy, and safe.

Even before I began the hectic college selection process, I knew in my heart that Notre Dame was for me. Not only had it become a familiar place to me, it would also be the place where my faith, education, and interests could all come together to make me the best person I can be. Knowing that I will attend Notre Dame next fall, I can't imagine spending my college years anywhere else. There is a remarkable mystique about Notre Dame, indescribable to those who don't know it. As Lou Holtz said, "If you were there, no explanation is necessary. If you weren't, no explanation is satisfactory." I look at my parents, and many of their dearest friends are classmates from Notre Dame. That alone says something about the school; it is a place where you form the deepest kind of friendships, ones that endure long after your graduation.

Although I'm not exactly sure what I want to study at Notre Dame—right now, I'm thinking about some sort of design. The wonderful thing about Notre Dame is that my possibilities and opportunities are endless, and whatever major I choose will be an outstanding educational experience for me and will prepare me for the road ahead. I am so grateful for your decision to make Notre Dame a coeducational institution almost thirty-five years ago, because I can't see myself anywhere else but Notre Dame. My four younger sisters will also be able to apply to Notre Dame, and, if any of them do end up there, I will be so glad that they will truly be able to have the ultimate college experience. I feel so blessed to be able to attend Notre Dame next fall. Thank you so much for making my dream come true, I truly could not have done it without you.

Very truly yours,

Mary M. ("Molly") Oelerich
Class of '11

# EPILOGUE

Maris Braun '08 (Student Body Vice President 2007-2008), Lourdes Meraz '09 (Sophomore Class President 2006-2007), Bridget Keating '08 (Junior Class President 2006-2007), Father Ted, Lizzi Shappell '07 (Student Body President 2006-2007), Liz Brown '08 (Student Body President 2007-2008), Charlotte Buhler '10 (Freshman Class President 2006-2007) in Father Ted's office on February 8, 2007. A thirty-fifth Notre Dame Coeducation anniversary poster, featuring this picture, may be purchased at www.thankingfatherted.com.

# Thanking Father Ted Foundation

## OFFICERS AND DIRECTORS

**President**
Ann Therese Darin Palmer '73, '75 MBA
Attorney/Freelance Writer, *Time, Fortune,* and
*Fortune Small Business* Magazines, *Chicago Tribune* Business Section
First Woman Director, ND Club of Chicago 1976

**Secretary**
The Honorable Sheila M. O'Brien '77, '80 JD
Justice, Illinois Appellate Court
2007 Rev. Charles F. Sorin Alumni Award for
Distinguished Service to the University

**Treasurer**
Anne Giffels '81
Director, PricewaterhouseCoopers, Chicago, Illinois

**Vice President**
Mary Davey Bliley '72
First Notre Dame Woman Undergraduate Degree
Recipient, Virginia

**Vice President**
Paulita Pike '93, '96 JD
Partner, Bell Boyd & Lloyd LLP, Chicago, Illinois

**Vice President**
Julie Webb '73
Attorney, Oak Brook, Illinois
Second Woman Director, Notre Dame Club of
Chicago, 1977

**Director**
Patricia Ann Romano Barry '84
First Notre Dame Woman Class President
Granger, Indiana

**Director**
Jean Collier '83
President, Notre Dame Alumni Association 2003

**Director**
Reverend Anne M. Dilenschneider '77
Pastor, United Methodist and United Church of
Christ, Montara, California

**Director**
Mary Hesburgh Flaherty '79
Board Chair, Marymount High School of Los Angeles
Board of Trustees and Women's Health Advocate
Chair, St. John's Hospital and Health Center,
California

**Director**
Melinda Henneberger '80
Author, *If They Only Listened to Us: What Women
Voters Want Poiticians to Hear* (2007)
*Newsweek* Contributing Editor

**Director**
Amy Treder Kelliher '88
Financial Advisor, AXA Advisors, Detroit, Michigan
Secretary, Notre Dame Club of Detroit 2007

**Director**
Tara Crane Kenney '82
First Woman Notre Dame Student Body Vice
President
Managing Director, Deutsche Bank Asset
Management, Boston, Massachusetts

**Director**
Christine Romano Klauer '79
Trustee, Holy Cross College, Notre Dame
Granger, Indiana

Patrice Purcell DeCorrevont '84
Managing Director, JPMorgan Chase & Co., Chicago,
    Illinois

Joya DeFoor '77
Treasurer, City of Los Angeles, California

The Honorable Mary Katherine Rochford Demetrio
    '76, '79 JD
Associate Judge, Cook County Circuit Court, Illinois

Julie Pierson Doyle '85
First Woman President, Notre Dame Monogram Club
Director, Educational Research, Education and
    Research Foundation, Virginia

Kathryn Faccenda '85
Vice President, Northern Trust Co., Chicago, Illinois

Elizabeth Fallon '76
First ND Woman's Tennis Team Captain 1973–1976
Vice President, Marketing, Planning, and
    Community Health, Brooks Health Systems,
    Florida

The Honorable Carol A. Falvey '82
Circuit Judge, Citrus County (Florida) Circuit Court

Peggy Foran '76, '79 JD
Senior Vice President, Associate General Counsel,
    and Corporate Secretary, Pfizer Inc., New York
    City

Celeste Volz Ford '78
CEO/Chairperson, Stellar Solutions Inc., California
Chairman, Notre Dame Fitzpatrick Engineering
    College Advisory Council

Patricia Fosmoe '93
Personal Financial Consultant, Ernst & Young,
    Chicago, Illinois

Carol Hackett Garagiola '77
Chief Judge, Livingston County (Michigan) Probate
    Court

Margaret Faccenda Green '86
Former Elementary School Teacher, Indianapolis,
    Indiana

The Honorable Piper D. Griffin '84
Judge, Civil District Court, New Orleans, Louisiana

Ann Gurucharri '03
2007 Council of Women World Leaders Fellow,
    Global Observatory of Women's Health, Madrid,
    Spain

Catherine O'Neill Friedman '02
Elementary School Teacher, Denver, Colorado

Amy Faulhaber Haddow '82
Development Associate, Alaska SeaLife Center

Susan Darin Hagan '76
First Woman Editor in Chief, *Dome* Yearbook, 1975
    Edition

Madeleine Hanna '08
Editor in Chief, *Observer* Newspaper 2007–2008

Sheila McDaniel Henry '87
First Notre Dame Student Woman Radio Station
    Manager, WVFI- FM 1986–1987

Kathryn Massman Hilliard '81, '84 MA
Publicity Director, Andrews McMeel Publishing,
    Kansas City, Missouri

Carol Hank Hoffman '78
Notre Dame Trustee, Minnesota

Maribeth Faccenda Hough '82
Realtor, New York

Monica Yant Kinney '93
Editor in Chief, *Observer* Newspaper 1992–1993

Yvonne Kobayashi '88
Research Scientist, University of Iowa College of
 Medicine

Brooke Norton Lais '02
First Notre Dame Woman Student Body President
 2001–2002

Kathleen C. Laurini '82
Deputy Director, Space Life Sciences Doctorate,
 NASA Johnson Space Center

The Honorable Diana Lewis '74, '82 JD
Trustee, Circuit Court Judge, Palm Beach County,
 Florida

Jennifer Liebenauer '05
Analyst, UBS Investment Bank, Chicago, Illinois

Sally Stanton MacKenzie '76
First Woman Editor in Chief, *Scholastic* Magazine
 1975–1976
Romance Novelist, Maryland

Sarah Hamilton Magill '86
Editor in Chief, *Observer* Newspaper 1985–1986

Kathryn Sobrero Markgraf '98
Captain, ND Women's Soccer Team 1997–1998
2000 Silver Olympic Medalist, Women's Soccer
2004 Gold Olympic Medalist, Women's Soccer

Roxanne O'Brien Martino '77
President, Harris Alternatives, LLC, Chicago, Illinois
Chairman, Notre Dame Mendoza Business College
 Advisory Council

Rosemary Mills-Russell '80
First Notre Dame Undergraduate Woman Editor in
 Chief, *Observer* Student Newspaper 1979–1980

Karen Phelps Moyer '87
Vice President, Moyer Foundation, Seattle,
 Washington

Mary Killeen Mullen '90
Manager, Special Events, Tampa Bay Buccaneers

Patricia Mullen '80
President and Chief Executive Officer,
 OrthoDiscovery Partners, LLC, New York City

Kristy Zloch Murphy '96
Television Actress, *The West Wing,* Virginia

Anne Cisle Murray '74
First Woman Director, Notre Dame Monogram Club
 1978–1984

Carmen Lund Nanni '93
Former Director, Notre Dame International Study
 Programs

Tawny Ryan Nelb '75
President, Nelb Archival Consulting, Inc., Michigan

Patricia O'Hara '74 JD
Dean, Notre Dame Law School
First Notre Dame Woman Vice President
 Vice President of Student Affairs 1990–1999

Keri Ochs Oxley '04
Trustee, Medical Student, Yale University Medical
 School

Cindy Buescher Parseghian '77
President, Ara Parseghian Medical Foundation,
 Arizona

Susan Oglesbee Payne '73
Economic Development Consultant, New York

Ruth Riley '01
Member, San Antonio Silver Stars
Olympic Gold Medal Winner
NCAA Irish Women's Basketball Championship Team
Member, Detroit Shock
2006 WNBA Champions

Shayla Keough Rumley '76
Trustee, Attorney, Atlanta, Georgia

Lee Ann Russo '77
Partner, Jones Day, Chicago, Illinois

Laura Jonaus Schumacher '85
General Counsel, Abbott Laboratories, North
   Chicago, Illinois

Elizabeth Shappell '07
Notre Dame Student Body President 2006–2007

Frances L. Shavers '90
Chief of Staff, Special Assistant to the President,
   University of Notre Dame

Carol Lally Shields '79, '05 Honorary
Ocular Oncologist, Wills Eye Hospital, Philadelphia,
   Pennsylvania

Elizabeth Bishop Shields '03
Notre Dame Student Body President 2002–2003

Carolyn Short '77
Former General Counsel, U.S. Senate Judiciary
   Committee
Partner, Reed, Smith, Shaw & McClay, Philadelphia,
   Pennsylvania

Elizabeth Anne Toomey '81
First Woman President, Notre Dame Alumni
   Association
Residential Realtor, Seattle, Washington

Claire J. Twist '82
Pediatric Hematologist-Oncologist
Lucile Packard Children's Hospital at Stanford
   University, Palo Alto, California

Susan M. Valdiserri '84
Professional and Executive Coach, IBM Corp.,
   Chicago, Illinois

The Honorable Martha Vazquez '75, '79 JD
U.S. District Court, New Mexico

Eleanor Walker '84
Radiation Oncologist, Henry Ford Hospital, Detroit,
   Michigan

Neilli Mullen Walsh '84
Attorney, Young Conaway Stargatt Taylor LLP,
   Delaware

Rosemary Hardart Wylie '82
General Manager, Travel 100 Group, Kenilworth,
   Illinois

The Honorable Susan Zwick '77, '80 JD
Circuit Court Judge, Cook County, Illinois